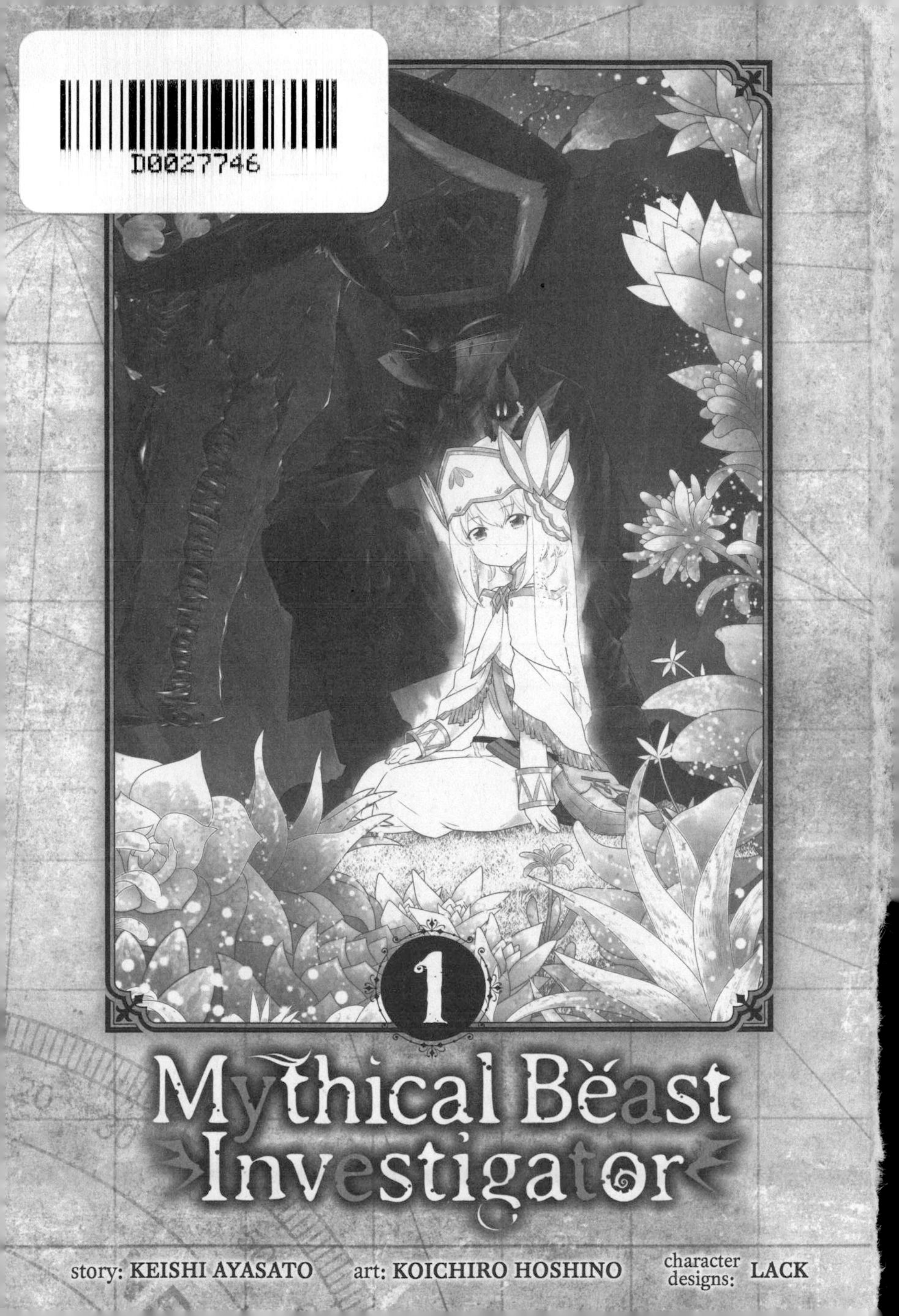
1

Mythical Beast Investigator

story: KEISHI AYASATO   art: KOICHIRO HOSHINO   character designs: LACK

contents

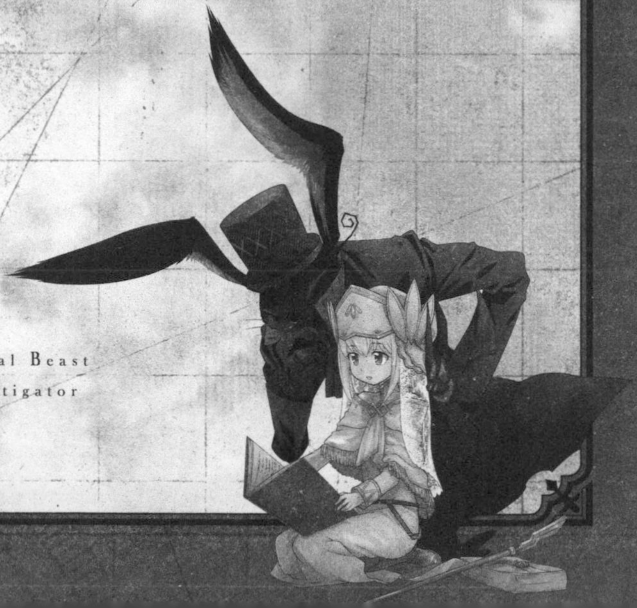

Mythical Beast
Investigator

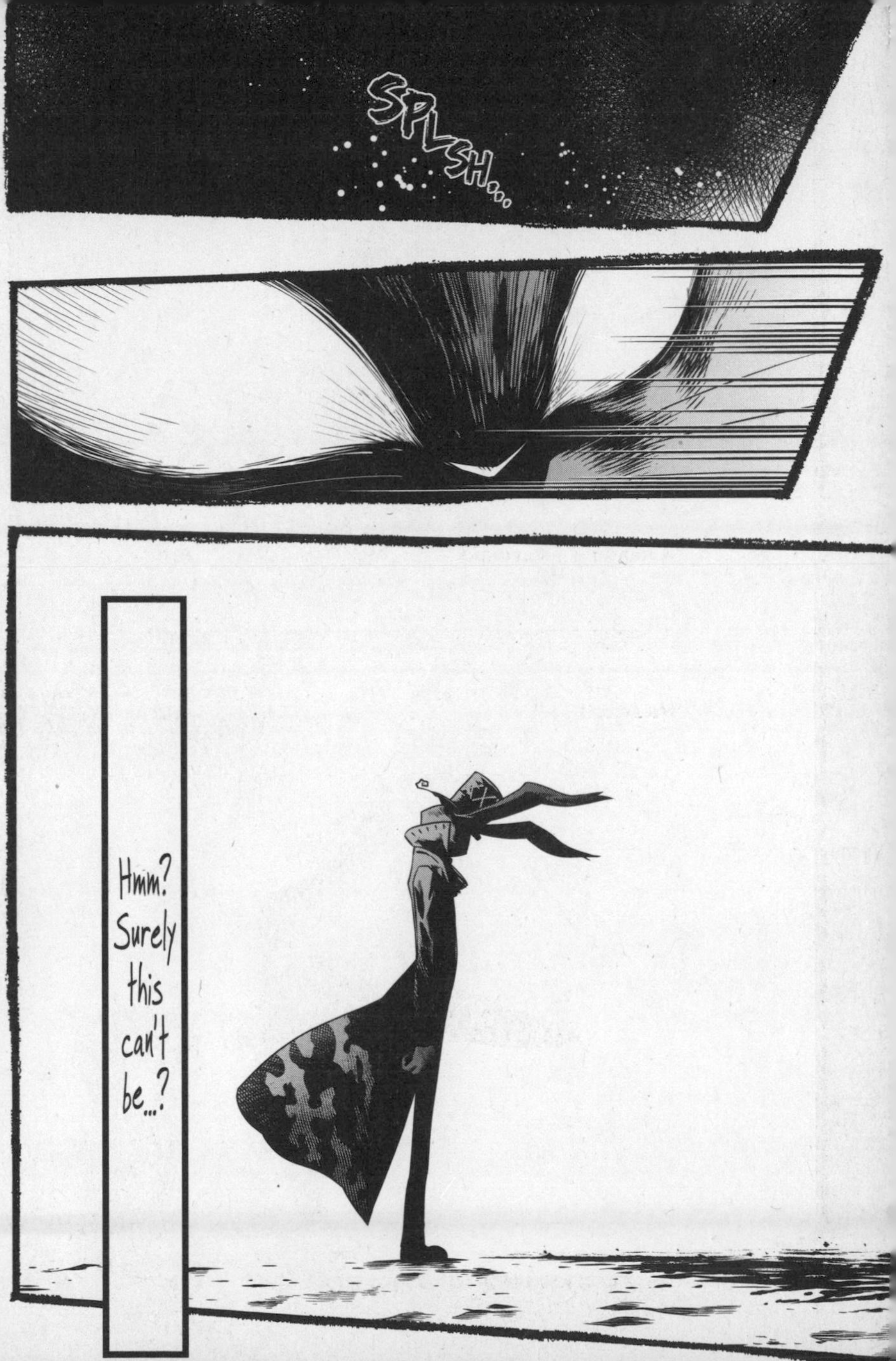
SPLSH...
Hmm? Surely this can't be...?

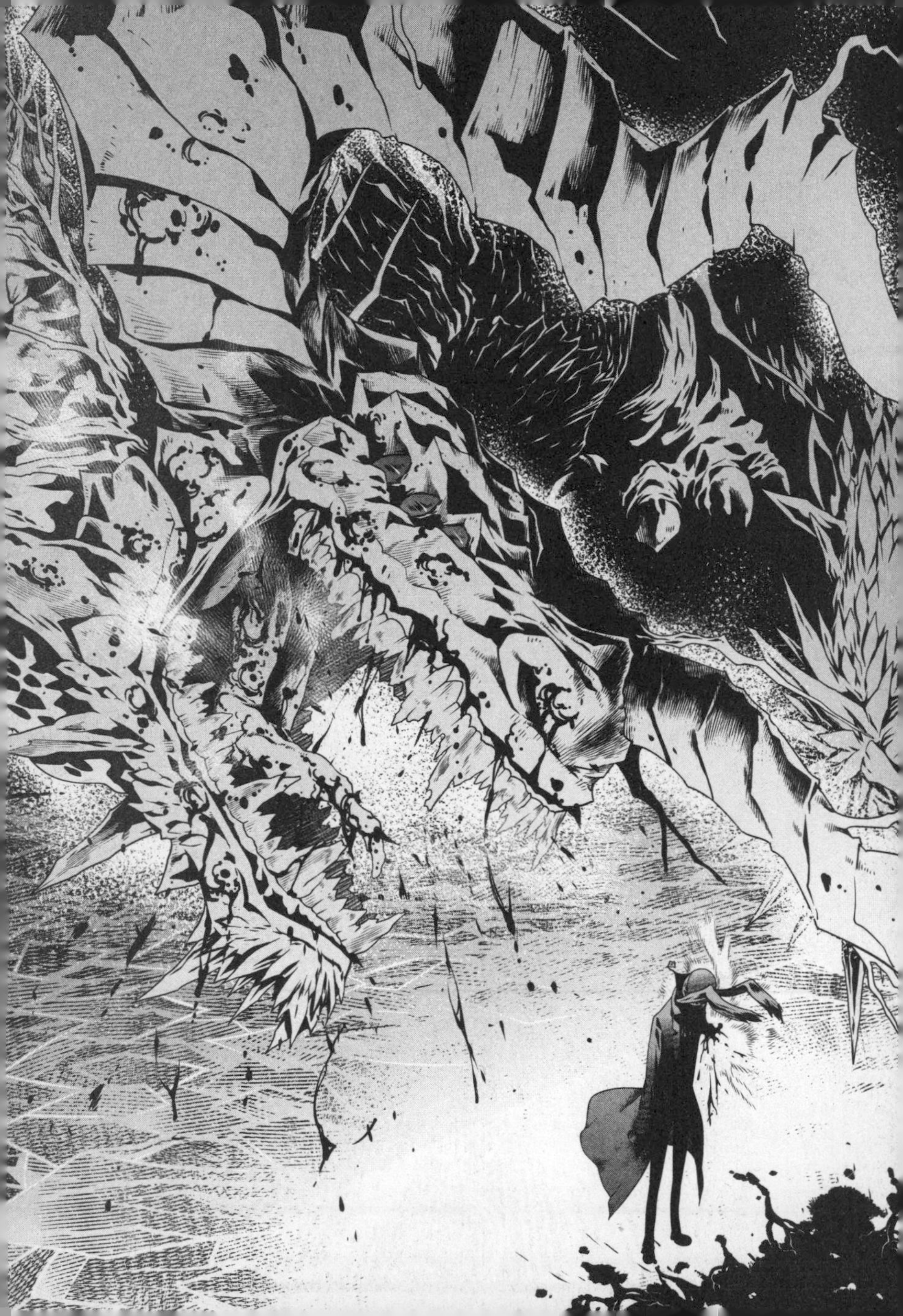

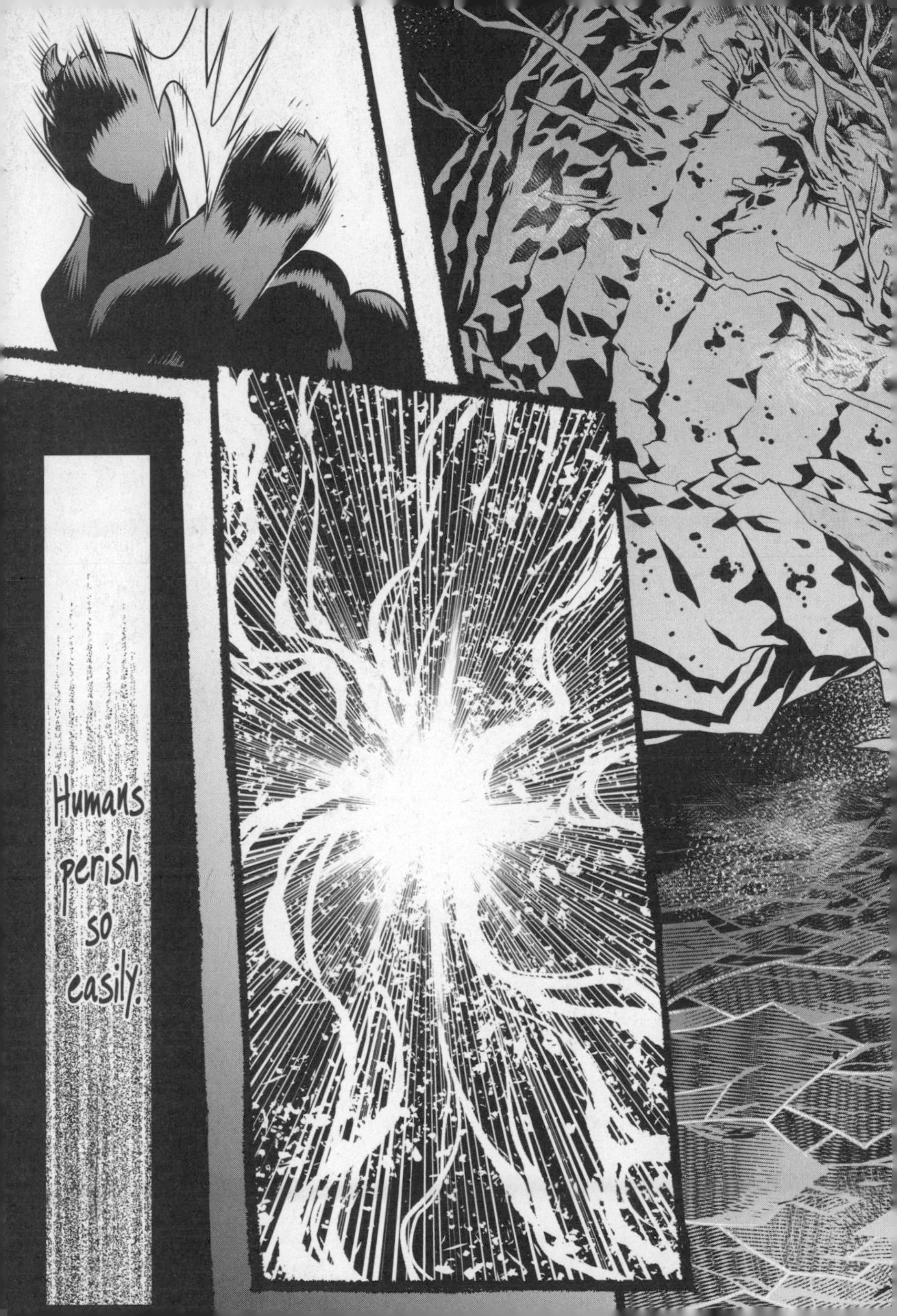
Humans perish so easily.

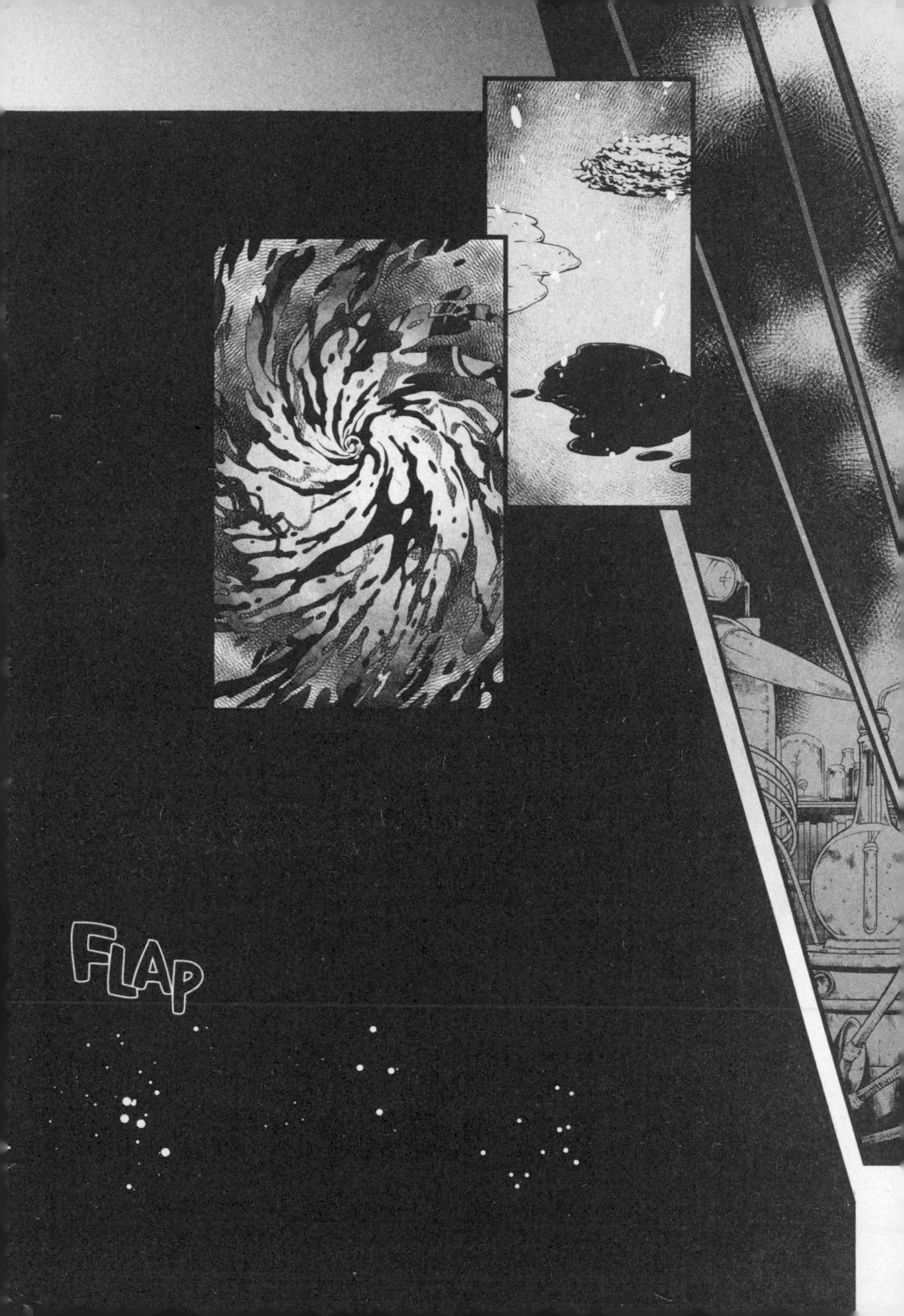
FLAP

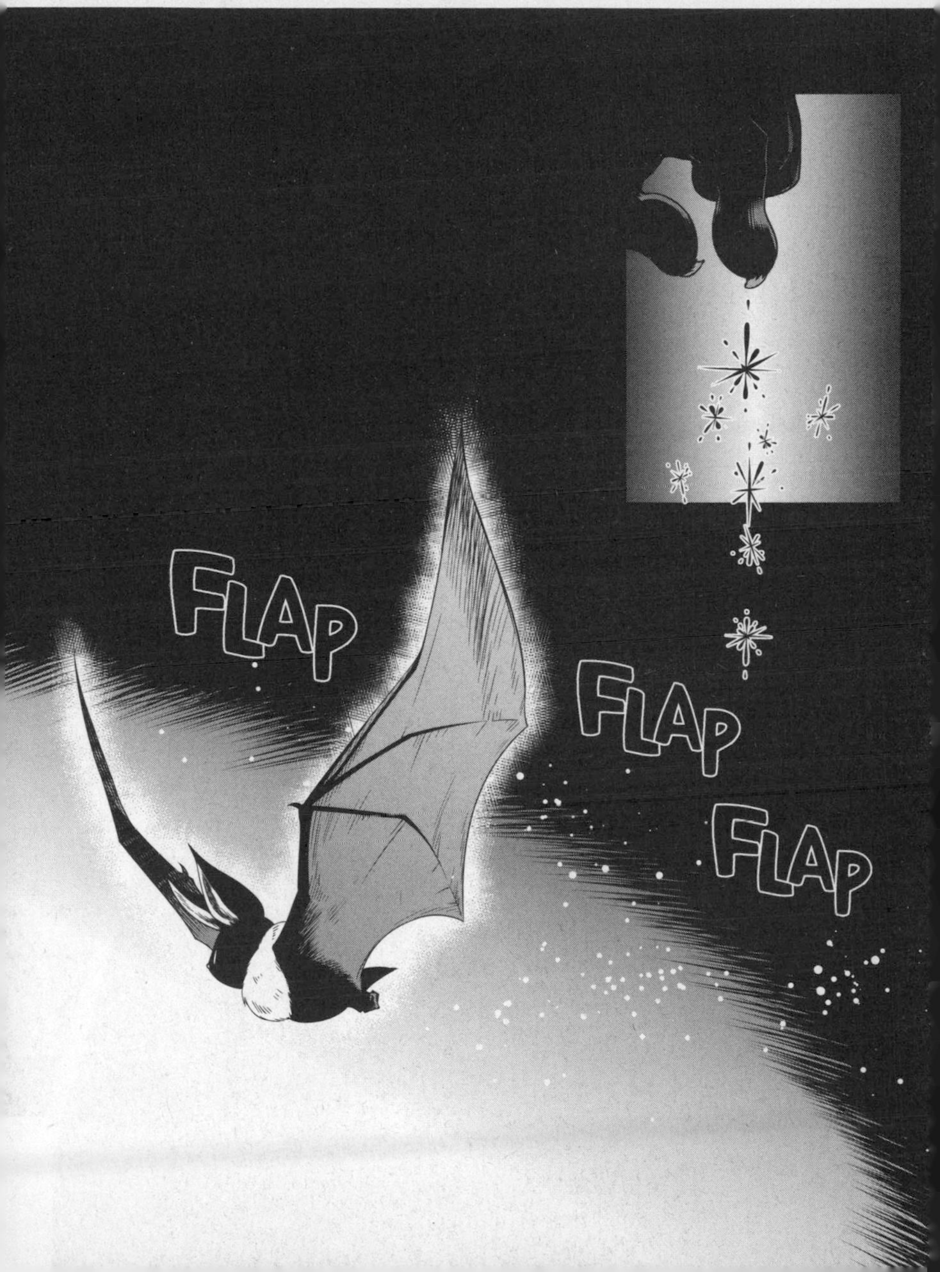
FLAP
FLAP
FLAP

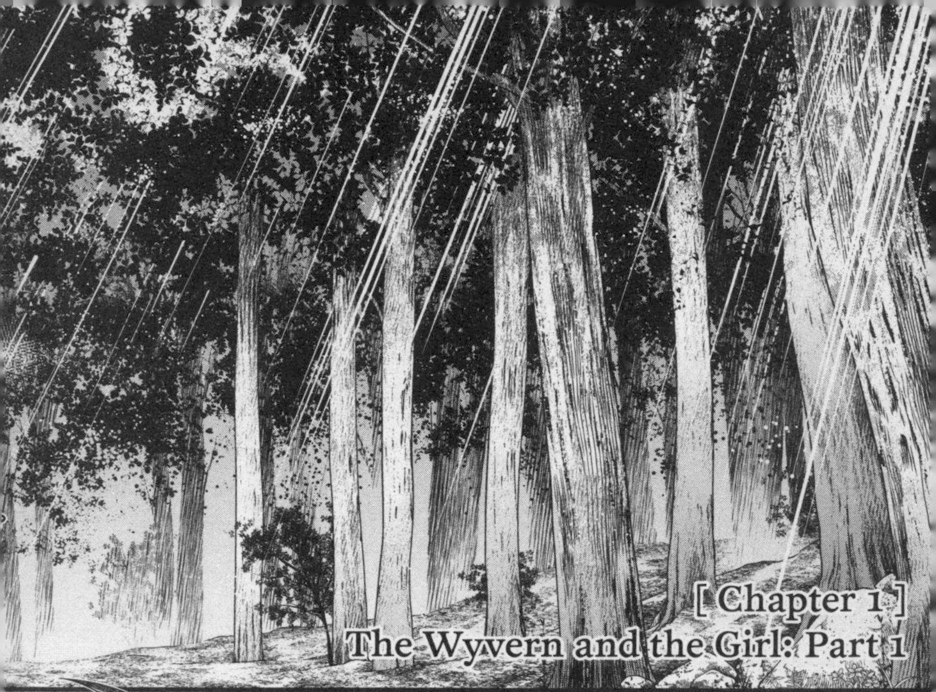
[Chapter 1]
The Wyvern and the Girl: Part 1

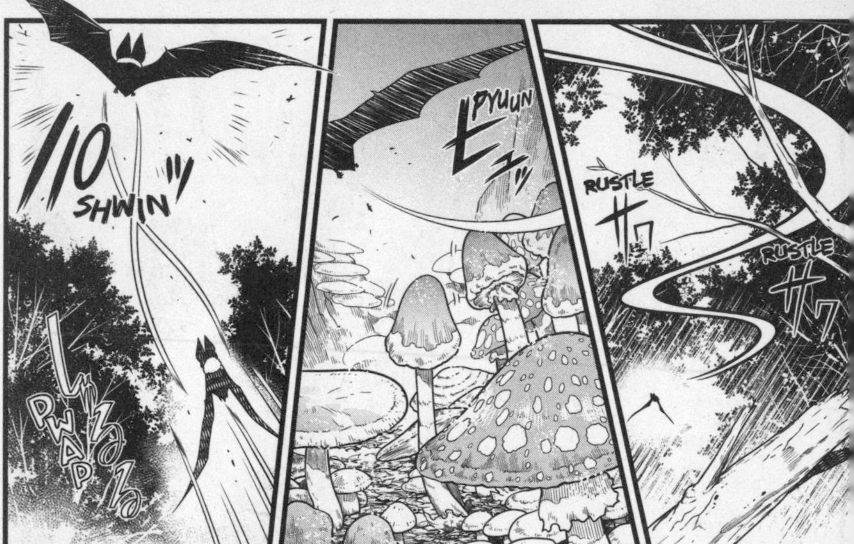
RUSTLE
RUSTLE
PYUUN
SHWIN
PWAP

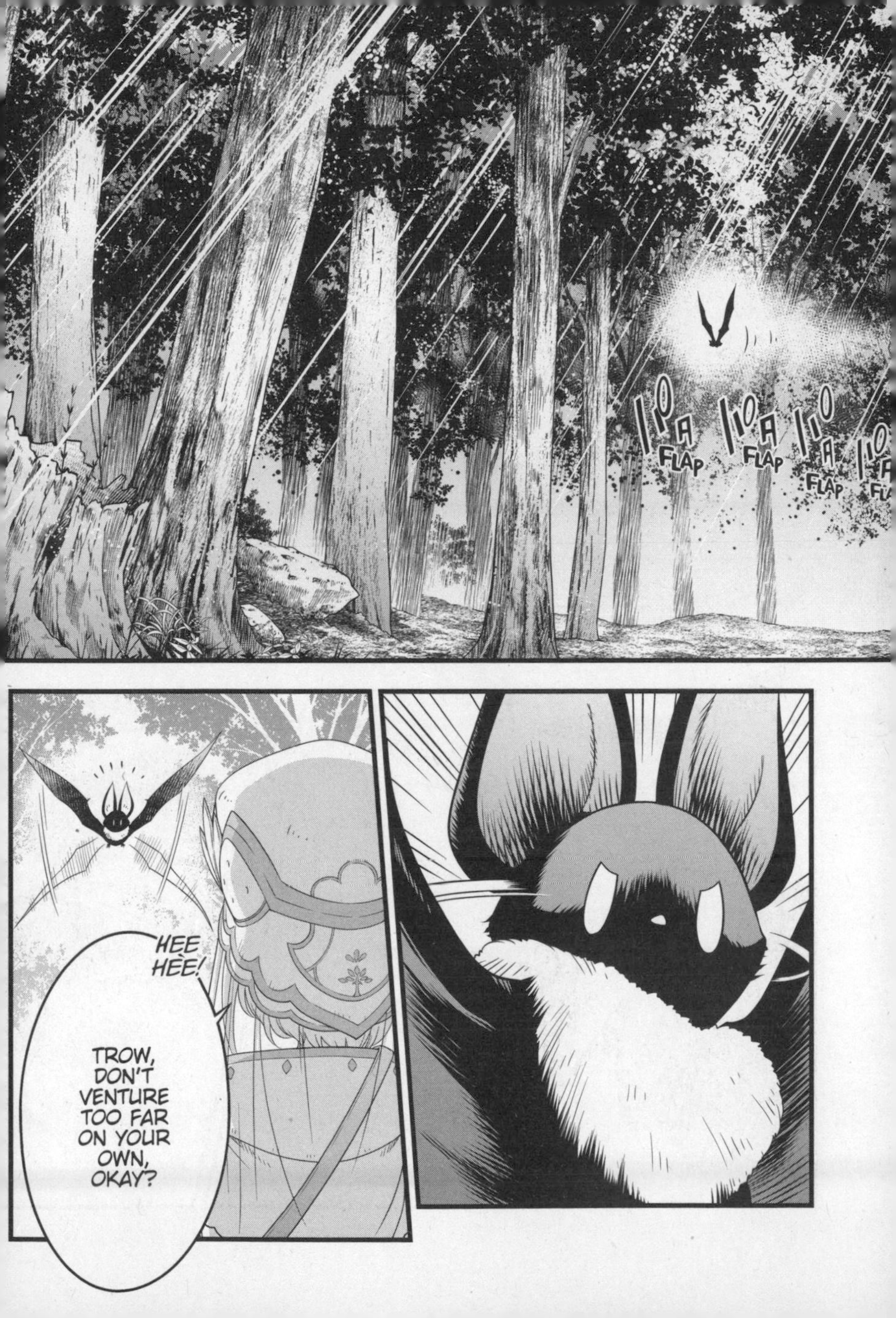
FLAP
FLAP
FLAP
FLAP
HEE HEE!
TROW, DON'T VENTURE TOO FAR ON YOUR OWN, OKAY?

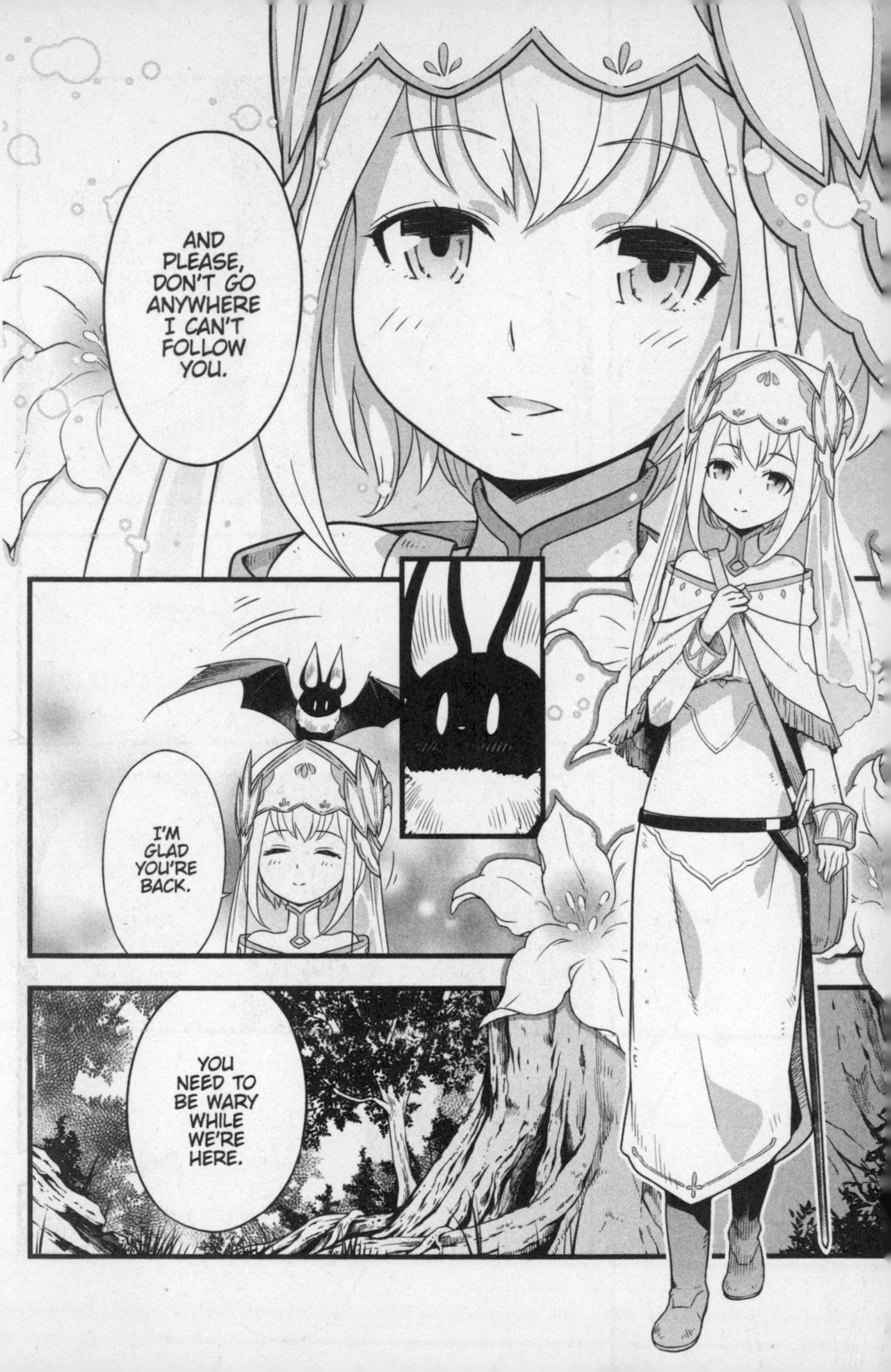
AND PLEASE, DON'T GO ANYWHERE I CAN'T FOLLOW YOU.
I'M GLAD YOU'RE BACK.
YOU NEED TO BE WARY WHILE WE'RE HERE.

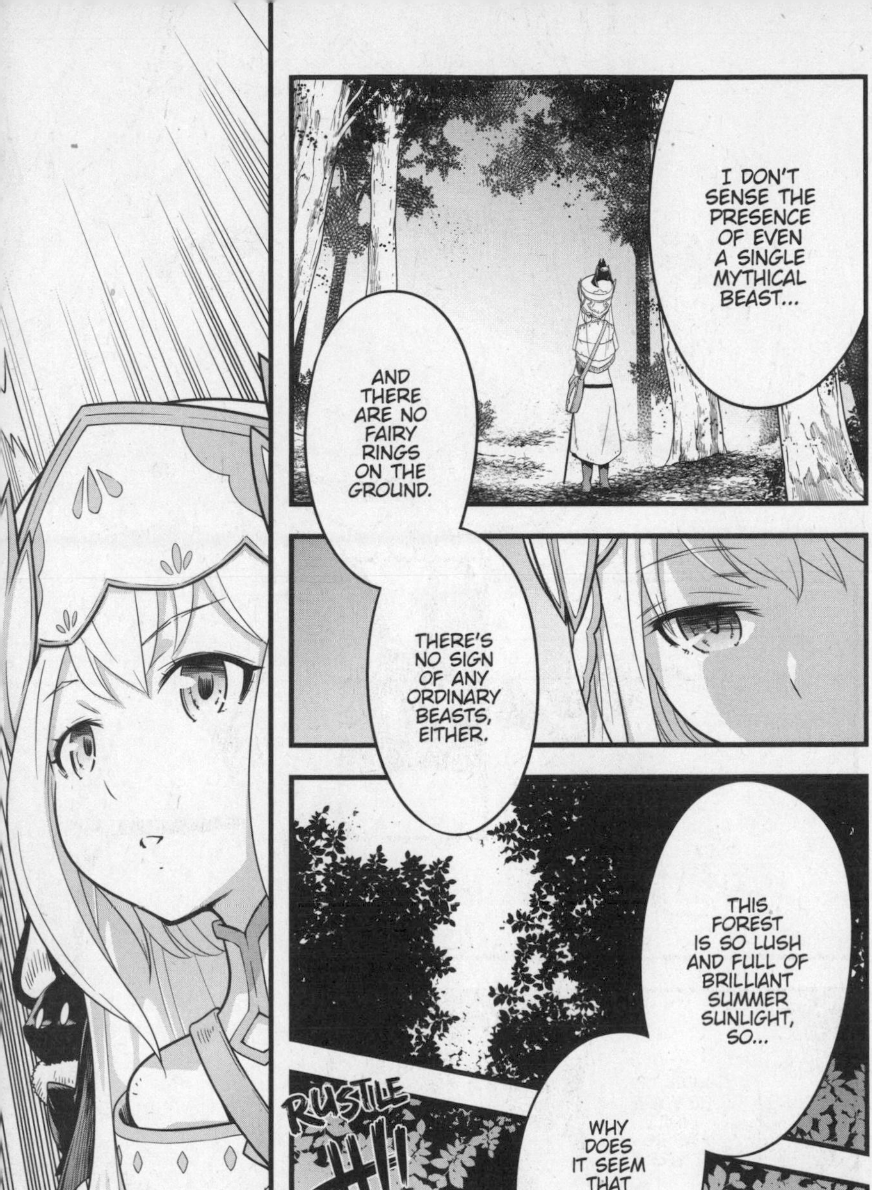
I DON'T SENSE THE PRESENCE OF EVEN A SINGLE MYTHICAL BEAST...
AND THERE ARE NO FAIRY RINGS ON THE GROUND.
THERE'S NO SIGN OF ANY ORDINARY BEASTS, EITHER.
THIS FOREST IS SO LUSH AND FULL OF BRILLIANT SUMMER SUNLIGHT, SO...
RUSTLE
WHY DOES IT SEEM THAT ALL ITS CREATURES HAVE FLED?

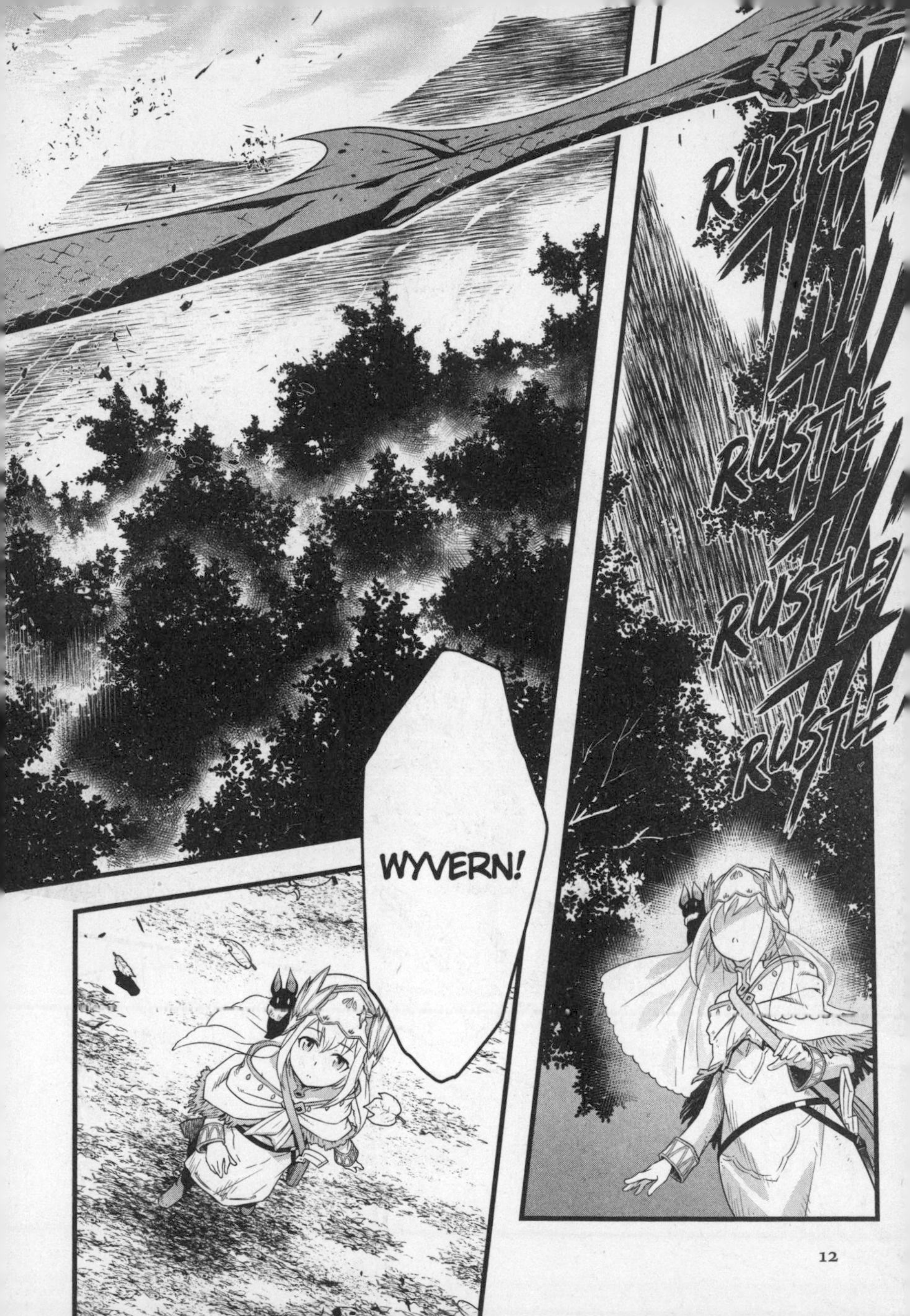
RUSTLE
RUSTLE
RUSTLE
RUSTLE
WYVERN!

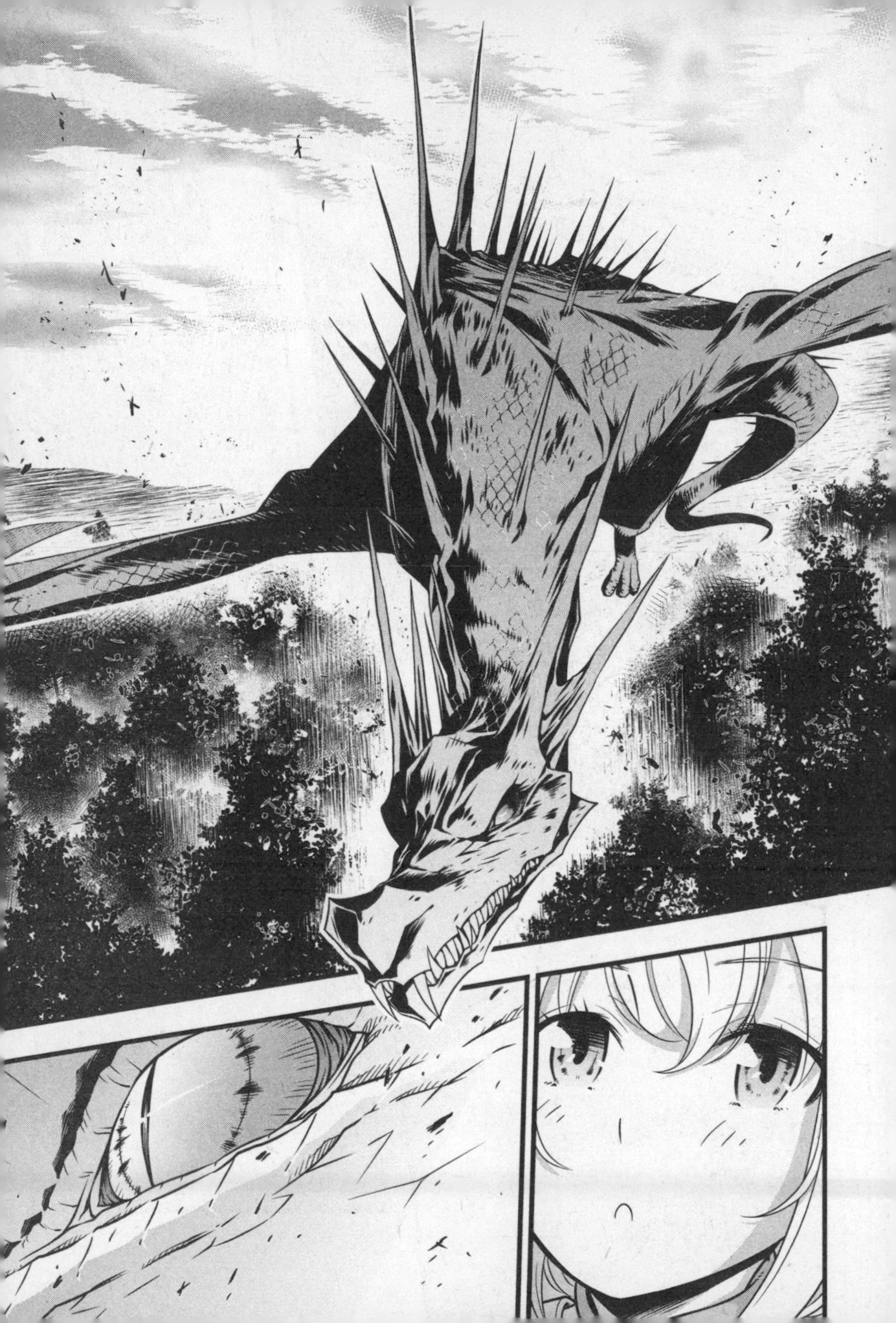

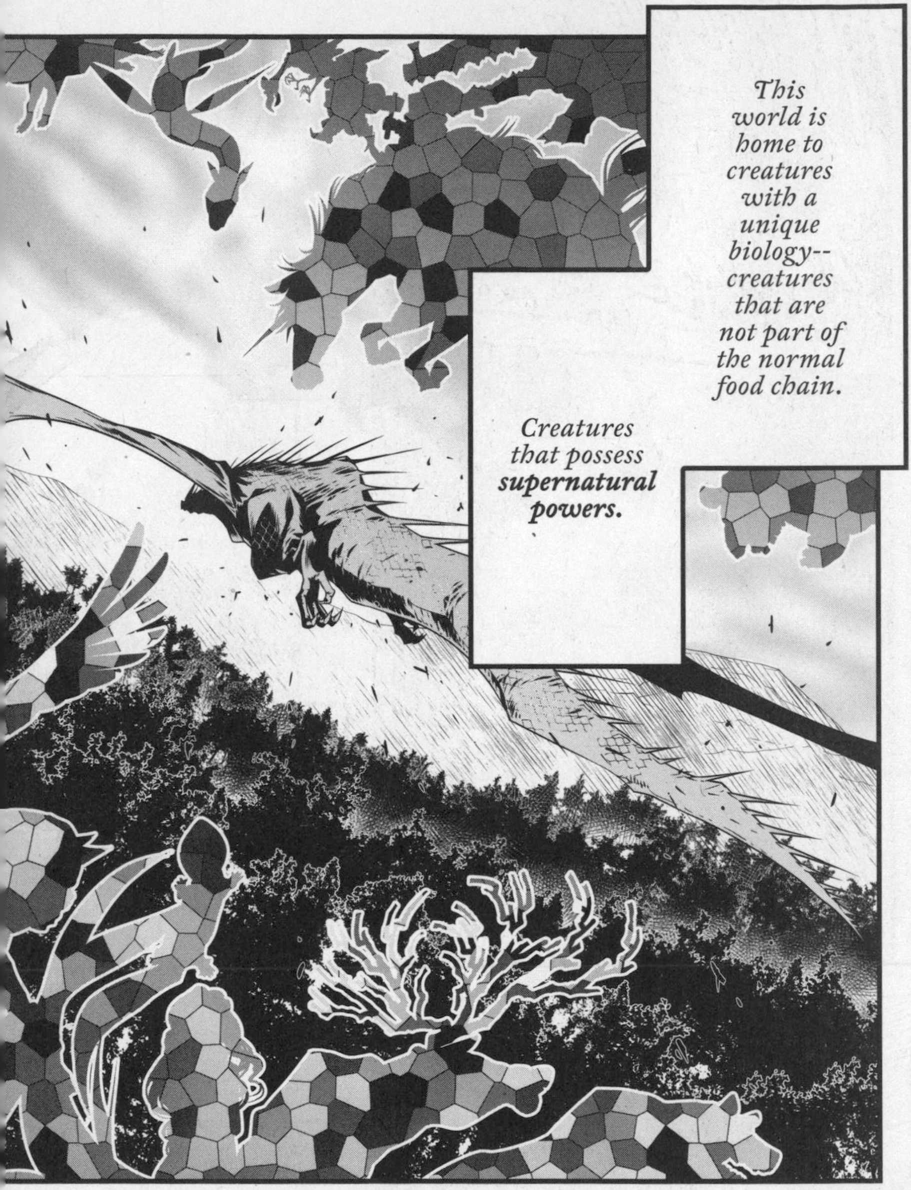
This world is home to creatures with a unique biology-- creatures that are not part of the normal food chain.
Creatures that possess **supernatural powers.**

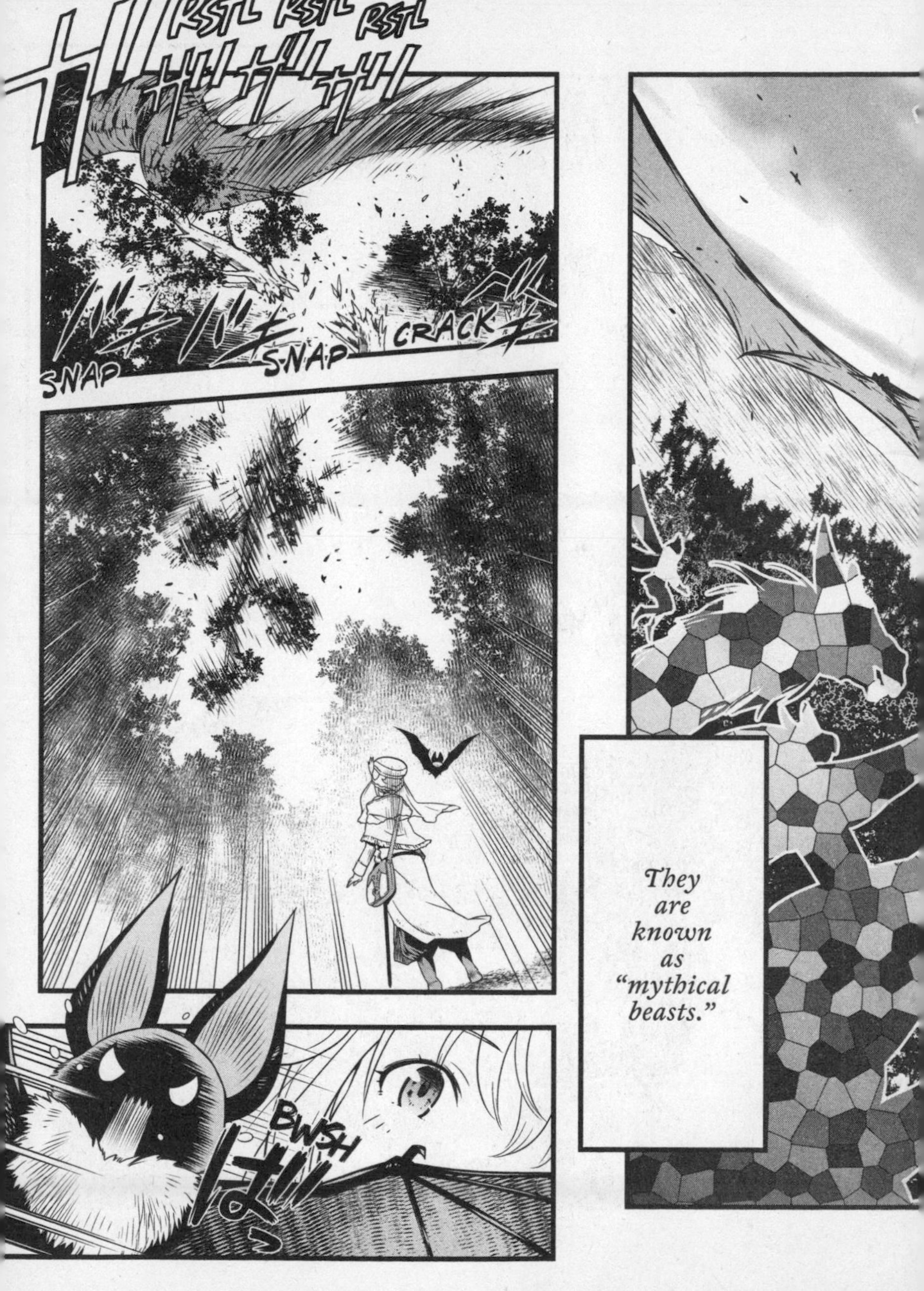
They are known as "mythical beasts."
RSTL RSTL RSTL
SNAP
SNAP
CRACK
BWSH

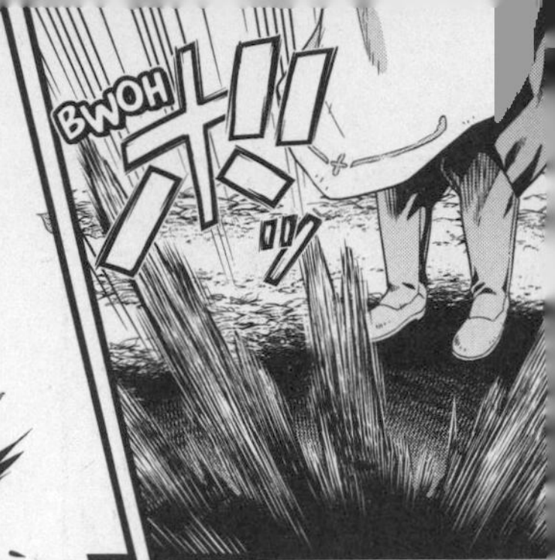
BWOH
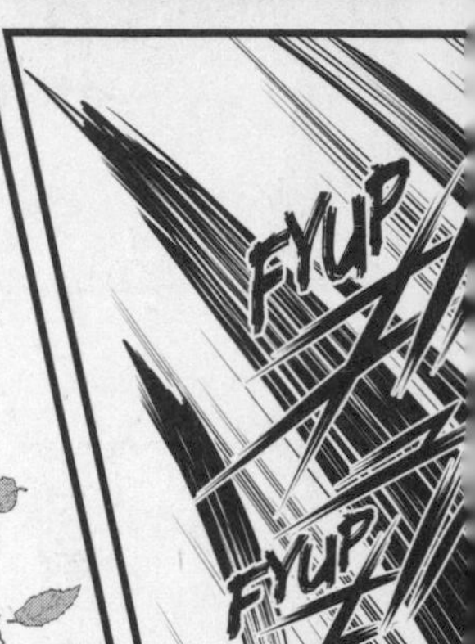
FYUP
FYUP
FYUP
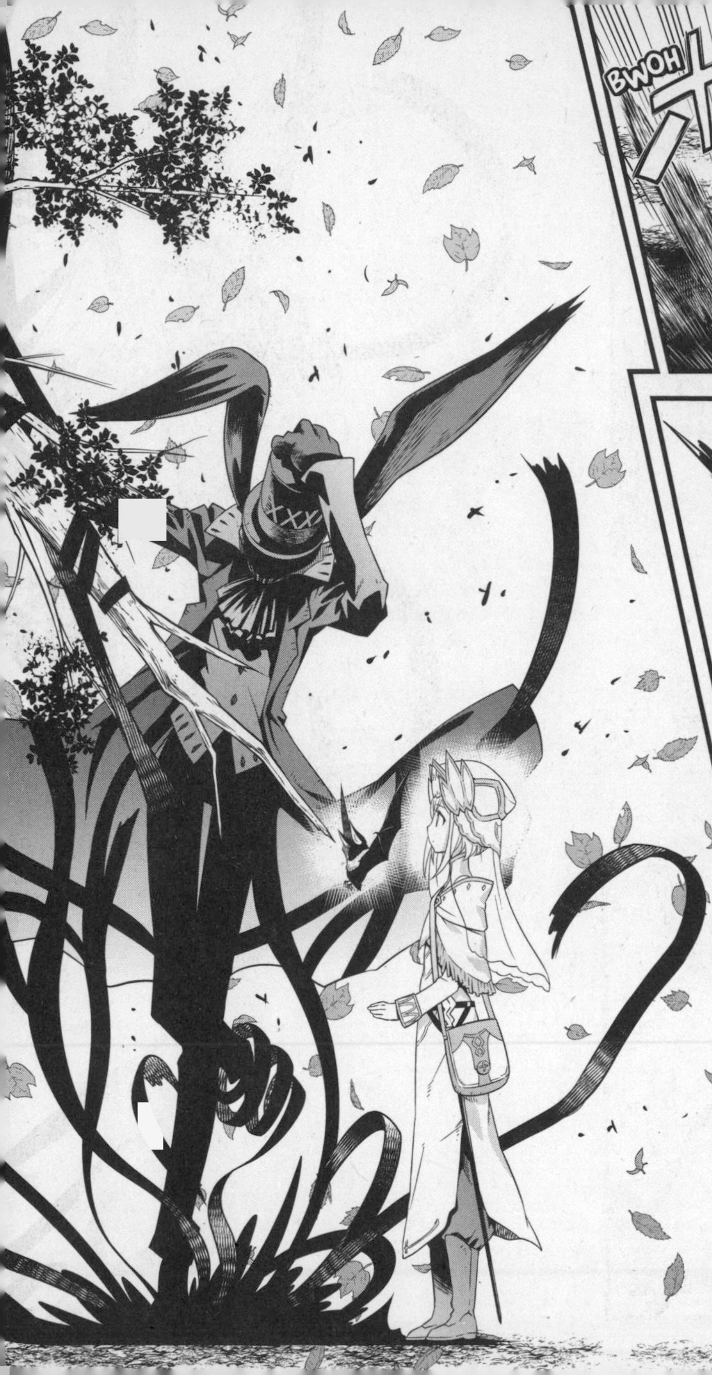

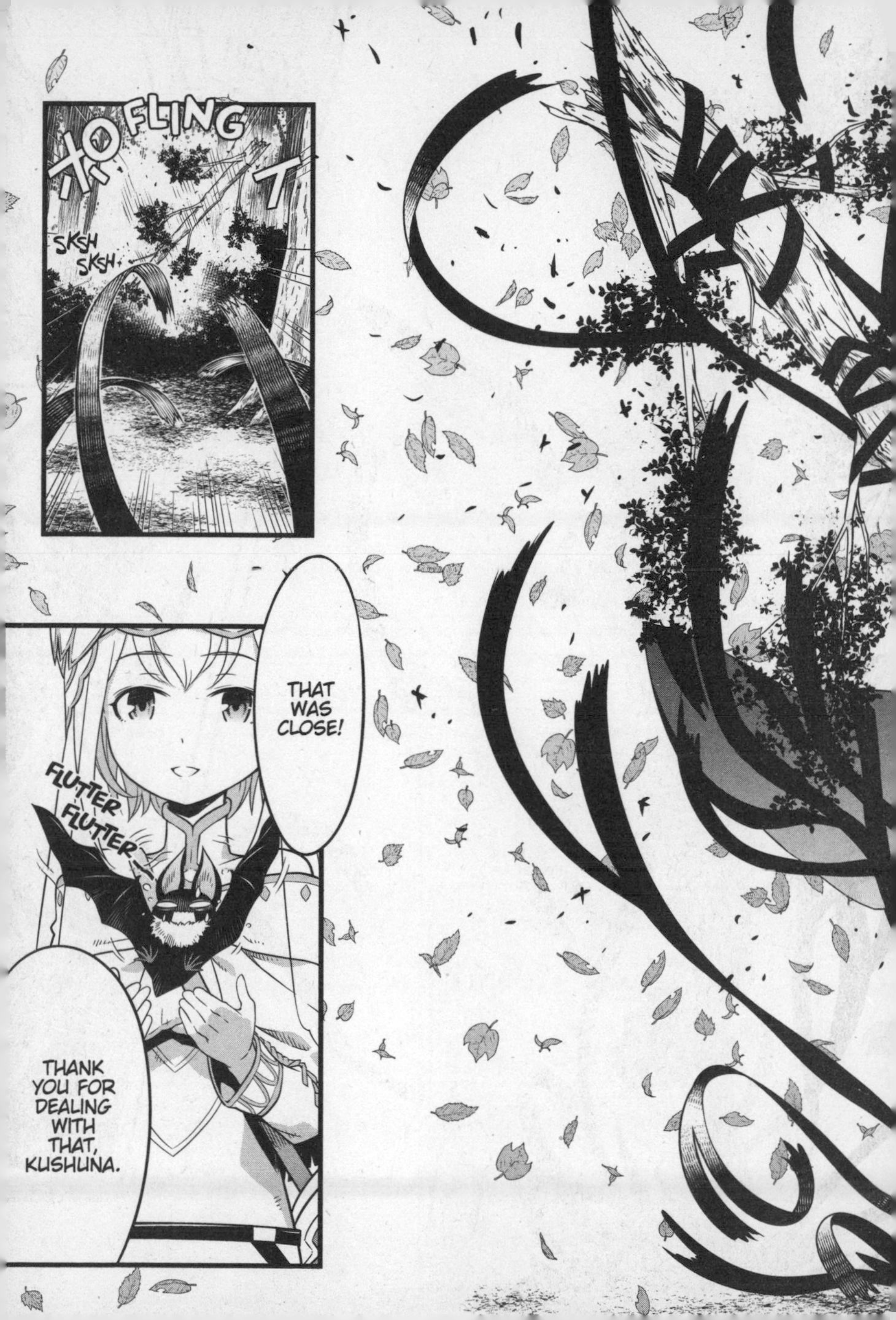
FLING
SKSH SKSH
THAT WAS CLOSE!
FLUTTER FLUTTER
THANK YOU FOR DEALING WITH THAT, KUSHUNA.

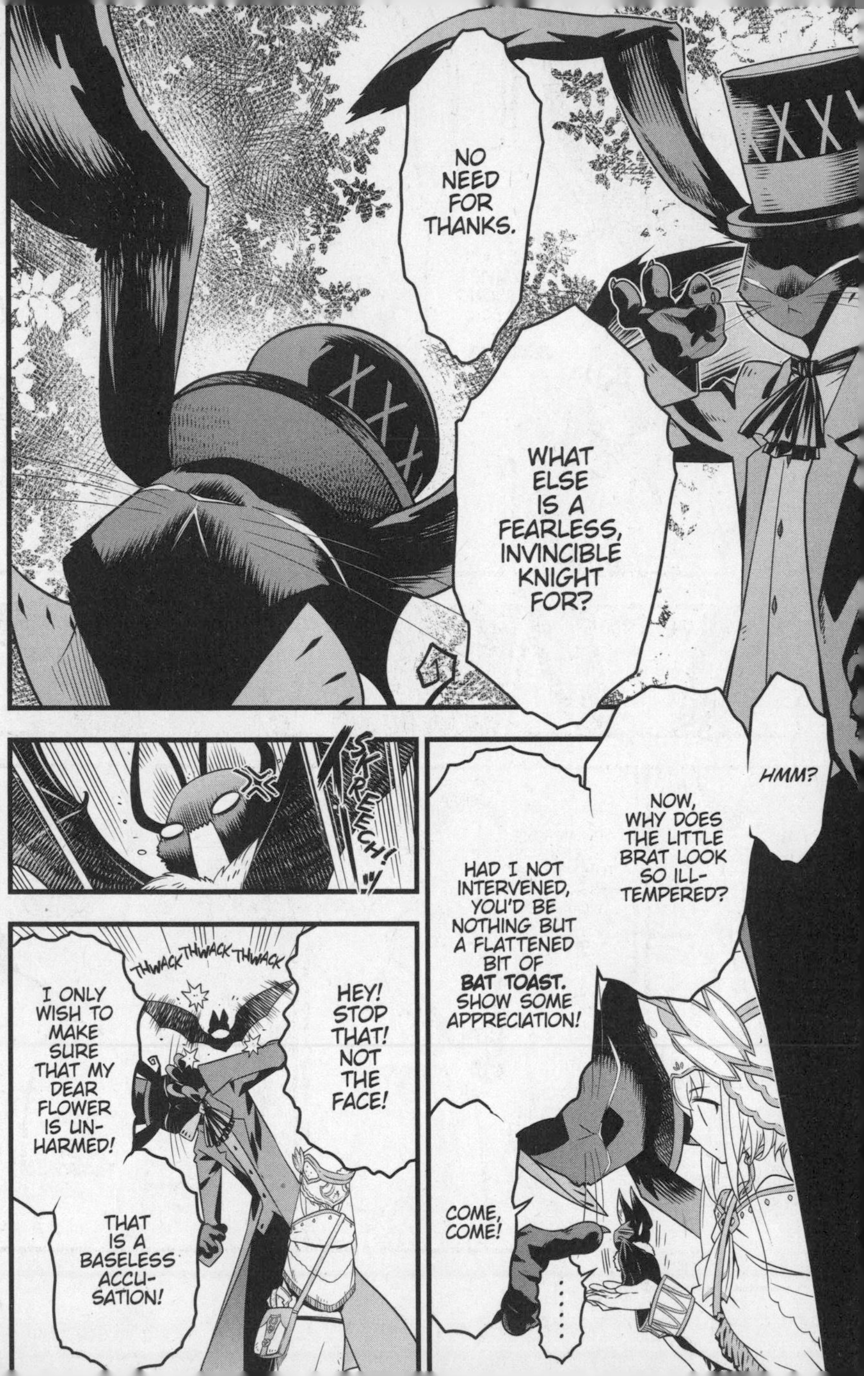
NO NEED FOR THANKS.
WHAT ELSE IS A FEARLESS, INVINCIBLE KNIGHT FOR?
HMM?
NOW, WHY DOES THE LITTLE BRAT LOOK SO ILL-TEMPERED?
HAD I NOT INTERVENED, YOU'D BE NOTHING BUT A FLATTENED BIT OF **BAT TOAST.** SHOW SOME APPRECIATION!
COME, COME!
......
SKREECH!
THWACK THWACK THWACK
HEY! STOP THAT! NOT THE FACE!
I ONLY WISH TO MAKE SURE THAT MY DEAR FLOWER IS UN-HARMED!
THAT IS A BASELESS ACCU-SATION!

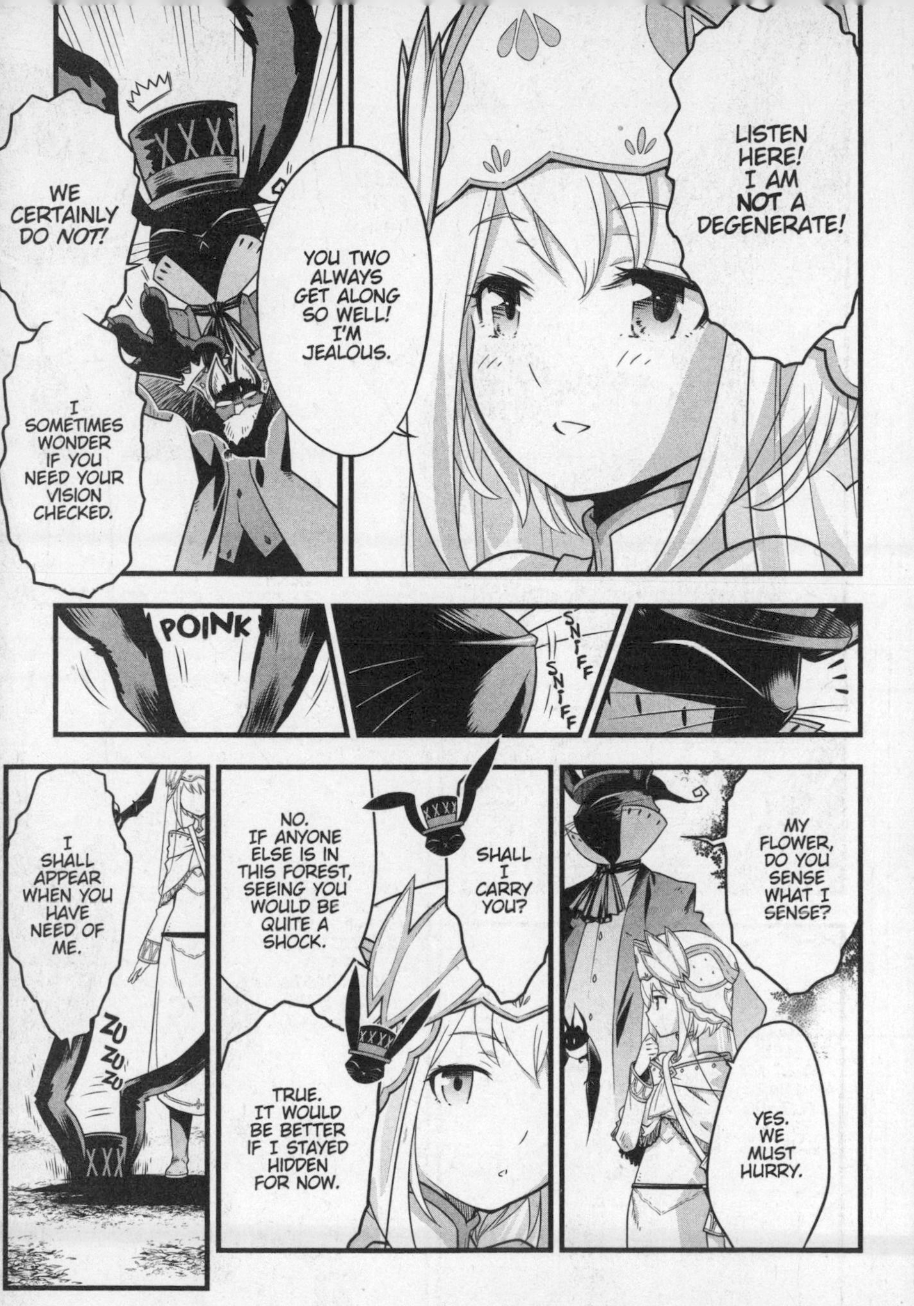
LISTEN HERE! I AM NOT A DEGENERATE!
YOU TWO ALWAYS GET ALONG SO WELL! I'M JEALOUS.
WE CERTAINLY DO NOT!
I SOMETIMES WONDER IF YOU NEED YOUR VISION CHECKED.
SNIFF SNIFF
POINK
MY FLOWER, DO YOU SENSE WHAT I SENSE?
YES. WE MUST HURRY.
SHALL I CARRY YOU?
NO. IF ANYONE ELSE IS IN THIS FOREST, SEEING YOU WOULD BE QUITE A SHOCK.
TRUE. IT WOULD BE BETTER IF I STAYED HIDDEN FOR NOW.
I SHALL APPEAR WHEN YOU HAVE NEED OF ME.
ZU ZU ZU

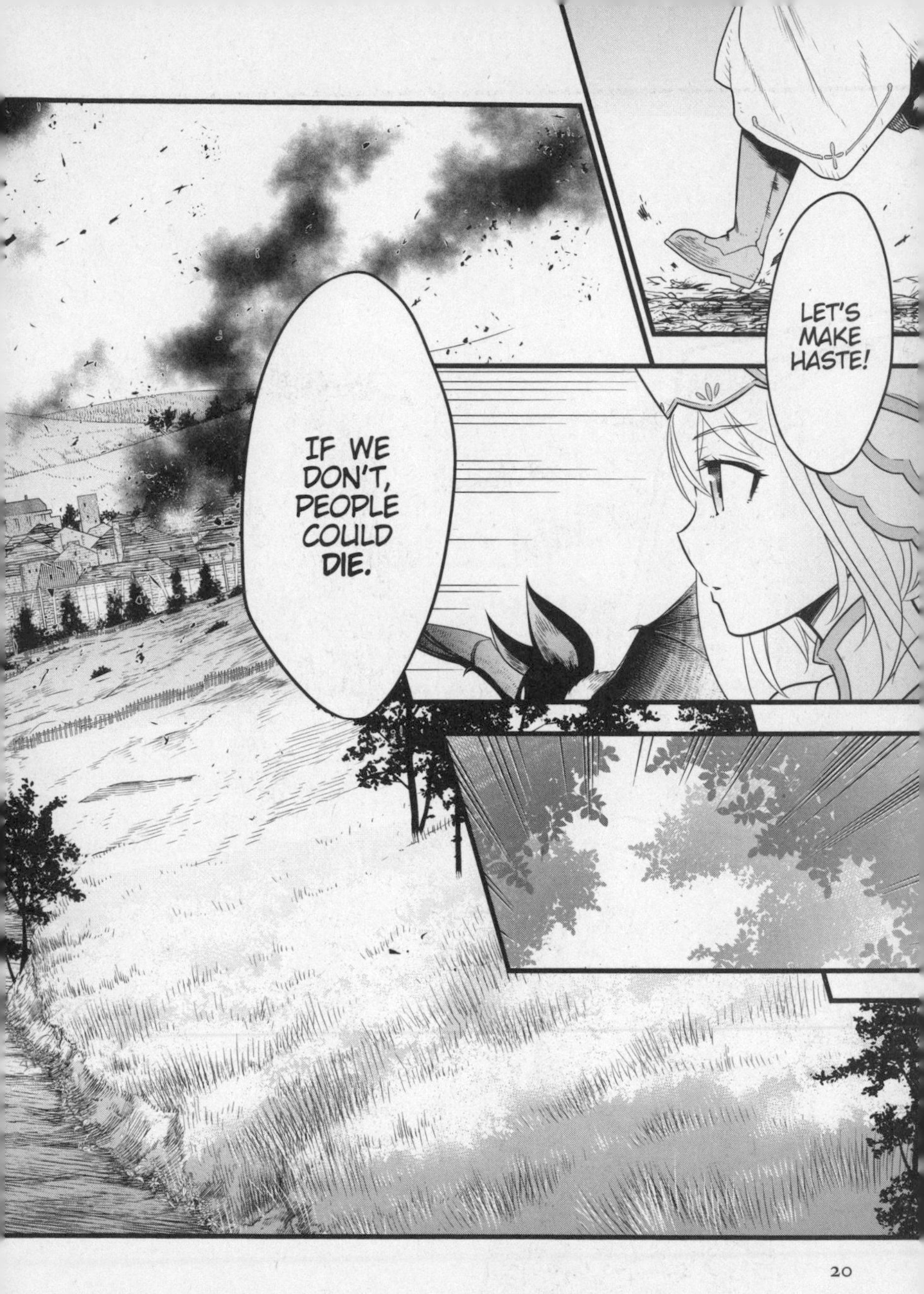
LET'S MAKE HASTE!
IF WE DON'T, PEOPLE COULD DIE.

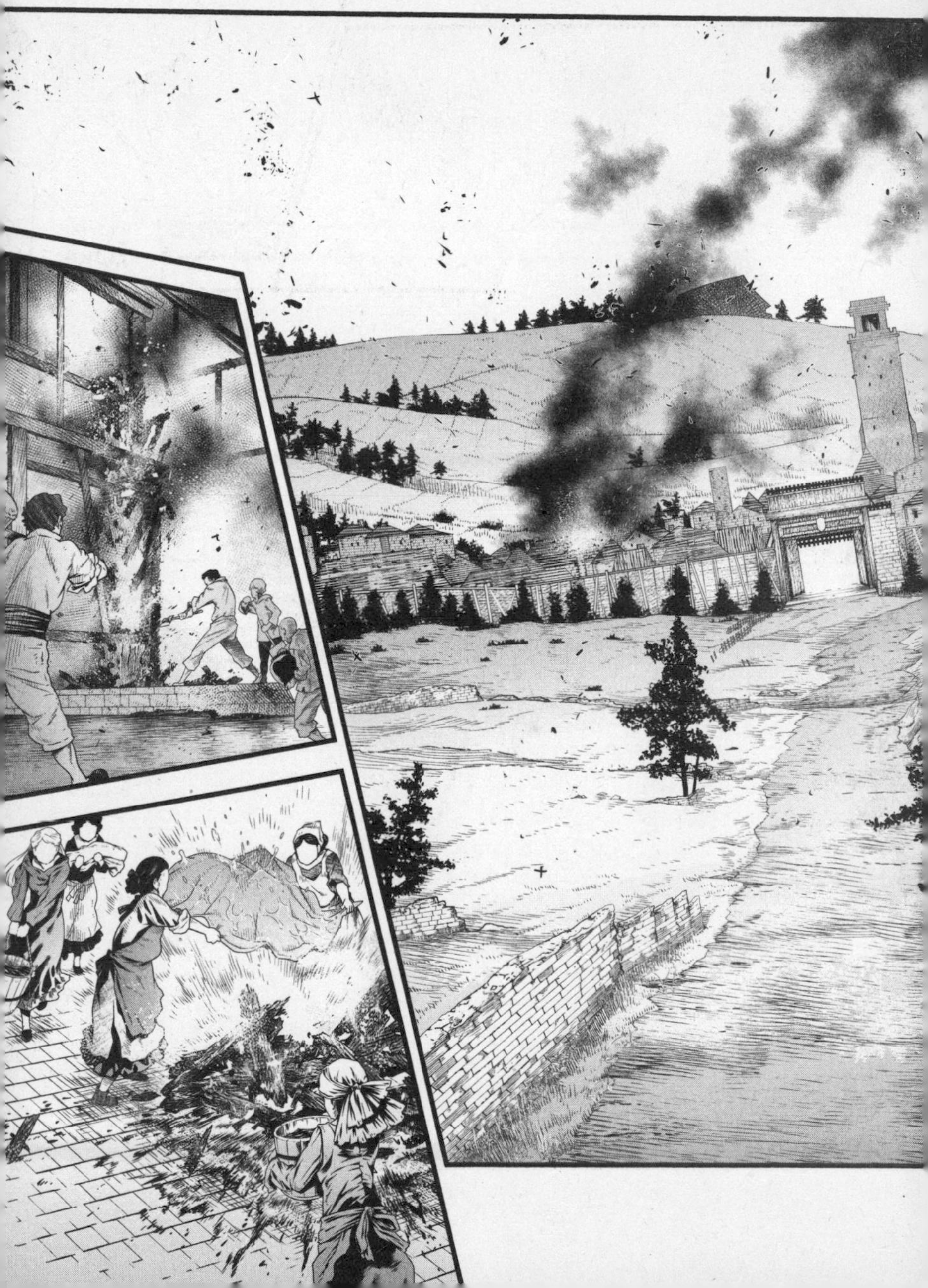

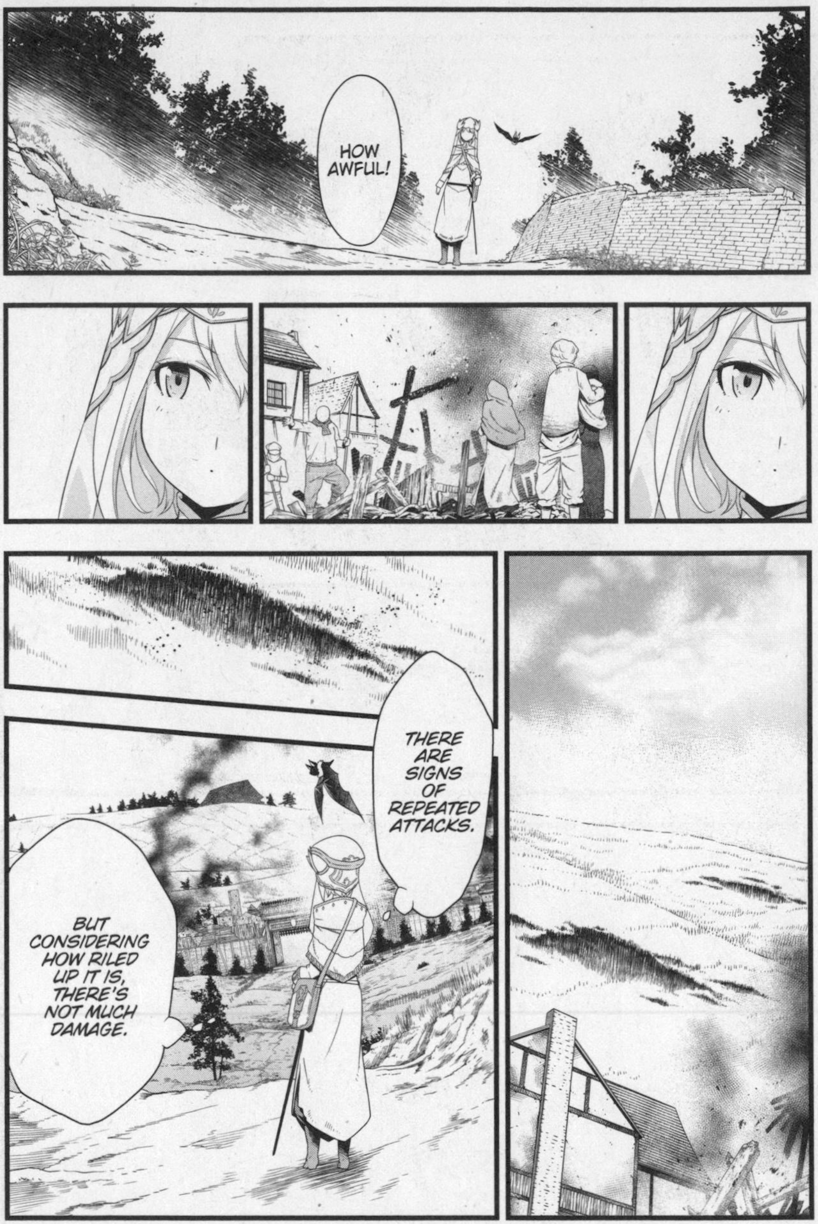
HOW AWFUL!
THERE ARE SIGNS OF REPEATED ATTACKS.
BUT CONSIDERING HOW RILED UP IT IS, THERE'S NOT MUCH DAMAGE.

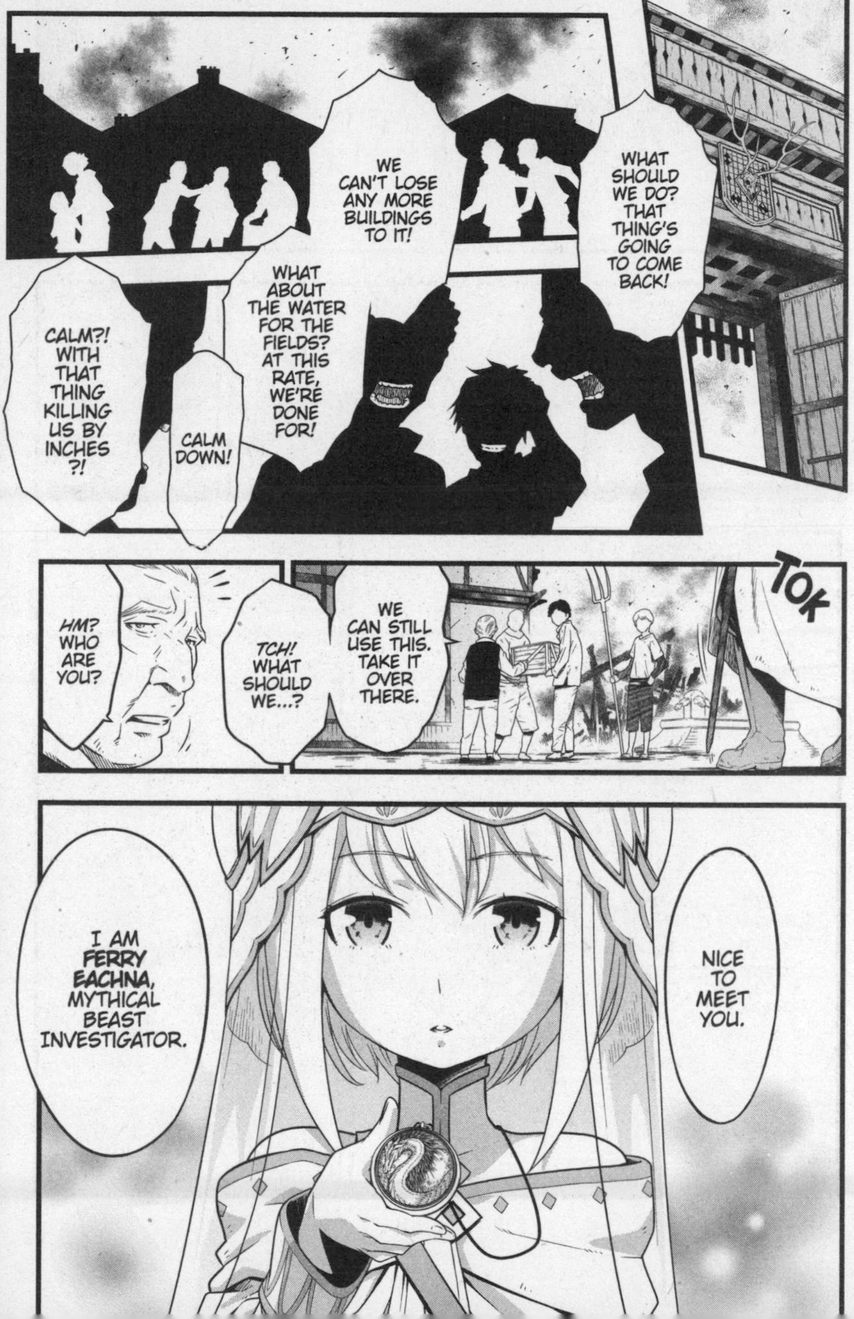
WHAT SHOULD WE DO? THAT THING'S GOING TO COME BACK!
WE CAN'T LOSE ANY MORE BUILDINGS TO IT!
WHAT ABOUT THE WATER FOR THE FIELDS? AT THIS RATE, WE'RE DONE FOR!
CALM DOWN!
CALM?! WITH THAT THING KILLING US BY INCHES?!
TOK
WE CAN STILL USE THIS. TAKE IT OVER THERE.
TCH! WHAT SHOULD WE...?
HM? WHO ARE YOU?
NICE TO MEET YOU.
I AM FERRY EACHNA, MYTHICAL BEAST INVESTIGATOR.

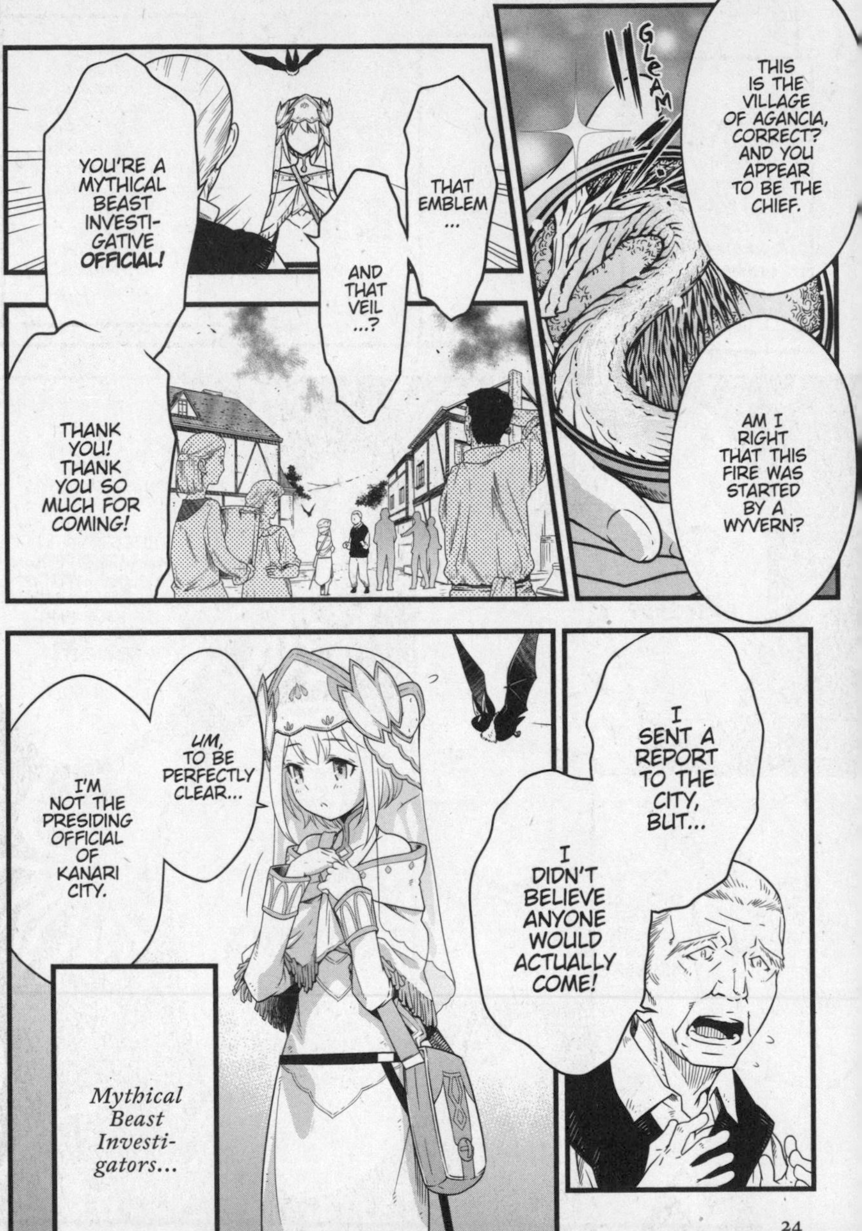
GLEAM
THIS IS THE VILLAGE OF AGANCIA, CORRECT? AND YOU APPEAR TO BE THE CHIEF.
AM I RIGHT THAT THIS FIRE WAS STARTED BY A WYVERN?
THAT EMBLEM...
AND THAT VEIL...?
YOU'RE A MYTHICAL BEAST INVESTI-GATIVE OFFICIAL!
THANK YOU! THANK YOU SO MUCH FOR COMING!
I SENT A REPORT TO THE CITY, BUT...
I DIDN'T BELIEVE ANYONE WOULD ACTUALLY COME!
UM, TO BE PERFECTLY CLEAR...
I'M NOT THE PRESIDING OFFICIAL OF KANARI CITY.
Mythical Beast Investi-gators...

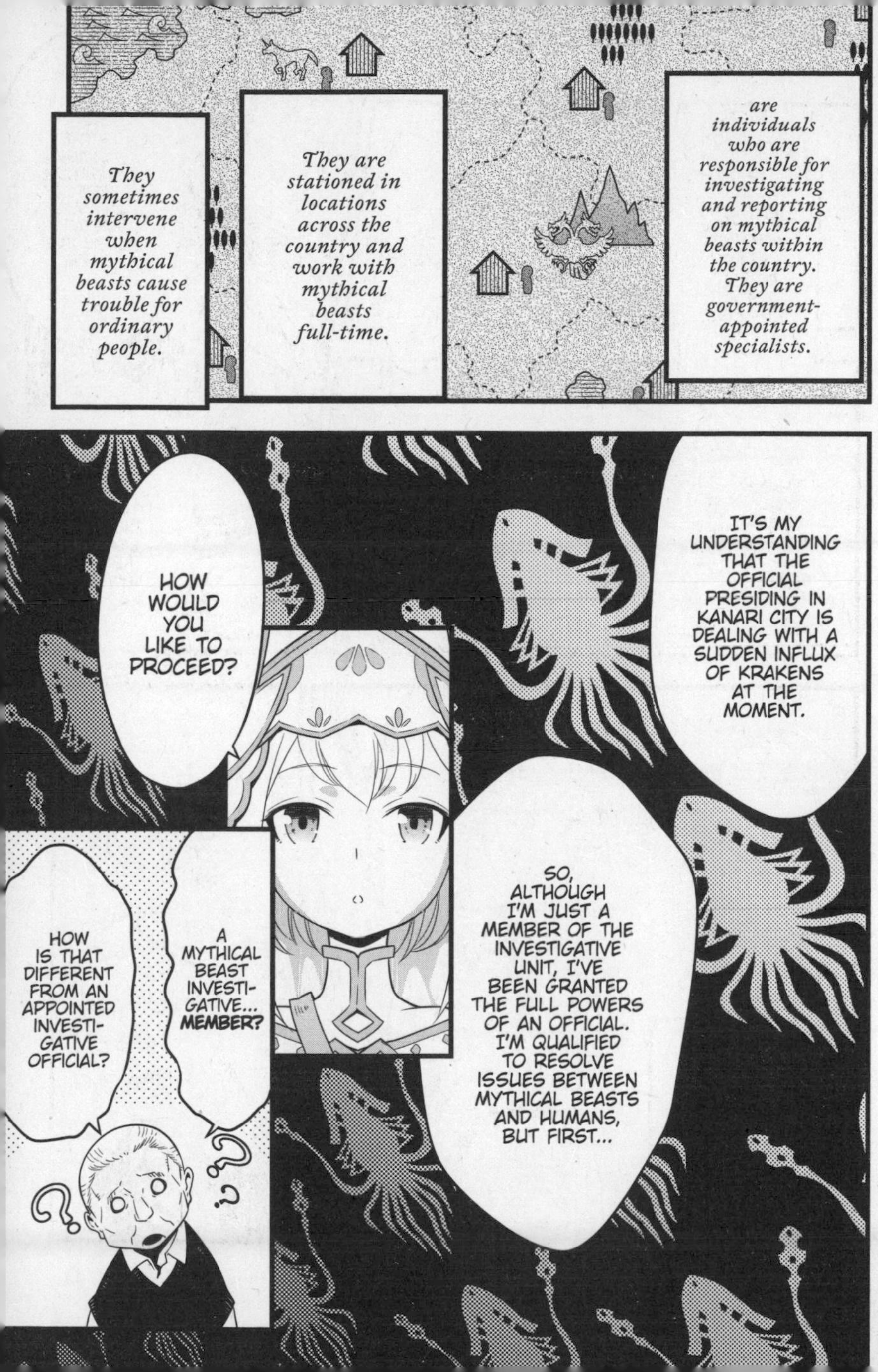
are individuals who are responsible for investigating and reporting on mythical beasts within the country. They are government-appointed specialists.
They are stationed in locations across the country and work with mythical beasts full-time.
They sometimes intervene when mythical beasts cause trouble for ordinary people.
IT'S MY UNDERSTANDING THAT THE OFFICIAL PRESIDING IN KANARI CITY IS DEALING WITH A SUDDEN INFLUX OF KRAKENS AT THE MOMENT.
HOW WOULD YOU LIKE TO PROCEED?
SO, ALTHOUGH I'M JUST A MEMBER OF THE INVESTIGATIVE UNIT, I'VE BEEN GRANTED THE FULL POWERS OF AN OFFICIAL. I'M QUALIFIED TO RESOLVE ISSUES BETWEEN MYTHICAL BEASTS AND HUMANS, BUT FIRST...
A MYTHICAL BEAST INVESTI-GATIVE... MEMBER?
HOW IS THAT DIFFERENT FROM AN APPOINTED INVESTI-GATIVE OFFICIAL?

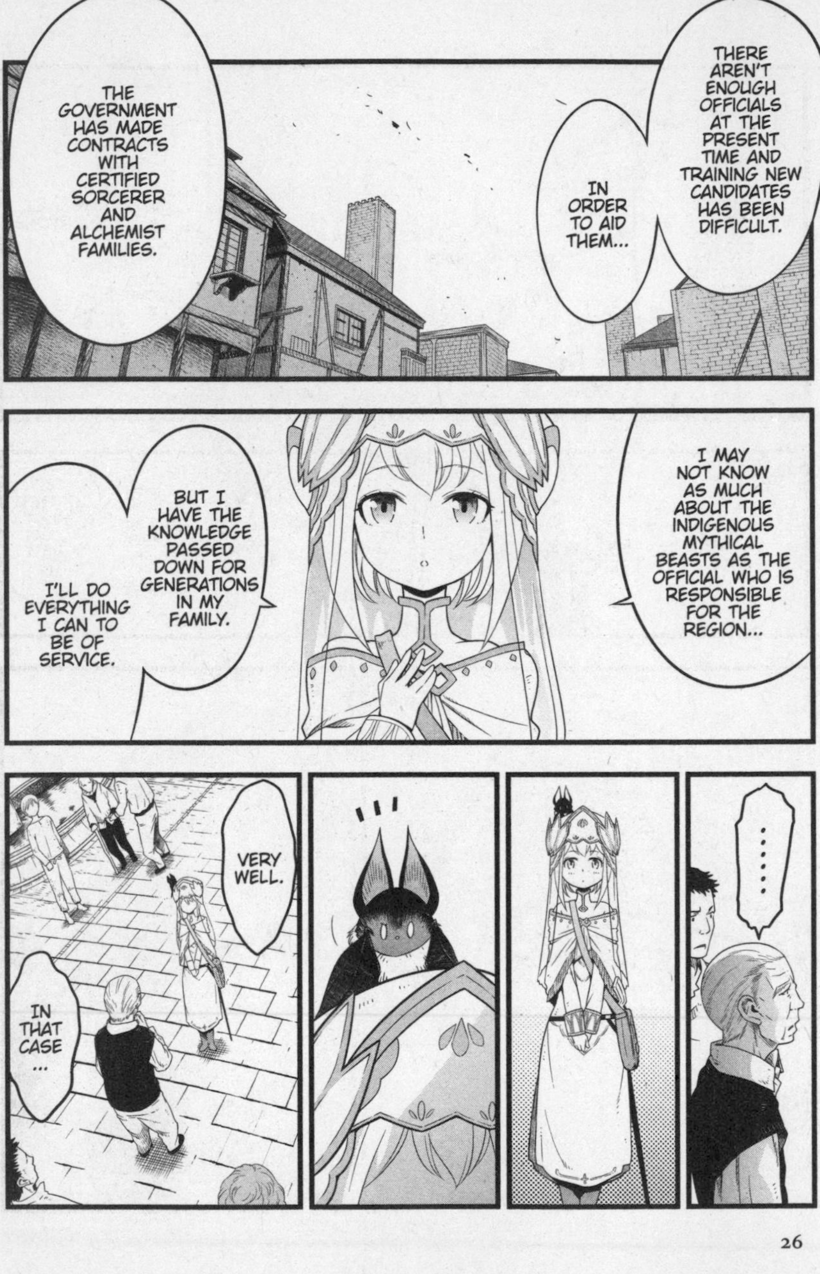
THERE AREN'T ENOUGH OFFICIALS AT THE PRESENT TIME AND TRAINING NEW CANDIDATES HAS BEEN DIFFICULT.
IN ORDER TO AID THEM...
THE GOVERNMENT HAS MADE CONTRACTS WITH CERTIFIED SORCERER AND ALCHEMIST FAMILIES.
I MAY NOT KNOW AS MUCH ABOUT THE INDIGENOUS MYTHICAL BEASTS AS THE OFFICIAL WHO IS RESPONSIBLE FOR THE REGION...
BUT I HAVE THE KNOWLEDGE PASSED DOWN FOR GENERATIONS IN MY FAMILY.
I'LL DO EVERYTHING I CAN TO BE OF SERVICE.
......
VERY WELL.
IN THAT CASE ...

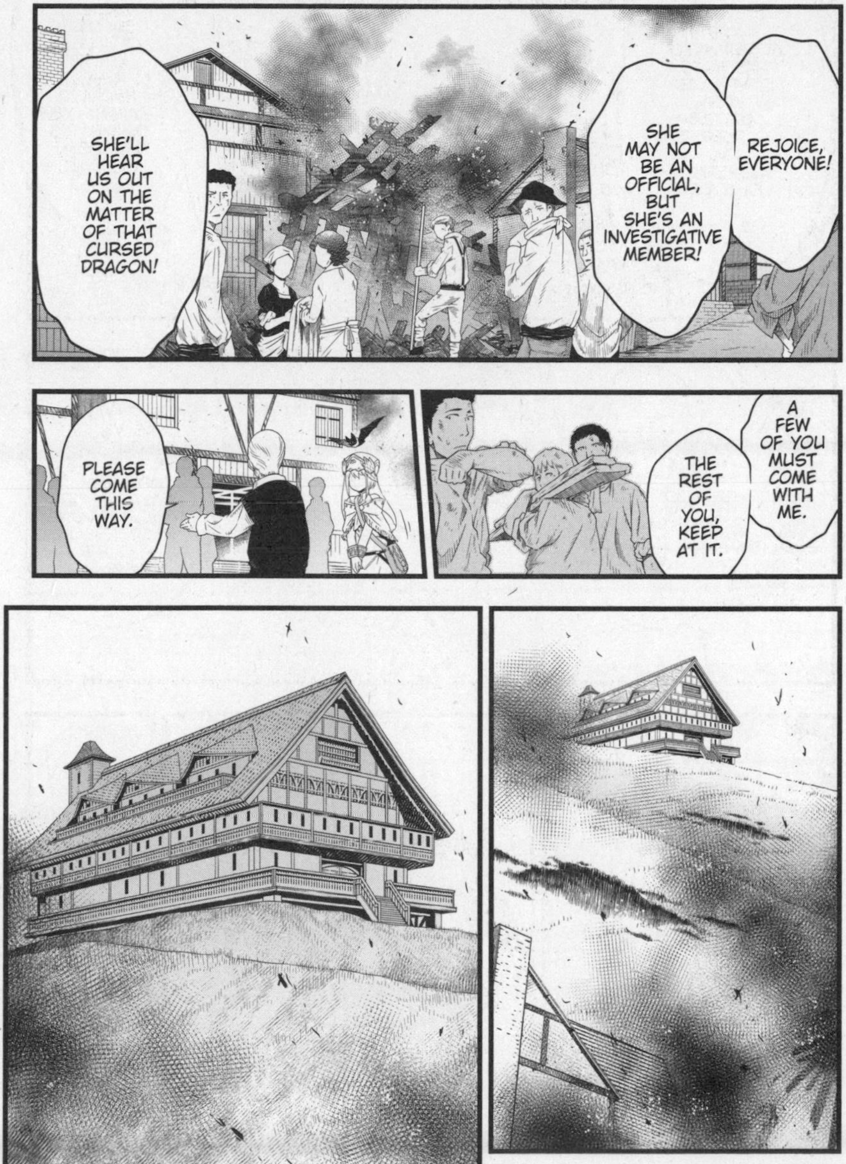
REJOICE, EVERYONE!
SHE MAY NOT BE AN OFFICIAL, BUT SHE'S AN INVESTIGATIVE MEMBER!
SHE'LL HEAR US OUT ON THE MATTER OF THAT CURSED DRAGON!
A FEW OF YOU MUST COME WITH ME.
THE REST OF YOU, KEEP AT IT.
PLEASE COME THIS WAY.

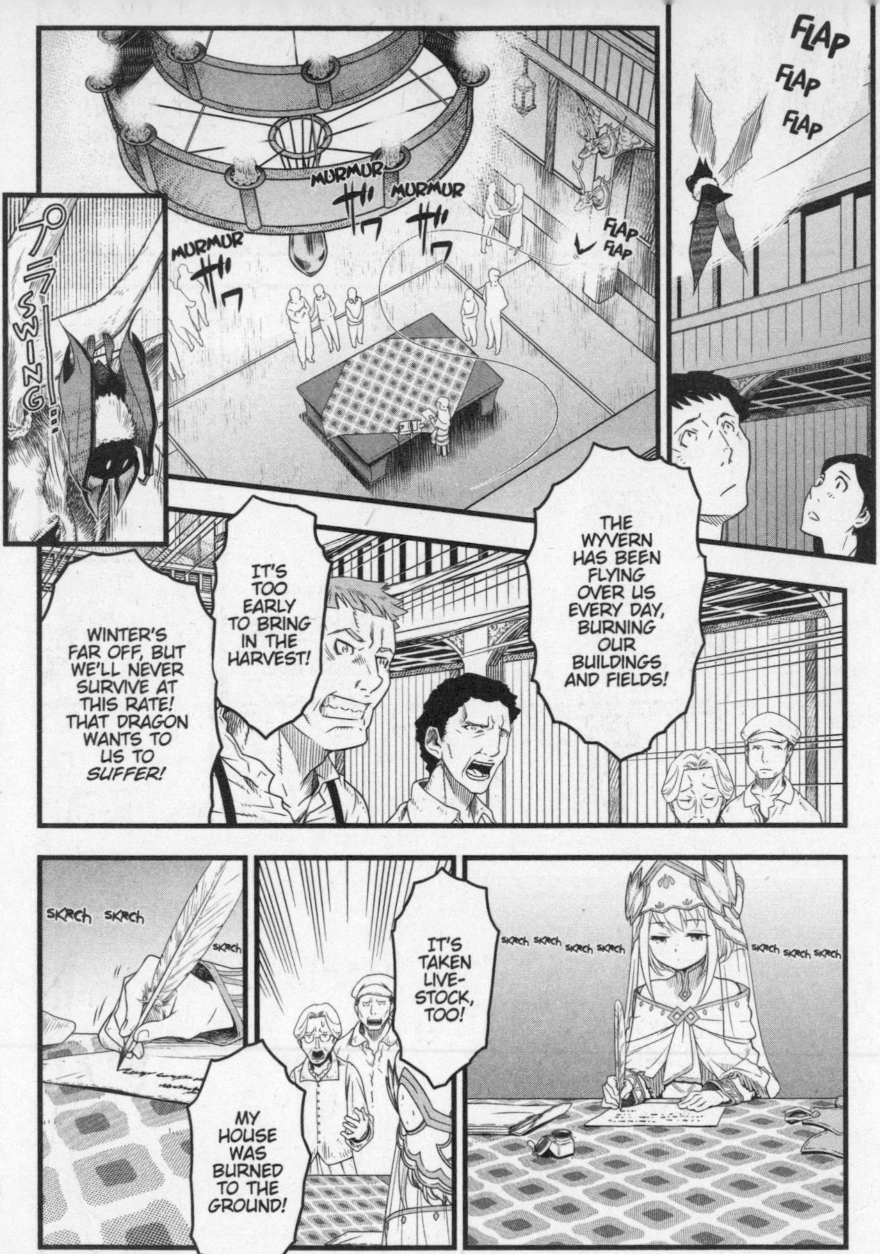
FLAP
FLAP
FLAP
MURMUR
MURMUR
MURMUR
FLAP FLAP
SWING!!
THE WYVERN HAS BEEN FLYING OVER US EVERY DAY, BURNING OUR BUILDINGS AND FIELDS!
IT'S TOO EARLY TO BRING IN THE HARVEST!
WINTER'S FAR OFF, BUT WE'LL NEVER SURVIVE AT THIS RATE! THAT DRAGON WANTS TO US TO SUFFER!
SKRCH SKRCH SKRCH SKRCH
SKRCH SKRCH SKRCH
IT'S TAKEN LIVE-STOCK, TOO!
MY HOUSE WAS BURNED TO THE GROUND!
SKRCH SKRCH
SKRCH

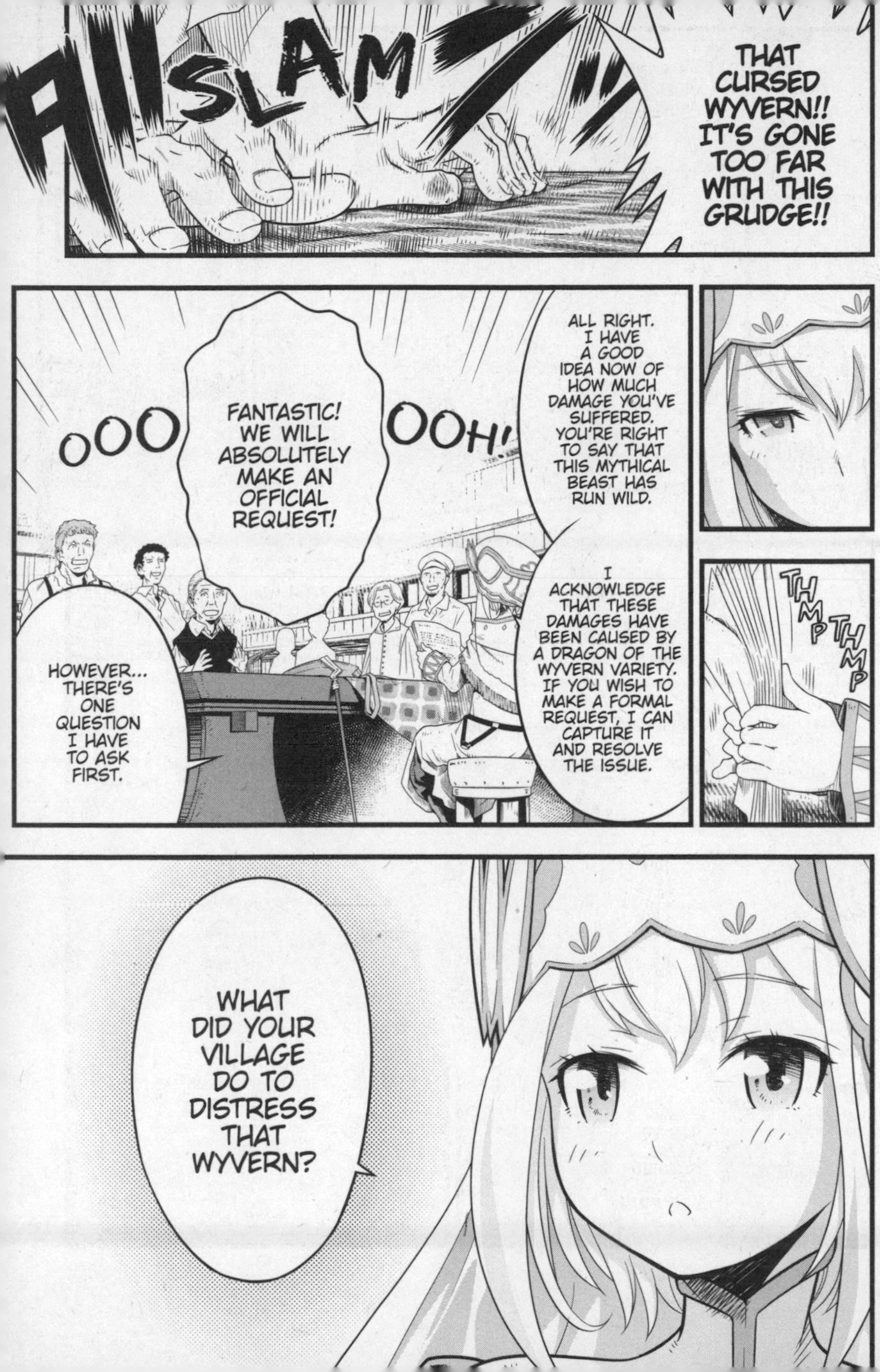
SLAM
THAT CURSED WYVERN!! IT'S GONE TOO FAR WITH THIS GRUDGE!!
THMP THMP
ALL RIGHT. I HAVE A GOOD IDEA NOW OF HOW MUCH DAMAGE YOU'VE SUFFERED. YOU'RE RIGHT TO SAY THAT THIS MYTHICAL BEAST HAS RUN WILD.
I ACKNOWLEDGE THAT THESE DAMAGES HAVE BEEN CAUSED BY A DRAGON OF THE WYVERN VARIETY. IF YOU WISH TO MAKE A FORMAL REQUEST, I CAN CAPTURE IT AND RESOLVE THE ISSUE.
OOOOOH!
FANTASTIC! WE WILL ABSOLUTELY MAKE AN OFFICIAL REQUEST!
HOWEVER... THERE'S ONE QUESTION I HAVE TO ASK FIRST.
WHAT DID YOUR VILLAGE DO TO DISTRESS THAT WYVERN?

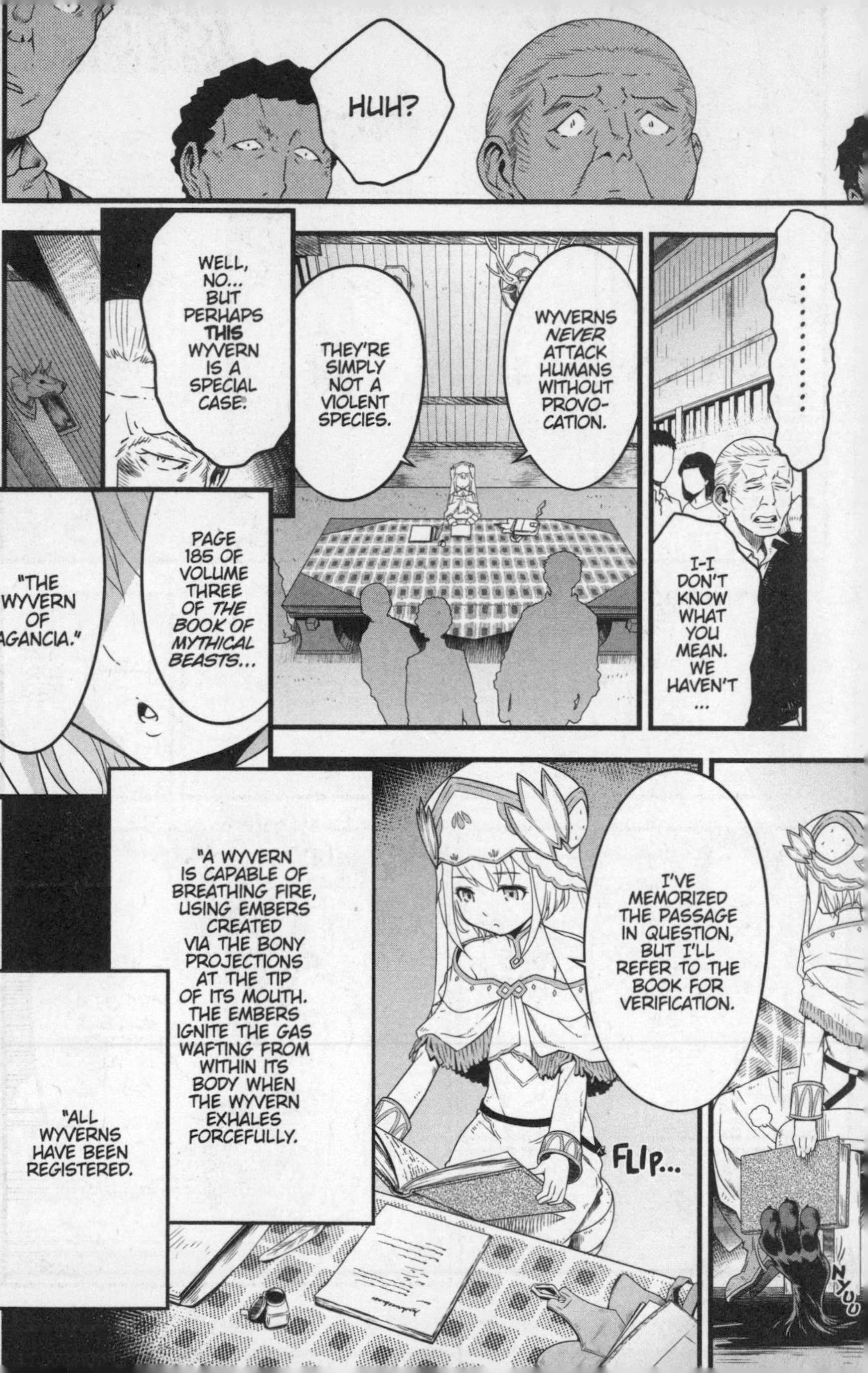
HUH?
......
I-I DON'T KNOW WHAT YOU MEAN. WE HAVEN'T ...
WYVERNS *NEVER* ATTACK HUMANS WITHOUT PROVOCATION.
THEY'RE SIMPLY NOT A VIOLENT SPECIES.
WELL, NO... BUT PERHAPS **THIS** WYVERN IS A SPECIAL CASE.
PAGE 185 OF VOLUME THREE OF *THE BOOK OF MYTHICAL BEASTS*...
"THE WYVERN OF AGANCIA."
I'VE MEMORIZED THE PASSAGE IN QUESTION, BUT I'LL REFER TO THE BOOK FOR VERIFICATION.
NYUU
FLIP...
"A WYVERN IS CAPABLE OF BREATHING FIRE, USING EMBERS CREATED VIA THE BONY PROJECTIONS AT THE TIP OF ITS MOUTH. THE EMBERS IGNITE THE GAS WAFTING FROM WITHIN ITS BODY WHEN THE WYVERN EXHALES FORCEFULLY.
"ALL WYVERNS HAVE BEEN REGISTERED.

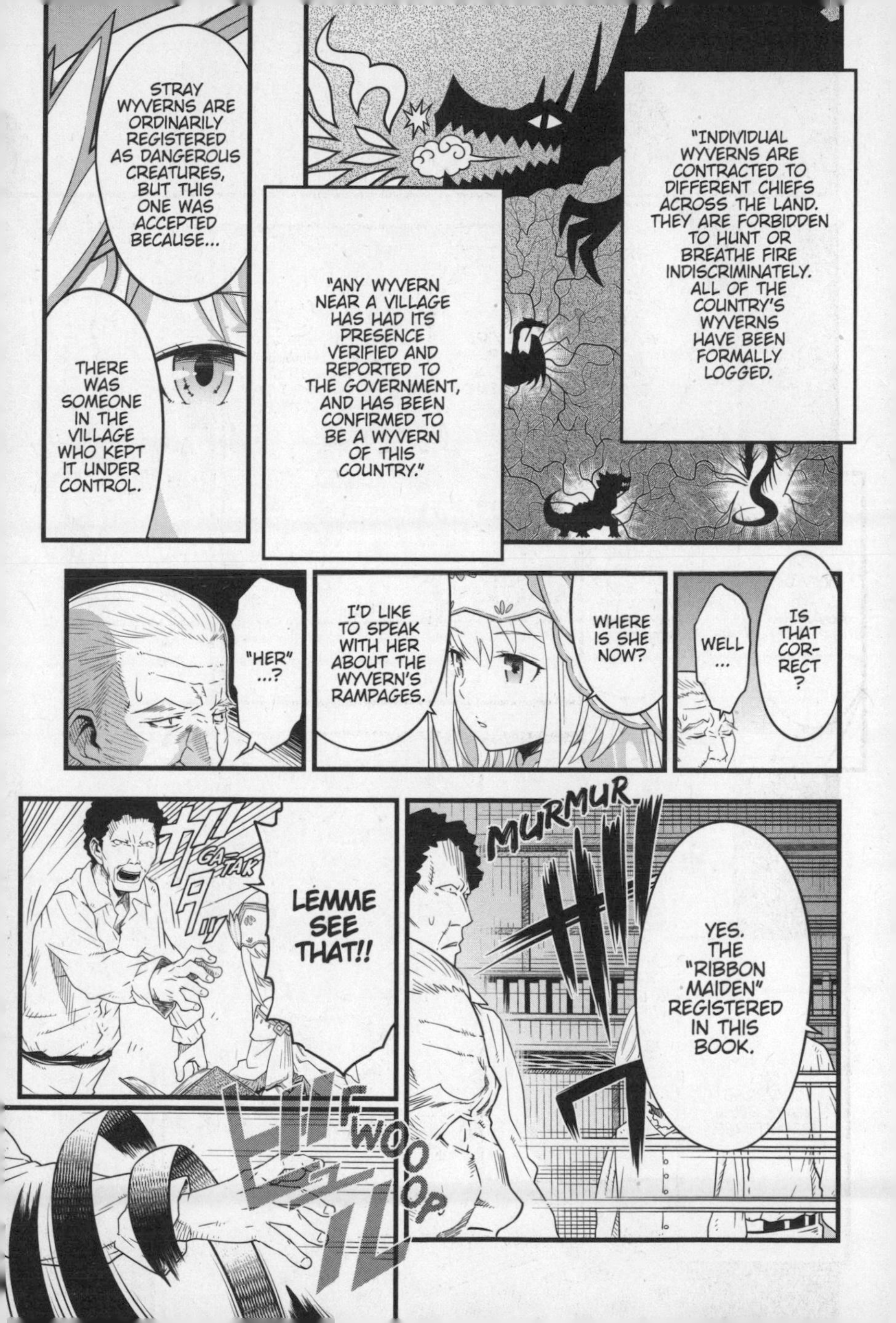
"INDIVIDUAL WYVERNS ARE CONTRACTED TO DIFFERENT CHIEFS ACROSS THE LAND. THEY ARE FORBIDDEN TO HUNT OR BREATHE FIRE INDISCRIMINATELY. ALL OF THE COUNTRY'S WYVERNS HAVE BEEN FORMALLY LOGGED.
"ANY WYVERN NEAR A VILLAGE HAS HAD ITS PRESENCE VERIFIED AND REPORTED TO THE GOVERNMENT, AND HAS BEEN CONFIRMED TO BE A WYVERN OF THIS COUNTRY."
STRAY WYVERNS ARE ORDINARILY REGISTERED AS DANGEROUS CREATURES, BUT THIS ONE WAS ACCEPTED BECAUSE...
THERE WAS SOMEONE IN THE VILLAGE WHO KEPT IT UNDER CONTROL.
IS THAT CORRECT?
WELL...
WHERE IS SHE NOW?
I'D LIKE TO SPEAK WITH HER ABOUT THE WYVERN'S RAMPAGES.
"HER"...?
MURMUR
YES. THE "RIBBON MAIDEN" REGISTERED IN THIS BOOK.
GATAK
LEMME SEE THAT!!
FWOOOP

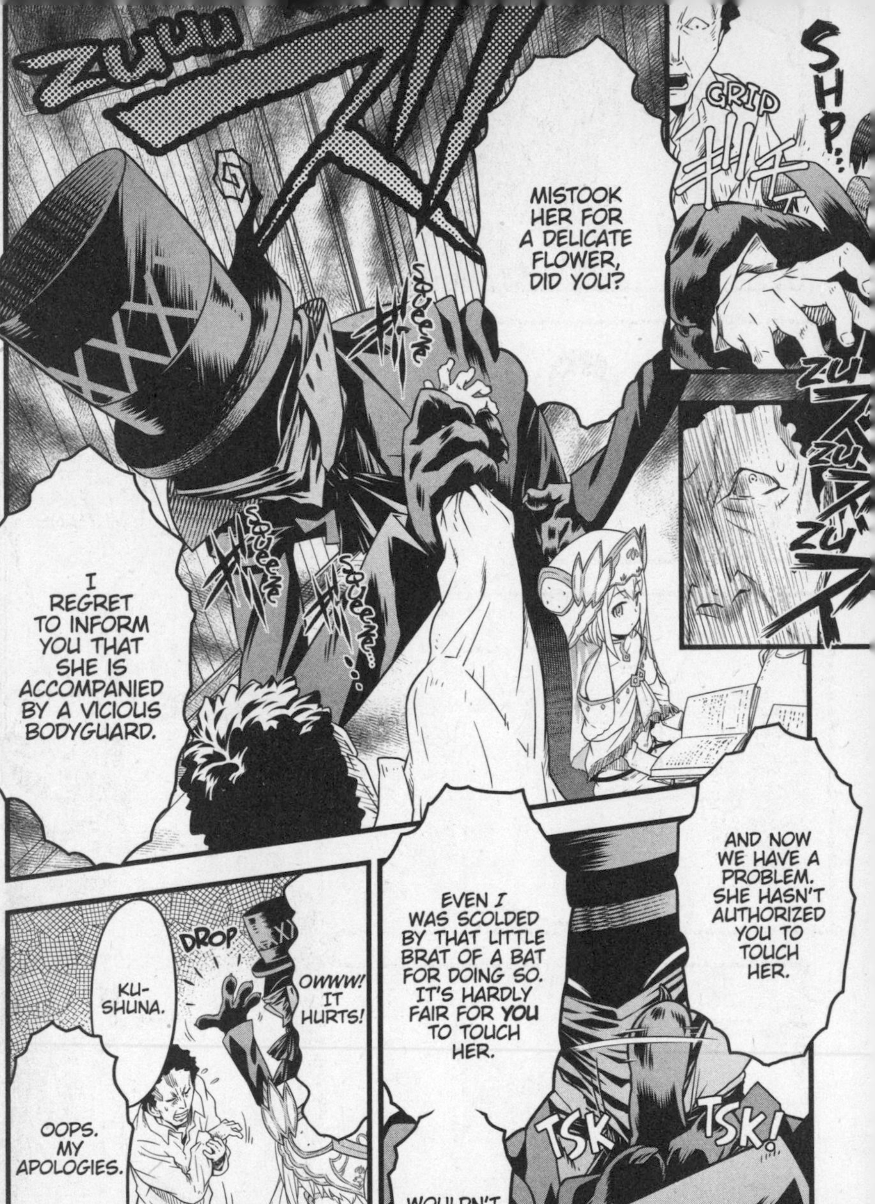
SHP...
GRIP
ZU
ZU
ZU
MISTOOK HER FOR A DELICATE FLOWER, DID YOU?
I REGRET TO INFORM YOU THAT SHE IS ACCOMPANIED BY A VICIOUS BODYGUARD.
AND NOW WE HAVE A PROBLEM. SHE HASN'T AUTHORIZED YOU TO TOUCH HER.
EVEN *I* WAS SCOLDED BY THAT LITTLE BRAT OF A BAT FOR DOING SO. IT'S HARDLY FAIR FOR **YOU** TO TOUCH HER.
TSK TSK!
WOULDN'T YOU AGREE?
KU-SHUNA.
DROP
OWWW! IT HURTS!
OOPS. MY APOLOGIES.

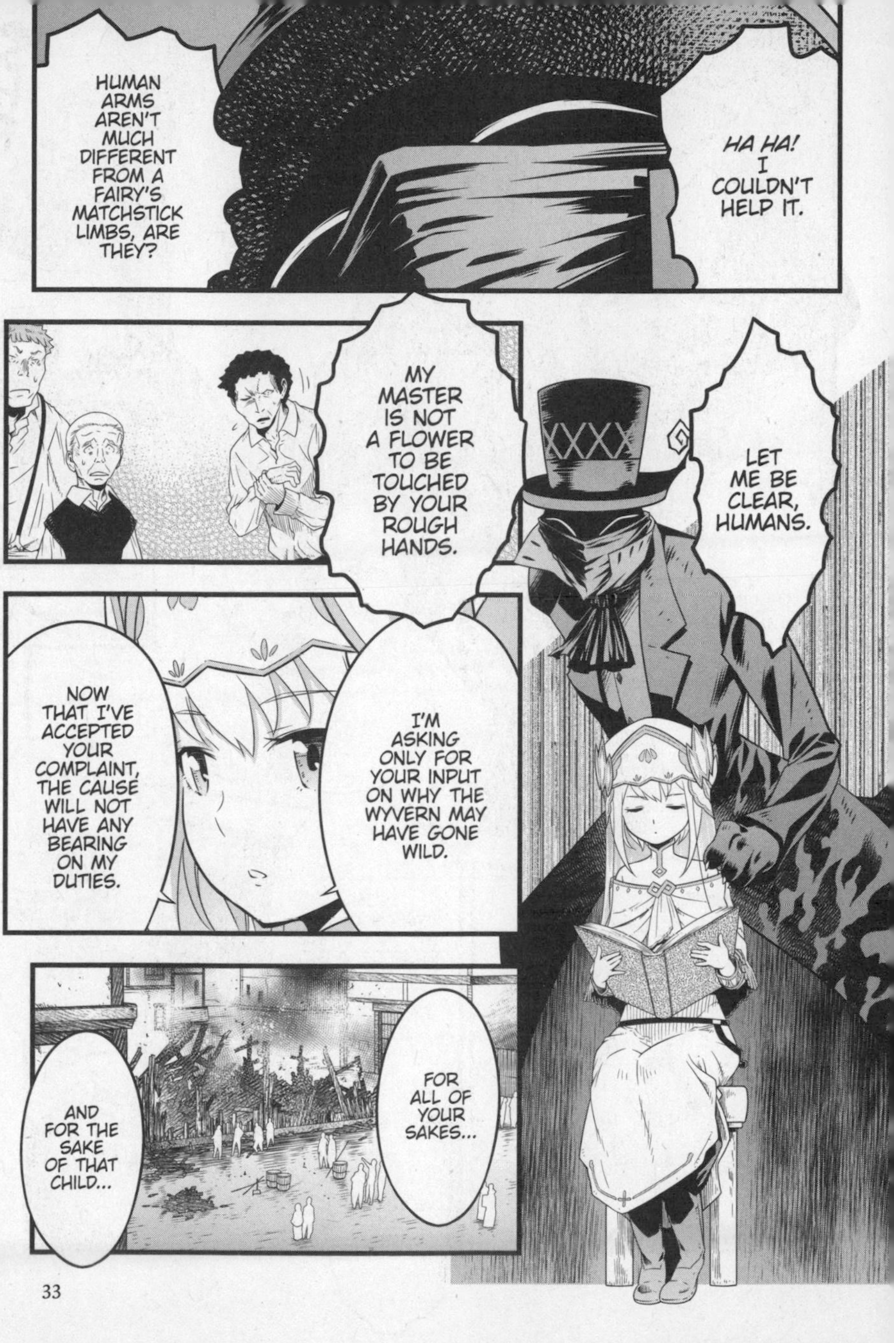
HA HA! I COULDN'T HELP IT.
HUMAN ARMS AREN'T MUCH DIFFERENT FROM A FAIRY'S MATCHSTICK LIMBS, ARE THEY?
LET ME BE CLEAR, HUMANS.
MY MASTER IS NOT A FLOWER TO BE TOUCHED BY YOUR ROUGH HANDS.
I'M ASKING ONLY FOR YOUR INPUT ON WHY THE WYVERN MAY HAVE GONE WILD.
NOW THAT I'VE ACCEPTED YOUR COMPLAINT, THE CAUSE WILL NOT HAVE ANY BEARING ON MY DUTIES.
FOR ALL OF YOUR SAKES...
AND FOR THE SAKE OF THAT CHILD...

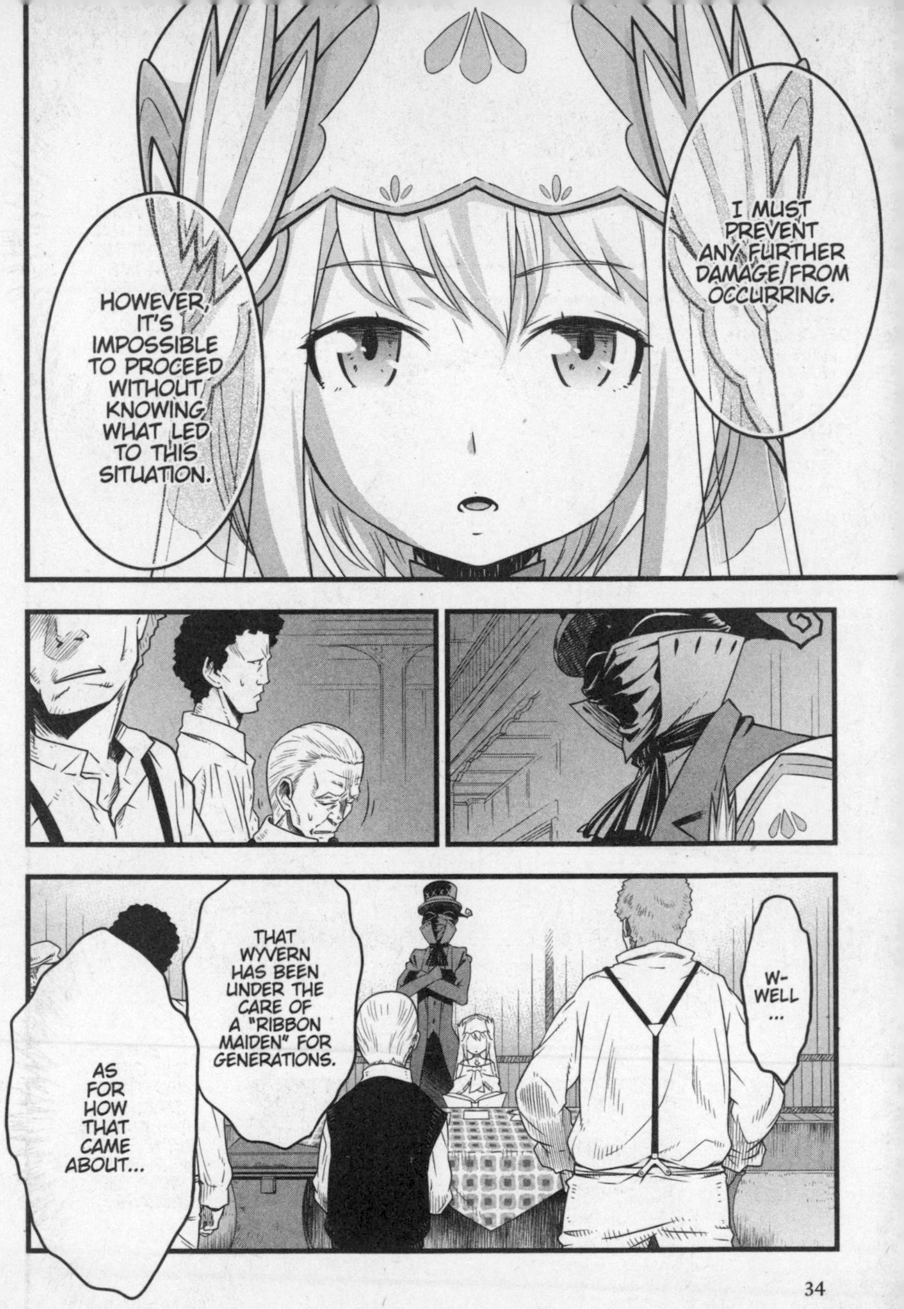
I MUST PREVENT ANY FURTHER DAMAGE FROM OCCURRING.
HOWEVER, IT'S IMPOSSIBLE TO PROCEED WITHOUT KNOWING WHAT LED TO THIS SITUATION.
W-WELL...
THAT WYVERN HAS BEEN UNDER THE CARE OF A "RIBBON MAIDEN" FOR GENERATIONS.
AS FOR HOW THAT CAME ABOUT...

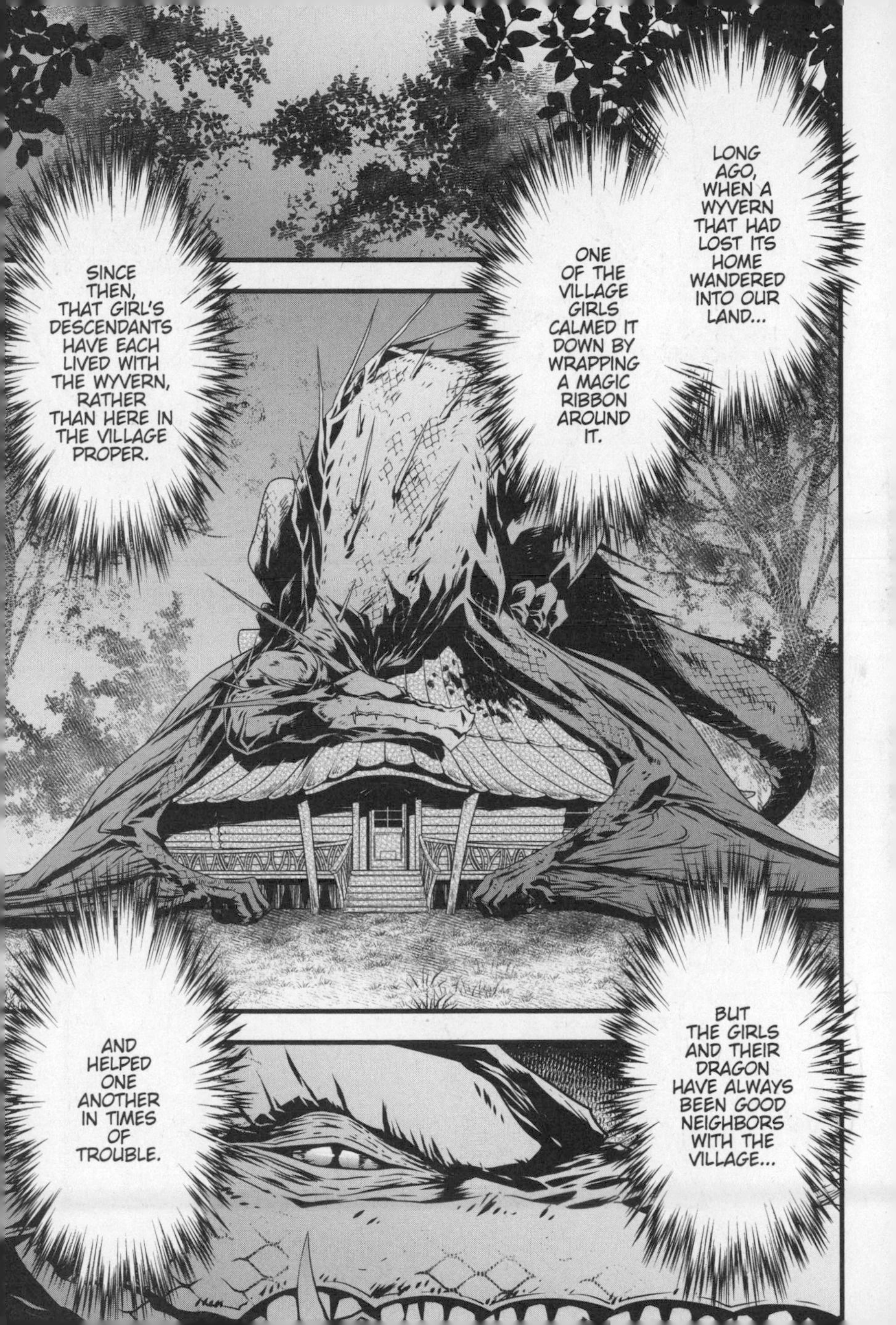
LONG AGO, WHEN A WYVERN THAT HAD LOST ITS HOME WANDERED INTO OUR LAND...
ONE OF THE VILLAGE GIRLS CALMED IT DOWN BY WRAPPING A MAGIC RIBBON AROUND IT.
SINCE THEN, THAT GIRL'S DESCENDANTS HAVE EACH LIVED WITH THE WYVERN, RATHER THAN HERE IN THE VILLAGE PROPER.
BUT THE GIRLS AND THEIR DRAGON HAVE ALWAYS BEEN GOOD NEIGHBORS WITH THE VILLAGE...
AND HELPED ONE ANOTHER IN TIMES OF TROUBLE.

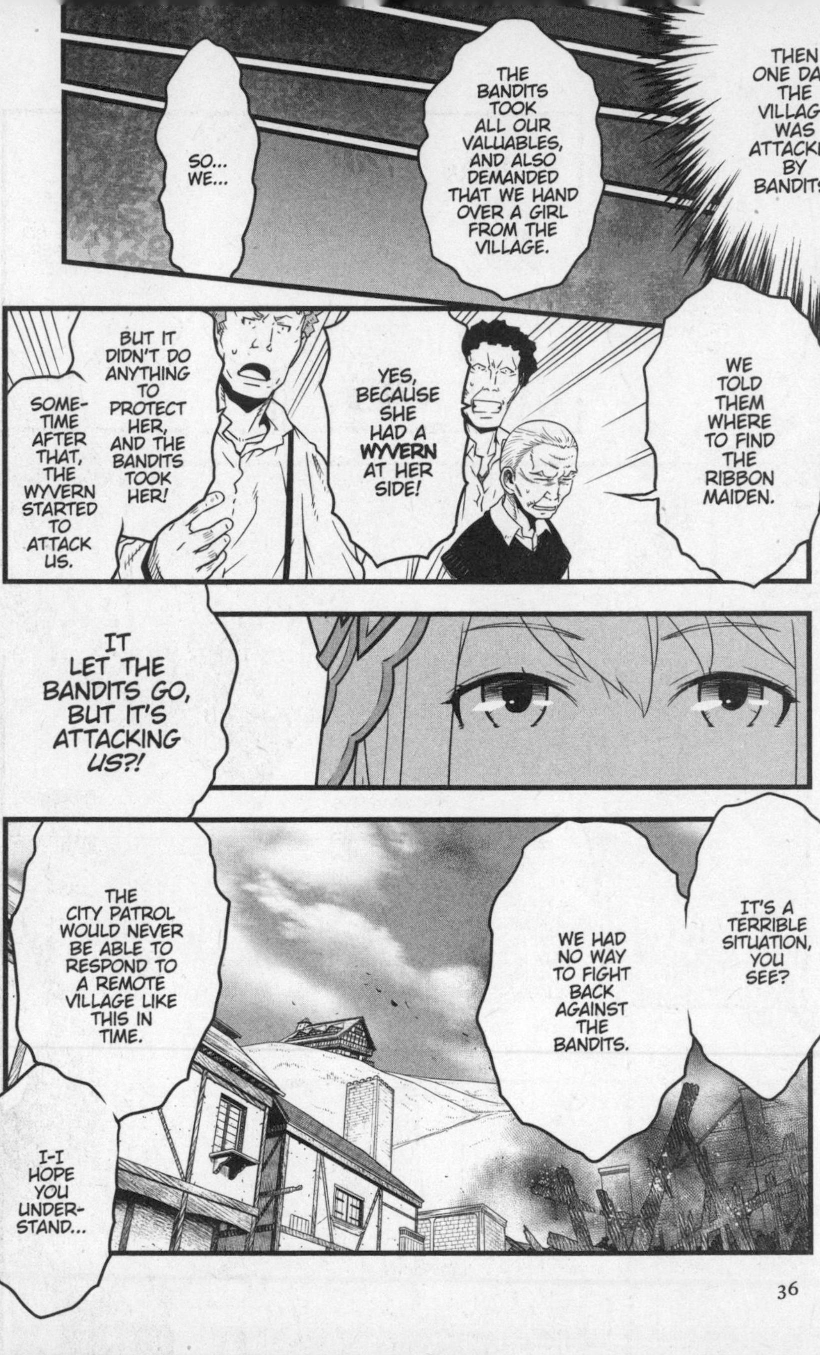
THEN ONE DAY, THE VILLAGE WAS ATTACKED BY BANDITS.
THE BANDITS TOOK ALL OUR VALUABLES, AND ALSO DEMANDED THAT WE HAND OVER A GIRL FROM THE VILLAGE.
SO... WE...
WE TOLD THEM WHERE TO FIND THE RIBBON MAIDEN.
YES, BECAUSE SHE HAD A **WYVERN** AT HER SIDE!
BUT IT DIDN'T DO ANYTHING TO PROTECT HER, AND THE BANDITS TOOK HER!
SOME-TIME AFTER THAT, THE WYVERN STARTED TO ATTACK US.
IT LET THE BANDITS GO, BUT IT'S ATTACKING *US?!*
IT'S A TERRIBLE SITUATION, YOU SEE?
WE HAD NO WAY TO FIGHT BACK AGAINST THE BANDITS.
THE CITY PATROL WOULD NEVER BE ABLE TO RESPOND TO A REMOTE VILLAGE LIKE THIS IN TIME.
I-I HOPE YOU UNDER-STAND...

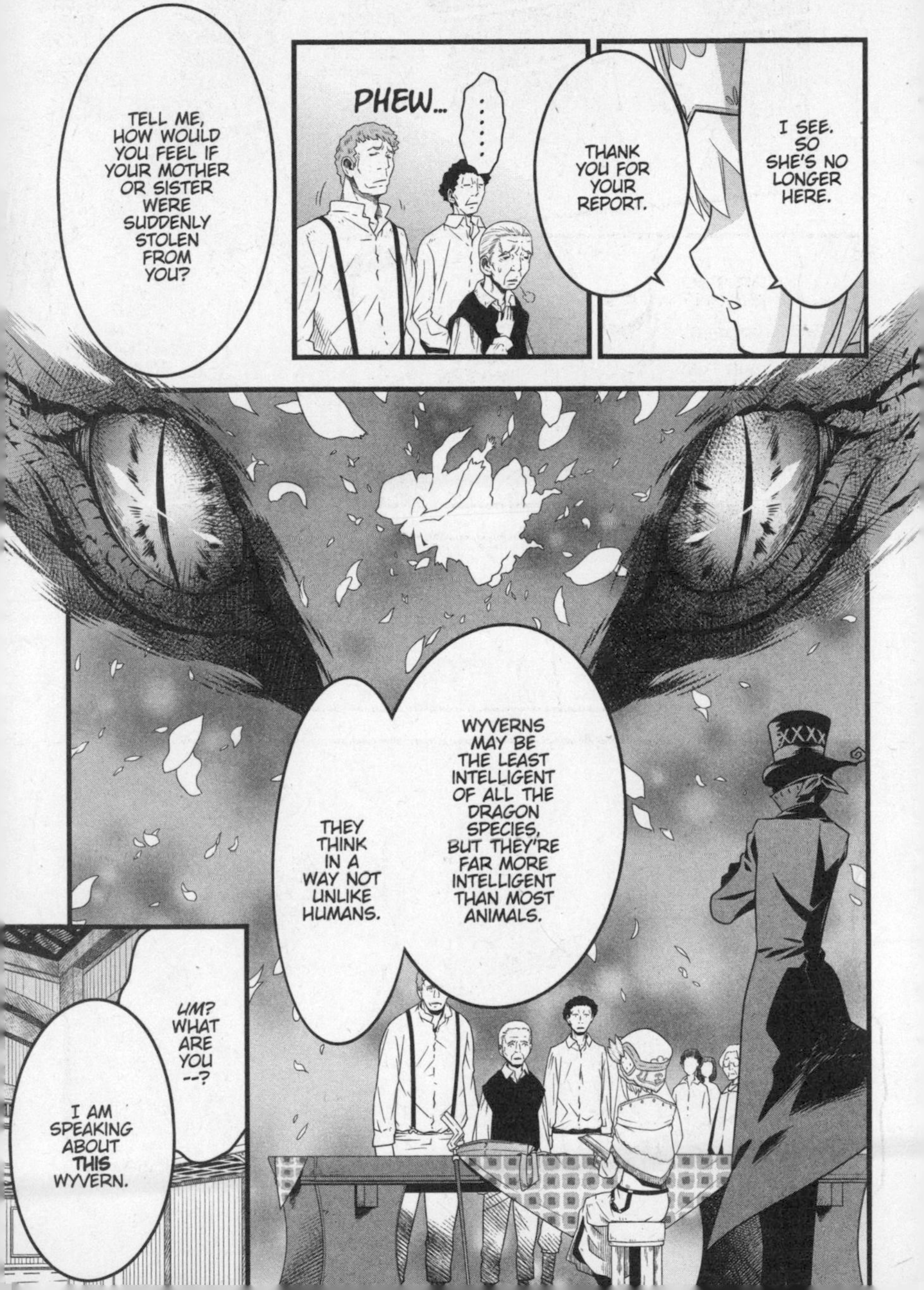
I SEE. SO SHE'S NO LONGER HERE.
THANK YOU FOR YOUR REPORT.
PHEW...
......
TELL ME, HOW WOULD YOU FEEL IF YOUR MOTHER OR SISTER WERE SUDDENLY STOLEN FROM YOU?
UM? WHAT ARE YOU --?
I AM SPEAKING ABOUT THIS WYVERN.
WYVERNS MAY BE THE LEAST INTELLIGENT OF ALL THE DRAGON SPECIES, BUT THEY'RE FAR MORE INTELLIGENT THAN MOST ANIMALS.
THEY THINK IN A WAY NOT UNLIKE HUMANS.

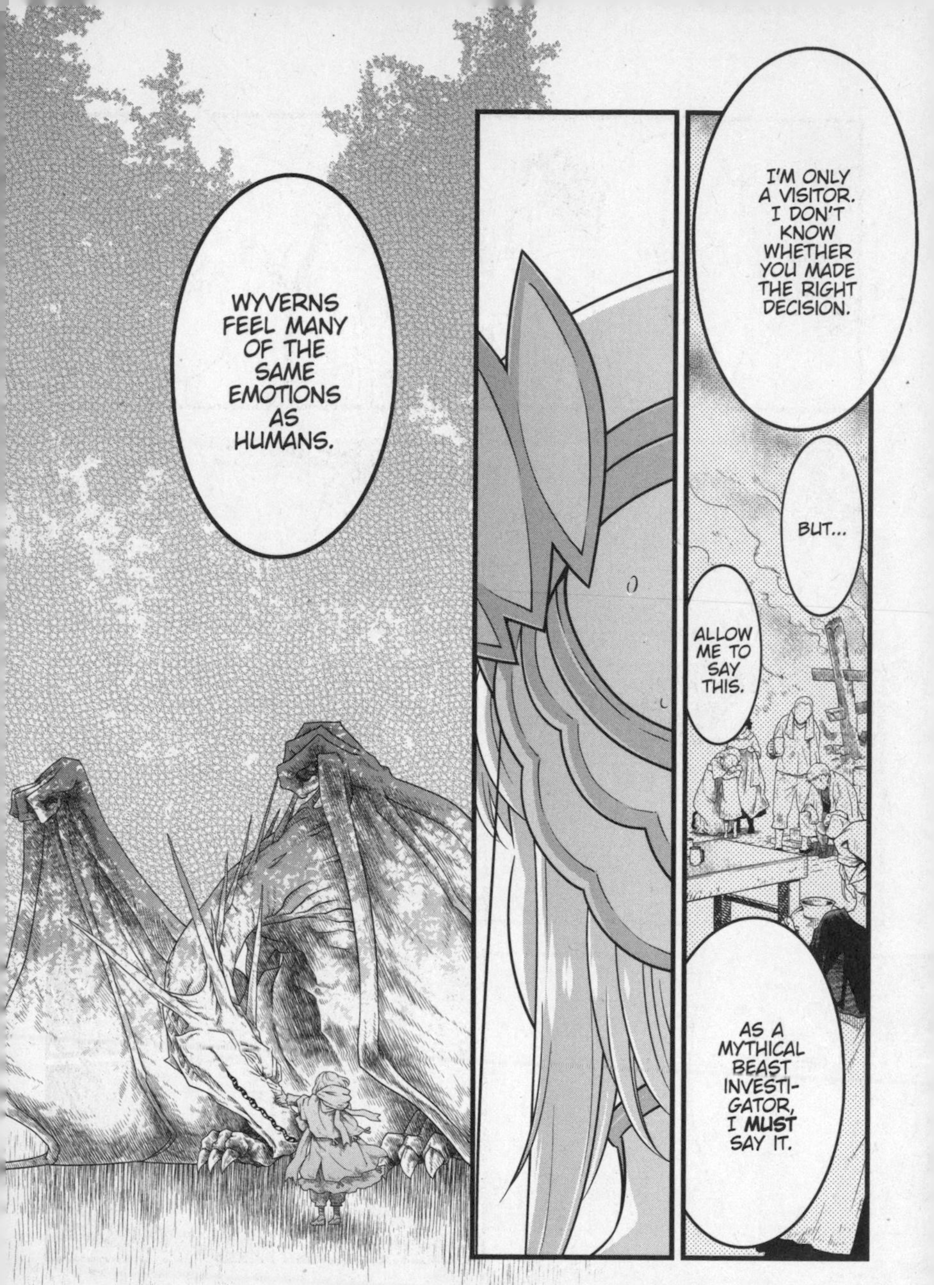
I'M ONLY A VISITOR. I DON'T KNOW WHETHER YOU MADE THE RIGHT DECISION.
BUT...
ALLOW ME TO SAY THIS.
AS A MYTHICAL BEAST INVESTIGATOR, I **MUST** SAY IT.
WYVERNS FEEL MANY OF THE SAME EMOTIONS AS HUMANS.

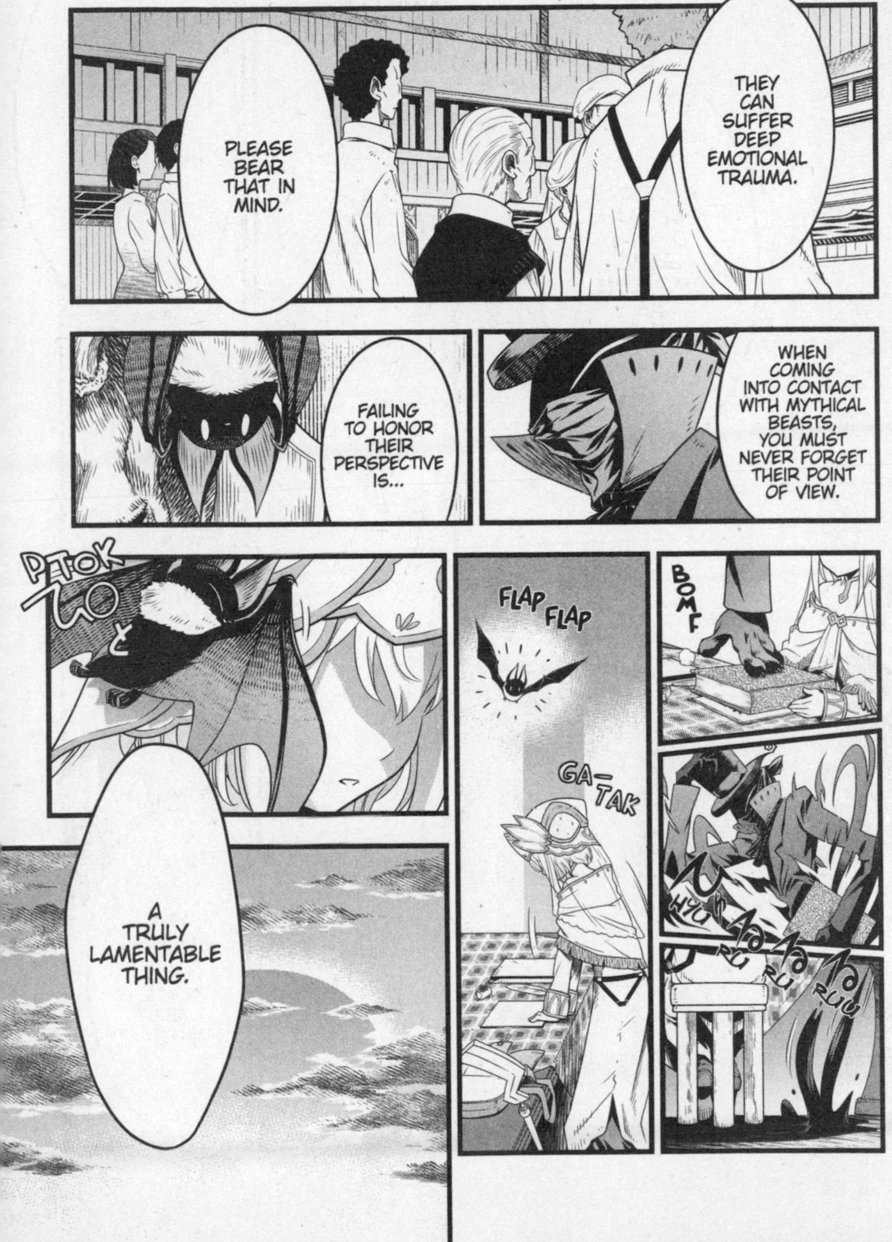
THEY CAN SUFFER DEEP EMOTIONAL TRAUMA.
PLEASE BEAR THAT IN MIND.
WHEN COMING INTO CONTACT WITH MYTHICAL BEASTS, YOU MUST NEVER FORGET THEIR POINT OF VIEW.
FAILING TO HONOR THEIR PERSPECTIVE IS...
BOMF
HYU RU RU RU RUU
FLAP FLAP
GA-TAK
PTOK
A TRULY LAMENTABLE THING.

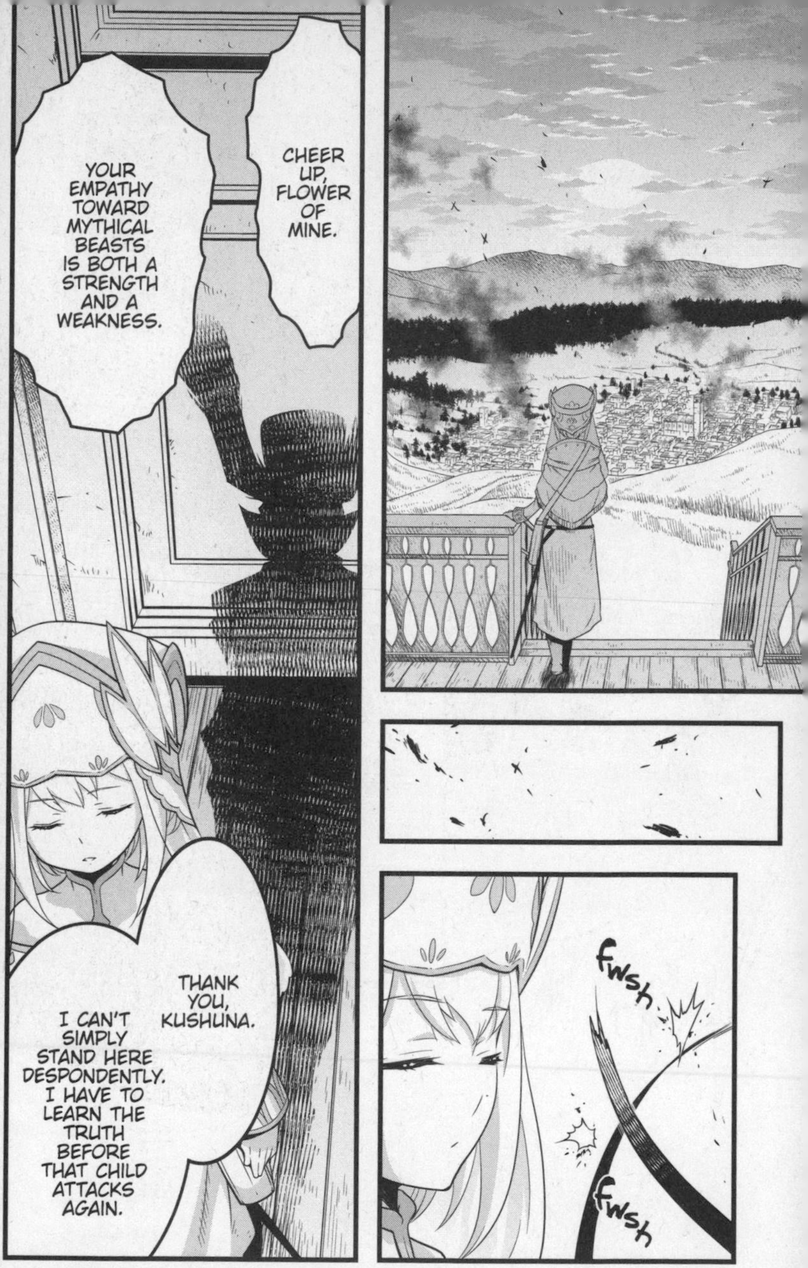
fwsh
fwsh
CHEER UP, FLOWER OF MINE.
YOUR EMPATHY TOWARD MYTHICAL BEASTS IS BOTH A STRENGTH AND A WEAKNESS.
THANK YOU, KUSHUNA.
I CAN'T SIMPLY STAND HERE DESPONDENTLY. I HAVE TO LEARN THE TRUTH BEFORE THAT CHILD ATTACKS AGAIN.

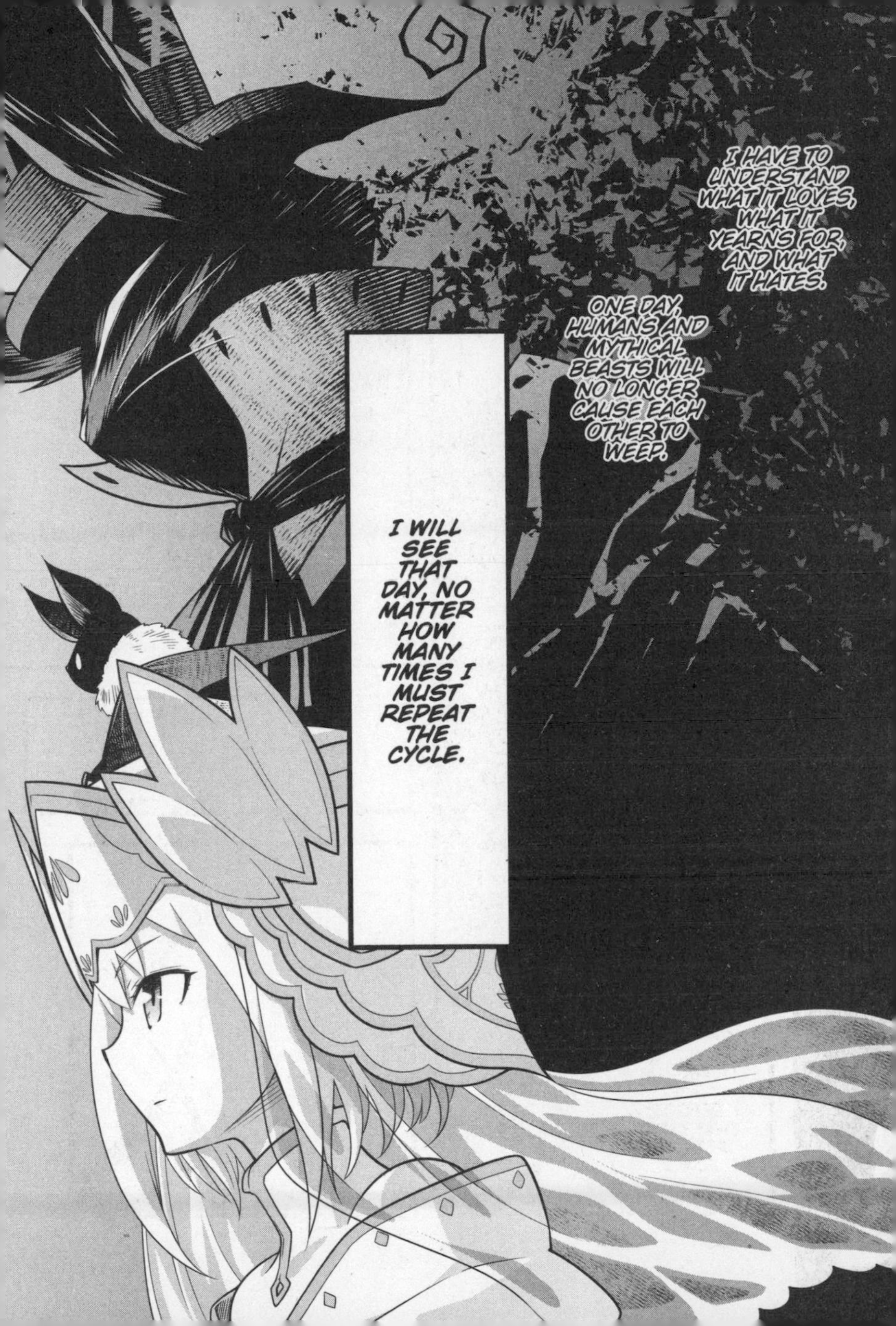
I HAVE TO UNDERSTAND WHAT IT LOVES, WHAT IT YEARNS FOR, AND WHAT IT HATES.
ONE DAY, HUMANS AND MYTHICAL BEASTS WILL NO LONGER CAUSE EACH OTHER TO WEEP.
I WILL SEE THAT DAY, NO MATTER HOW MANY TIMES I MUST REPEAT THE CYCLE.

Mythical Bĕast
Investigator

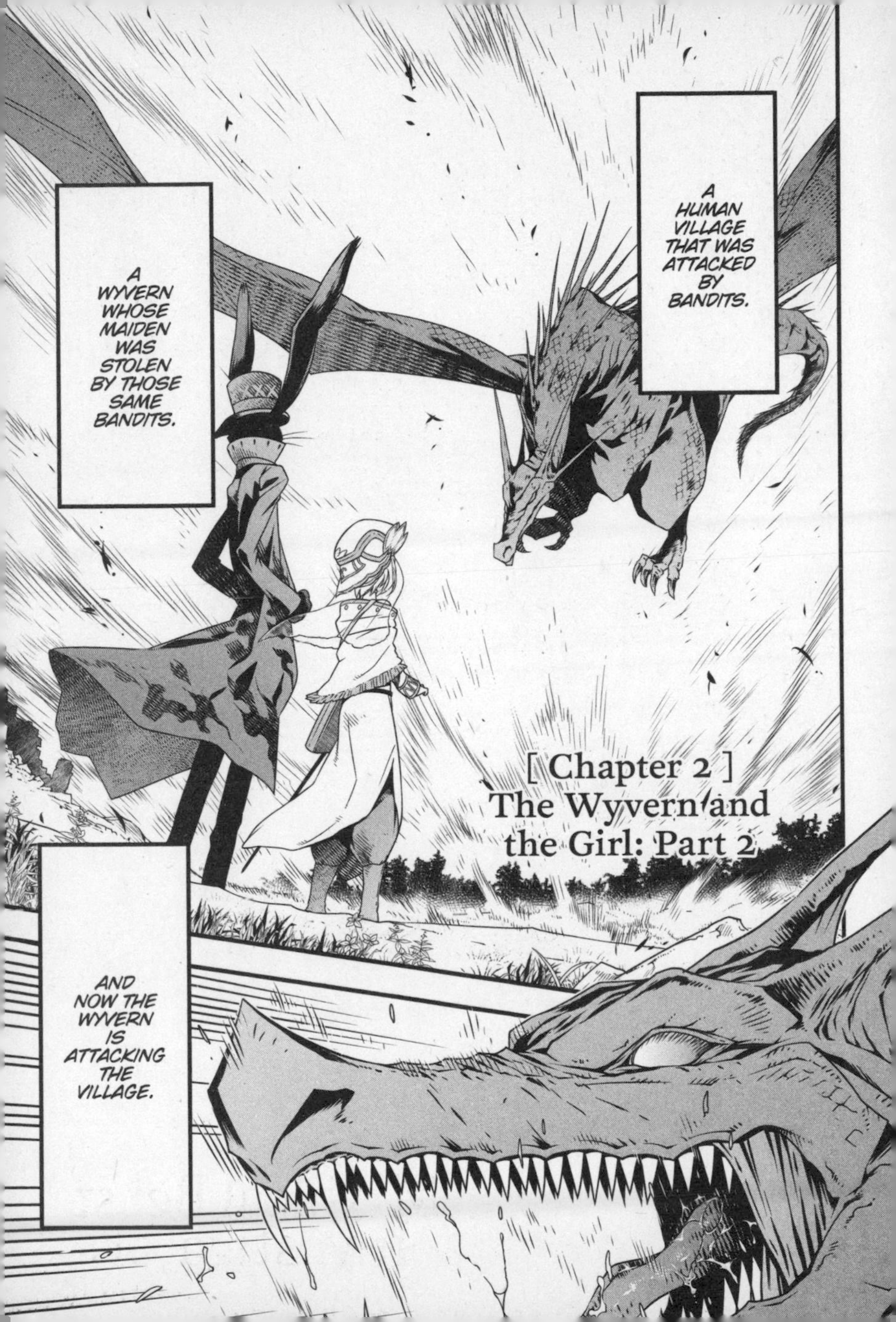
A HUMAN VILLAGE THAT WAS ATTACKED BY BANDITS.
A WYVERN WHOSE MAIDEN WAS STOLEN BY THOSE SAME BANDITS.
[Chapter 2]
The Wyvern and the Girl: Part 2
AND NOW THE WYVERN IS ATTACKING THE VILLAGE.

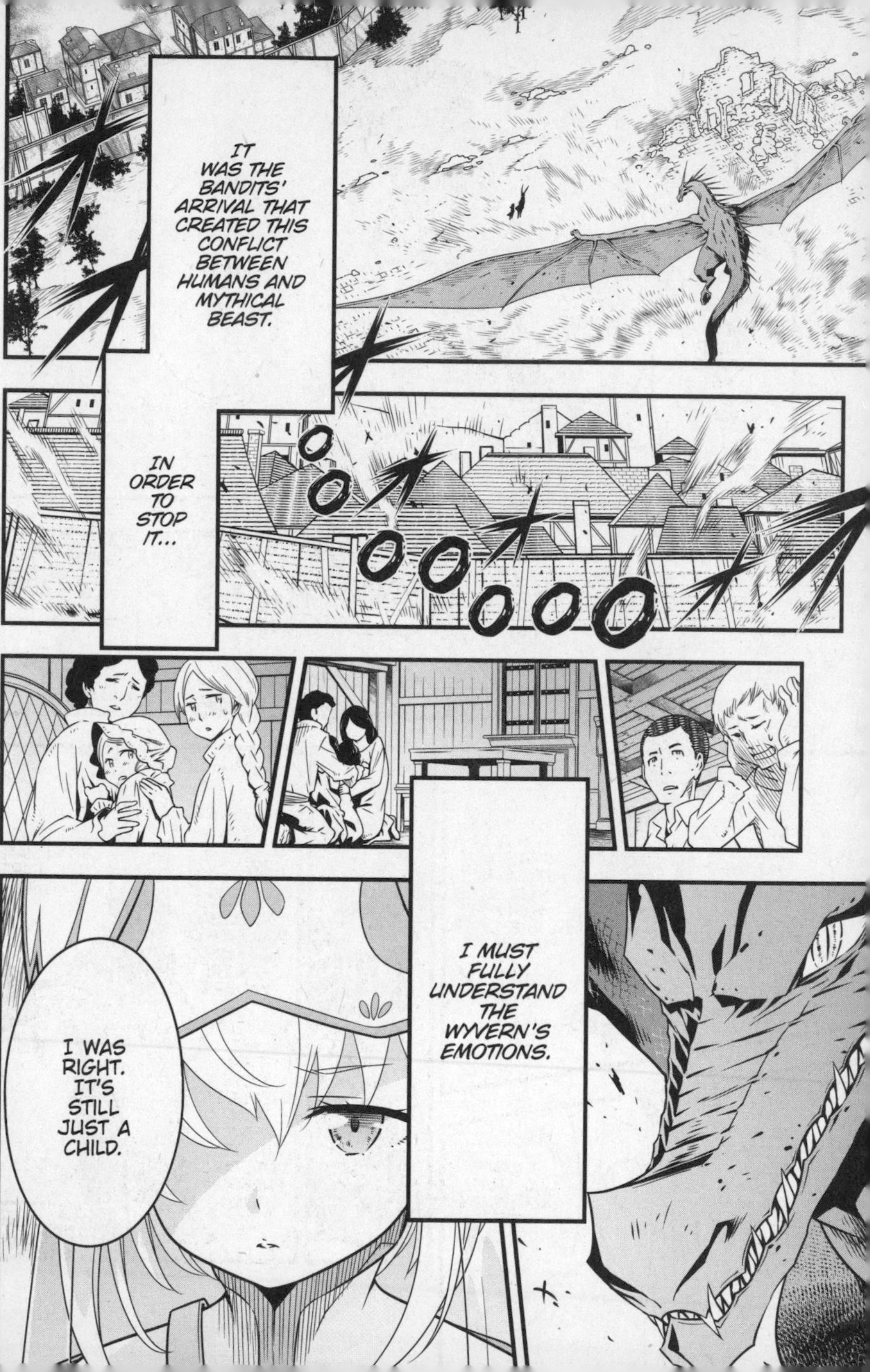
IT WAS THE BANDITS' ARRIVAL THAT CREATED THIS CONFLICT BETWEEN HUMANS AND MYTHICAL BEAST.
IN ORDER TO STOP IT...
I MUST FULLY UNDERSTAND THE WYVERN'S EMOTIONS.
I WAS RIGHT. IT'S STILL JUST A CHILD.

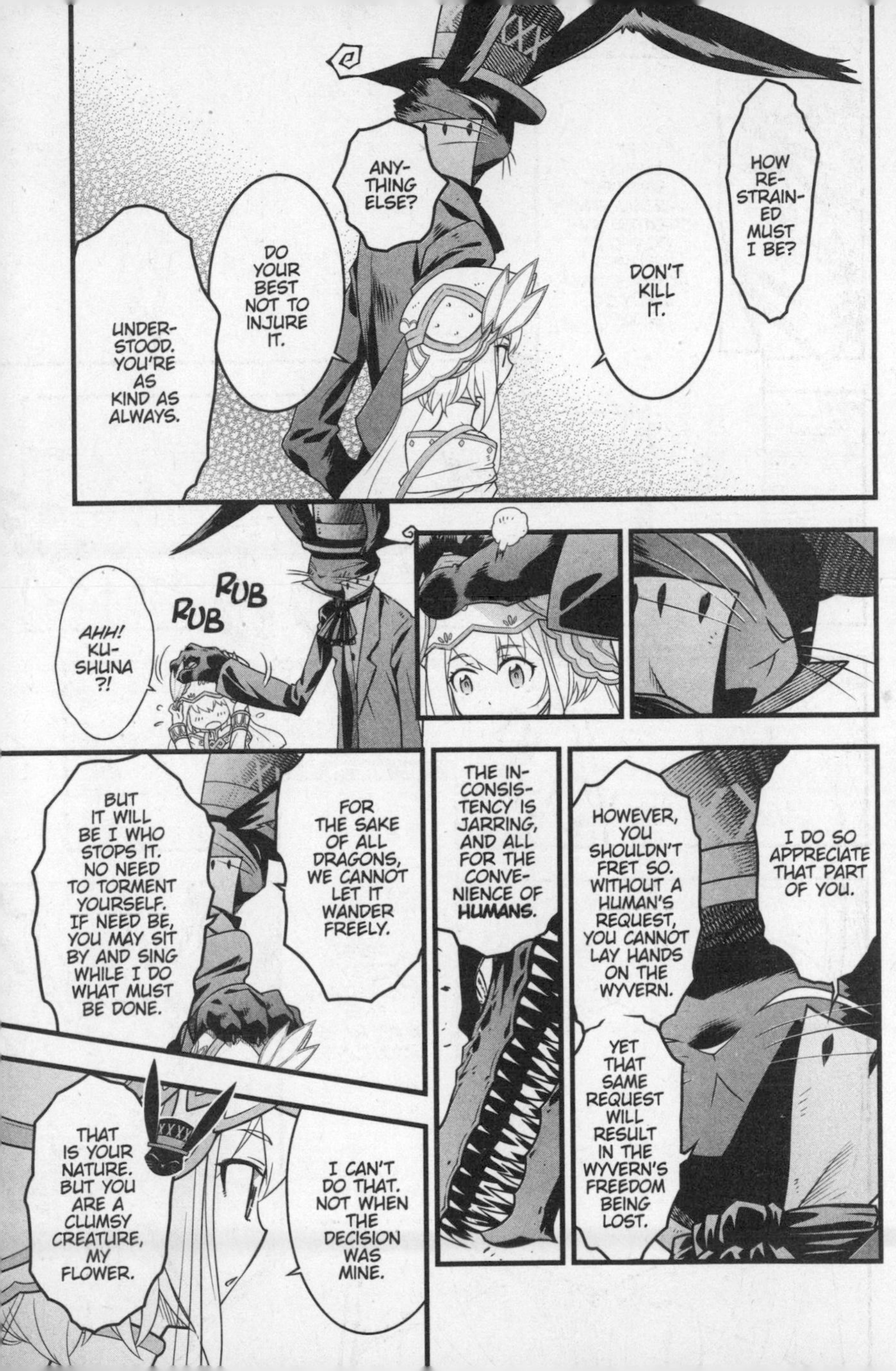
HOW RE-STRAIN-ED MUST I BE?
DON'T KILL IT.
ANY-THING ELSE?
DO YOUR BEST NOT TO INJURE IT.
UNDER-STOOD. YOU'RE AS KIND AS ALWAYS.
RUB
RUB
AHH! KU-SHUNA?!
I DO SO APPRECIATE THAT PART OF YOU.
HOWEVER, YOU SHOULDN'T FRET SO. WITHOUT A HUMAN'S REQUEST, YOU CANNOT LAY HANDS ON THE WYVERN.
YET THAT SAME REQUEST WILL RESULT IN THE WYVERN'S FREEDOM BEING LOST.
THE IN-CONSIS-TENCY IS JARRING, AND ALL FOR THE CONVE-NIENCE OF **HUMANS.**
FOR THE SAKE OF ALL DRAGONS, WE CANNOT LET IT WANDER FREELY.
BUT IT WILL BE I WHO STOPS IT. NO NEED TO TORMENT YOURSELF. IF NEED BE, YOU MAY SIT BY AND SING WHILE I DO WHAT MUST BE DONE.
I CAN'T DO THAT. NOT WHEN THE DECISION WAS MINE.
THAT IS YOUR NATURE. BUT YOU ARE A CLUMSY CREATURE, MY FLOWER.

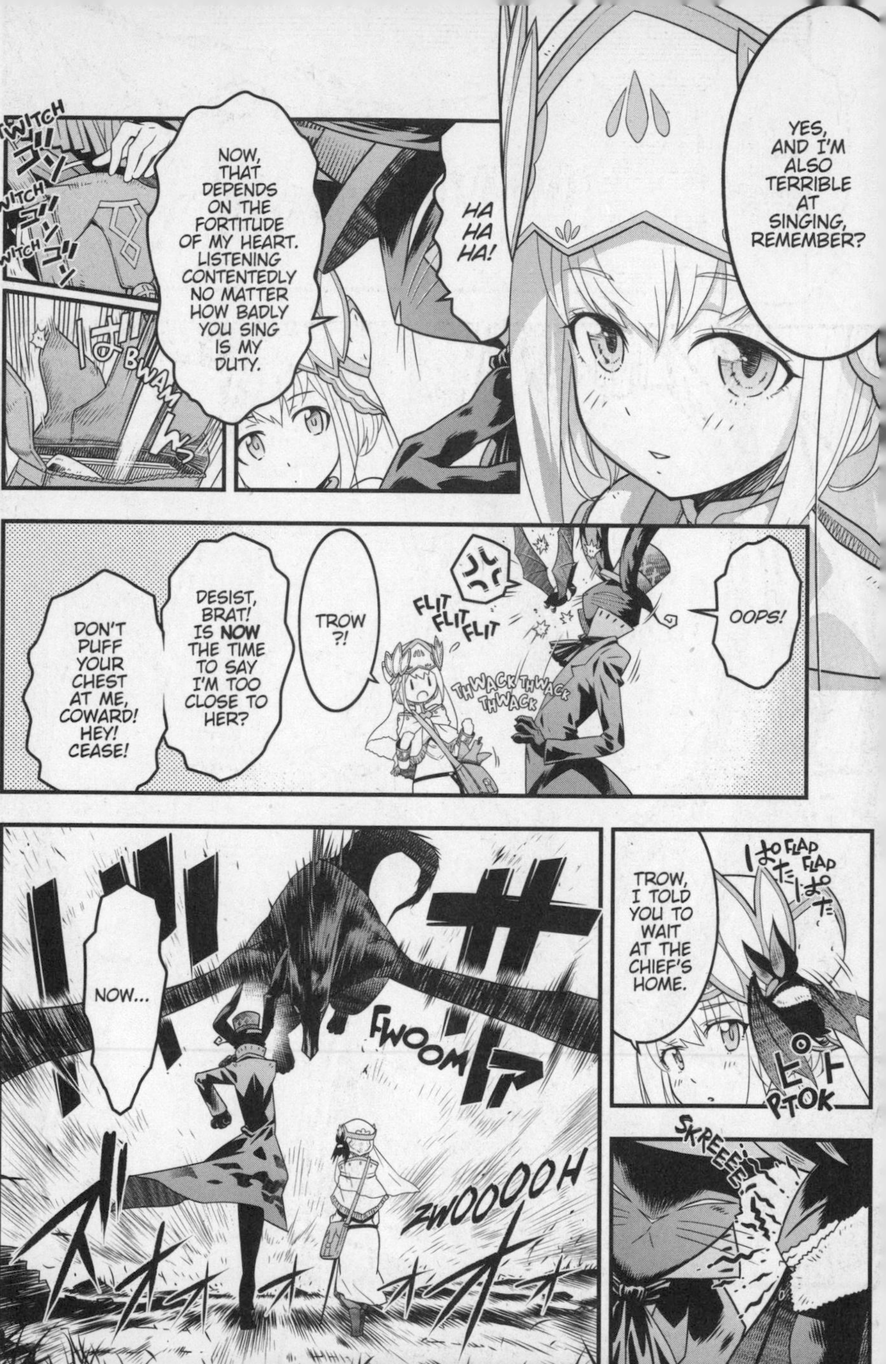
YES, AND I'M ALSO TERRIBLE AT SINGING, REMEMBER?
HA HA HA!
NOW, THAT DEPENDS ON THE FORTITUDE OF MY HEART. LISTENING CONTENTEDLY NO MATTER HOW BADLY YOU SING IS MY DUTY.
TWITCH
TWITCH
TWITCH
BWAM
OOPS!
FLIT FLIT FLIT
THWACK THWACK THWACK
TROW ?!
DESIST, BRAT! IS NOW THE TIME TO SAY I'M TOO CLOSE TO HER?
DON'T PUFF YOUR CHEST AT ME, COWARD! HEY! CEASE!
TROW, I TOLD YOU TO WAIT AT THE CHIEF'S HOME.
FLAP FLAP
P-TOK
SKREEEE
NOW...
FWOOM
ZWOOOOOH

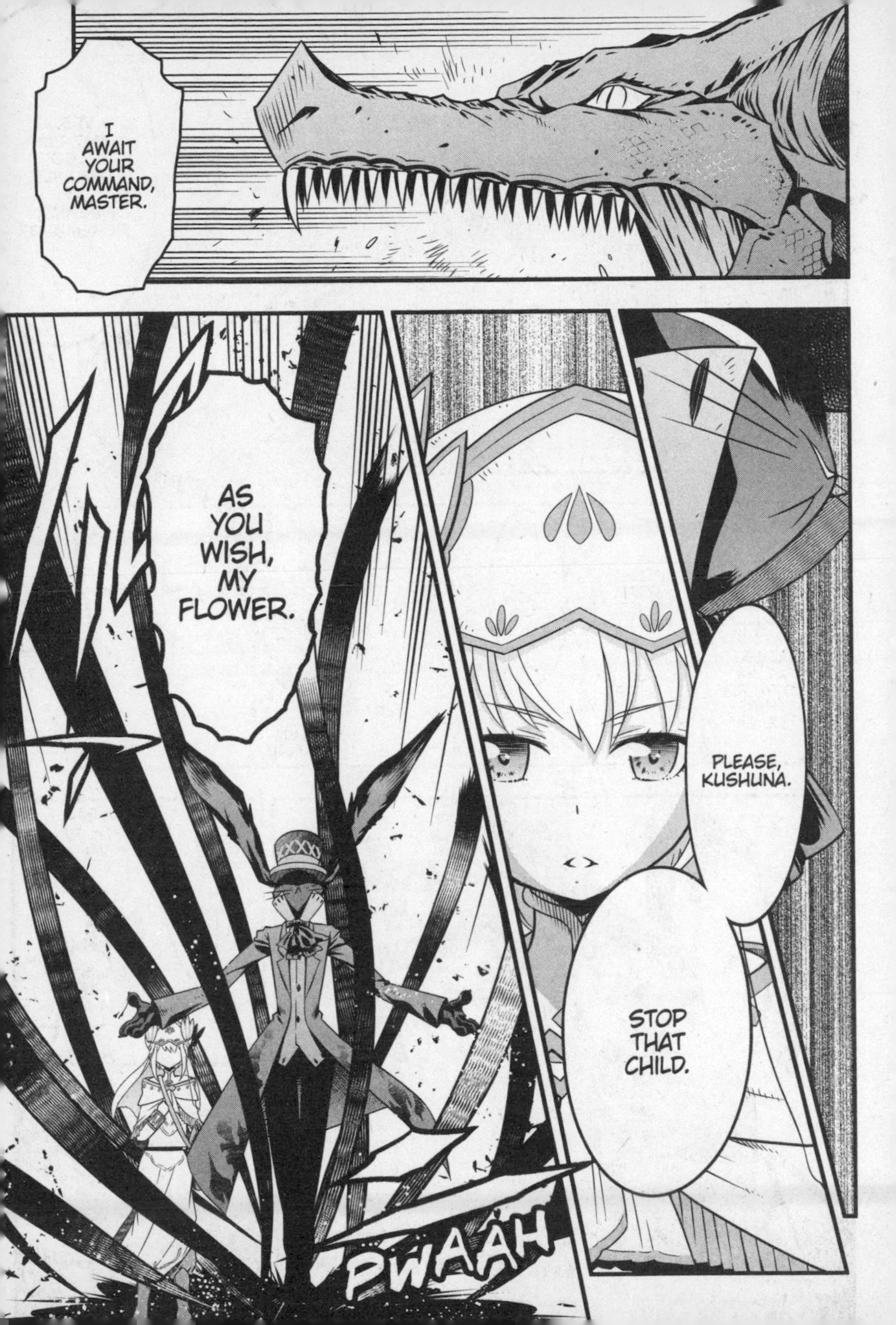
I AWAIT YOUR COMMAND, MASTER.
PLEASE, KUSHUNA.
STOP THAT CHILD.
AS YOU WISH, MY FLOWER.
PWAAH

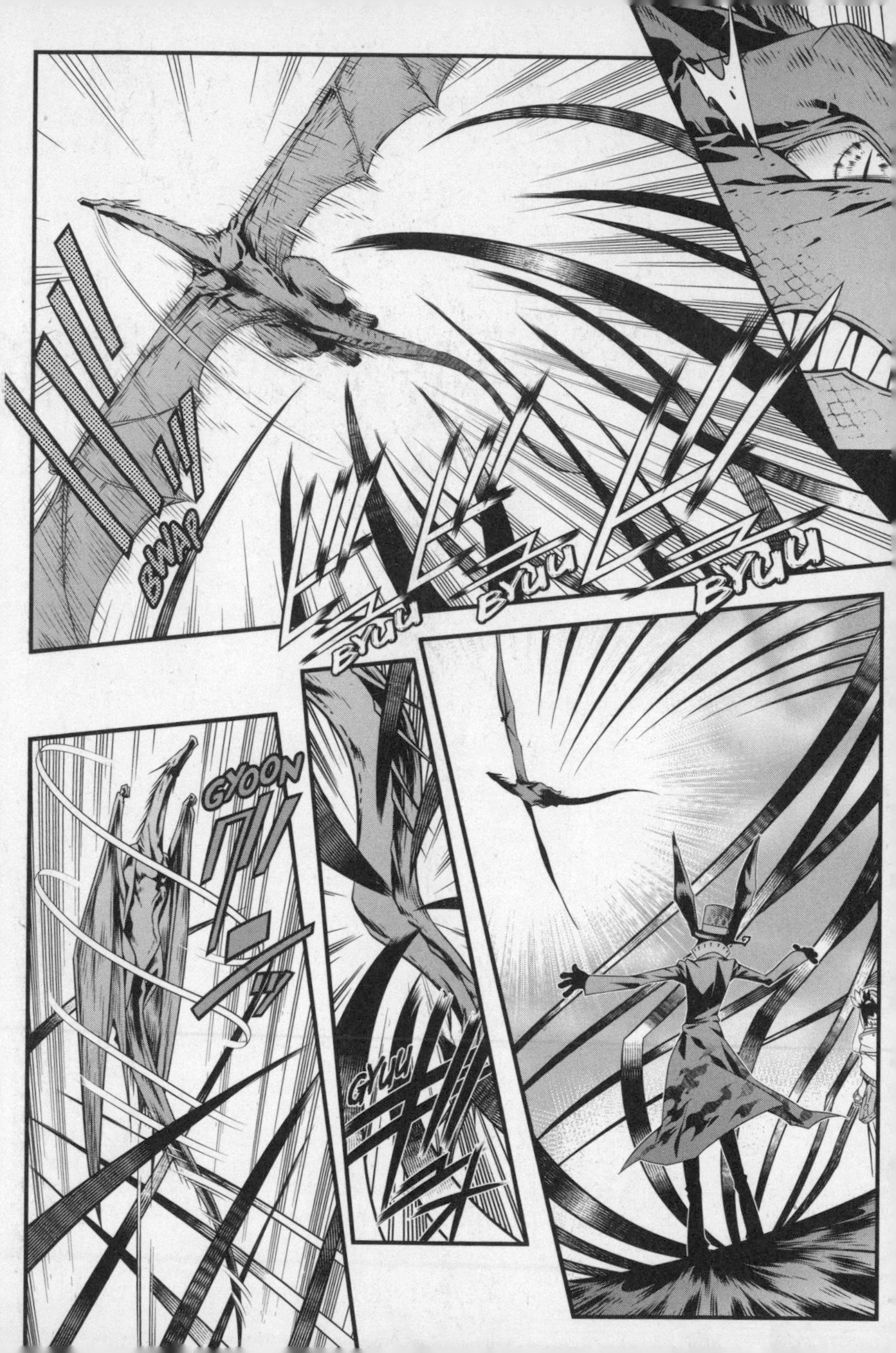
BWAP
BYUU BYUU BYUU BYUU
GYOON
GYUU

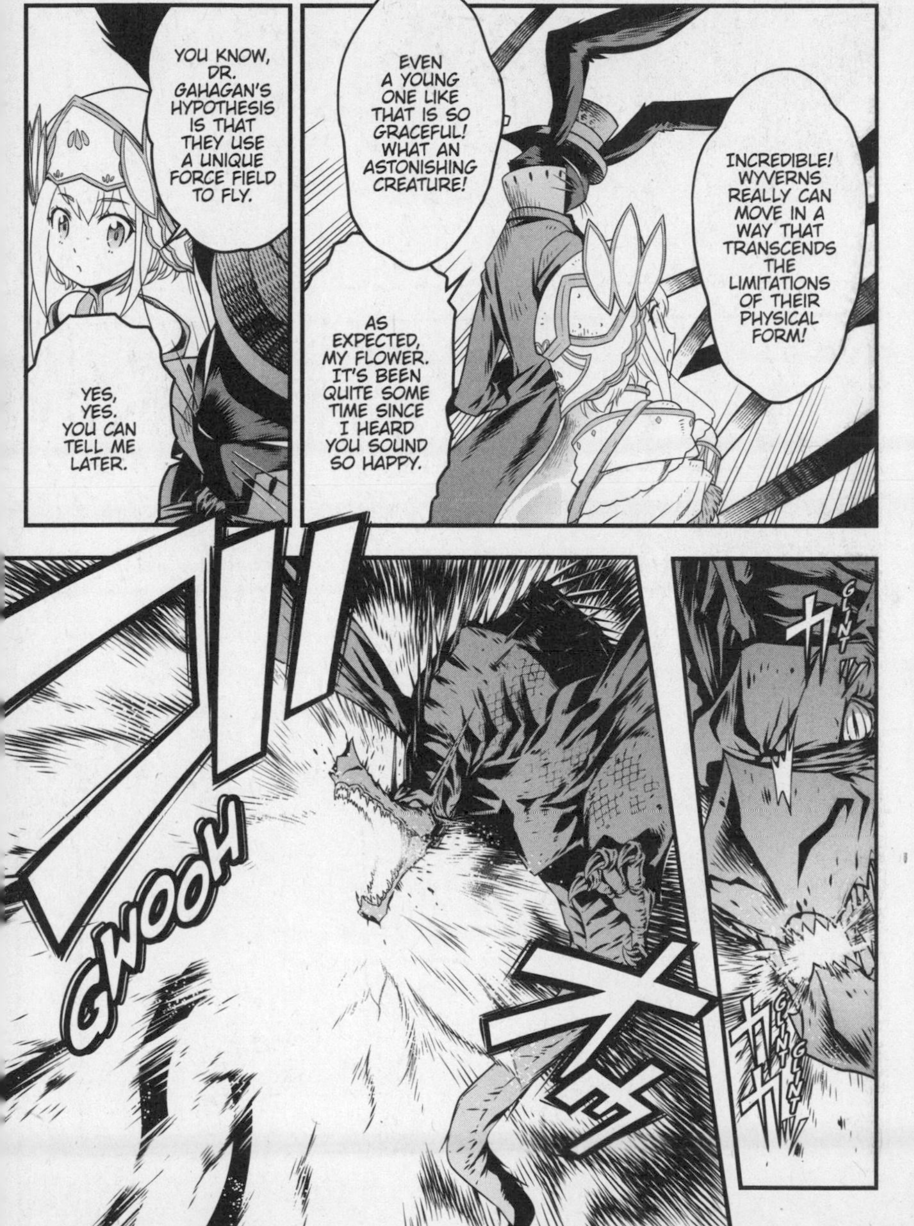
INCREDIBLE! WYVERNS REALLY CAN MOVE IN A WAY THAT TRANSCENDS THE LIMITATIONS OF THEIR PHYSICAL FORM!
EVEN A YOUNG ONE LIKE THAT IS SO GRACEFUL! WHAT AN ASTONISHING CREATURE!
AS EXPECTED, MY FLOWER. IT'S BEEN QUITE SOME TIME SINCE I HEARD YOU SOUND SO HAPPY.
YOU KNOW, DR. GAHAGAN'S HYPOTHESIS IS THAT THEY USE A UNIQUE FORCE FIELD TO FLY.
YES, YES. YOU CAN TELL ME LATER.
GLINT
GLINT
GLINT
GWOOH

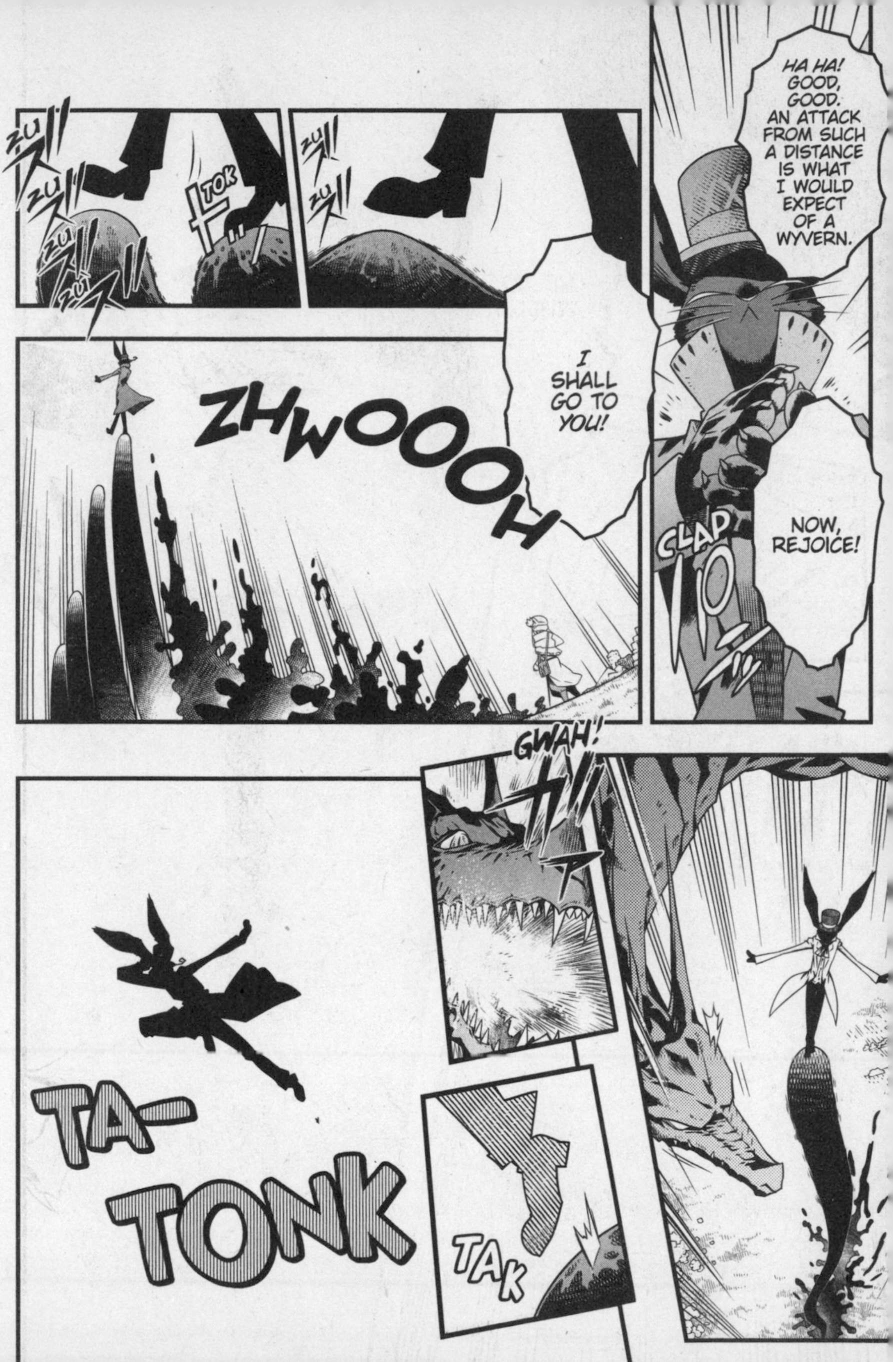
HA HA! GOOD, GOOD. AN ATTACK FROM SUCH A DISTANCE IS WHAT I WOULD EXPECT OF A WYVERN.
CLAP
NOW, REJOICE!
I SHALL GO TO YOU!
ZU ZU
ZU ZU ZU ZU
TOK
ZHWOOOOH
GWAH!
TAK
TA-TONK

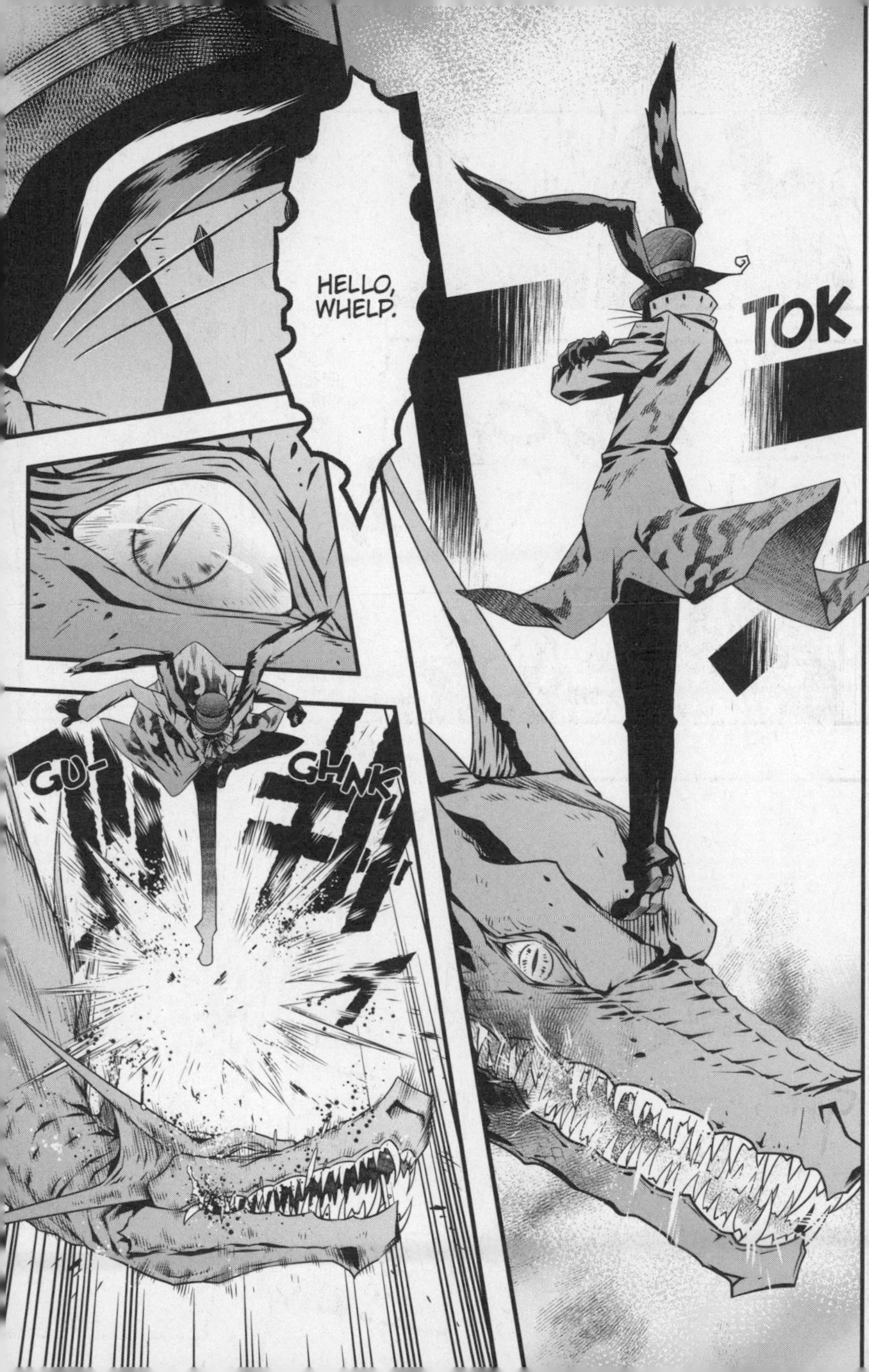
TOK
HELLO, WHELP.
GU-
GHNK

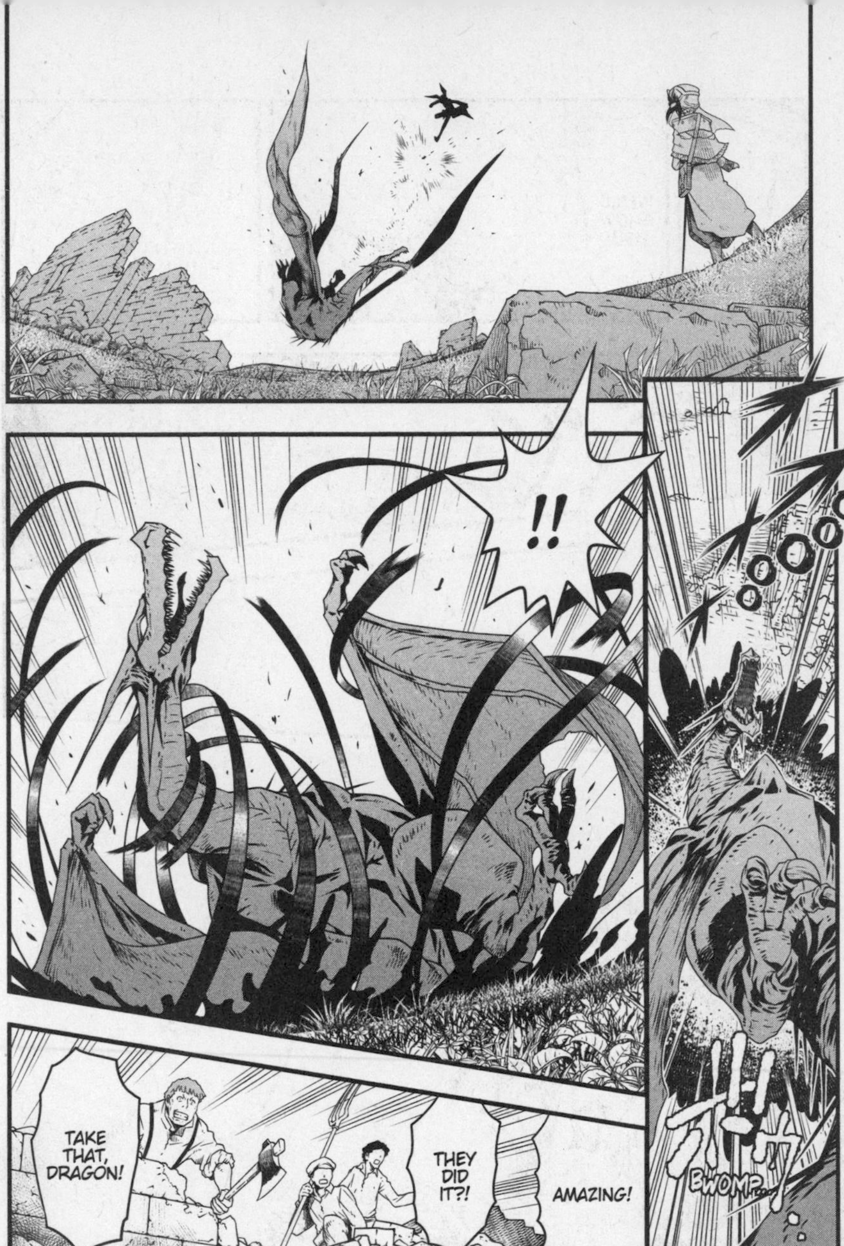
BWOMP...
!!
AMAZING!
THEY DID IT?!
TAKE THAT, DRAGON!

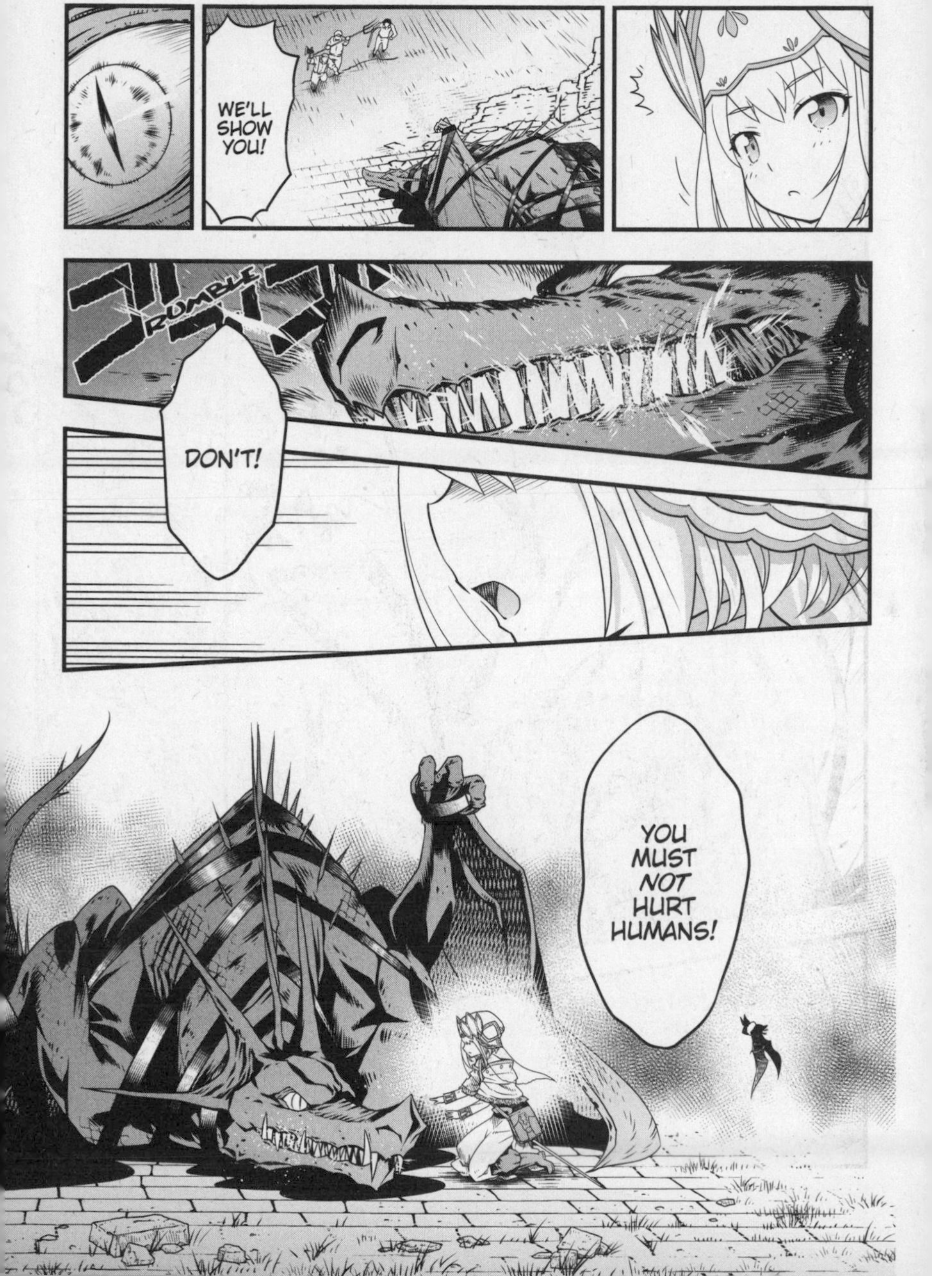
WE'LL SHOW YOU!
RUMBLE
DON'T!
YOU MUST *NOT* HURT HUMANS!

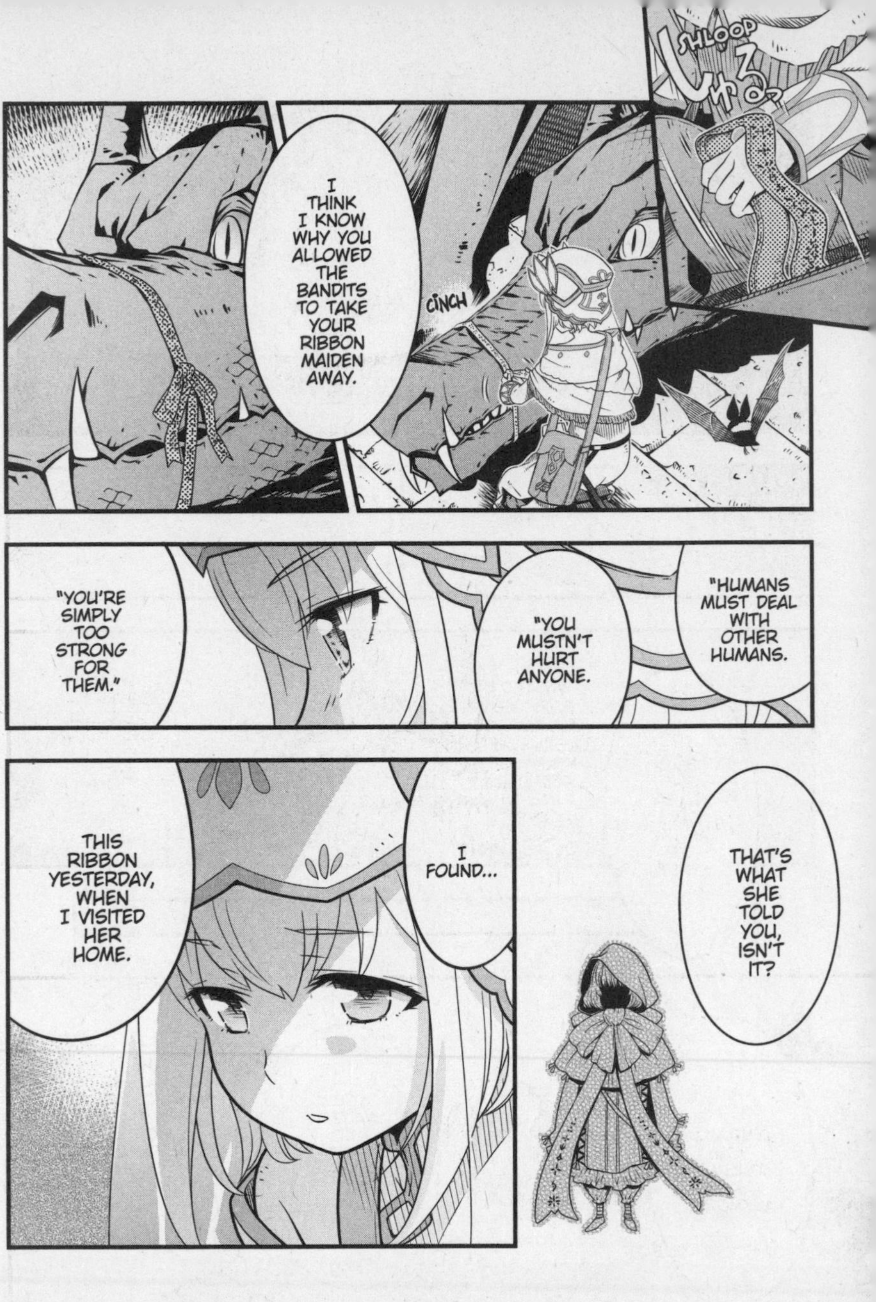
SHLOOP
CINCH
I THINK I KNOW WHY YOU ALLOWED THE BANDITS TO TAKE YOUR RIBBON MAIDEN AWAY.
"HUMANS MUST DEAL WITH OTHER HUMANS.
"YOU MUSTN'T HURT ANYONE.
"YOU'RE SIMPLY TOO STRONG FOR THEM."
THAT'S WHAT SHE TOLD YOU, ISN'T IT?
I FOUND...
THIS RIBBON YESTERDAY, WHEN I VISITED HER HOME.

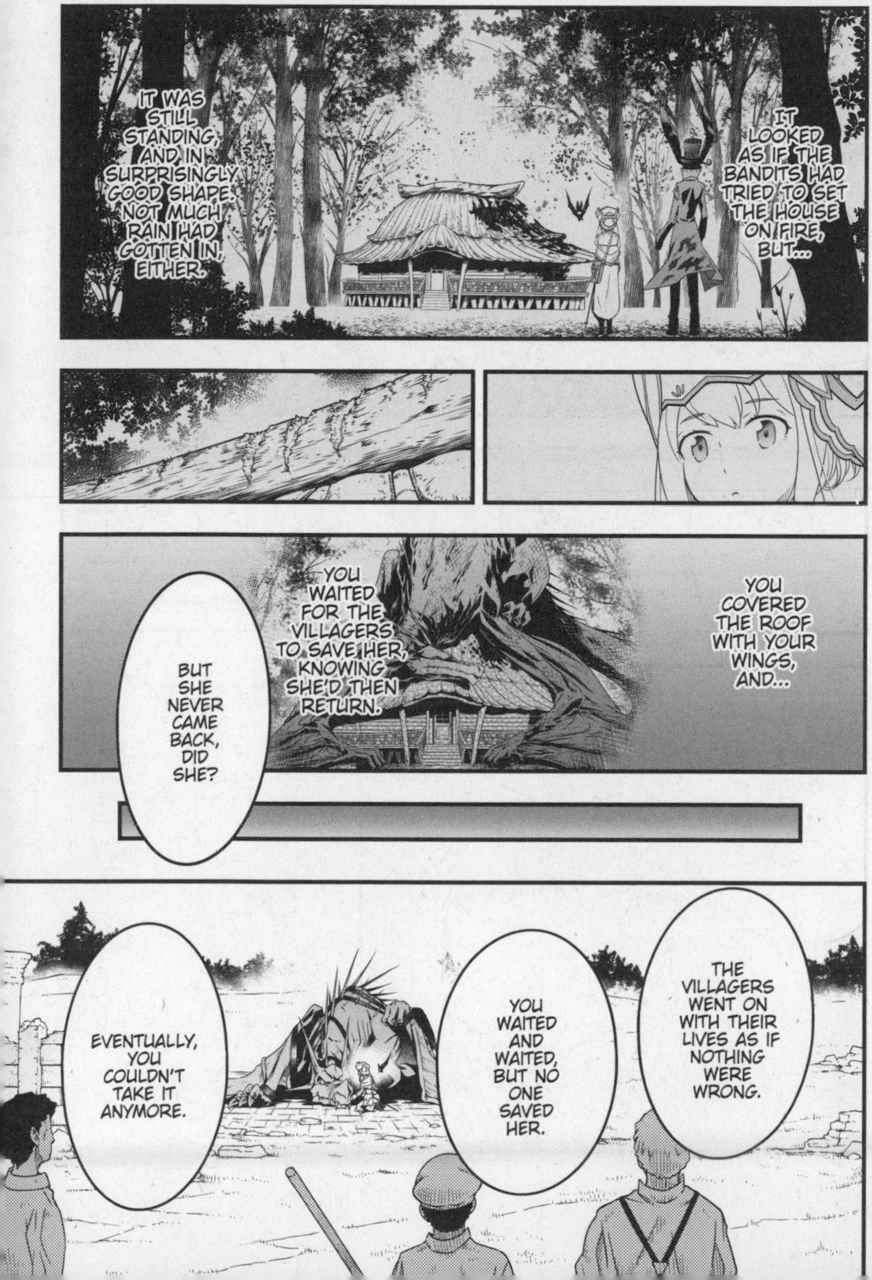
IT LOOKED AS IF THE BANDITS HAD TRIED TO SET THE HOUSE ON FIRE, BUT...
IT WAS STILL STANDING, AND IN SURPRISINGLY GOOD SHAPE. NOT MUCH RAIN HAD GOTTEN IN, EITHER.
YOU COVERED THE ROOF WITH YOUR WINGS, AND...
YOU WAITED FOR THE VILLAGERS TO SAVE HER, KNOWING SHE'D THEN RETURN.
BUT SHE NEVER CAME BACK, DID SHE?
THE VILLAGERS WENT ON WITH THEIR LIVES AS IF NOTHING WERE WRONG.
YOU WAITED AND WAITED, BUT NO ONE SAVED HER.
EVENTUALLY, YOU COULDN'T TAKE IT ANYMORE.

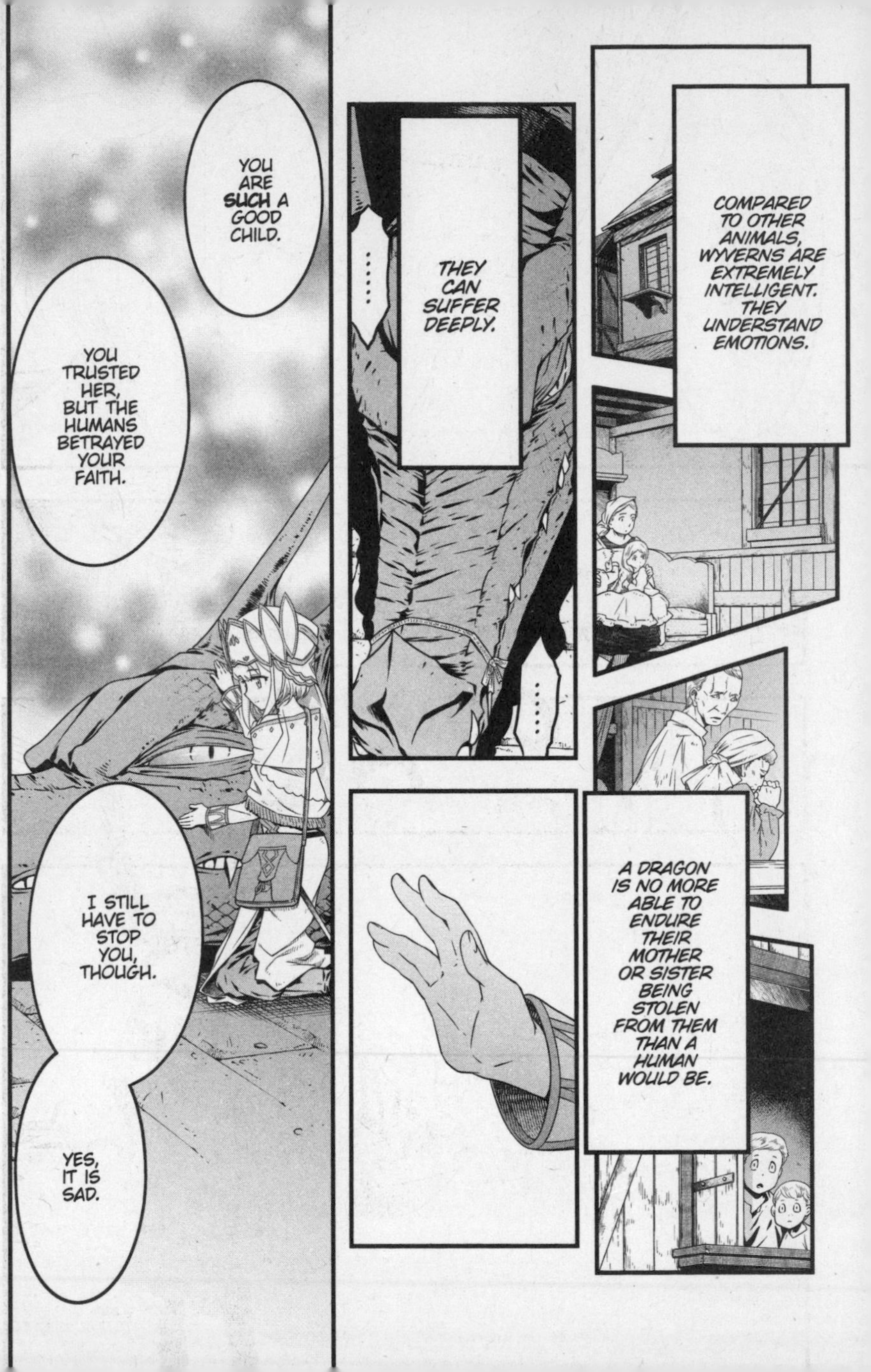
COMPARED TO OTHER ANIMALS, WYVERNS ARE EXTREMELY INTELLIGENT. THEY UNDERSTAND EMOTIONS.
THEY CAN SUFFER DEEPLY.
......
......
A DRAGON IS NO MORE ABLE TO ENDURE THEIR MOTHER OR SISTER BEING STOLEN FROM THEM THAN A HUMAN WOULD BE.
YOU ARE SUCH A GOOD CHILD.
YOU TRUSTED HER, BUT THE HUMANS BETRAYED YOUR FAITH.
I STILL HAVE TO STOP YOU, THOUGH.
YES, IT IS SAD.

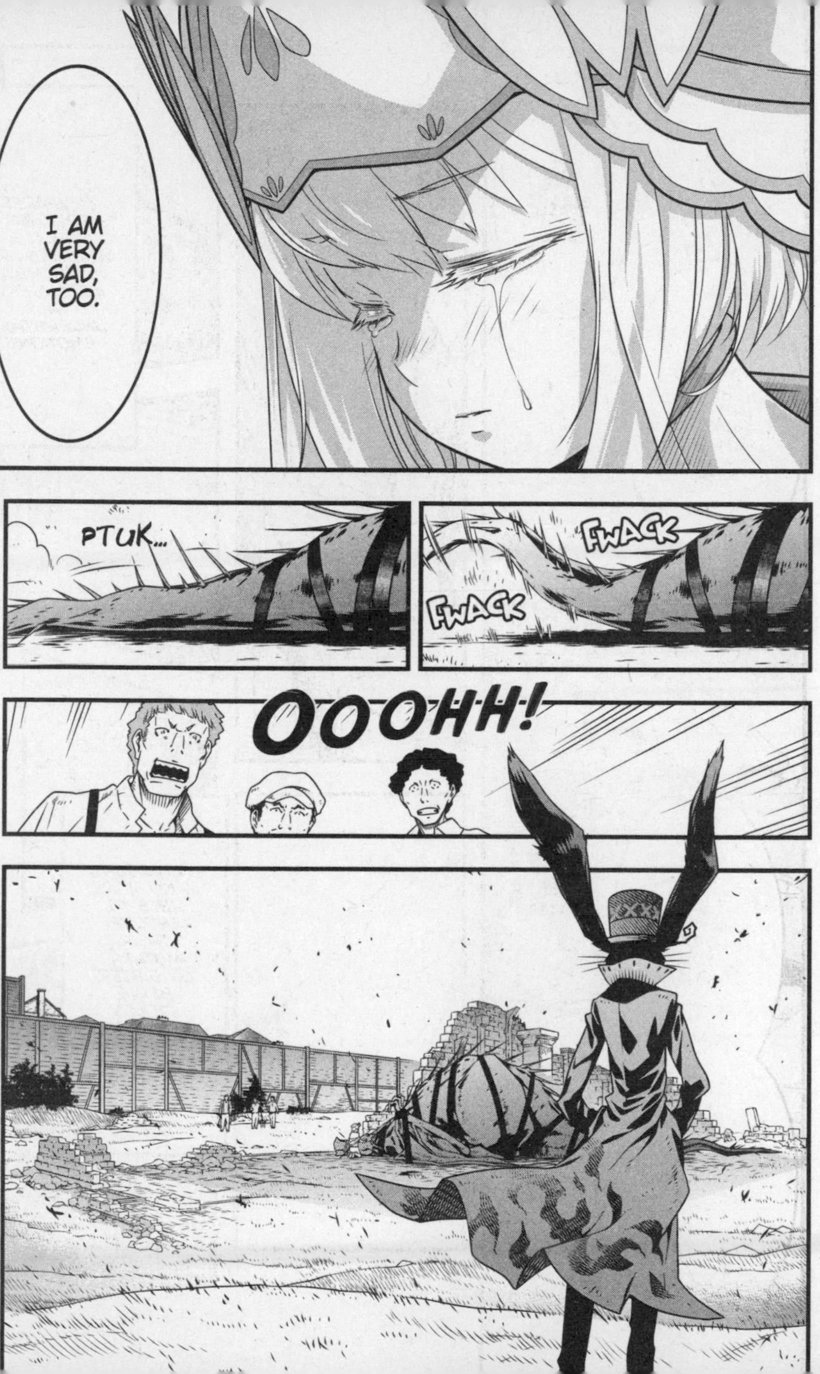
I AM VERY SAD, TOO.
FWACK
FWACK
PTUK...
OOOHH!

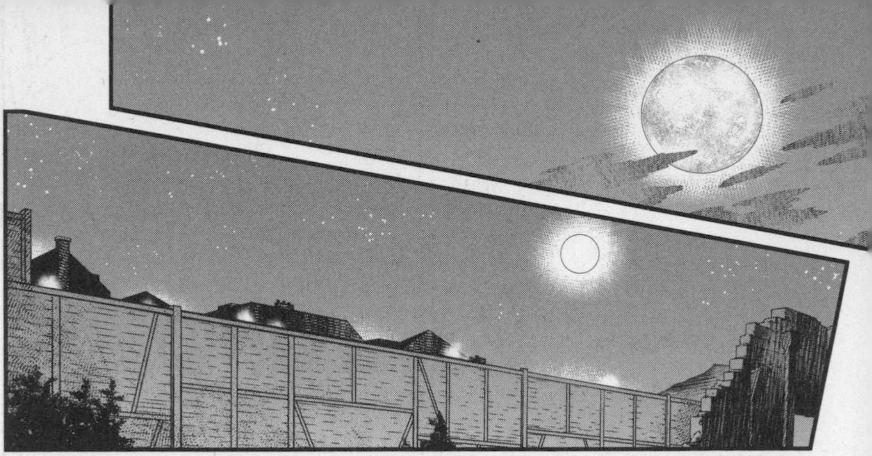

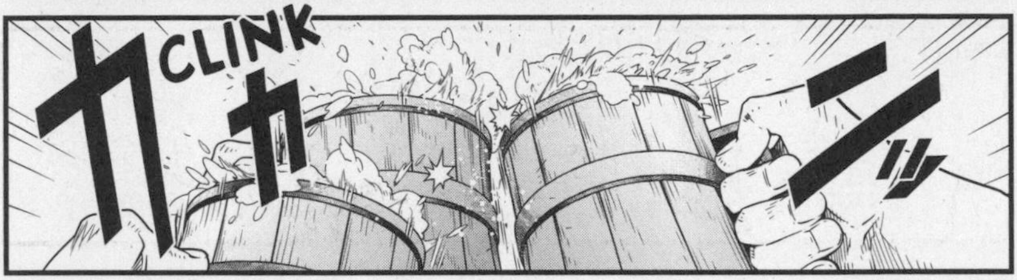
カカーンッ
CLINK

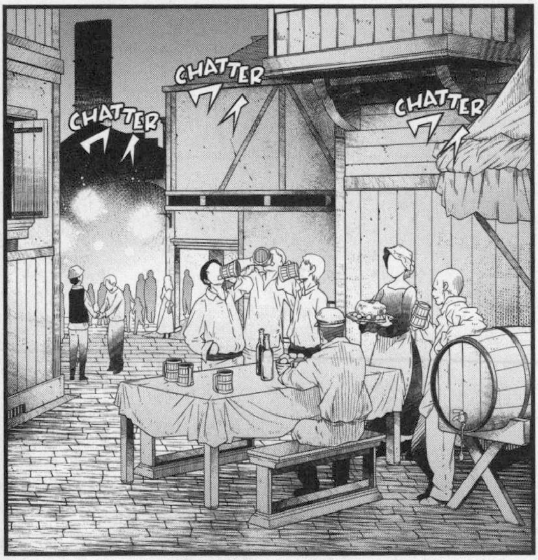
CHATTER
ワイ
CHATTER
ワイ
CHATTER
ワイ

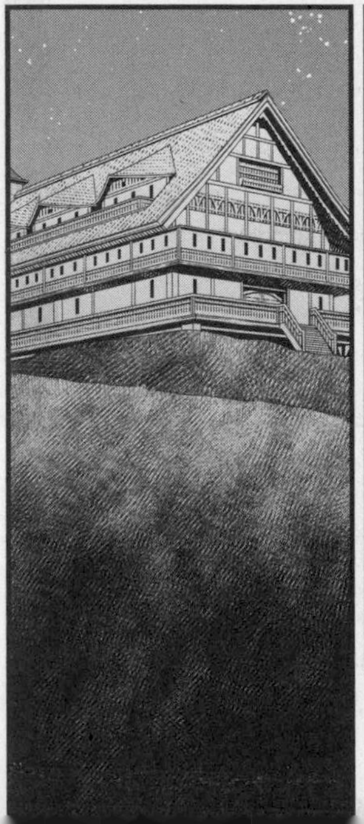

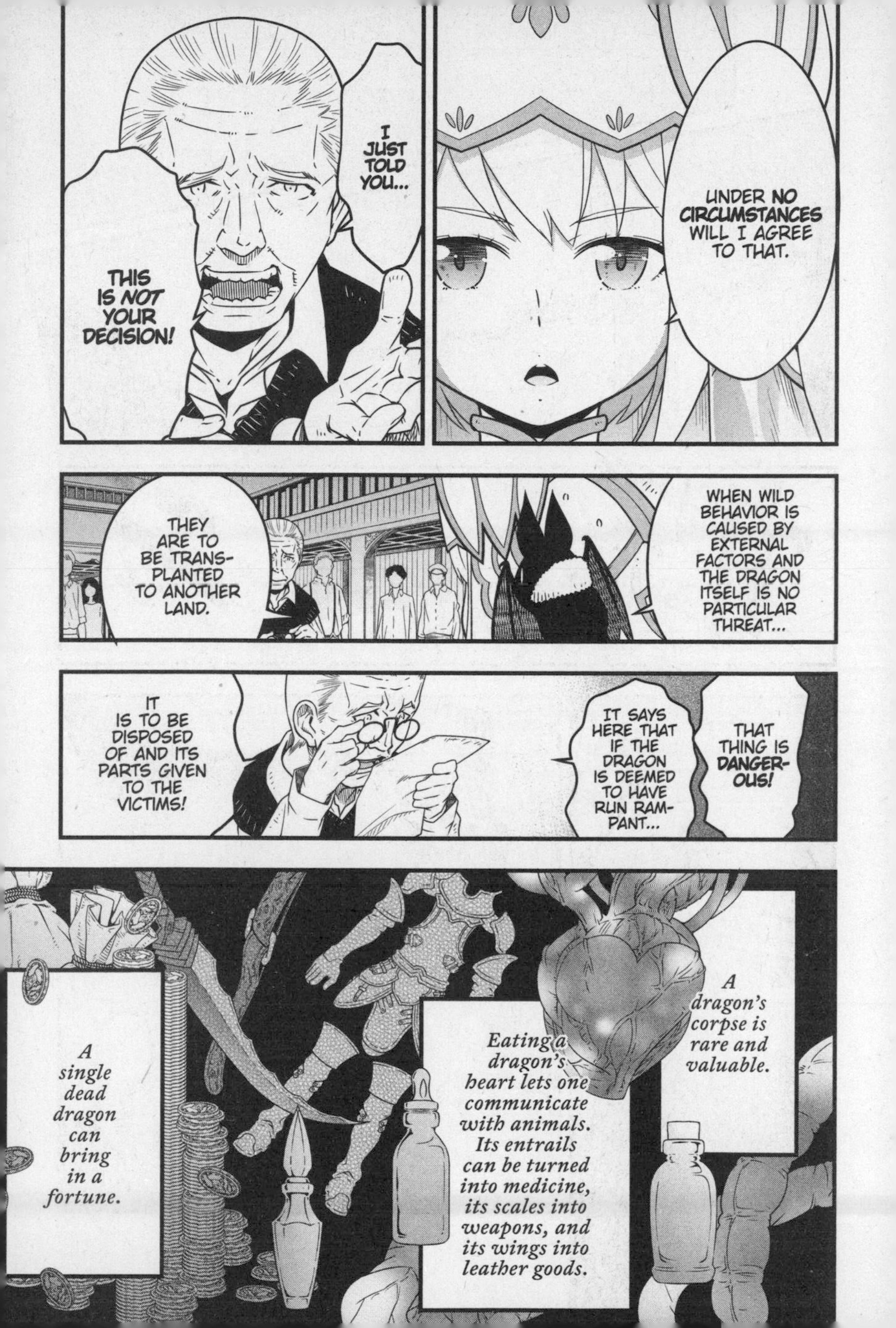
UNDER NO CIRCUMSTANCES WILL I AGREE TO THAT.
I JUST TOLD YOU...
THIS IS NOT YOUR DECISION!
WHEN WILD BEHAVIOR IS CAUSED BY EXTERNAL FACTORS AND THE DRAGON ITSELF IS NO PARTICULAR THREAT...
THEY ARE TO BE TRANS-PLANTED TO ANOTHER LAND.
THAT THING IS DANGER-OUS!
IT SAYS HERE THAT IF THE DRAGON IS DEEMED TO HAVE RUN RAM-PANT...
IT IS TO BE DISPOSED OF AND ITS PARTS GIVEN TO THE VICTIMS!
A dragon's corpse is rare and valuable.
Eating a dragon's heart lets one communicate with animals. Its entrails can be turned into medicine, its scales into weapons, and its wings into leather goods.
A single dead dragon can bring in a fortune.

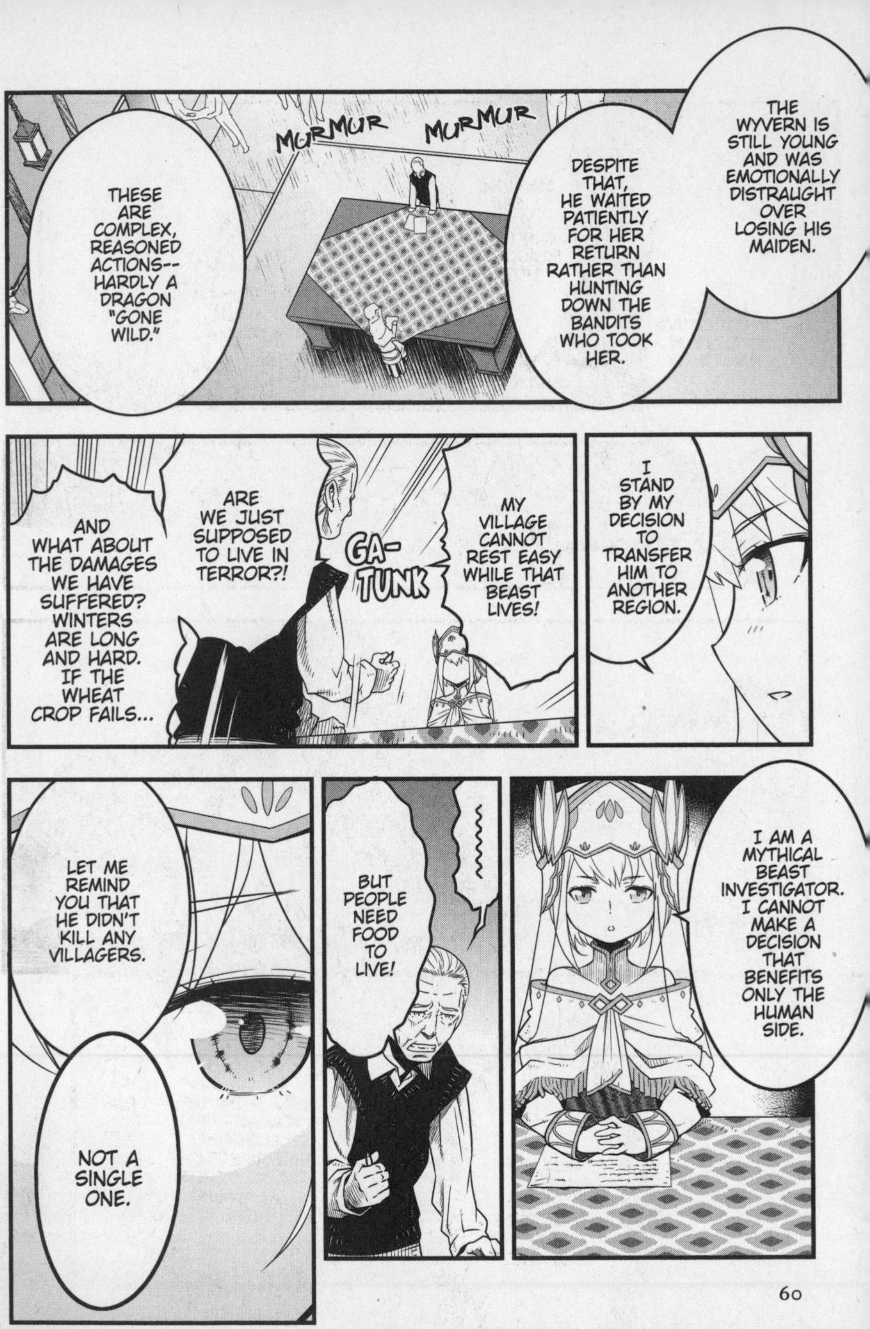
MURMUR MURMUR
THE WYVERN IS STILL YOUNG AND WAS EMOTIONALLY DISTRAUGHT OVER LOSING HIS MAIDEN.
DESPITE THAT, HE WAITED PATIENTLY FOR HER RETURN RATHER THAN HUNTING DOWN THE BANDITS WHO TOOK HER.
THESE ARE COMPLEX, REASONED ACTIONS--HARDLY A DRAGON "GONE WILD."
I STAND BY MY DECISION TO TRANSFER HIM TO ANOTHER REGION.
MY VILLAGE CANNOT REST EASY WHILE THAT BEAST LIVES!
GA-TUNK
ARE WE JUST SUPPOSED TO LIVE IN TERROR?!
AND WHAT ABOUT THE DAMAGES WE HAVE SUFFERED? WINTERS ARE LONG AND HARD. IF THE WHEAT CROP FAILS...
I AM A MYTHICAL BEAST INVESTIGATOR. I CANNOT MAKE A DECISION THAT BENEFITS ONLY THE HUMAN SIDE.
BUT PEOPLE NEED FOOD TO LIVE!
LET ME REMIND YOU THAT HE DIDN'T KILL ANY VILLAGERS.
NOT A SINGLE ONE.

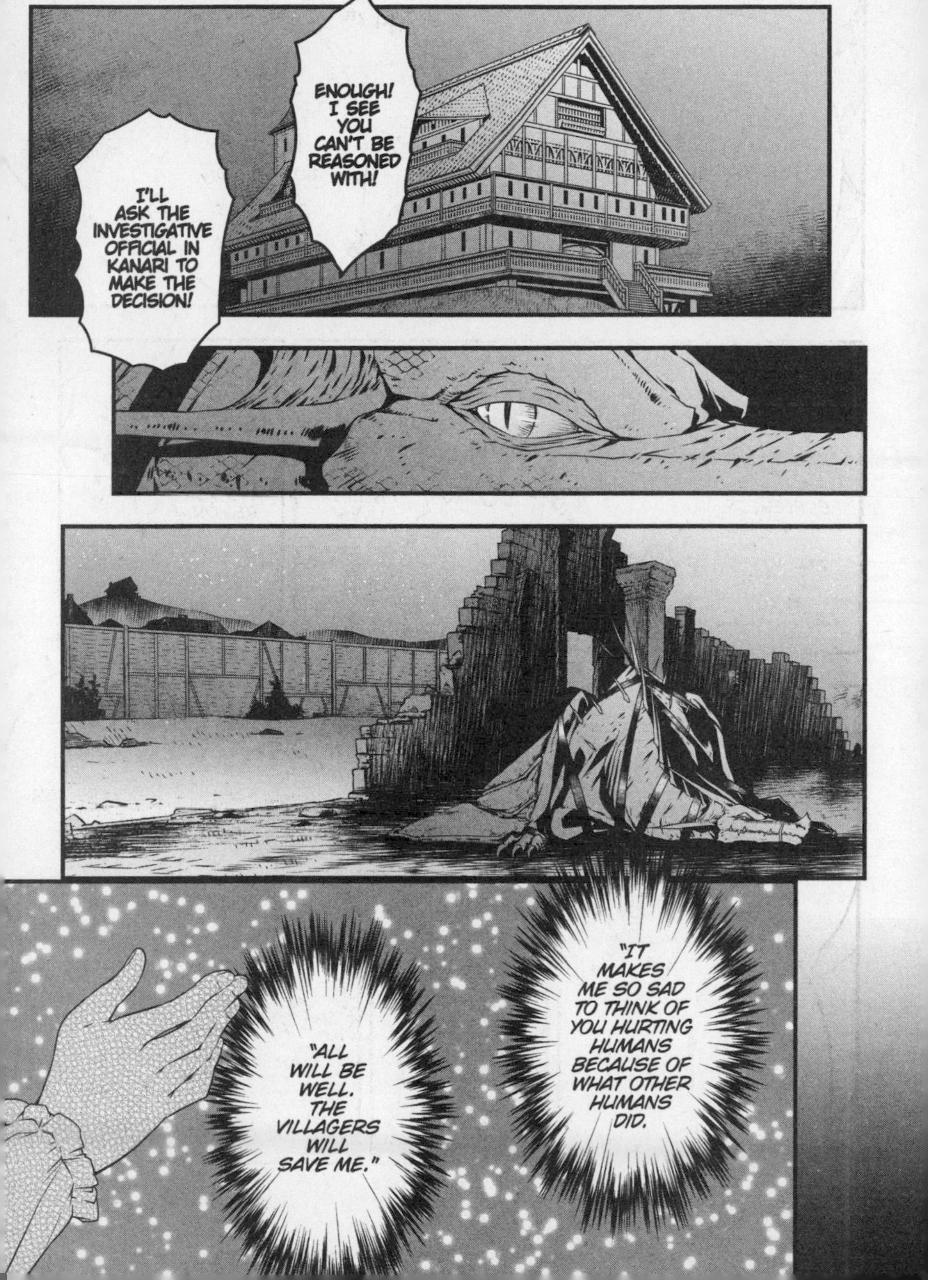
ENOUGH! I SEE YOU CAN'T BE REASONED WITH!
I'LL ASK THE INVESTIGATIVE OFFICIAL IN KANARI TO MAKE THE DECISION!
"IT MAKES ME SO SAD TO THINK OF YOU HURTING HUMANS BECAUSE OF WHAT OTHER HUMANS DID.
"ALL WILL BE WELL. THE VILLAGERS WILL SAVE ME."

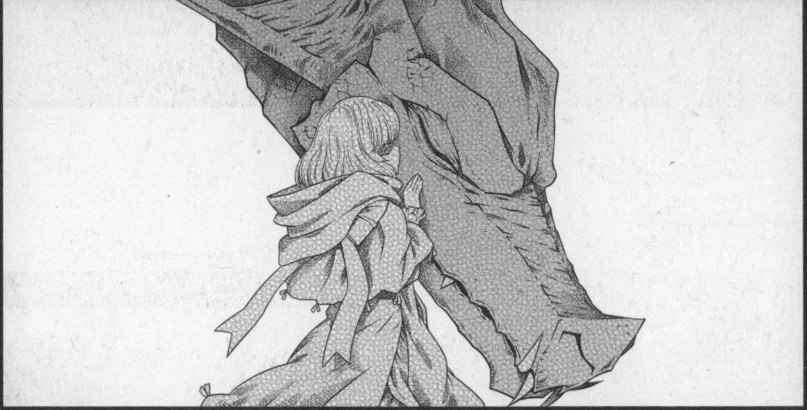

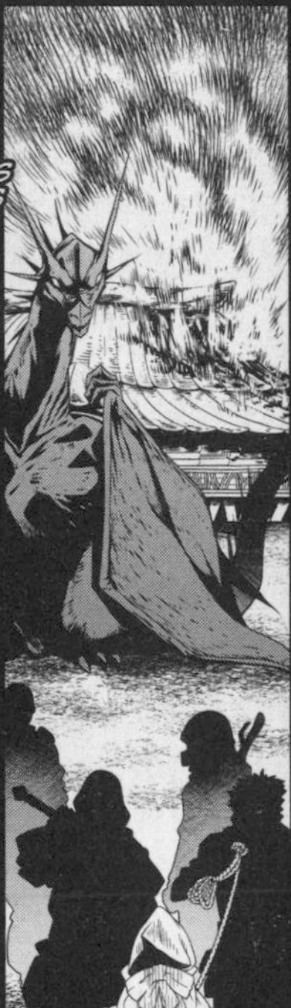
MY MAIDEN'S SPECIES IS WEAK AND SHORT-LIVED, BUT INTEL-LIGENT.

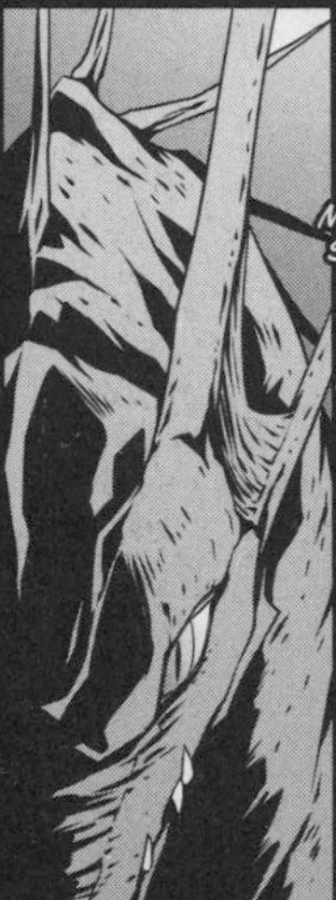
SHE HAS NEVER LIED TO ME.

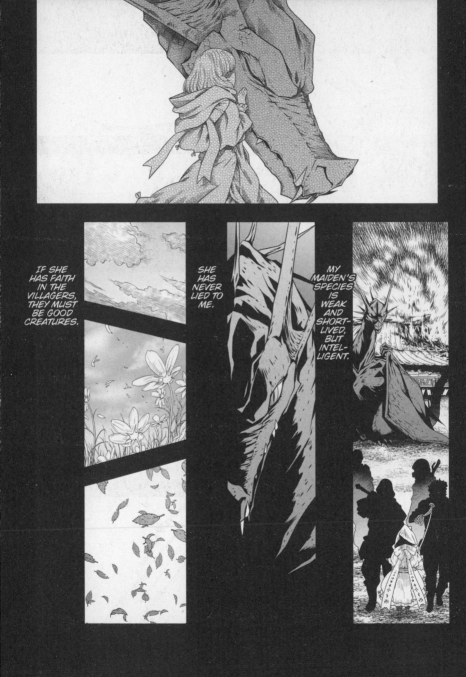

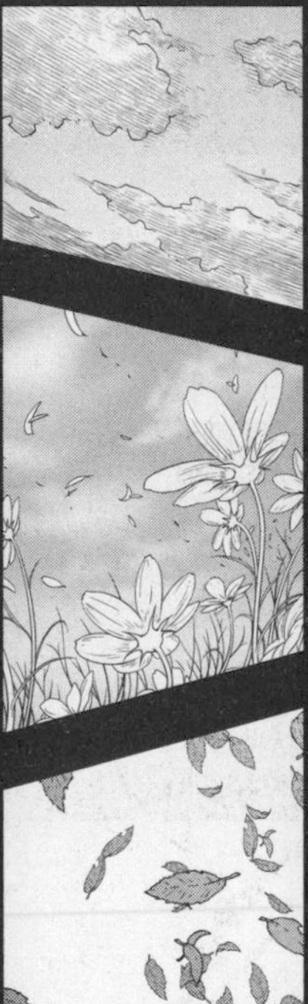
IF SHE HAS FAITH IN THE VILLAGERS, THEY MUST BE GOOD CREATURES.

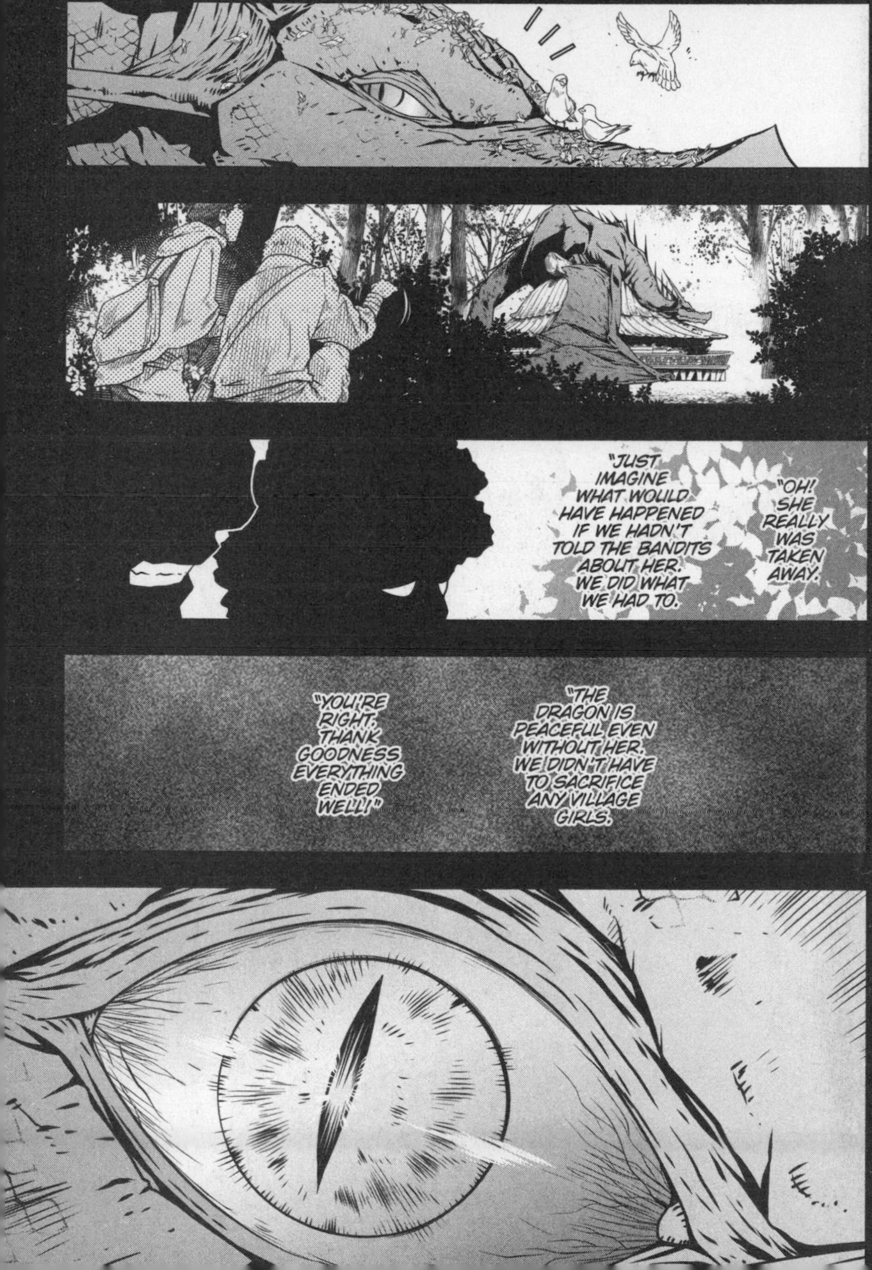
"OH! SHE REALLY WAS TAKEN AWAY.
"JUST IMAGINE WHAT WOULD HAVE HAPPENED IF WE HADN'T TOLD THE BANDITS ABOUT HER. WE DID WHAT WE HAD TO.
"THE DRAGON IS PEACEFUL EVEN WITHOUT HER. WE DIDN'T HAVE TO SACRIFICE ANY VILLAGE GIRLS.
"YOU'RE RIGHT. THANK GOODNESS EVERYTHING ENDED WELL!"

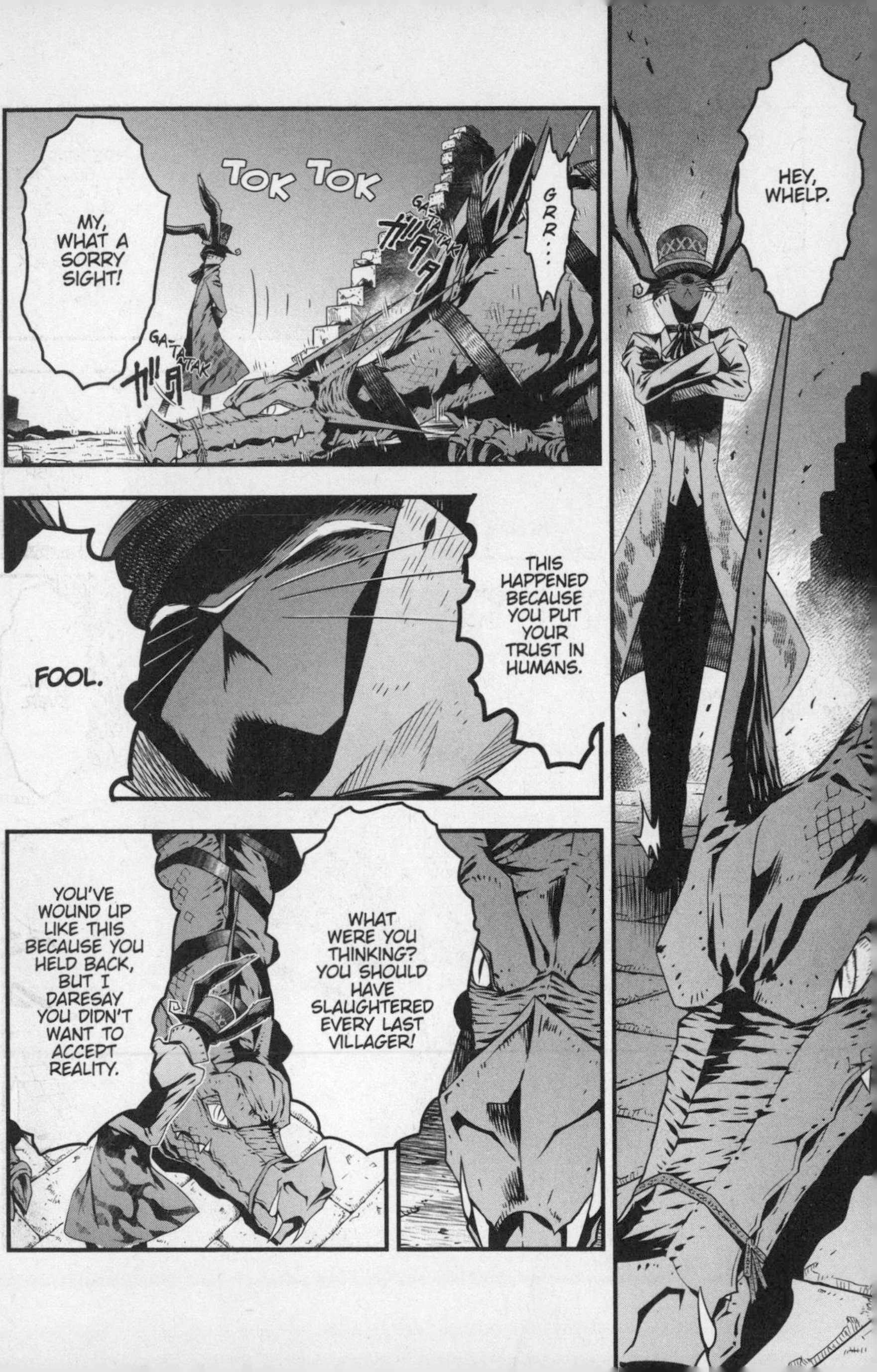
HEY, WHELP.
GRR...
TOK TOK
GA-TATAK
MY, WHAT A SORRY SIGHT!
GA-TATAK
THIS HAPPENED BECAUSE YOU PUT YOUR TRUST IN HUMANS.
FOOL.
WHAT WERE YOU THINKING? YOU SHOULD HAVE SLAUGHTERED EVERY LAST VILLAGER!
YOU'VE WOUND UP LIKE THIS BECAUSE YOU HELD BACK, BUT I DARESAY YOU DIDN'T WANT TO ACCEPT REALITY.

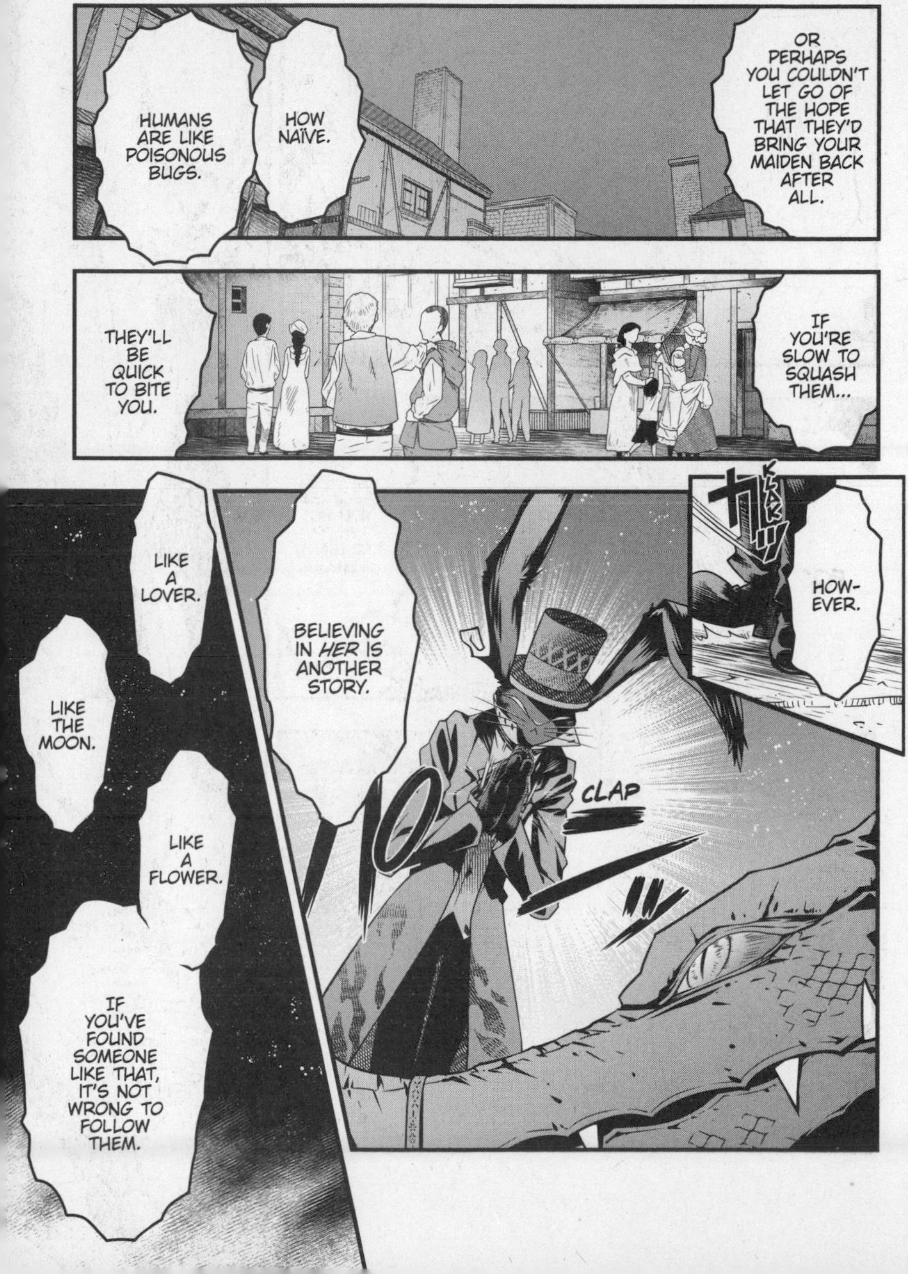
OR PERHAPS YOU COULDN'T LET GO OF THE HOPE THAT THEY'D BRING YOUR MAIDEN BACK AFTER ALL.
HOW NAÏVE.
HUMANS ARE LIKE POISONOUS BUGS.
IF YOU'RE SLOW TO SQUASH THEM...
THEY'LL BE QUICK TO BITE YOU.
KAK
HOW-EVER.
BELIEVING IN *HER* IS ANOTHER STORY.
CLAP
LIKE A LOVER.
LIKE THE MOON.
LIKE A FLOWER.
IF YOU'VE FOUND SOMEONE LIKE THAT, IT'S NOT WRONG TO FOLLOW THEM.

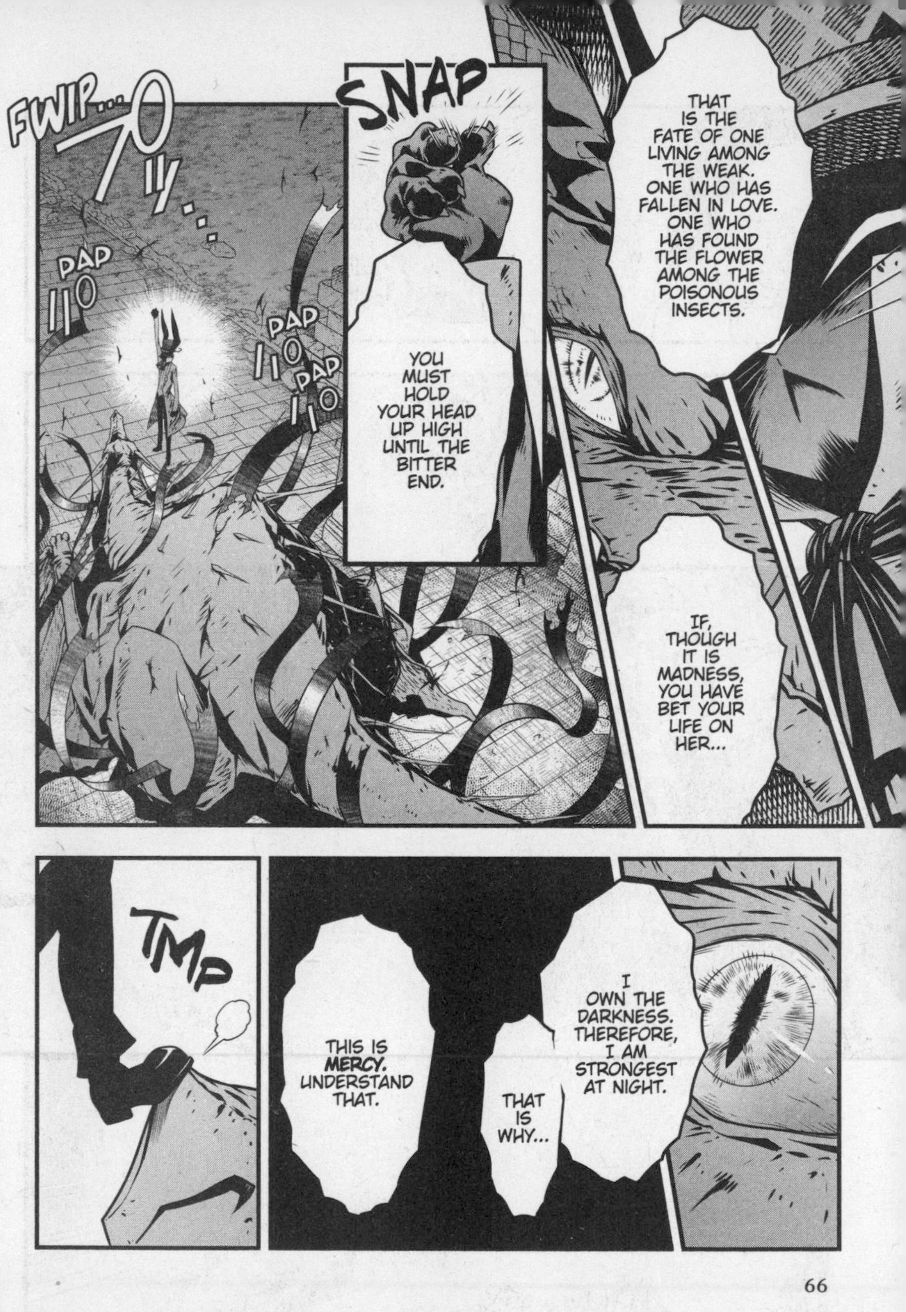
THAT IS THE FATE OF ONE LIVING AMONG THE WEAK. ONE WHO HAS FALLEN IN LOVE. ONE WHO HAS FOUND THE FLOWER AMONG THE POISONOUS INSECTS.
IF, THOUGH IT IS MADNESS, YOU HAVE BET YOUR LIFE ON HER...
SNAP
YOU MUST HOLD YOUR HEAD UP HIGH UNTIL THE BITTER END.
FWIP...
PAP
PAP
PAP
I OWN THE DARKNESS. THEREFORE, I AM STRONGEST AT NIGHT.
THAT IS WHY...
THIS IS **MERCY**. UNDERSTAND THAT.
TMP

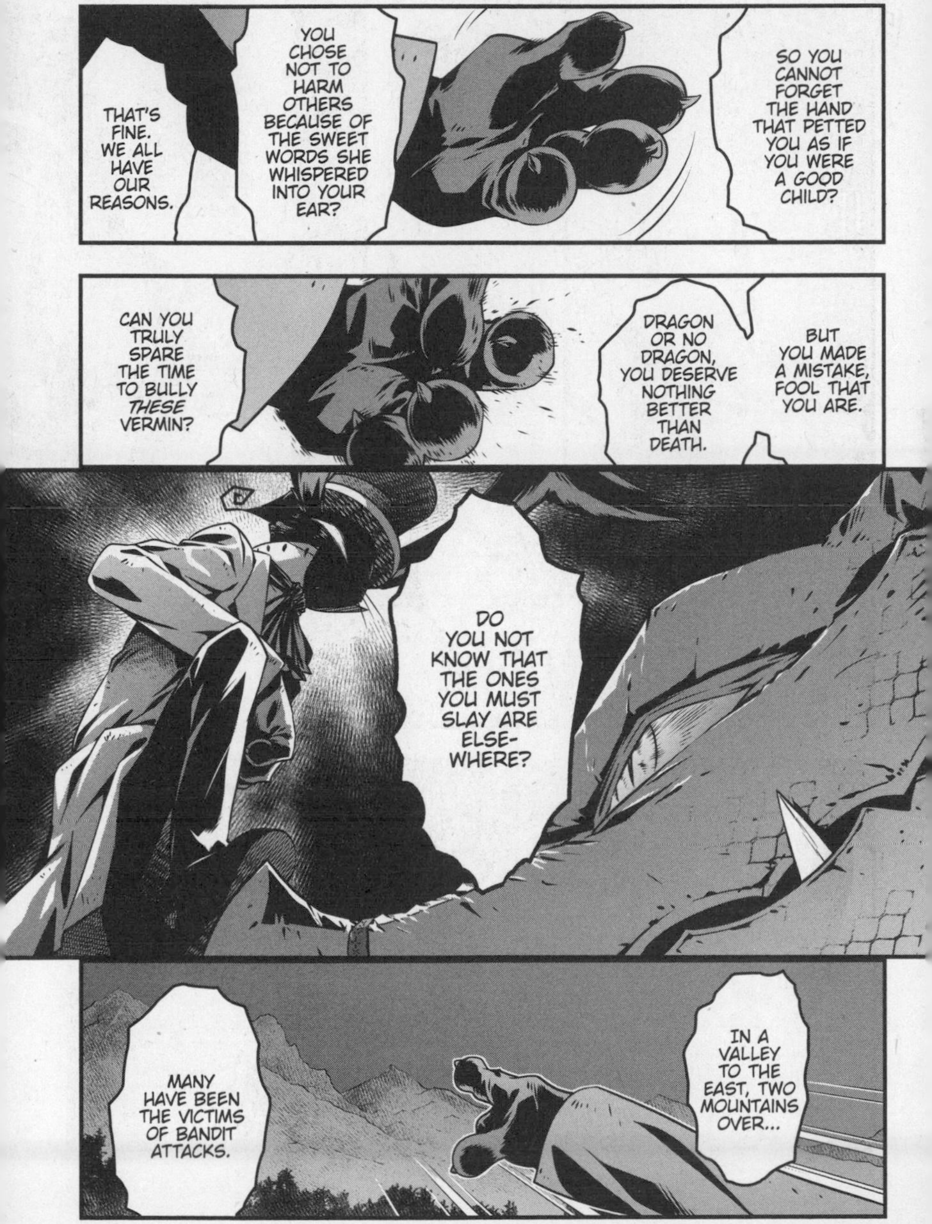
SO YOU CANNOT FORGET THE HAND THAT PETTED YOU AS IF YOU WERE A GOOD CHILD?
YOU CHOSE NOT TO HARM OTHERS BECAUSE OF THE SWEET WORDS SHE WHISPERED INTO YOUR EAR?
THAT'S FINE. WE ALL HAVE OUR REASONS.
BUT YOU MADE A MISTAKE, FOOL THAT YOU ARE.
DRAGON OR NO DRAGON, YOU DESERVE NOTHING BETTER THAN DEATH.
CAN YOU TRULY SPARE THE TIME TO BULLY *THESE* VERMIN?
DO YOU NOT KNOW THAT THE ONES YOU MUST SLAY ARE ELSE-WHERE?
IN A VALLEY TO THE EAST, TWO MOUNTAINS OVER...
MANY HAVE BEEN THE VICTIMS OF BANDIT ATTACKS.

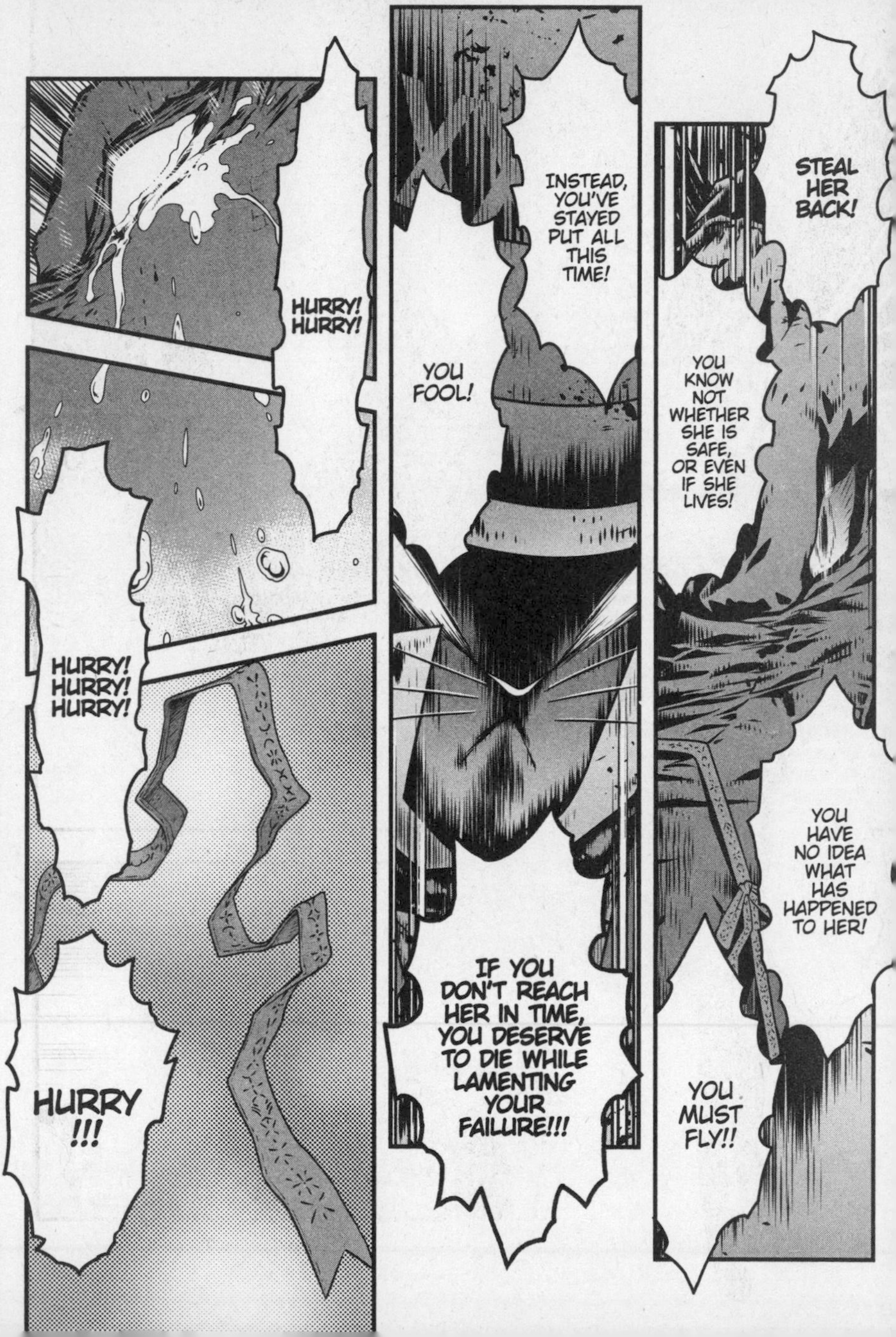
STEAL HER BACK!
YOU KNOW NOT WHETHER SHE IS SAFE, OR EVEN IF SHE LIVES!
YOU HAVE NO IDEA WHAT HAS HAPPENED TO HER!
YOU MUST FLY!!
INSTEAD, YOU'VE STAYED PUT ALL THIS TIME!
YOU FOOL!
IF YOU DON'T REACH HER IN TIME, YOU DESERVE TO DIE WHILE LAMENTING YOUR FAILURE!!!
HURRY! HURRY!
HURRY! HURRY! HURRY!
HURRY !!!

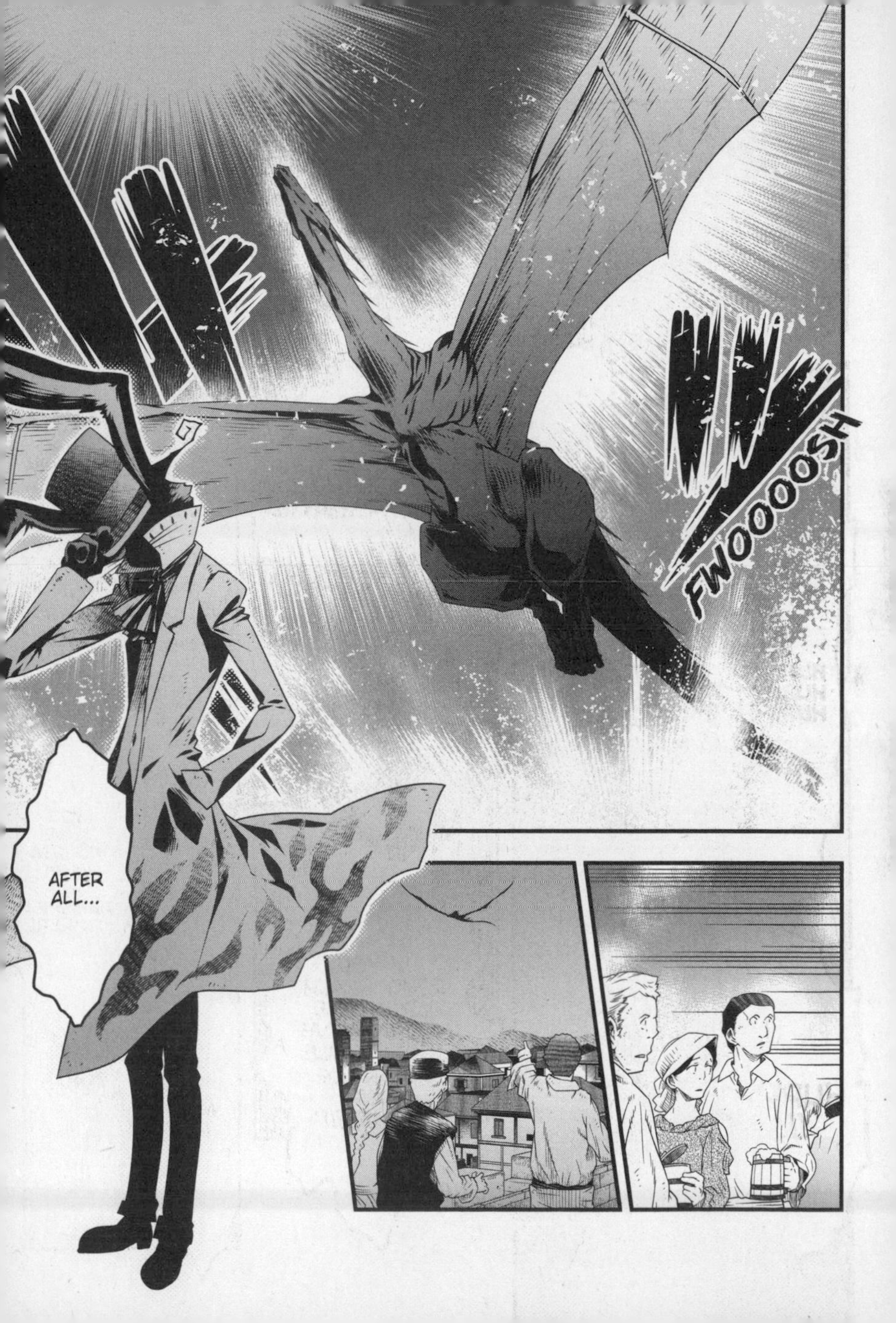
FWOOOOSH
AFTER ALL...

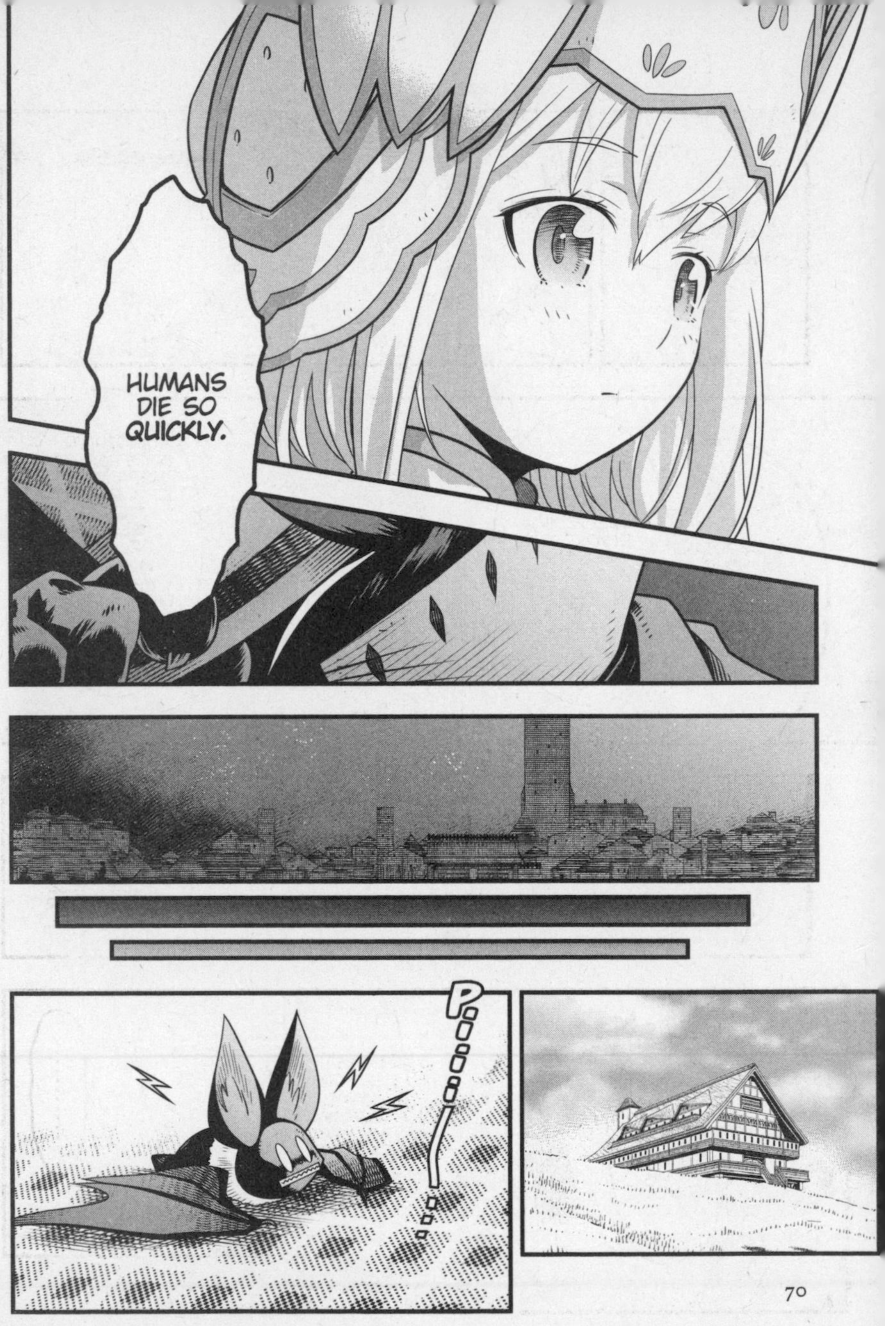
HUMANS DIE SO QUICKLY.
P...

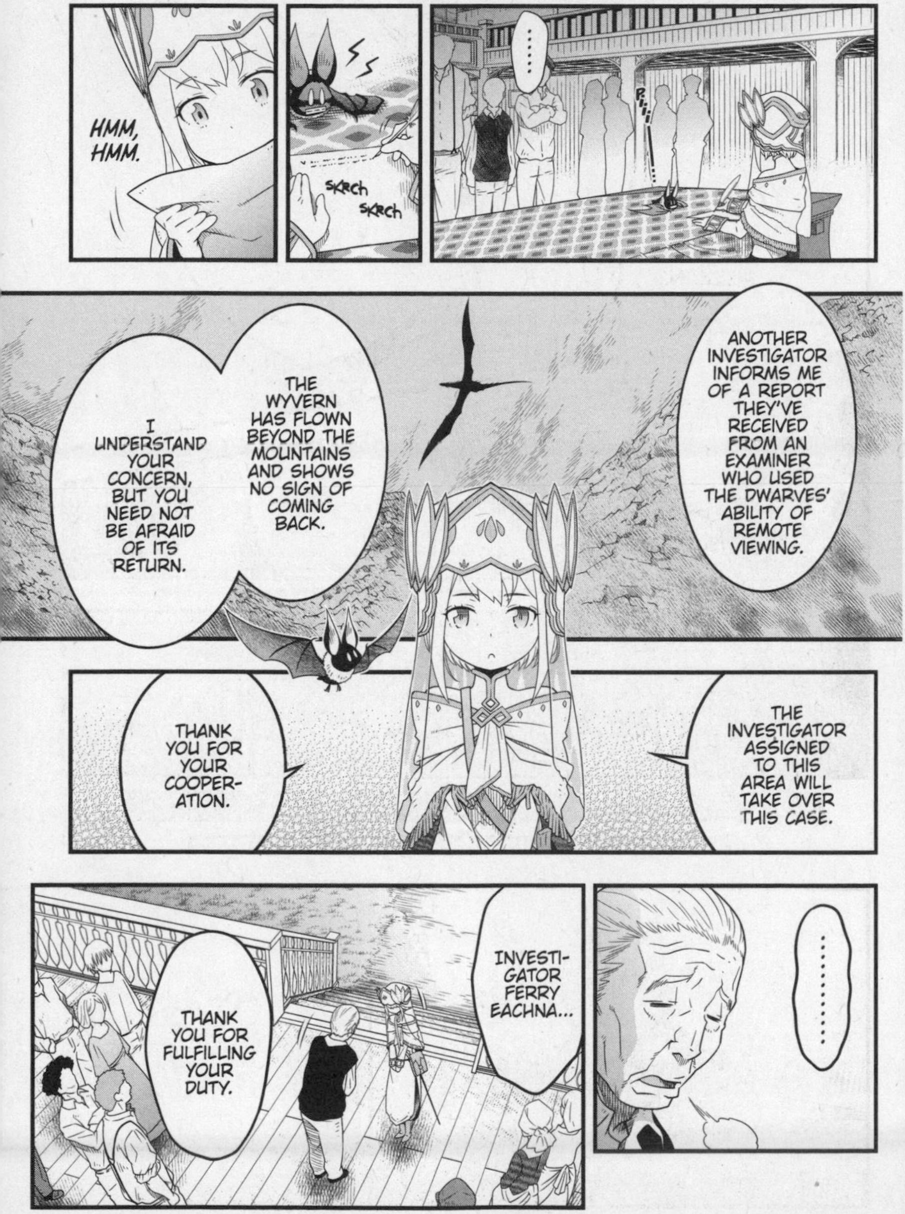
......
SKRCH
SKRCH
HMM, HMM.
ANOTHER INVESTIGATOR INFORMS ME OF A REPORT THEY'VE RECEIVED FROM AN EXAMINER WHO USED THE DWARVES' ABILITY OF REMOTE VIEWING.
THE WYVERN HAS FLOWN BEYOND THE MOUNTAINS AND SHOWS NO SIGN OF COMING BACK.
I UNDERSTAND YOUR CONCERN, BUT YOU NEED NOT BE AFRAID OF ITS RETURN.
THE INVESTIGATOR ASSIGNED TO THIS AREA WILL TAKE OVER THIS CASE.
THANK YOU FOR YOUR COOPER-ATION.
......
INVESTI-GATOR FERRY EACHNA...
THANK YOU FOR FULFILLING YOUR DUTY.

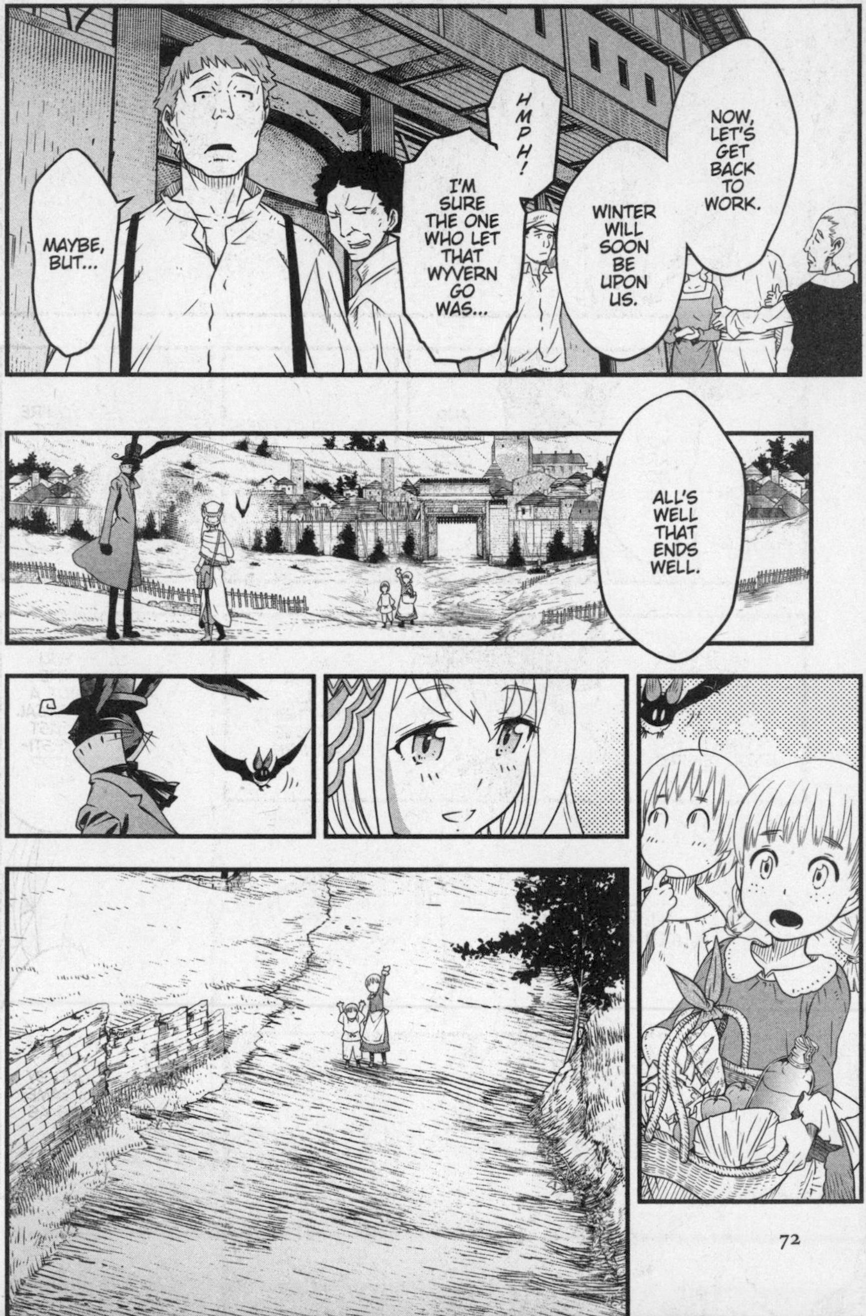
NOW, LET'S GET BACK TO WORK.
WINTER WILL SOON BE UPON US.
HMPH!
I'M SURE THE ONE WHO LET THAT WYVERN GO WAS...
MAYBE, BUT...
ALL'S WELL THAT ENDS WELL.

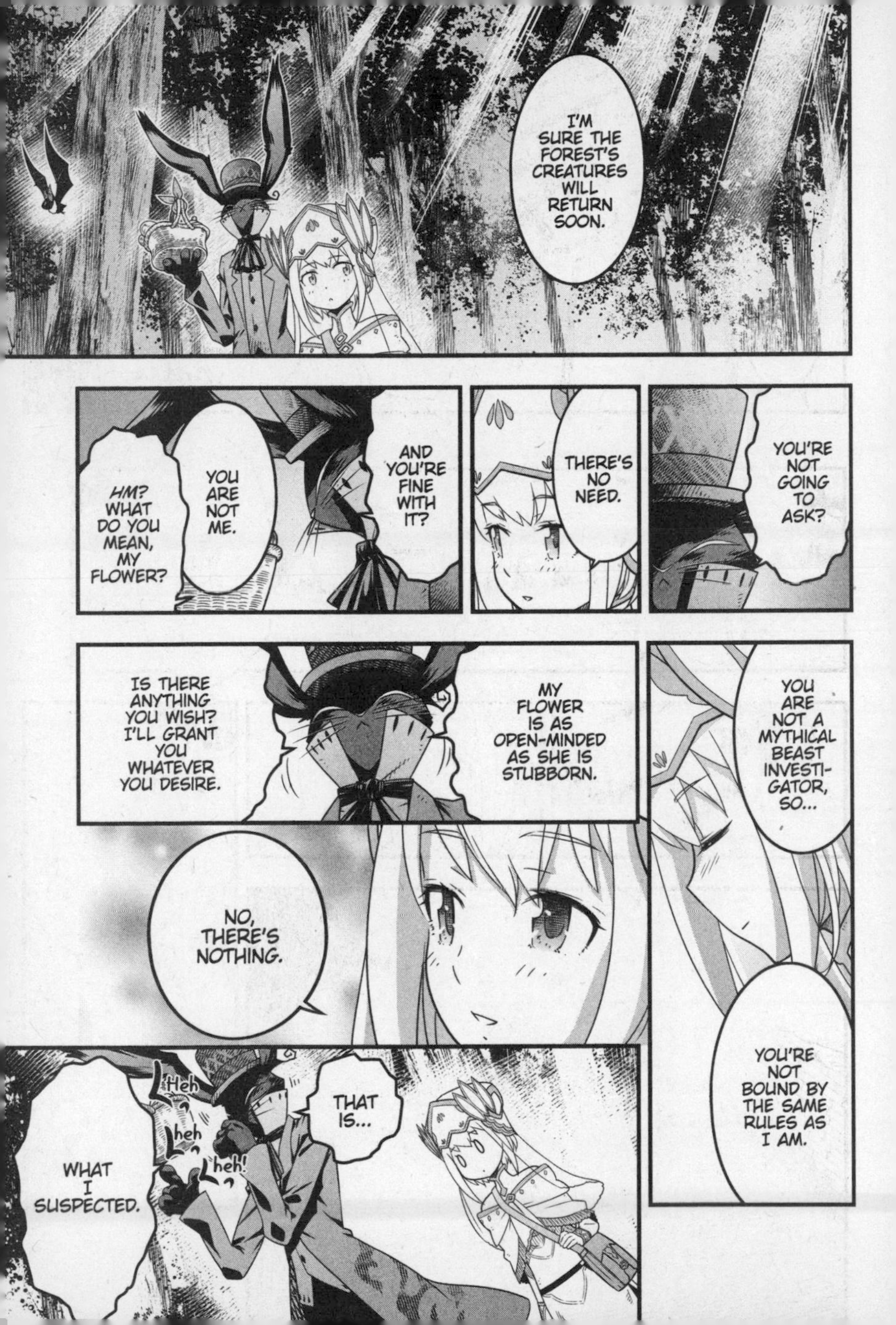
I'M SURE THE FOREST'S CREATURES WILL RETURN SOON.
YOU'RE NOT GOING TO ASK?
THERE'S NO NEED.
AND YOU'RE FINE WITH IT?
YOU ARE NOT ME.
HM? WHAT DO YOU MEAN, MY FLOWER?
YOU ARE NOT A MYTHICAL BEAST INVESTIGATOR, SO...
YOU'RE NOT BOUND BY THE SAME RULES AS I AM.
MY FLOWER IS AS OPEN-MINDED AS SHE IS STUBBORN.
IS THERE ANYTHING YOU WISH? I'LL GRANT YOU WHATEVER YOU DESIRE.
NO, THERE'S NOTHING.
THAT IS...
Heh heh heh!
WHAT I SUSPECTED.

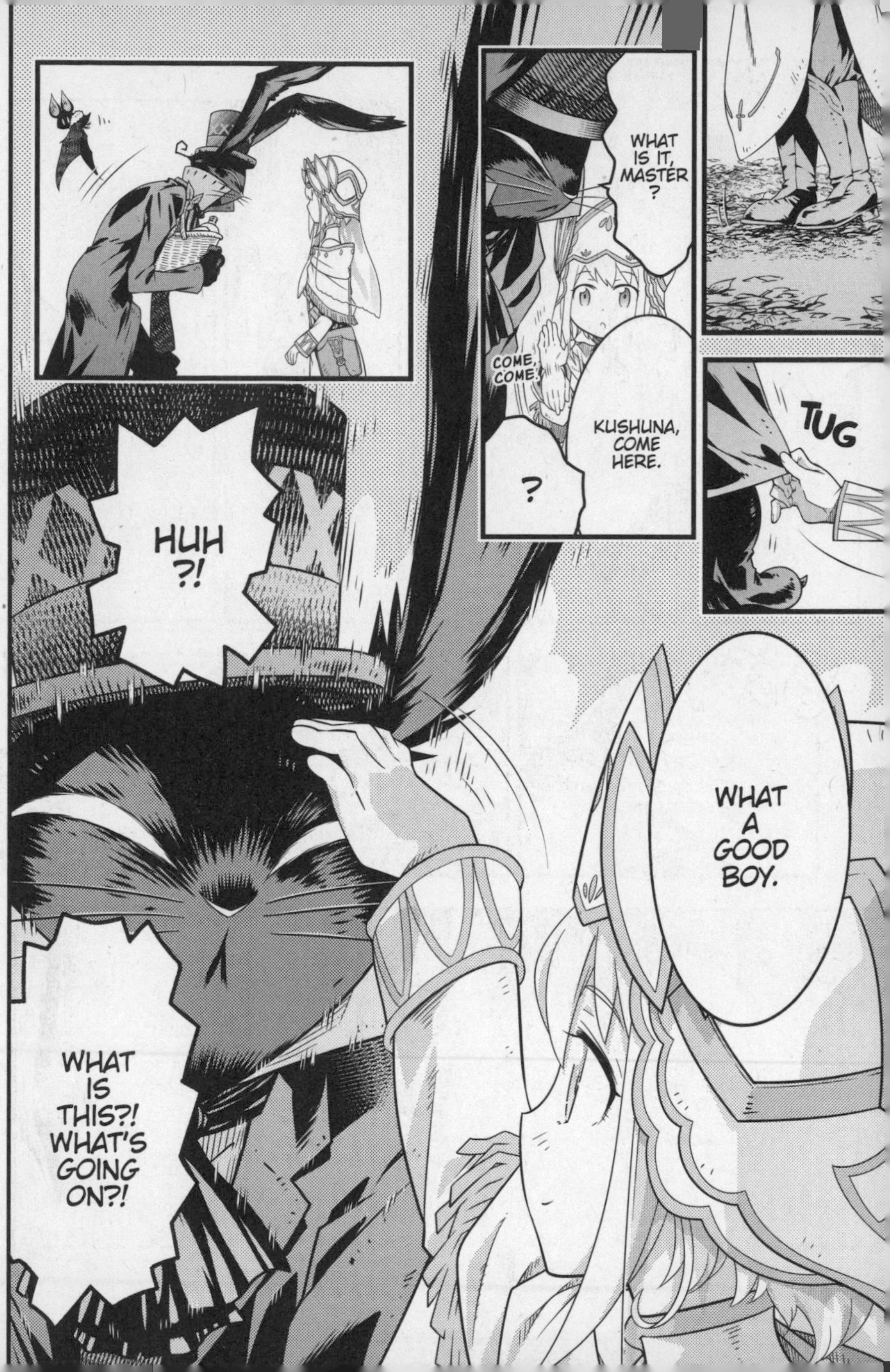
TUG
WHAT IS IT, MASTER?
KUSHUNA, COME HERE.
COME, COME.
?
WHAT A GOOD BOY.
HUH?!
WHAT IS THIS?! WHAT'S GOING ON?!

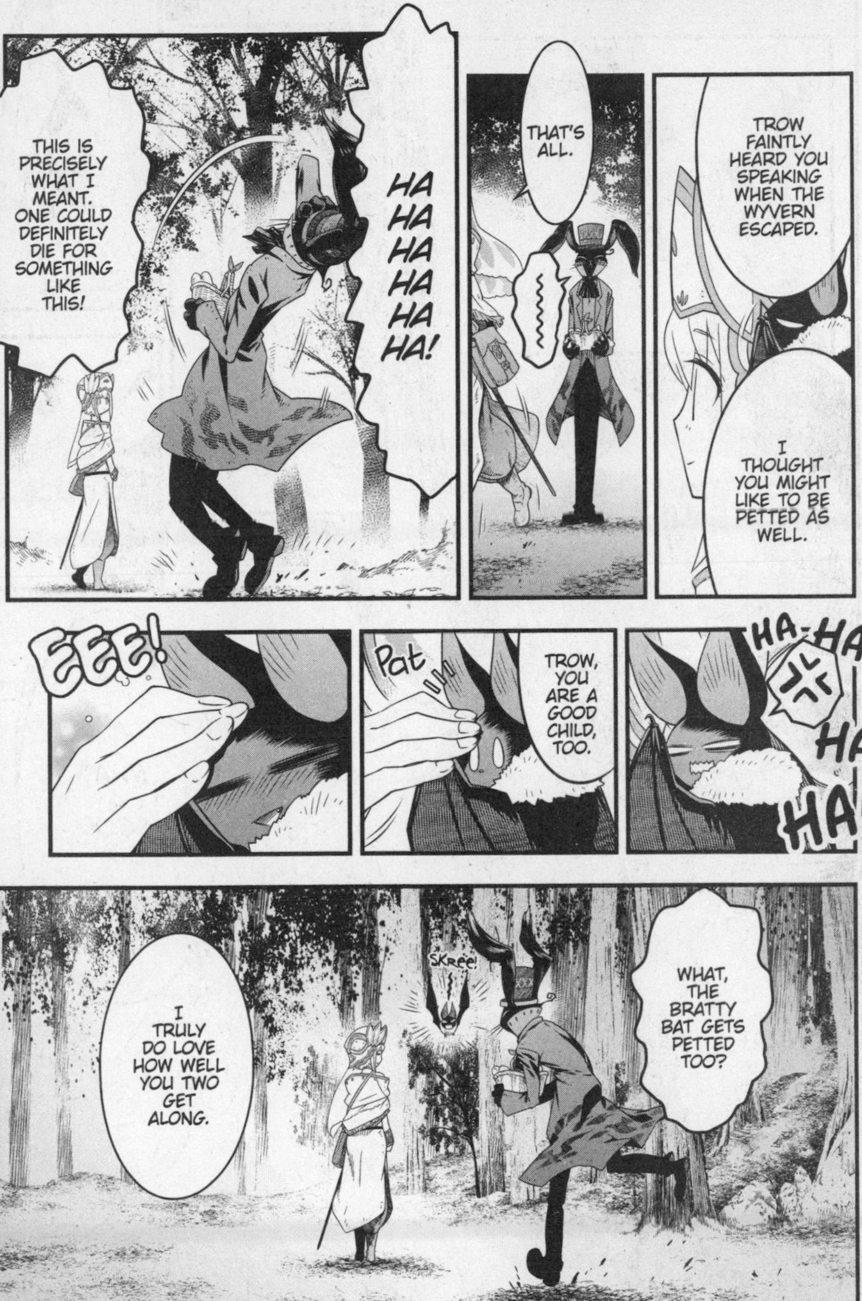
TROW FAINTLY HEARD YOU SPEAKING WHEN THE WYVERN ESCAPED.
I THOUGHT YOU MIGHT LIKE TO BE PETTED AS WELL.
THAT'S ALL.
HA HA HA HA HA HA!
THIS IS PRECISELY WHAT I MEANT. ONE COULD DEFINITELY DIE FOR SOMETHING LIKE THIS!
HA-HA HA HA!
Pat
TROW, YOU ARE A GOOD CHILD, TOO.
EEE!
WHAT, THE BRATTY BAT GETS PETTED TOO?
SKree!
I TRULY DO LOVE HOW WELL YOU TWO GET ALONG.

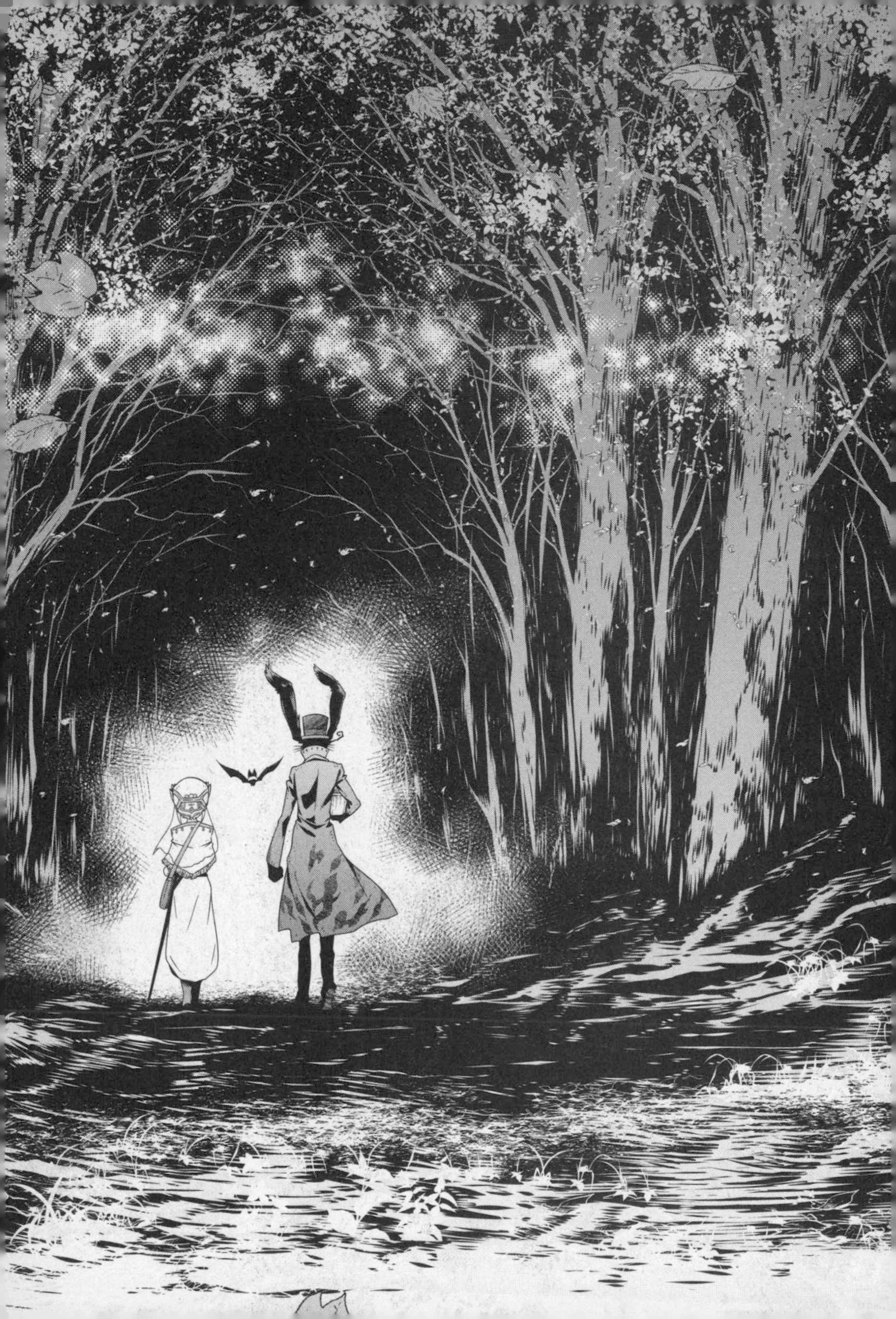

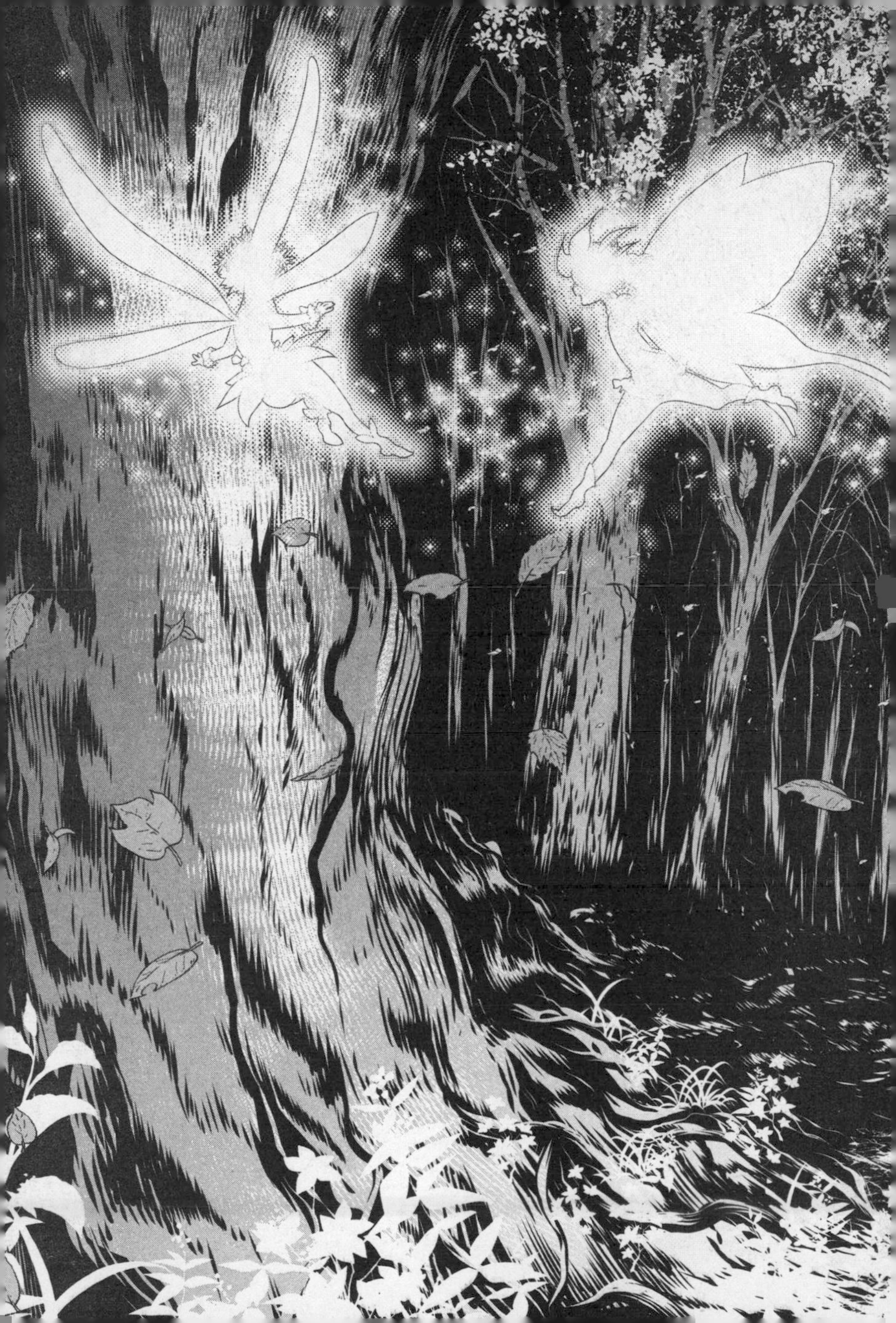

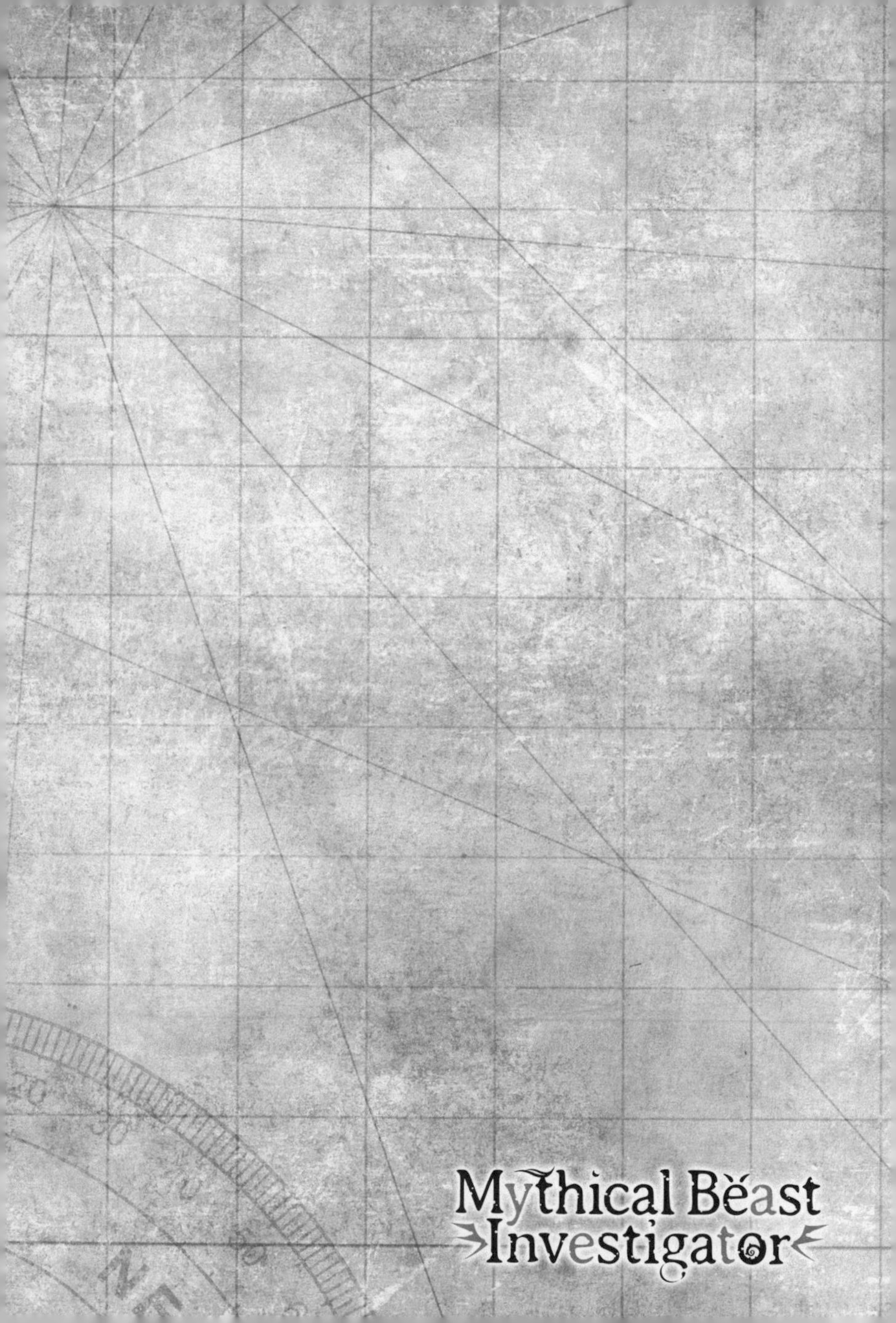
Mythical Beast Investigator

About the Wyvern and the Girl

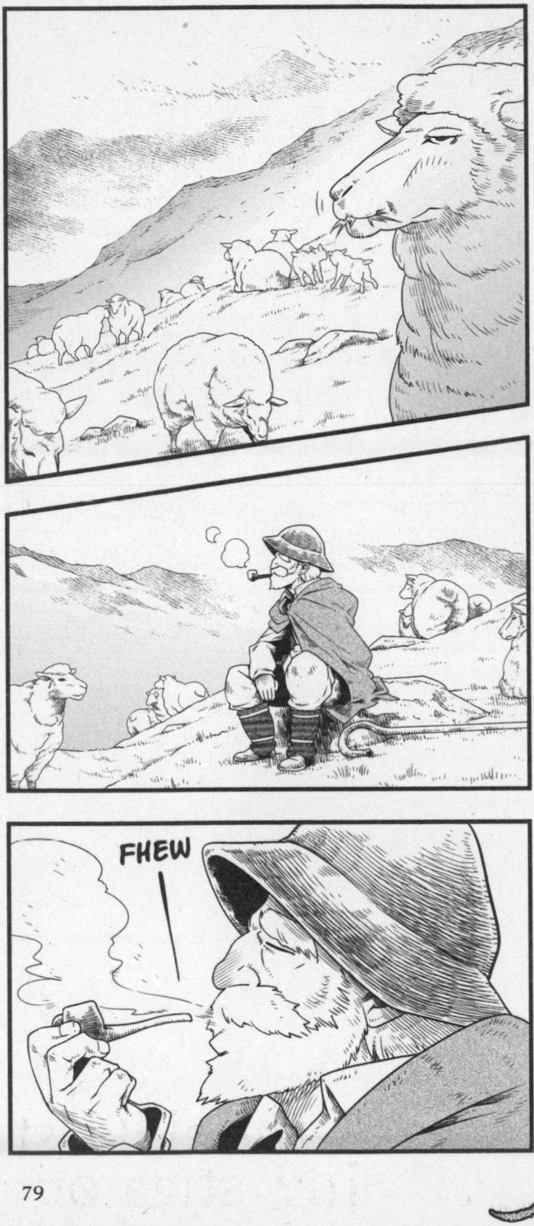
FHEW

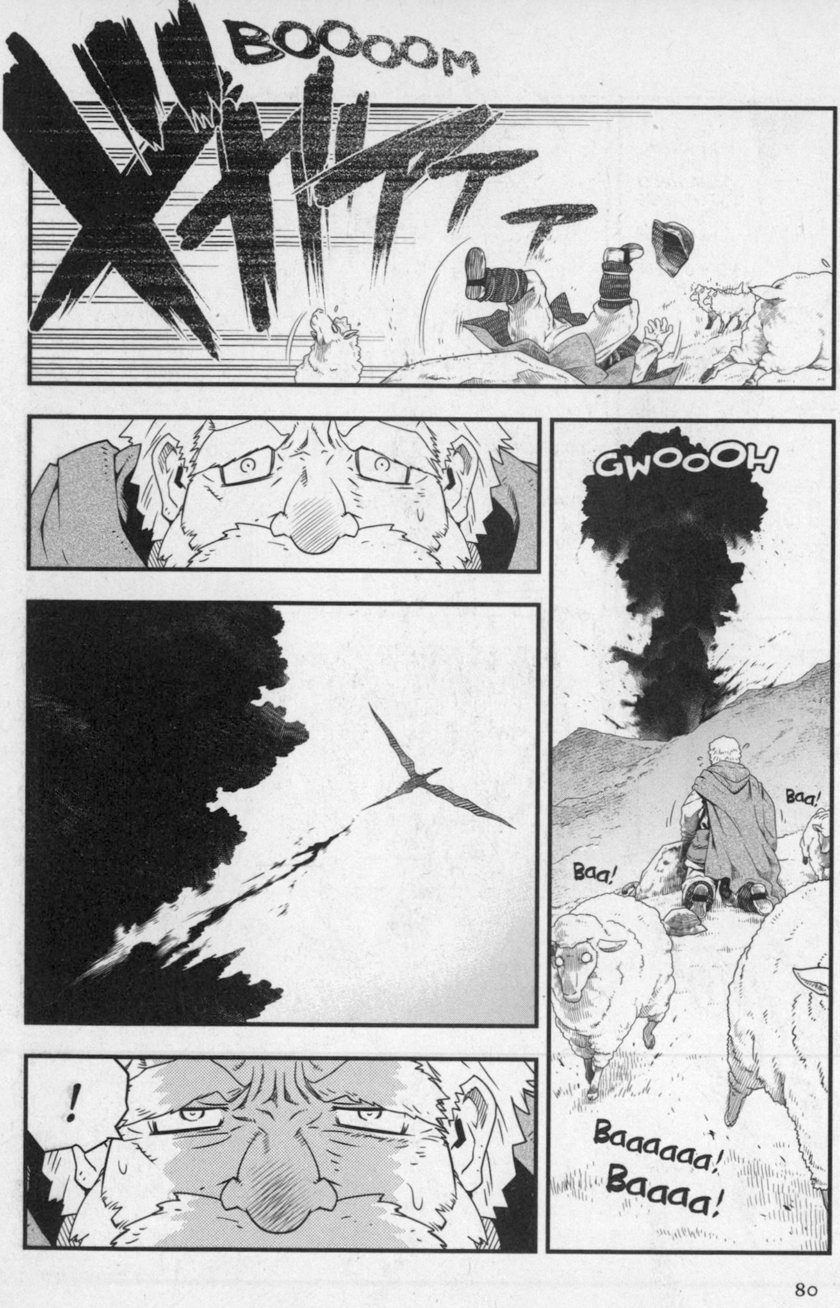
BOOOOM
GWOOOH
Baa!
Baa!
Baaaaaa!
Baaaa!
!

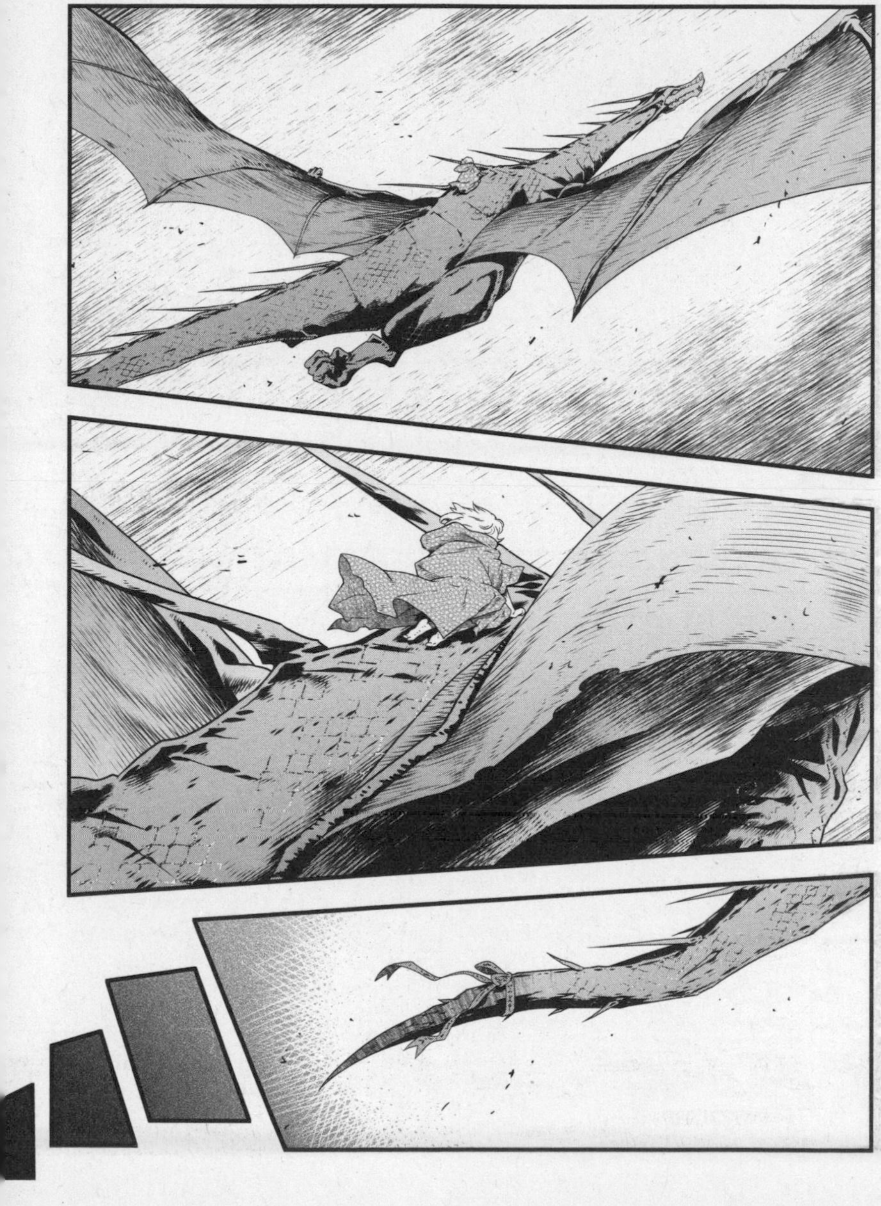

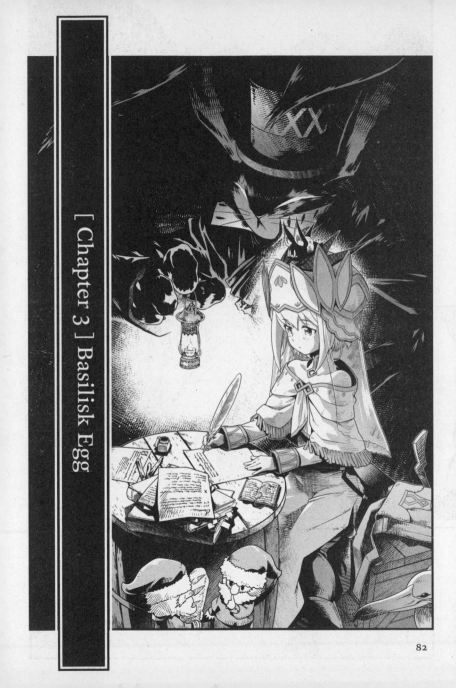

[Chapter 3] Basilisk Egg

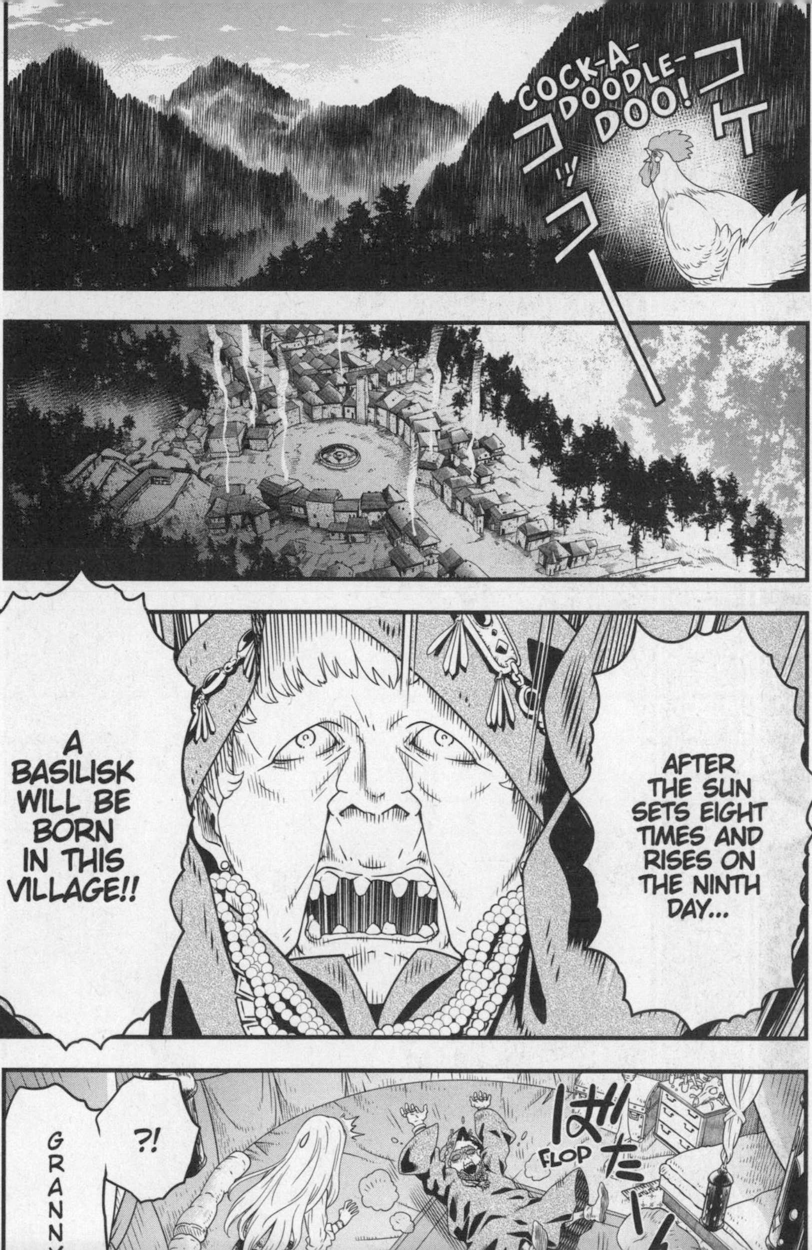

COCK-A-DOODLE-DOO!
コケコッコー
AFTER THE SUN SETS EIGHT TIMES AND RISES ON THE NINTH DAY...
A BASILISK WILL BE BORN IN THIS VILLAGE!!
FLOP
ばったーん
?!
GRANNY!

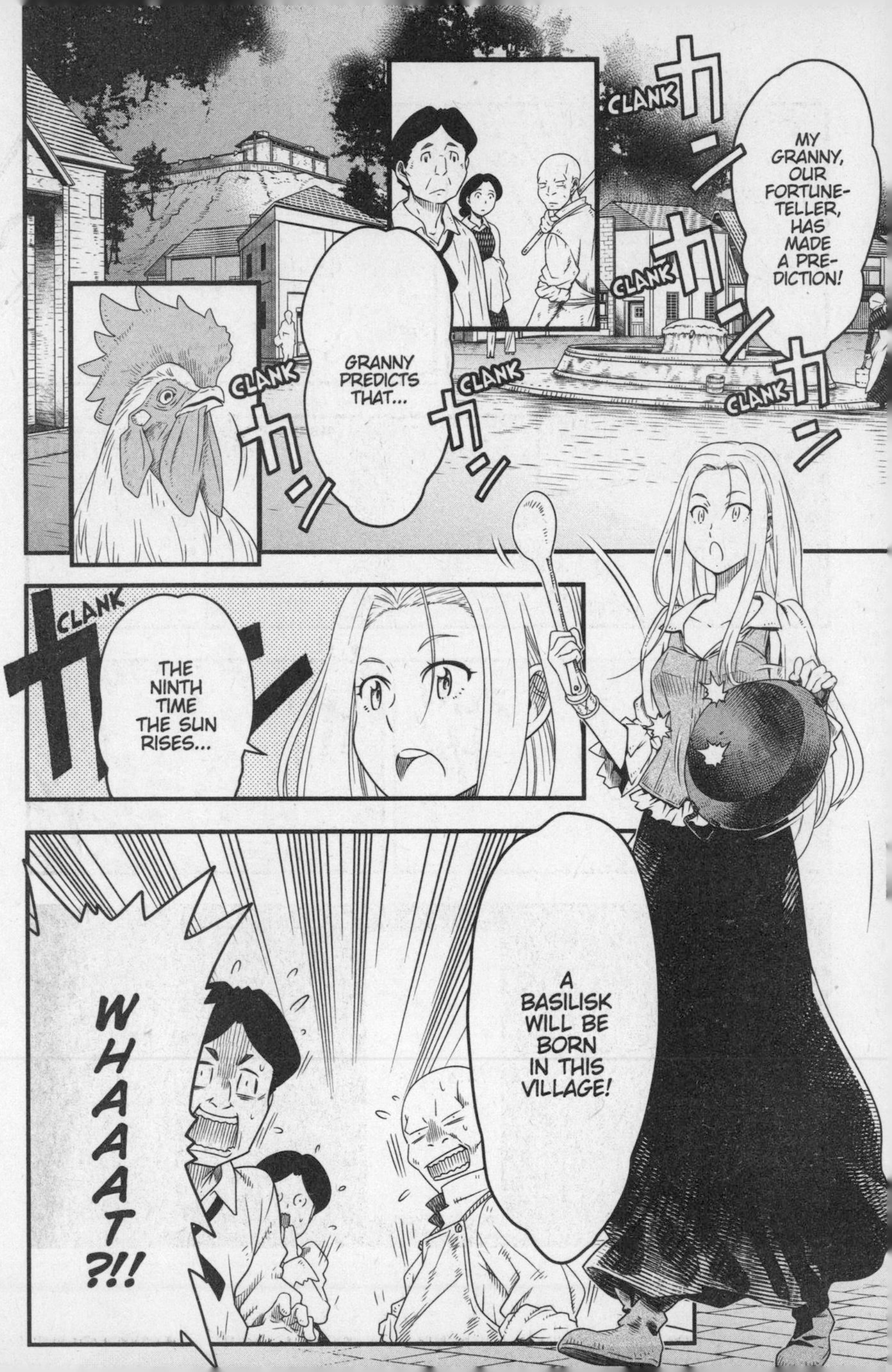
CLANK
CLANK
MY GRANNY, OUR FORTUNE-TELLER, HAS MADE A PRE-DICTION!
CLANK
CLANK
GRANNY PREDICTS THAT...
CLANK
CLANK
THE NINTH TIME THE SUN RISES...
A BASILISK WILL BE BORN IN THIS VILLAGE!
WHAAAT ?!!

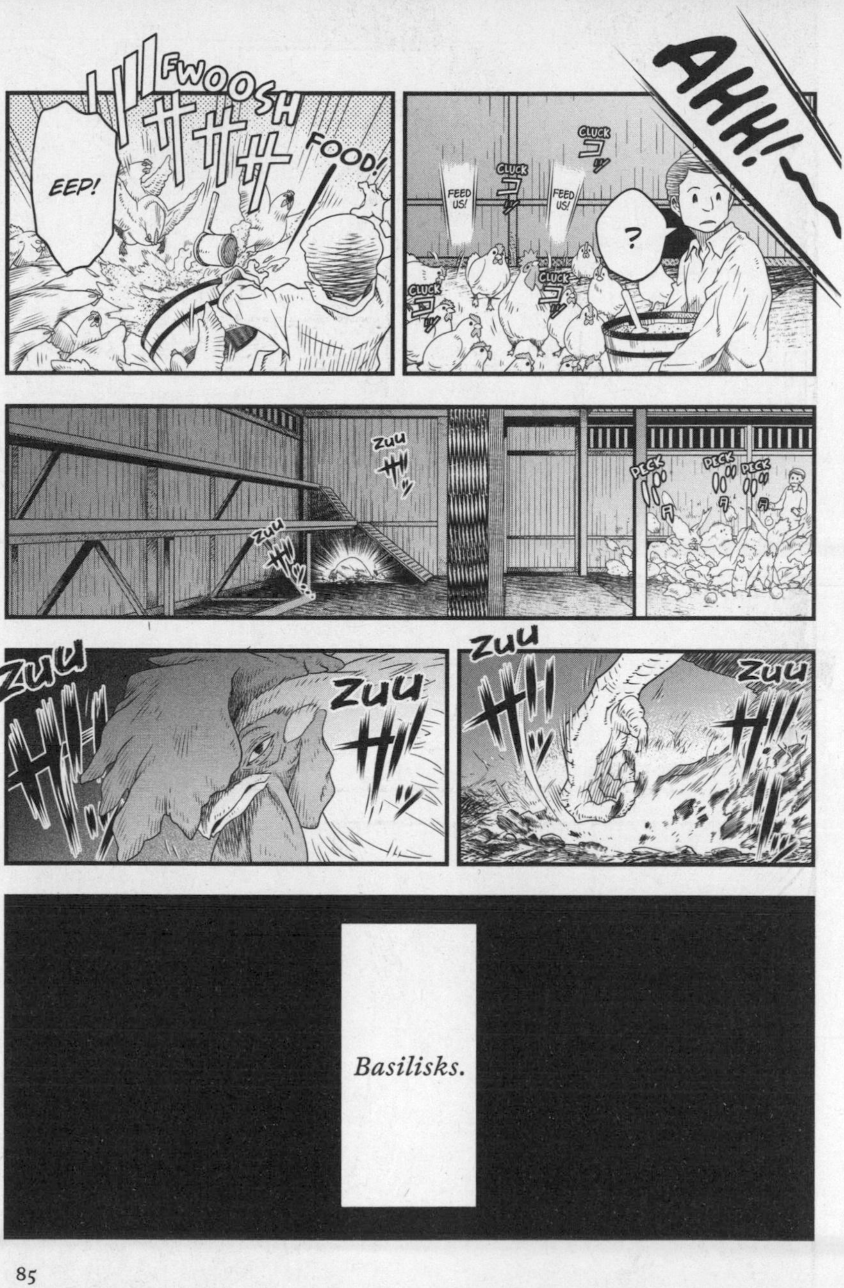
AHH!~
CLUCK
FEED US!
CLUCK
FEED US!
?
CLUCK
CLUCK
FWOOSH
FOOD!
EEP!
PECK
PECK
PECK
ZUU
ZUU
ZUU
ZUU
ZUU
ZUU
Basilisks.

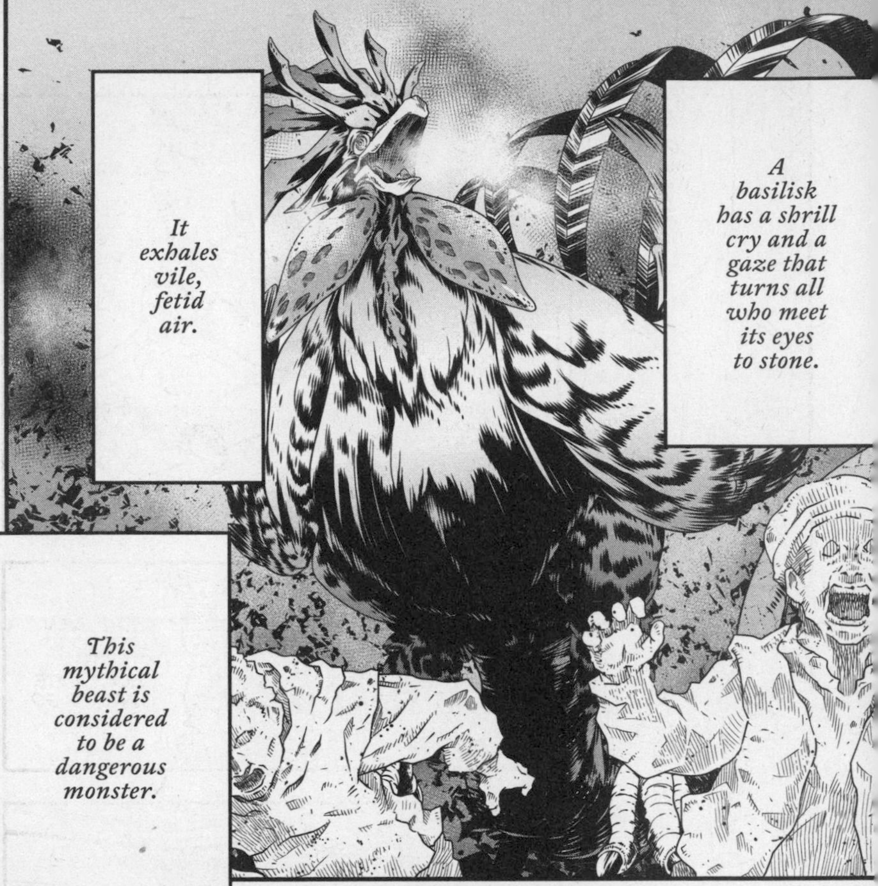
A basilisk has a shrill cry and a gaze that turns all who meet its eyes to stone.
It exhales vile, fetid air.
This mythical beast is considered to be a dangerous monster.

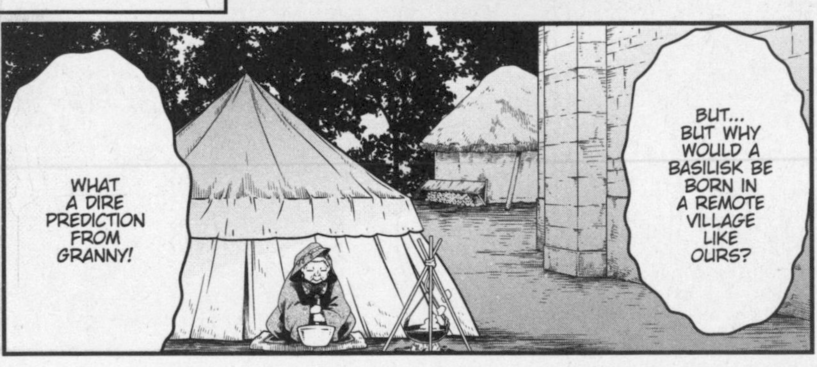
BUT... BUT WHY WOULD A BASILISK BE BORN IN A REMOTE VILLAGE LIKE OURS?
WHAT A DIRE PREDICTION FROM GRANNY!

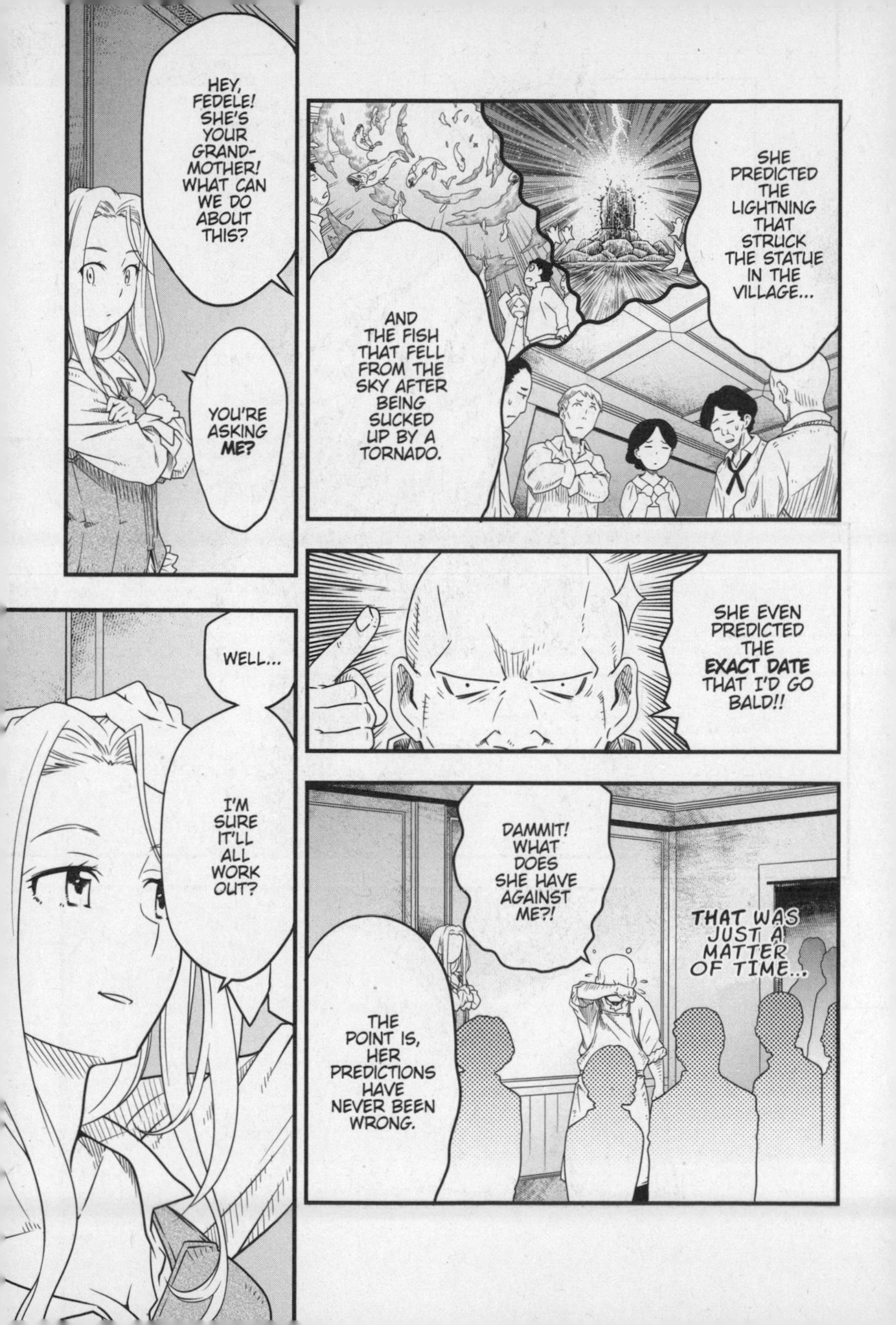
SHE PREDICTED THE LIGHTNING THAT STRUCK THE STATUE IN THE VILLAGE...
AND THE FISH THAT FELL FROM THE SKY AFTER BEING SUCKED UP BY A TORNADO.
SHE EVEN PREDICTED THE **EXACT DATE** THAT I'D GO BALD!!
DAMMIT! WHAT DOES SHE HAVE AGAINST ME?!
THAT WAS JUST A MATTER OF TIME...
THE POINT IS, HER PREDICTIONS HAVE NEVER BEEN WRONG.
HEY, FEDELE! SHE'S YOUR GRAND-MOTHER! WHAT CAN WE DO ABOUT THIS?
YOU'RE ASKING **ME?**
WELL...
I'M SURE IT'LL ALL WORK OUT?

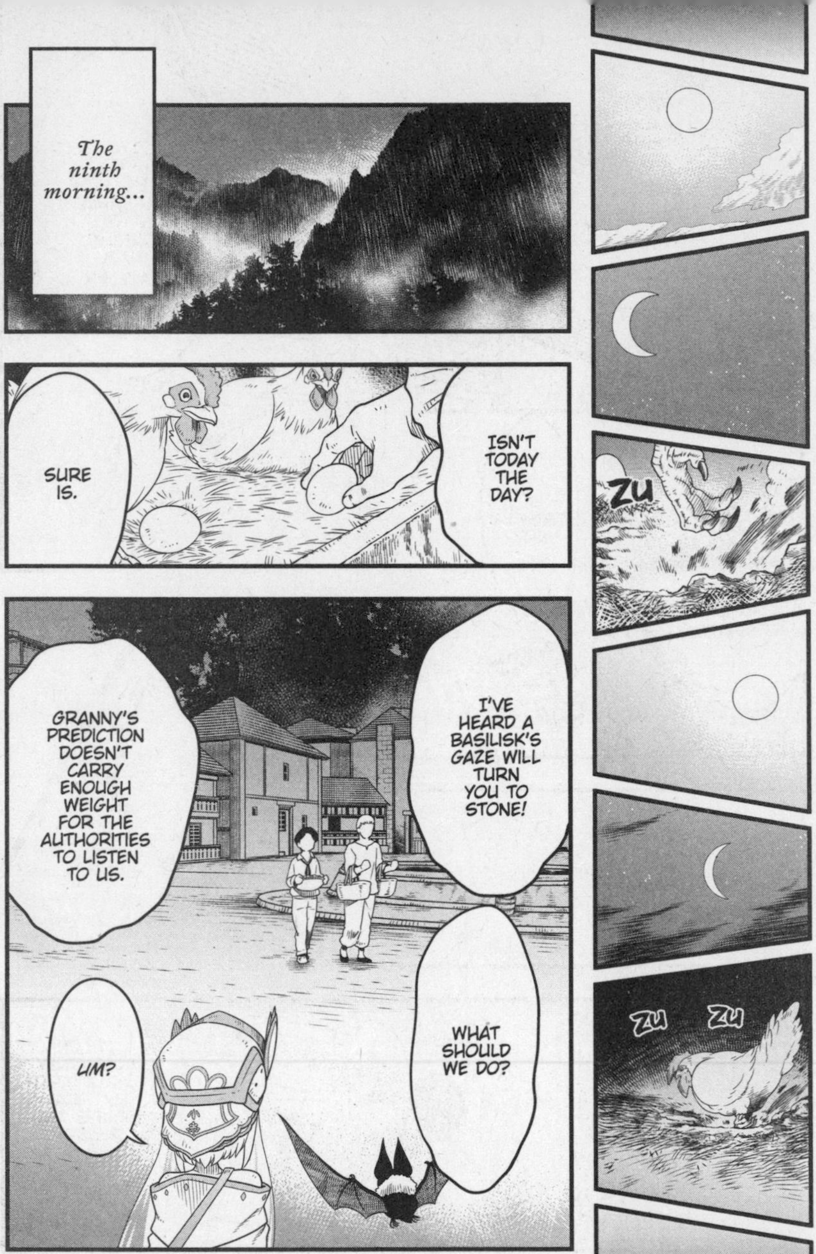
ZU
ZU ZU
The ninth morning...
ISN'T TODAY THE DAY?
SURE IS.
I'VE HEARD A BASILISK'S GAZE WILL TURN YOU TO STONE!
GRANNY'S PREDICTION DOESN'T CARRY ENOUGH WEIGHT FOR THE AUTHORITIES TO LISTEN TO US.
WHAT SHOULD WE DO?
UM?

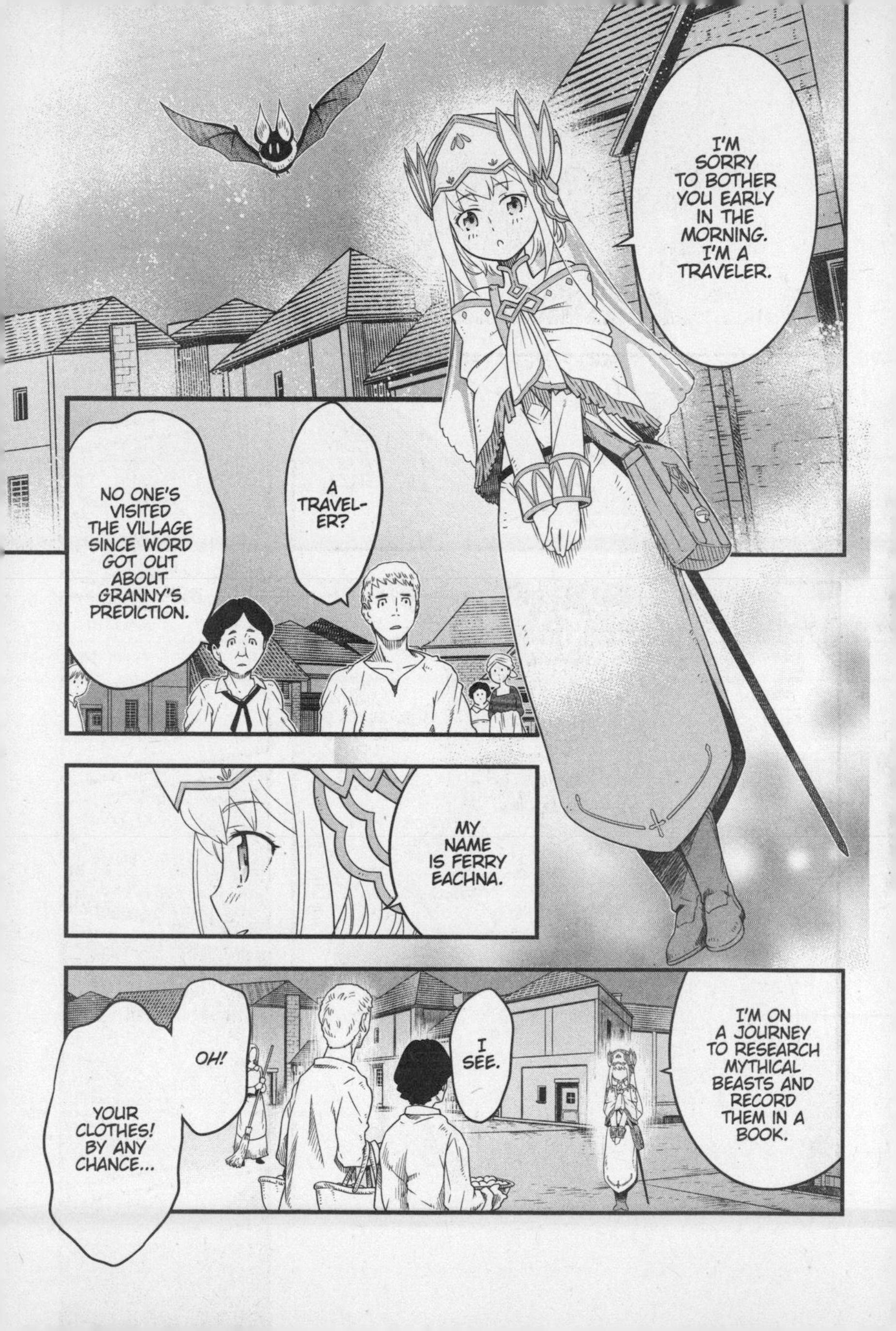
I'M SORRY TO BOTHER YOU EARLY IN THE MORNING. I'M A TRAVELER.
A TRAVEL-ER?
NO ONE'S VISITED THE VILLAGE SINCE WORD GOT OUT ABOUT GRANNY'S PREDICTION.
MY NAME IS FERRY EACHNA.
I'M ON A JOURNEY TO RESEARCH MYTHICAL BEASTS AND RECORD THEM IN A BOOK.
I SEE.
OH!
YOUR CLOTHES! BY ANY CHANCE...

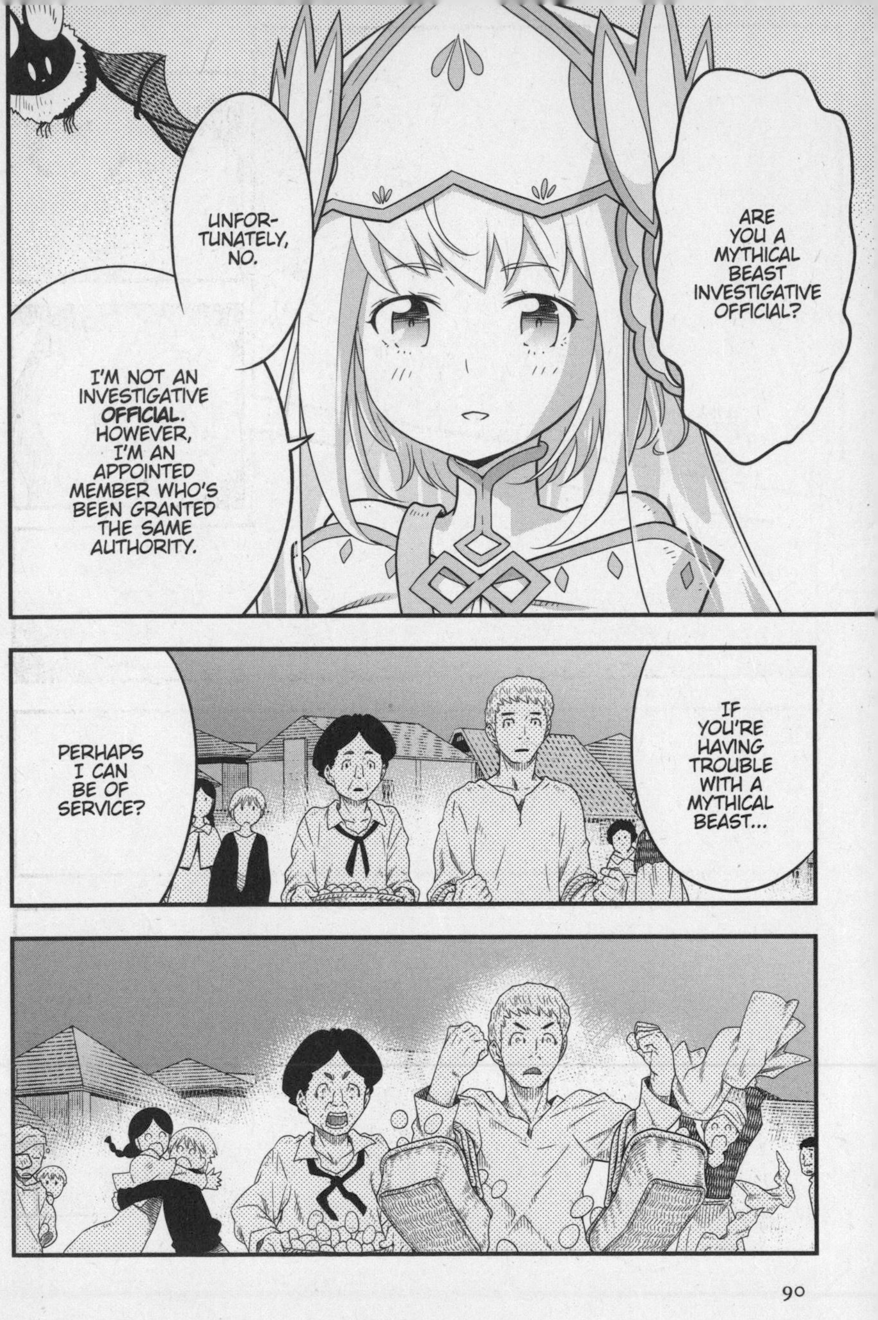
ARE YOU A MYTHICAL BEAST INVESTIGATIVE OFFICIAL?
UNFOR-TUNATELY, NO.
I'M NOT AN INVESTIGATIVE OFFICIAL. HOWEVER, I'M AN APPOINTED MEMBER WHO'S BEEN GRANTED THE SAME AUTHORITY.
IF YOU'RE HAVING TROUBLE WITH A MYTHICAL BEAST...
PERHAPS I CAN BE OF SERVICE?

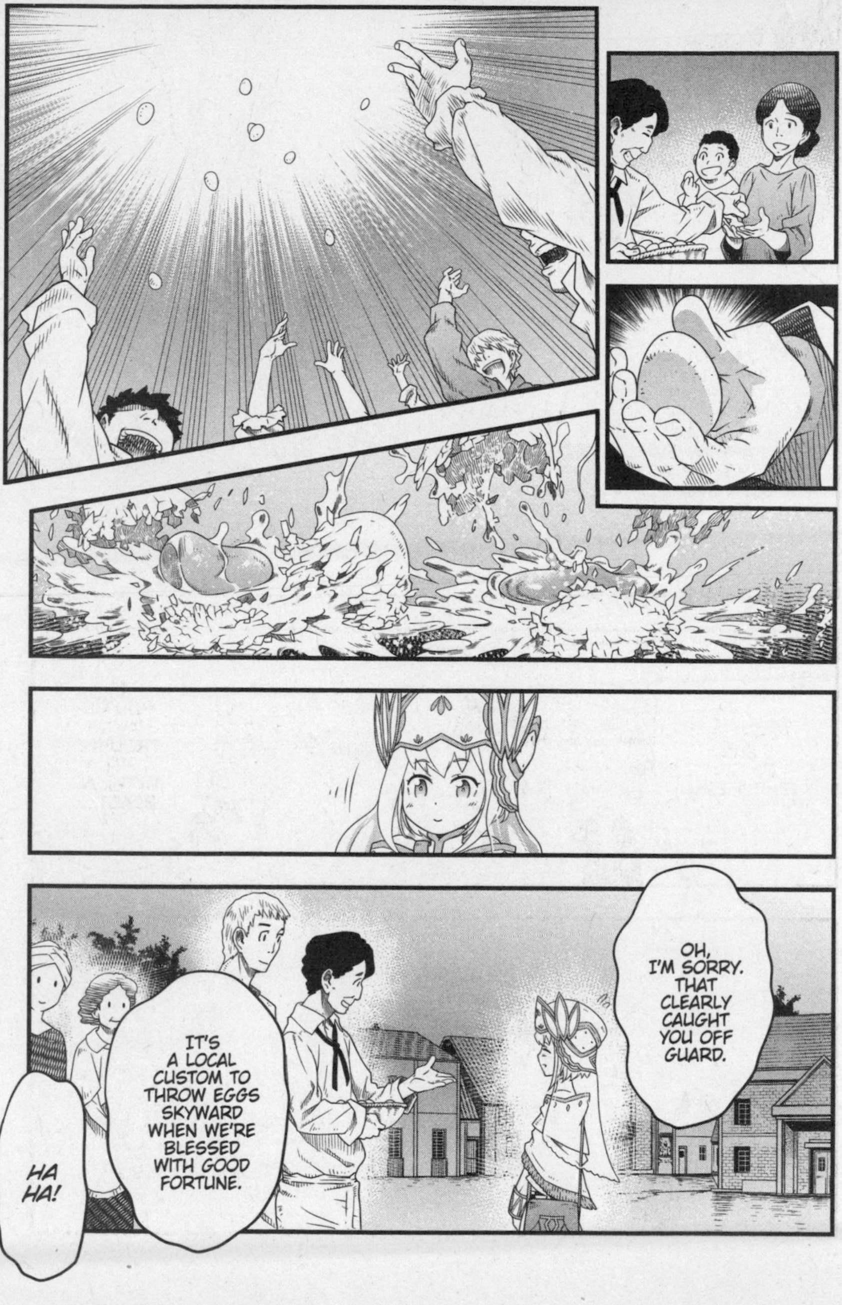
OH, I'M SORRY. THAT CLEARLY CAUGHT YOU OFF GUARD.
IT'S A LOCAL CUSTOM TO THROW EGGS SKYWARD WHEN WE'RE BLESSED WITH GOOD FORTUNE.
HA HA!

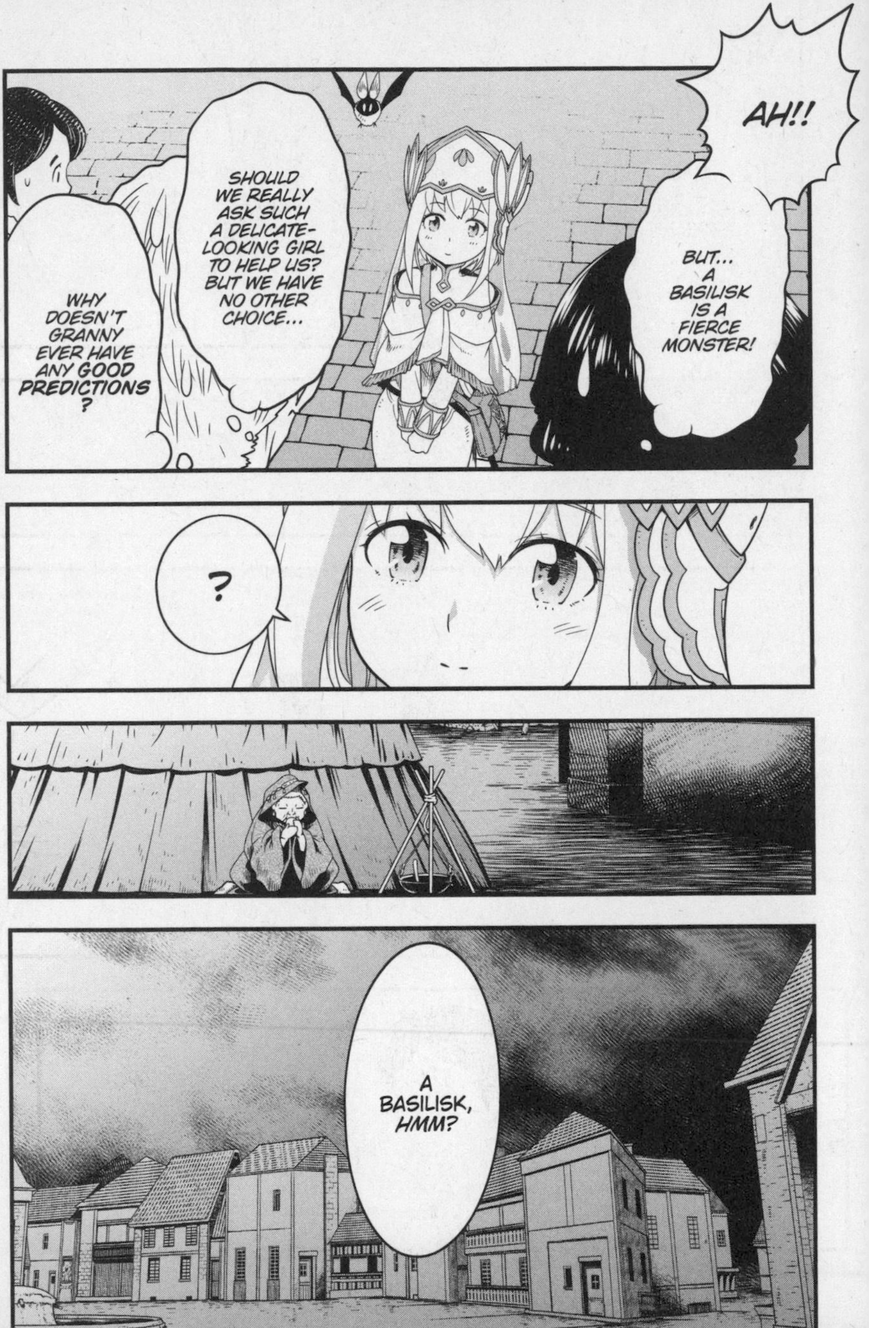
AH!!
BUT... A BASILISK IS A FIERCE MONSTER!
SHOULD WE REALLY ASK SUCH A DELICATE-LOOKING GIRL TO HELP US? BUT WE HAVE NO OTHER CHOICE...
WHY DOESN'T GRANNY EVER HAVE ANY GOOD PREDICTIONS?
?
A BASILISK, HMM?

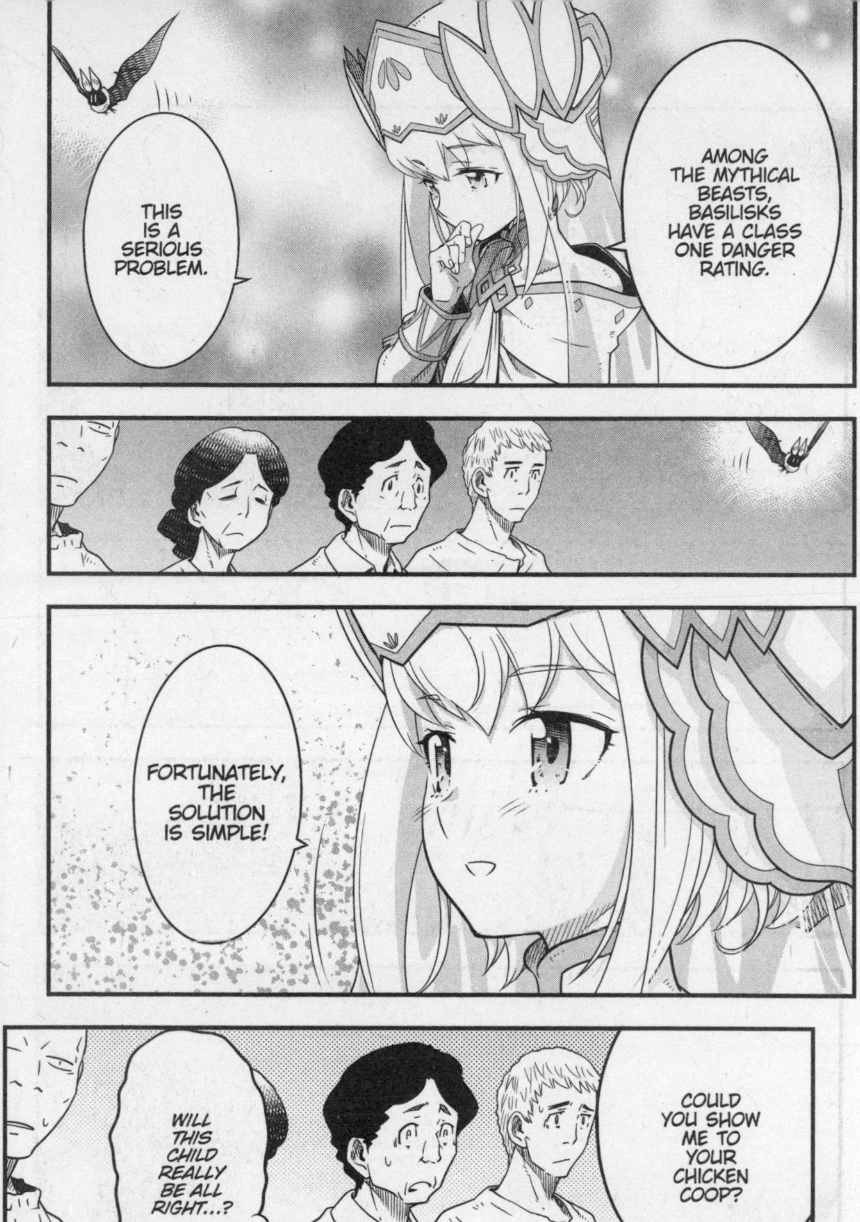
AMONG THE MYTHICAL BEASTS, BASILISKS HAVE A CLASS ONE DANGER RATING.
THIS IS A SERIOUS PROBLEM.
FORTUNATELY, THE SOLUTION IS SIMPLE!
COULD YOU SHOW ME TO YOUR CHICKEN COOP?
WILL THIS CHILD REALLY BE ALL RIGHT...?

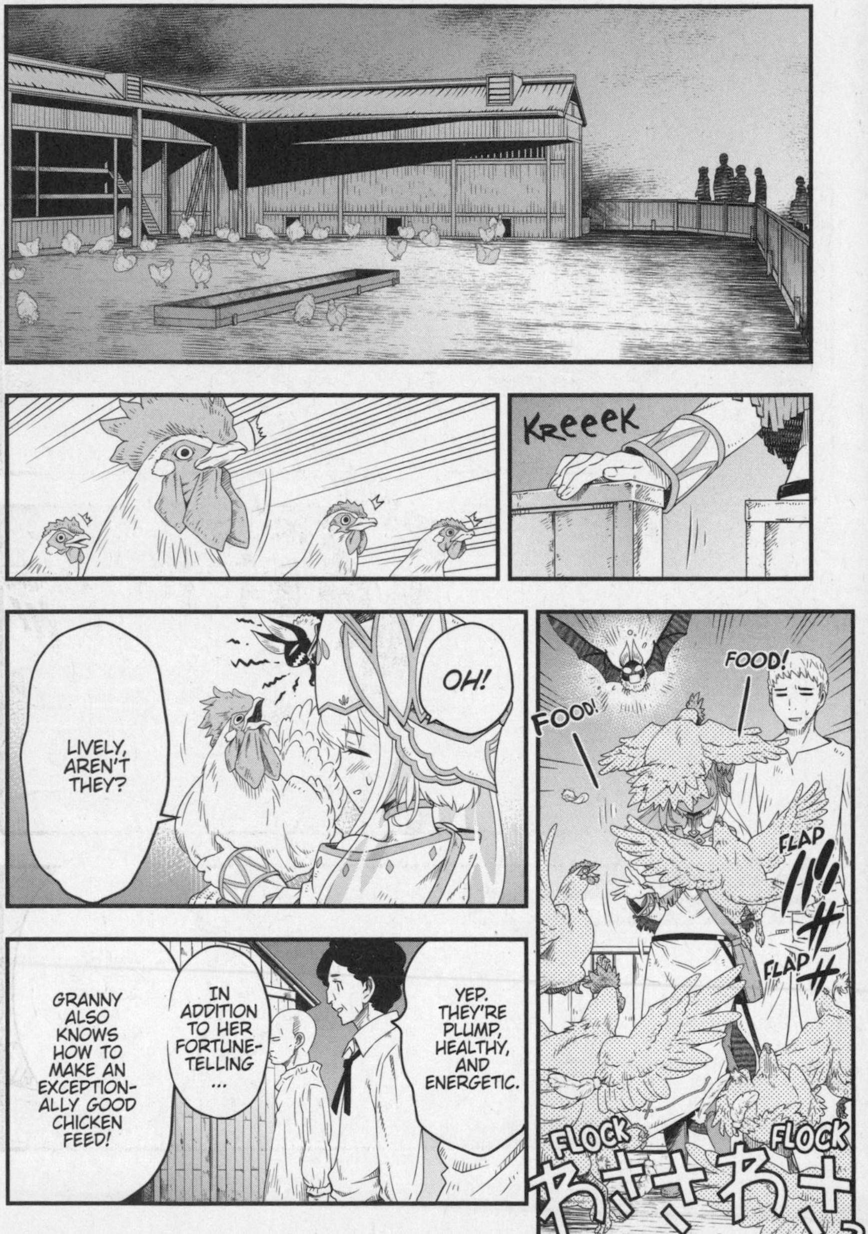
KREEEK
FOOD!
FOOD!
FLAP
FLAP
FLOCK
FLOCK
わさわさっ
OH!
LIVELY, AREN'T THEY?
YEP. THEY'RE PLUMP, HEALTHY, AND ENERGETIC.
IN ADDITION TO HER FORTUNE-TELLING...
GRANNY ALSO KNOWS HOW TO MAKE AN EXCEPTION-ALLY GOOD CHICKEN FEED!

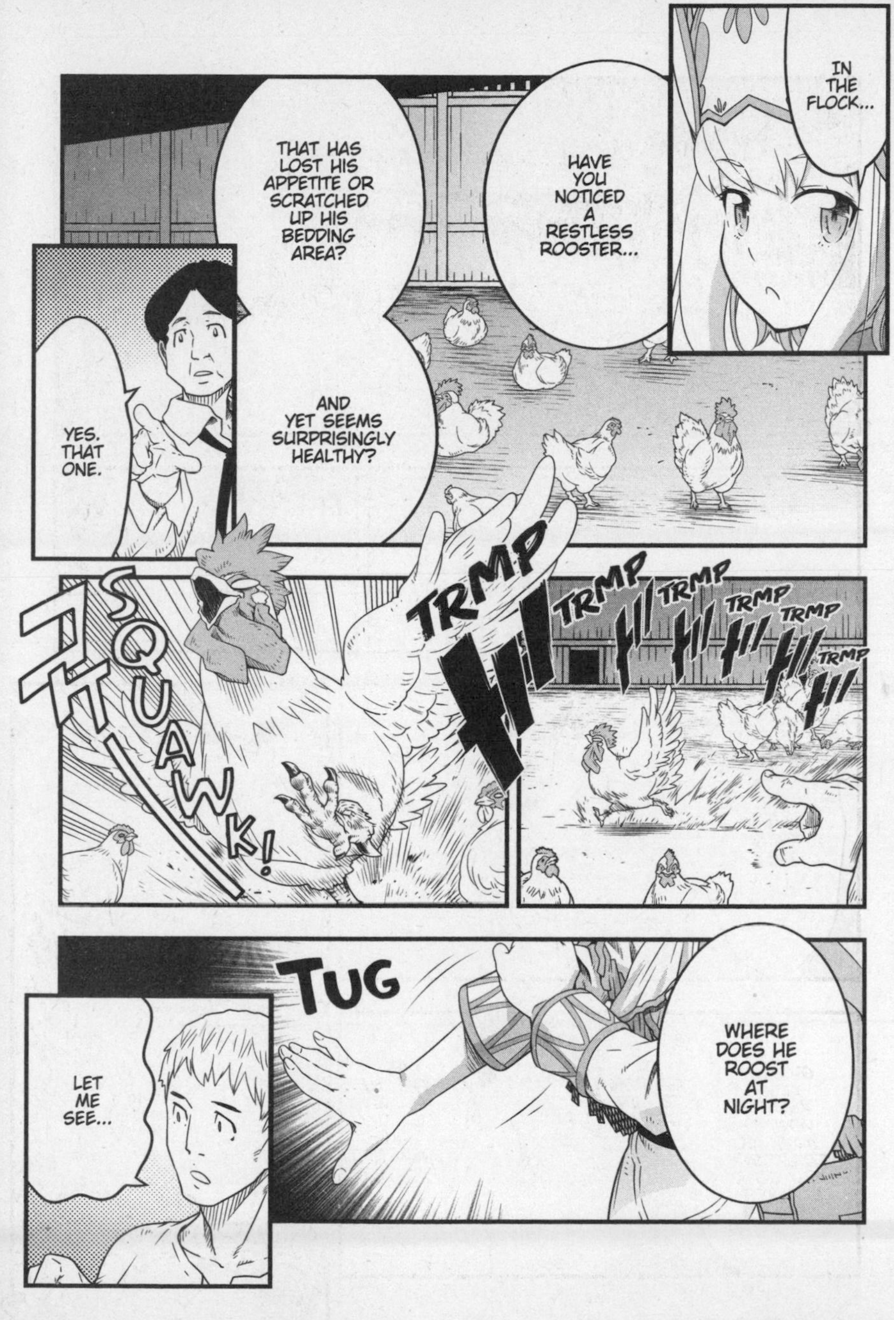
IN THE FLOCK...
HAVE YOU NOTICED A RESTLESS ROOSTER...
THAT HAS LOST HIS APPETITE OR SCRATCHED UP HIS BEDDING AREA?
AND YET SEEMS SURPRISINGLY HEALTHY?
YES. THAT ONE.
TRMP
TRMP
TRMP
TRMP
TRMP
TRMP
SQUAWK!
WHERE DOES HE ROOST AT NIGHT?
TUG
LET ME SEE...

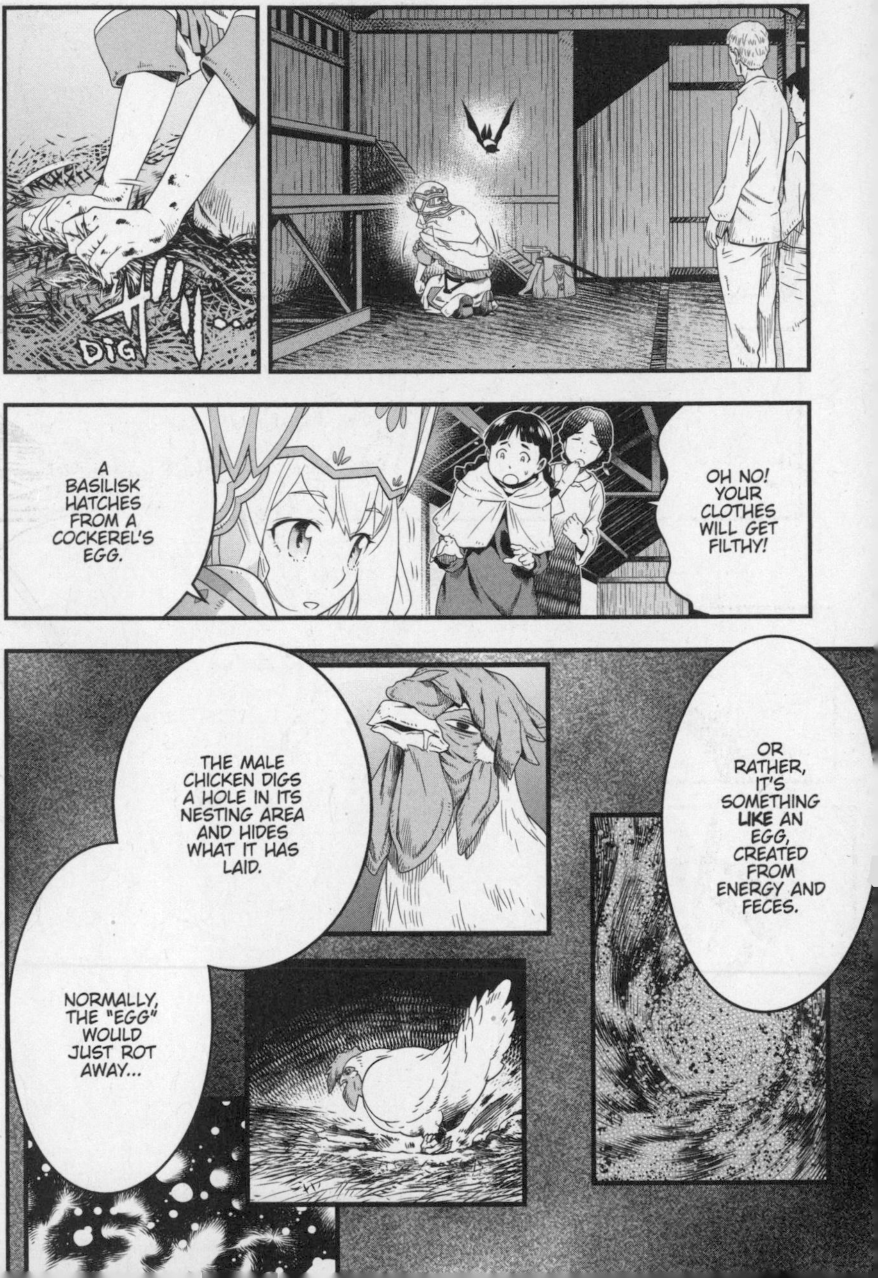
DIG
OH NO! YOUR CLOTHES WILL GET FILTHY!
A BASILISK HATCHES FROM A COCKEREL'S EGG.
OR RATHER, IT'S SOMETHING LIKE AN EGG, CREATED FROM ENERGY AND FECES.
THE MALE CHICKEN DIGS A HOLE IN ITS NESTING AREA AND HIDES WHAT IT HAS LAID.
NORMALLY, THE "EGG" WOULD JUST ROT AWAY...

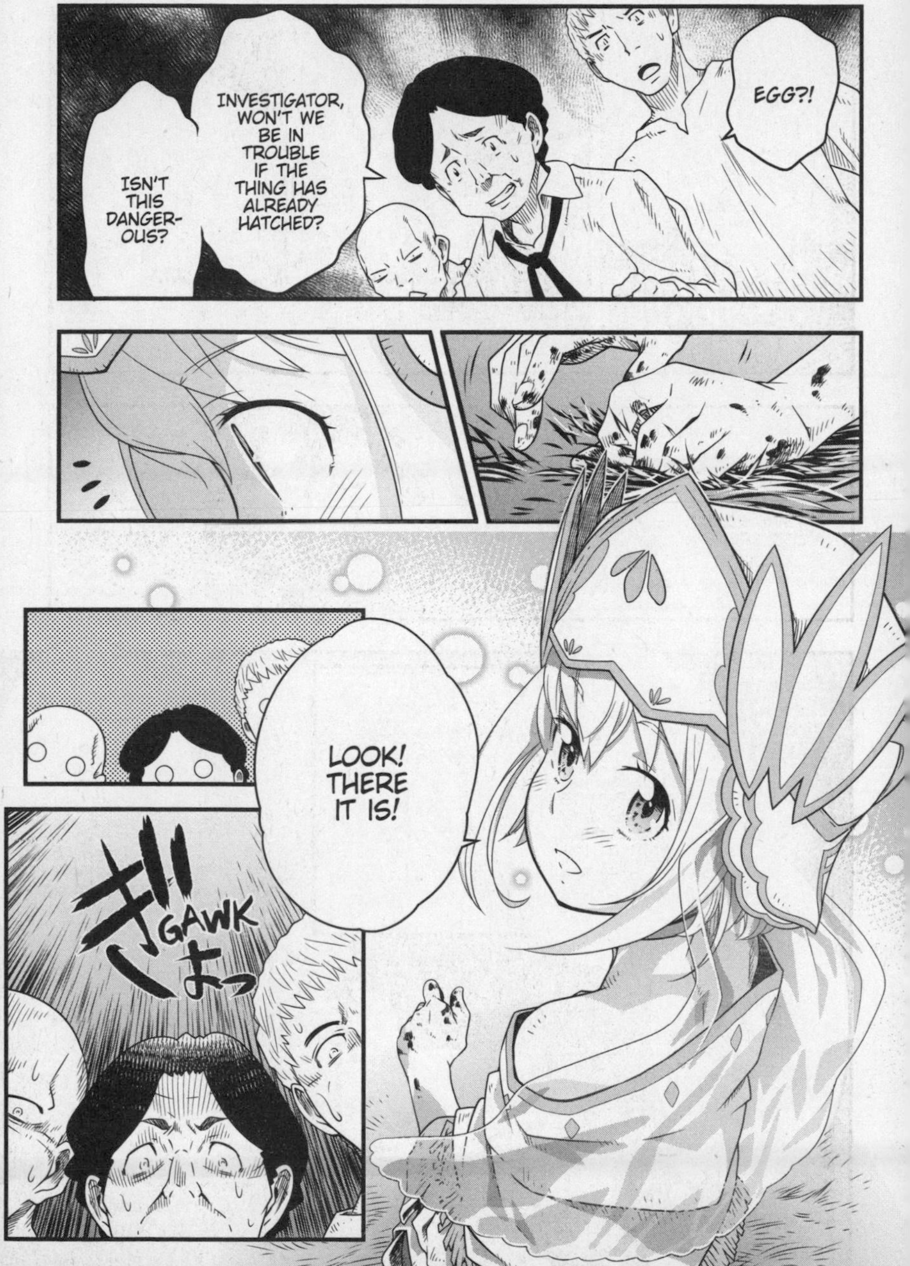
EGG?!
INVESTIGATOR, WON'T WE BE IN TROUBLE IF THE THING HAS ALREADY HATCHED?
ISN'T THIS DANGER-OUS?
LOOK! THERE IT IS!
ぎょっ
GAWK

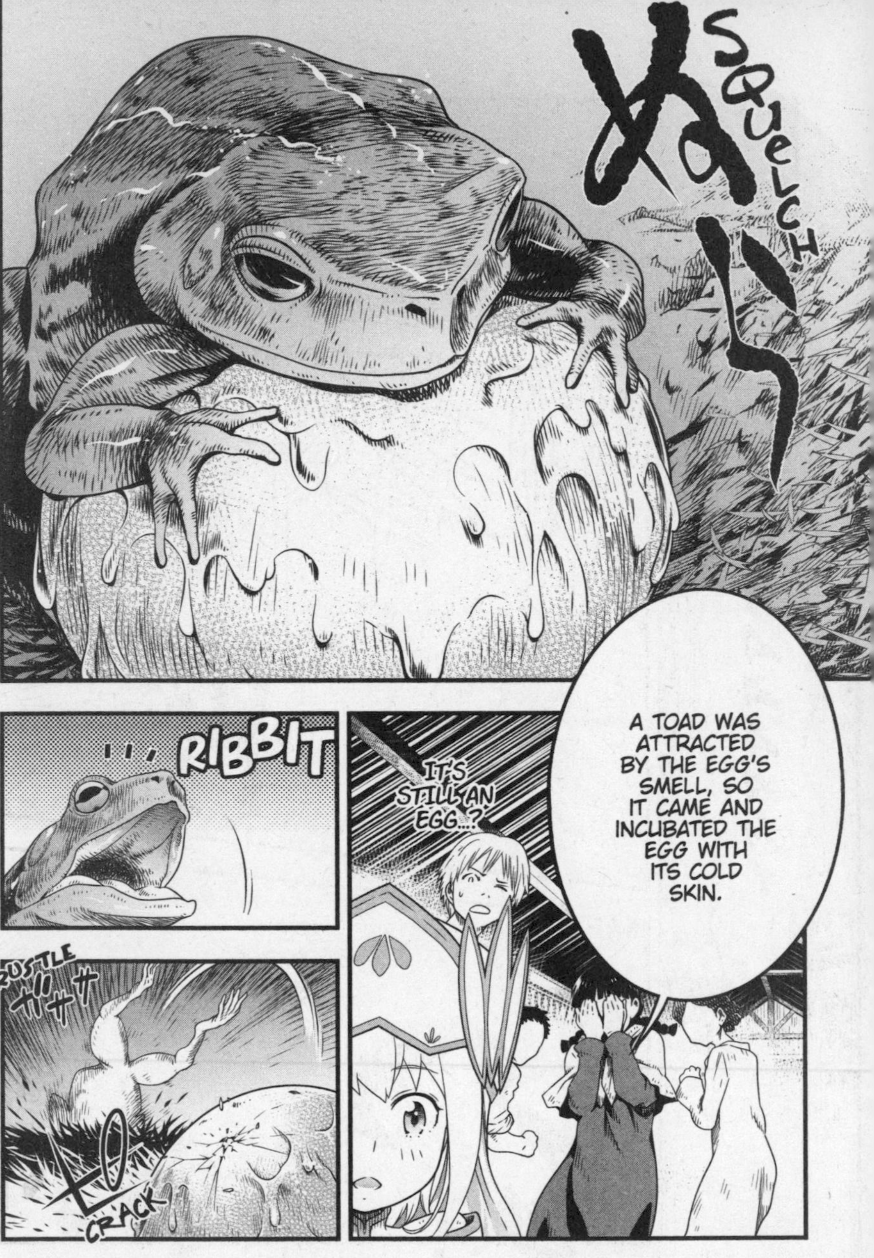
SQUELCH
A TOAD WAS ATTRACTED BY THE EGG'S SMELL, SO IT CAME AND INCUBATED THE EGG WITH ITS COLD SKIN.
IT'S STILL AN EGG...?
RIBBIT
RUSTLE
CRACK

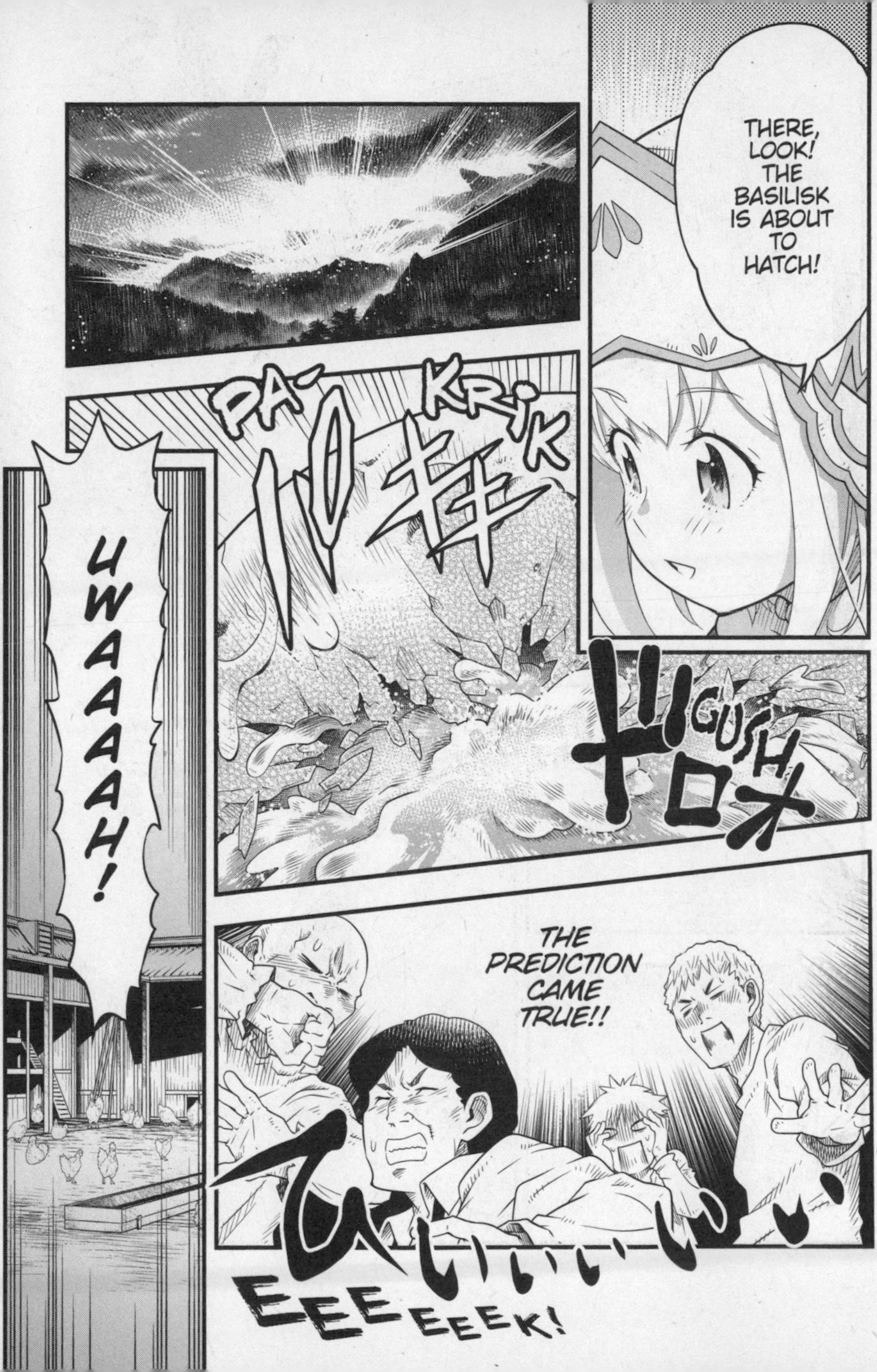

THERE, LOOK! THE BASILISK IS ABOUT TO HATCH!
PA- KRIK
GUSH
THE PREDICTION CAME TRUE!!
EEEEEEK!
UWAAAAAH!

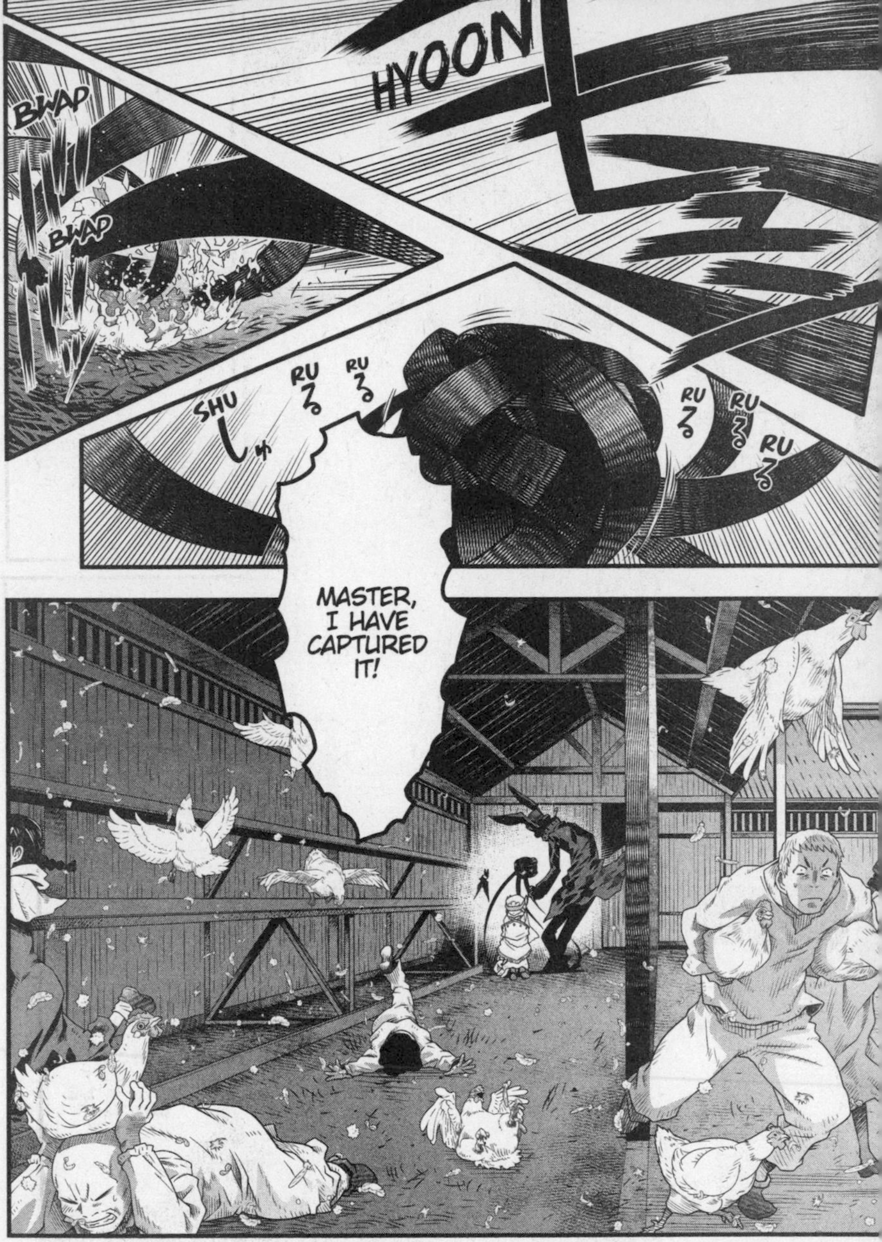
HYOON
BWAP
BWAP
SHU しゅ
RU る
RU る
RU る
RU る
RU る
MASTER, I HAVE CAPTURED IT!

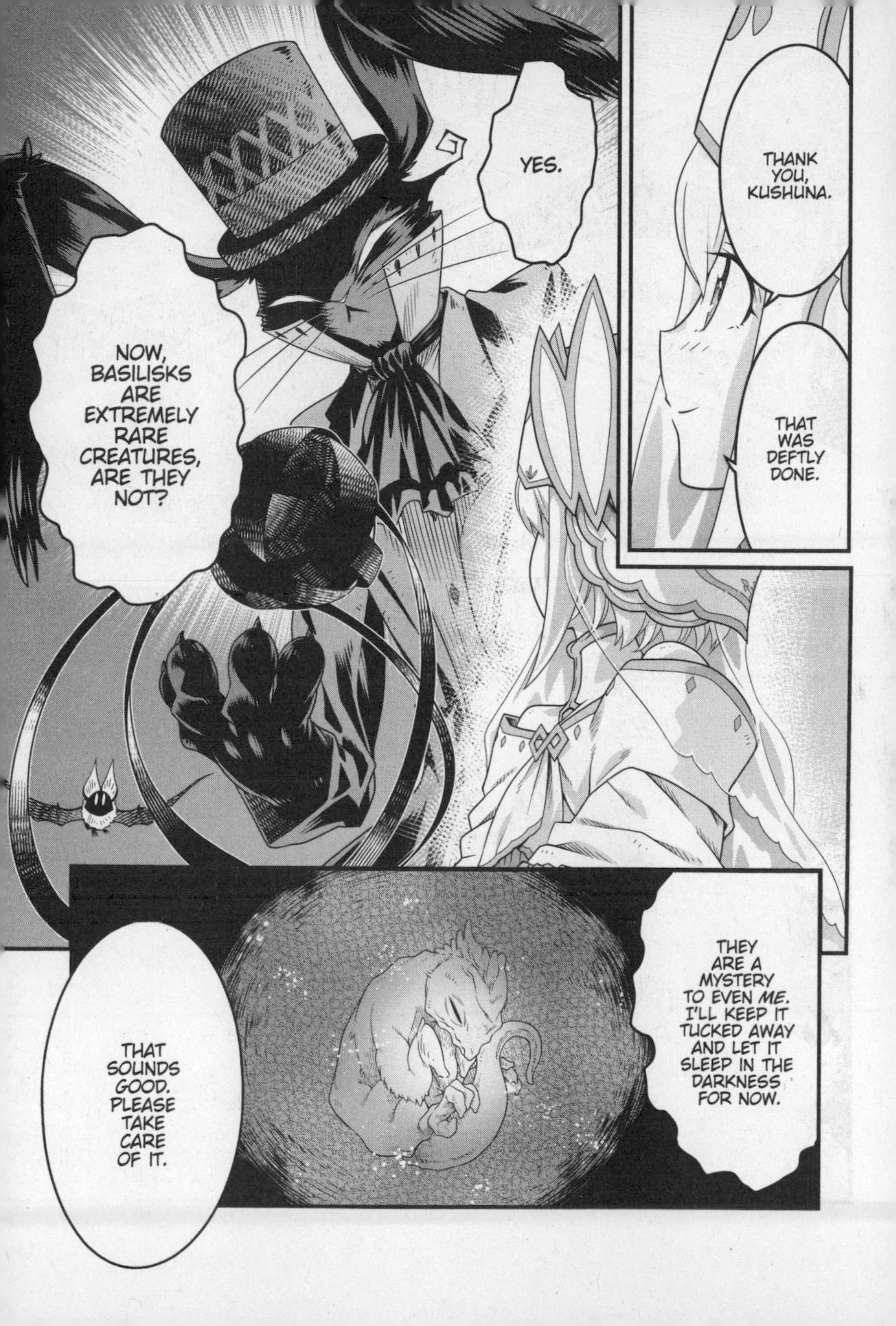
THANK YOU, KUSHUNA.
THAT WAS DEFTLY DONE.
YES.
NOW, BASILISKS ARE EXTREMELY RARE CREATURES, ARE THEY NOT?
THEY ARE A MYSTERY TO EVEN *ME*. I'LL KEEP IT TUCKED AWAY AND LET IT SLEEP IN THE DARKNESS FOR NOW.
THAT SOUNDS GOOD. PLEASE TAKE CARE OF IT.

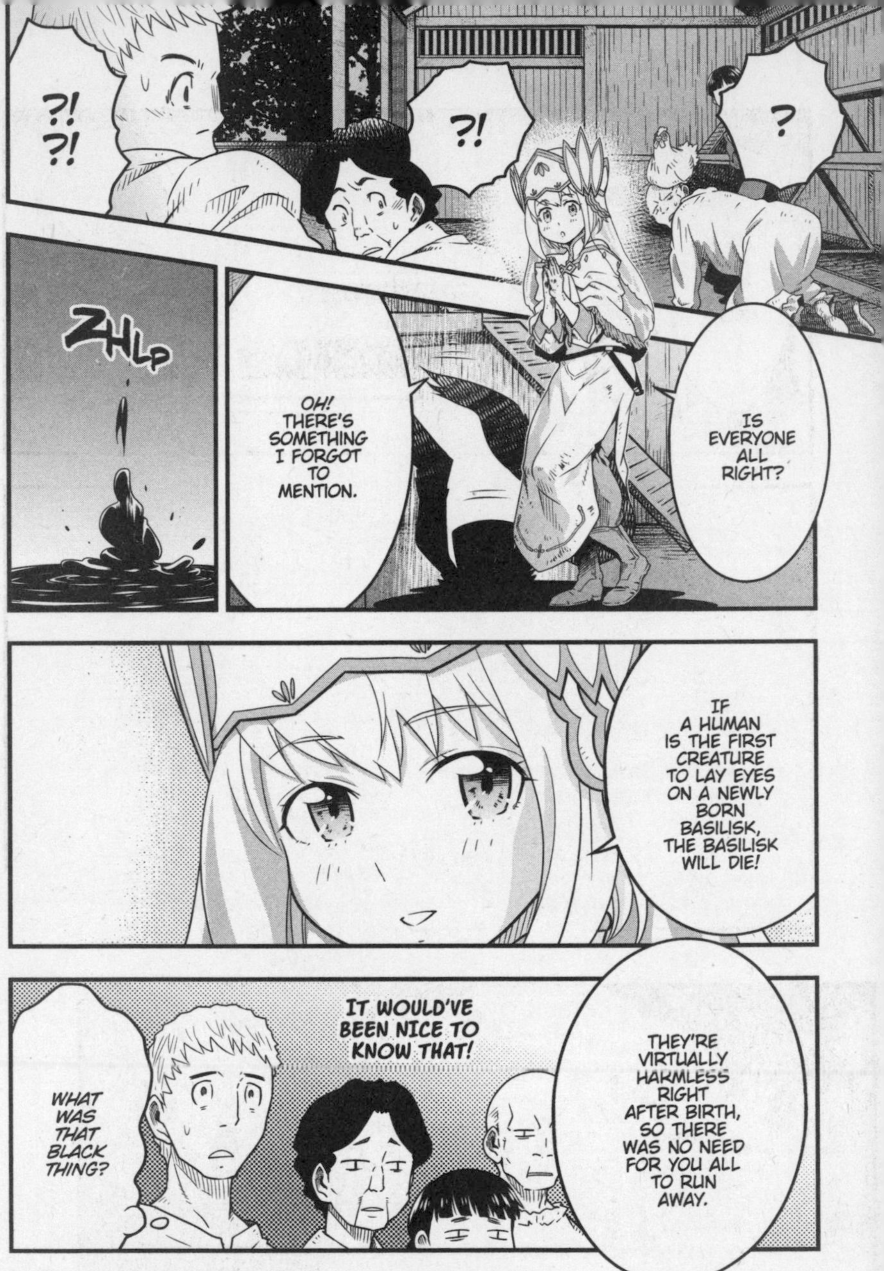
?
?!
?! ?!
IS EVERYONE ALL RIGHT?
OH! THERE'S SOMETHING I FORGOT TO MENTION.
ZHLP
IF A HUMAN IS THE FIRST CREATURE TO LAY EYES ON A NEWLY BORN BASILISK, THE BASILISK WILL DIE!
THEY'RE VIRTUALLY HARMLESS RIGHT AFTER BIRTH, SO THERE WAS NO NEED FOR YOU ALL TO RUN AWAY.
IT WOULD'VE BEEN NICE TO KNOW THAT!
WHAT WAS THAT BLACK THING?

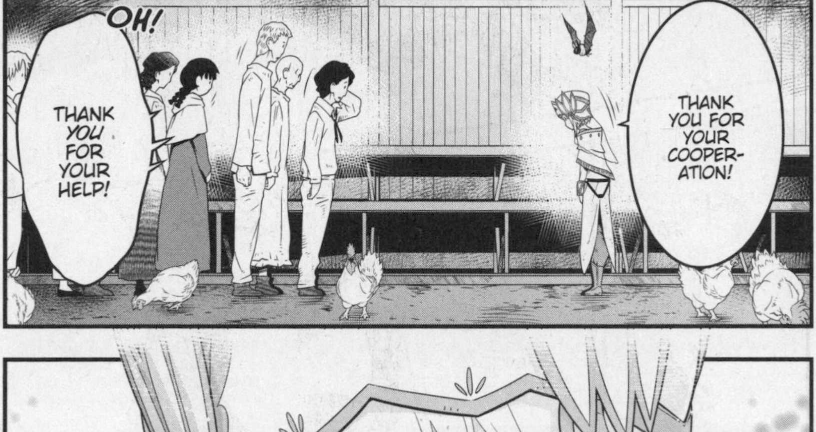
THANK YOU FOR YOUR COOPERATION!
OH!
THANK YOU FOR YOUR HELP!
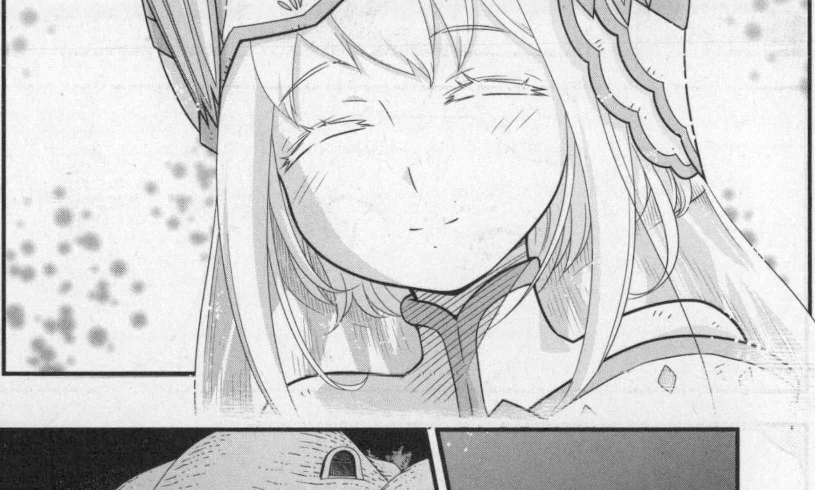
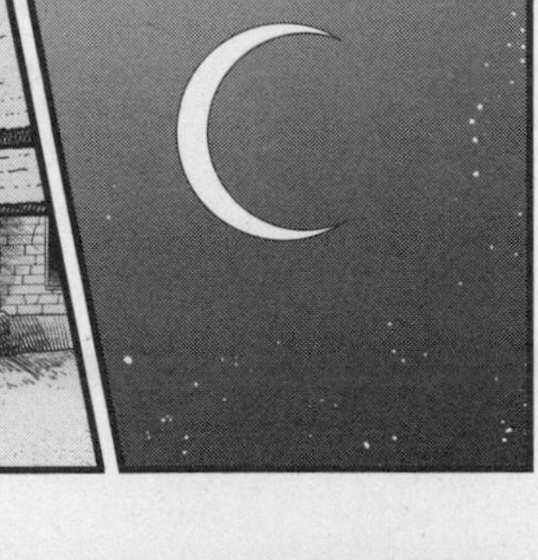
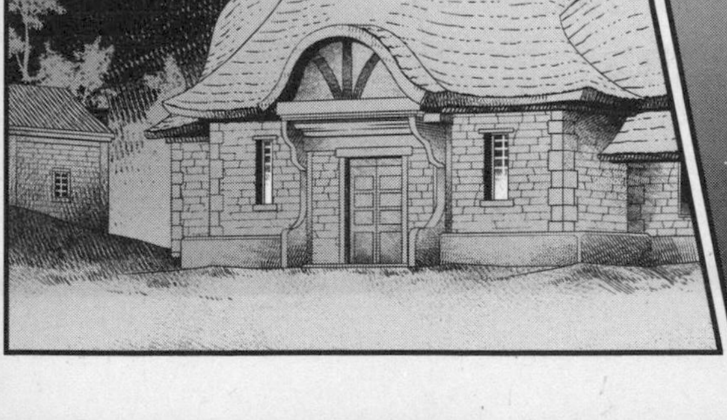

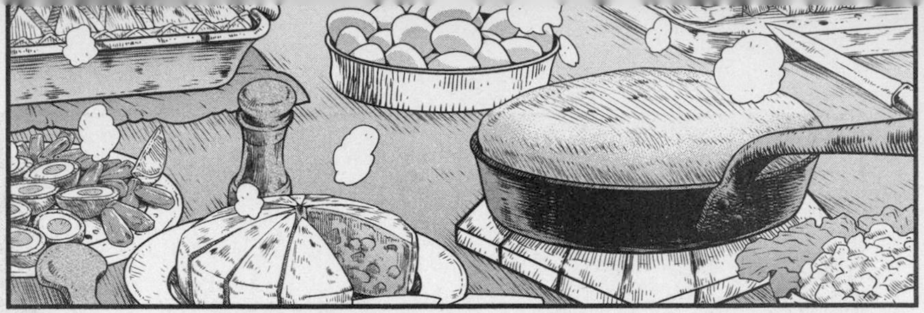

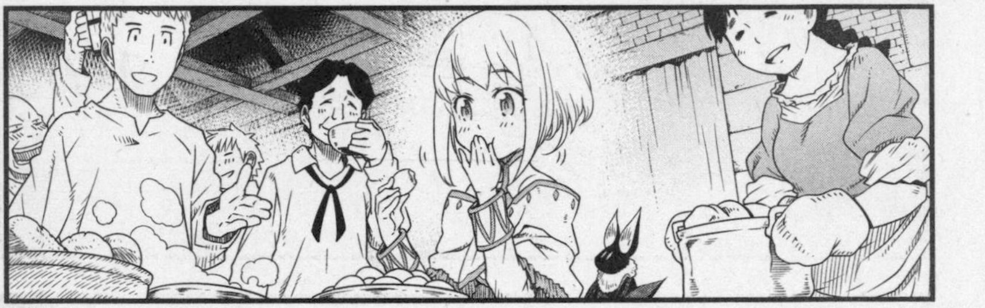

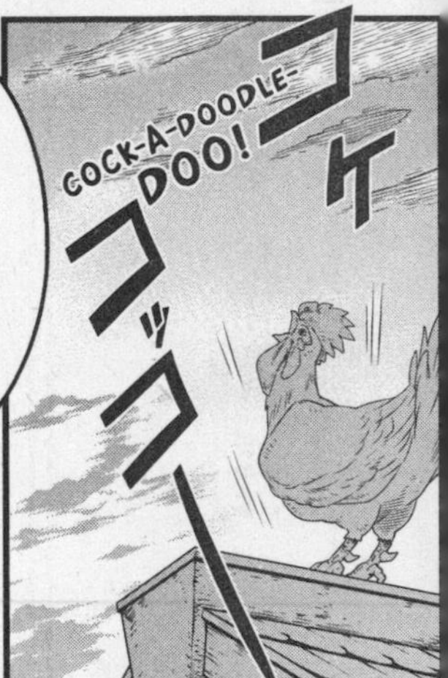
コケコッコー
COCK-A-DOODLE-DOO!

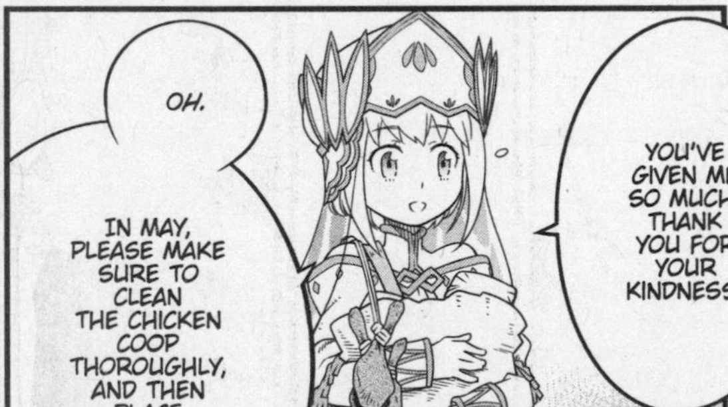
YOU'VE GIVEN ME SO MUCH! THANK YOU FOR YOUR KINDNESS.
OH.
IN MAY, PLEASE MAKE SURE TO CLEAN THE CHICKEN COOP THOROUGHLY, AND THEN PLACE HORNBEAM BRANCHES AROUND IT.

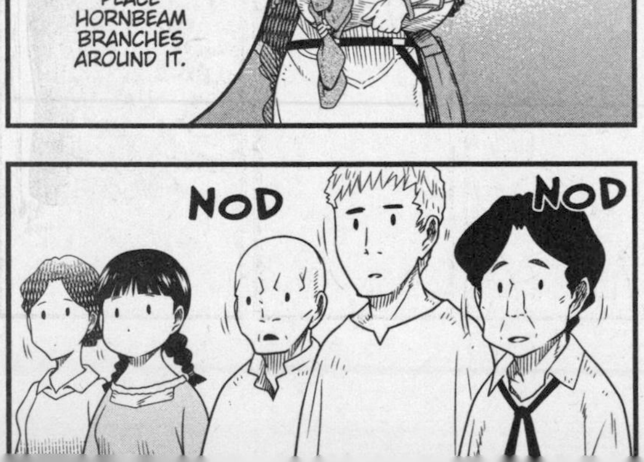
NOD
NOD

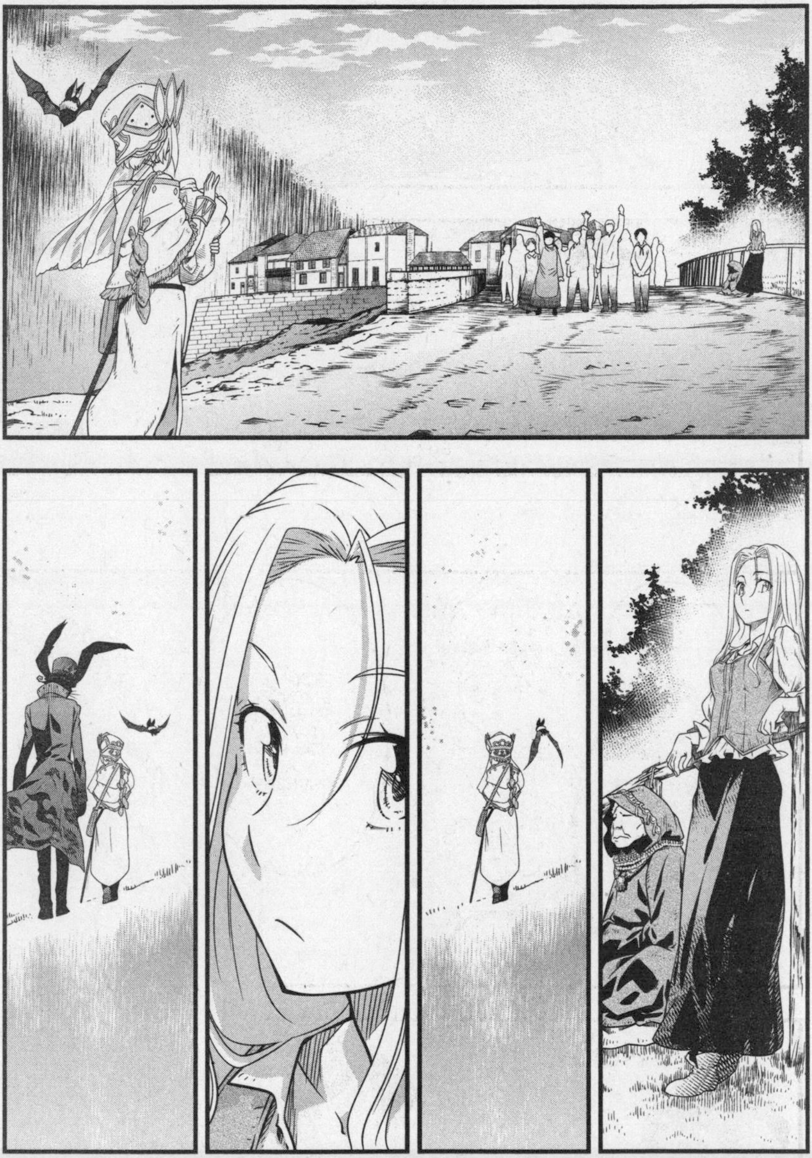

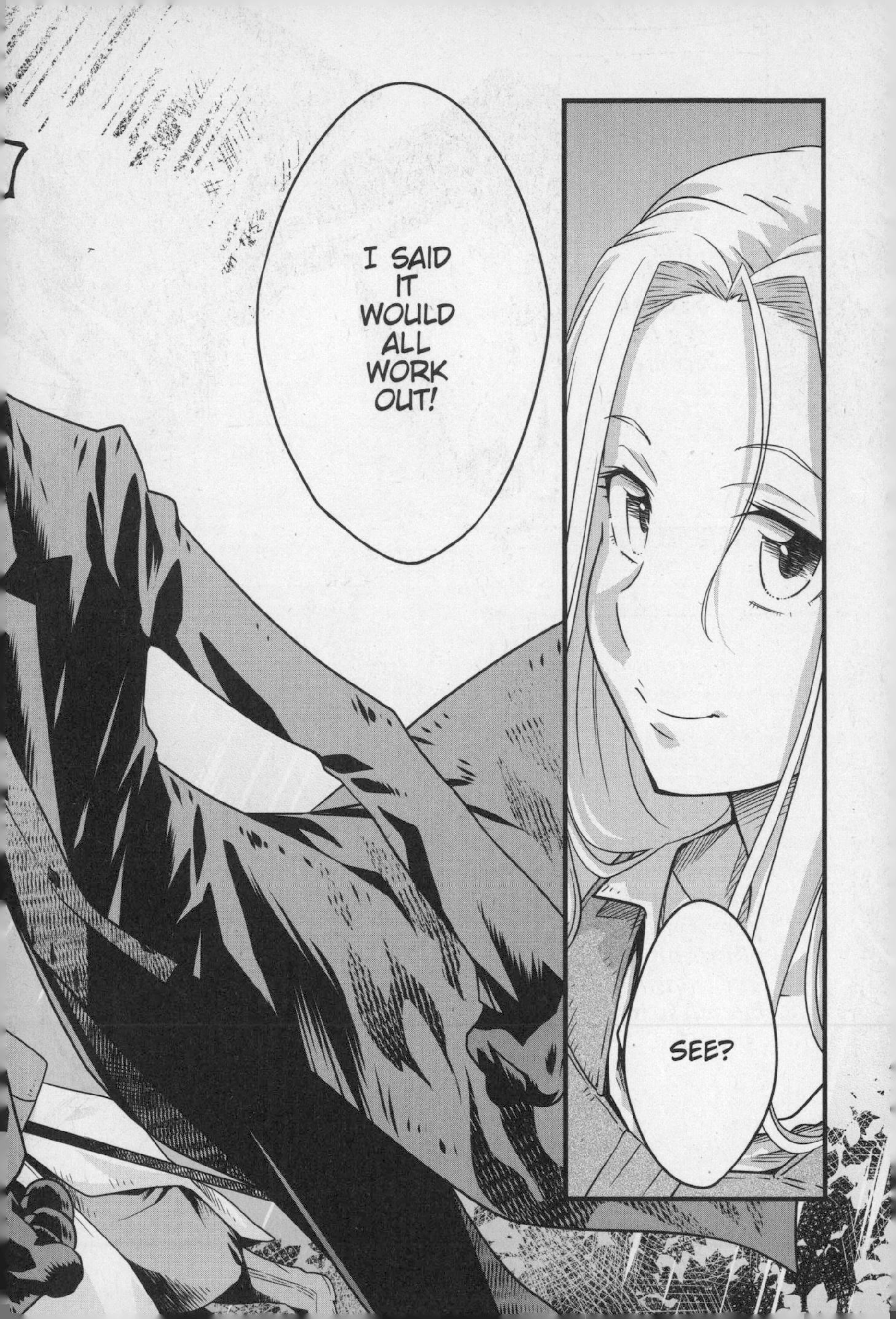
I SAID IT WOULD ALL WORK OUT!
SEE?

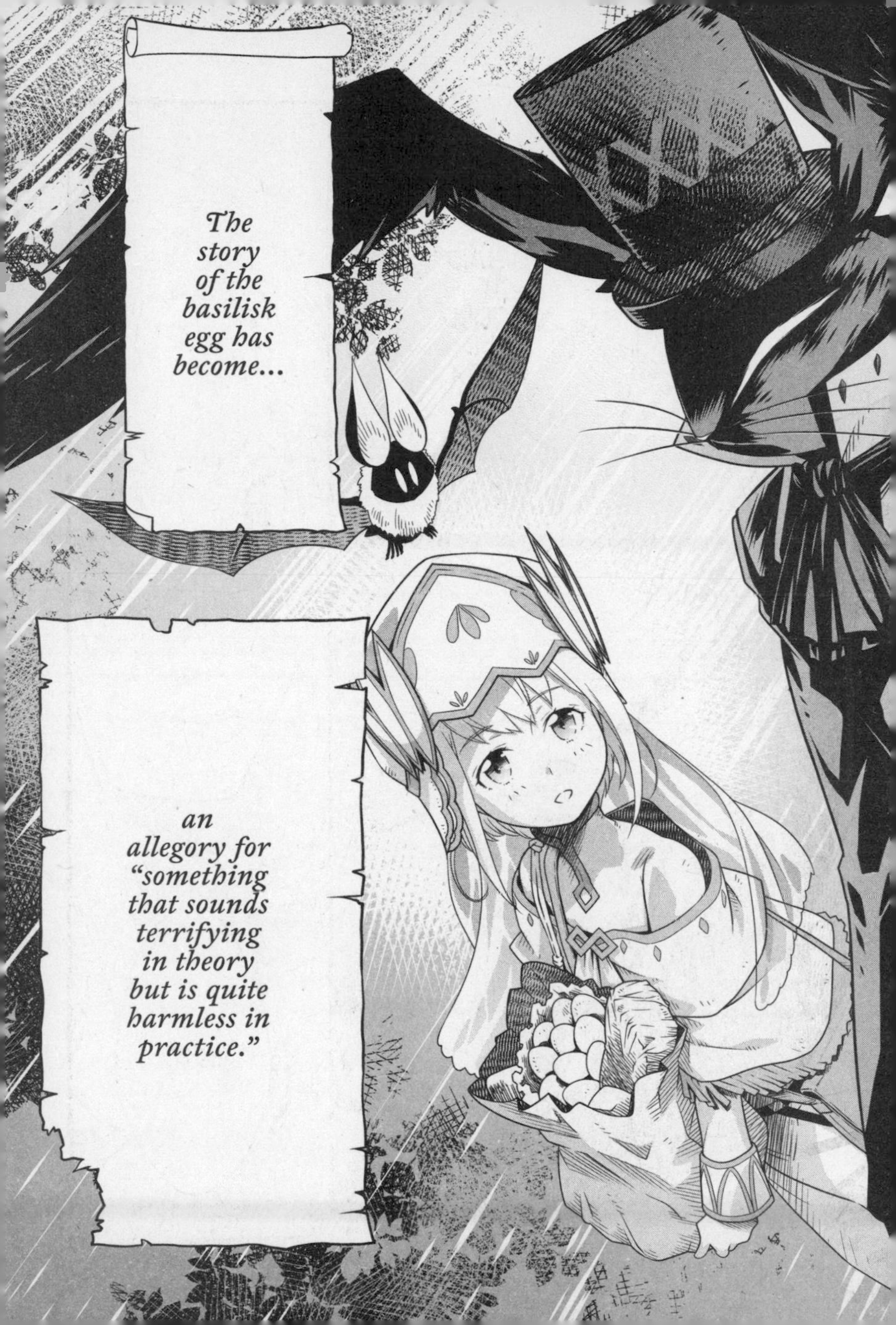
The story of the basilisk egg has become...
an allegory for "something that sounds terrifying in theory but is quite harmless in practice."

Mythical Beast Investigator

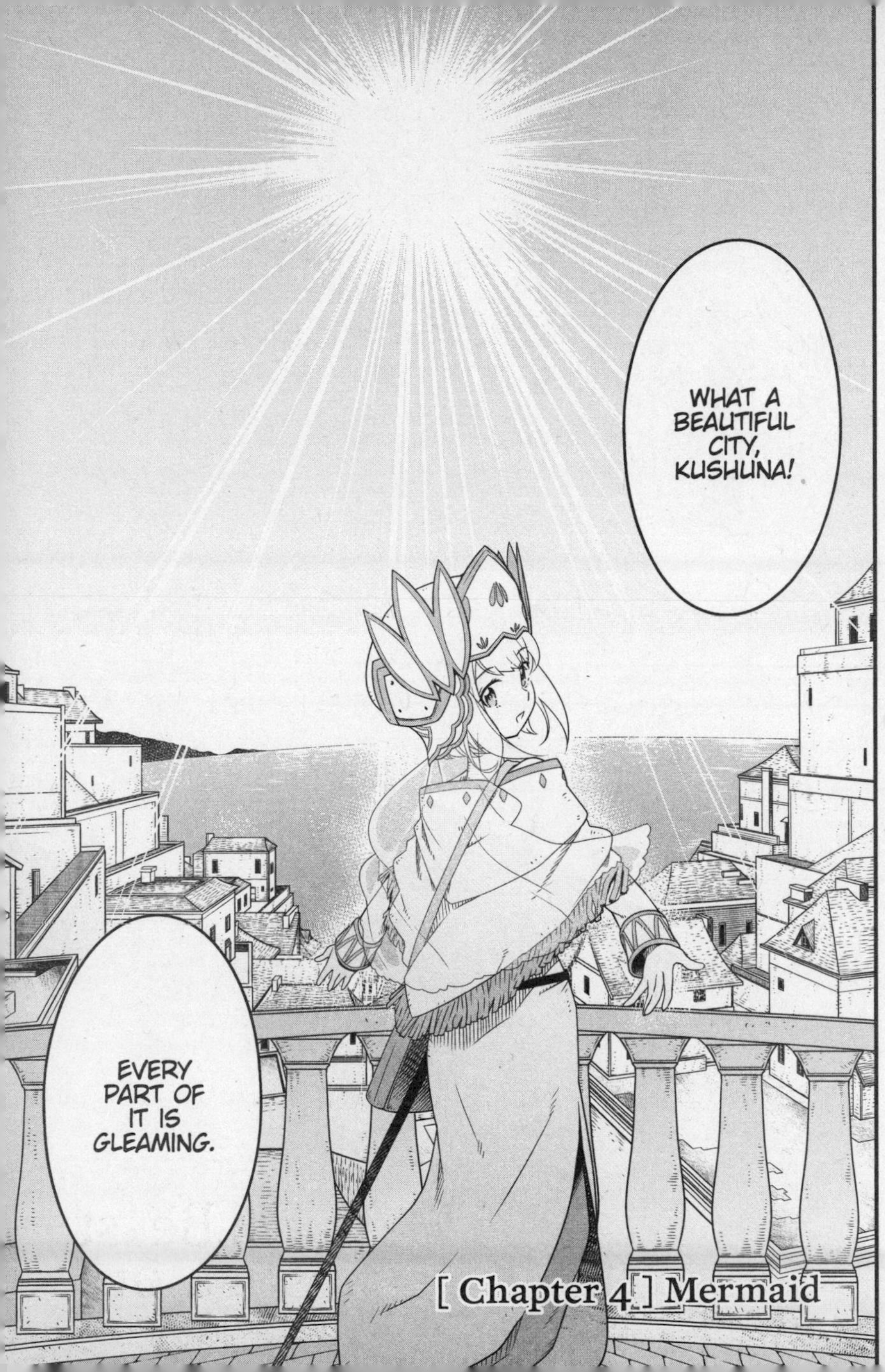
WHAT A BEAUTIFUL CITY, KUSHUNA!
EVERY PART OF IT IS GLEAMING.
[Chapter 4] Mermaid

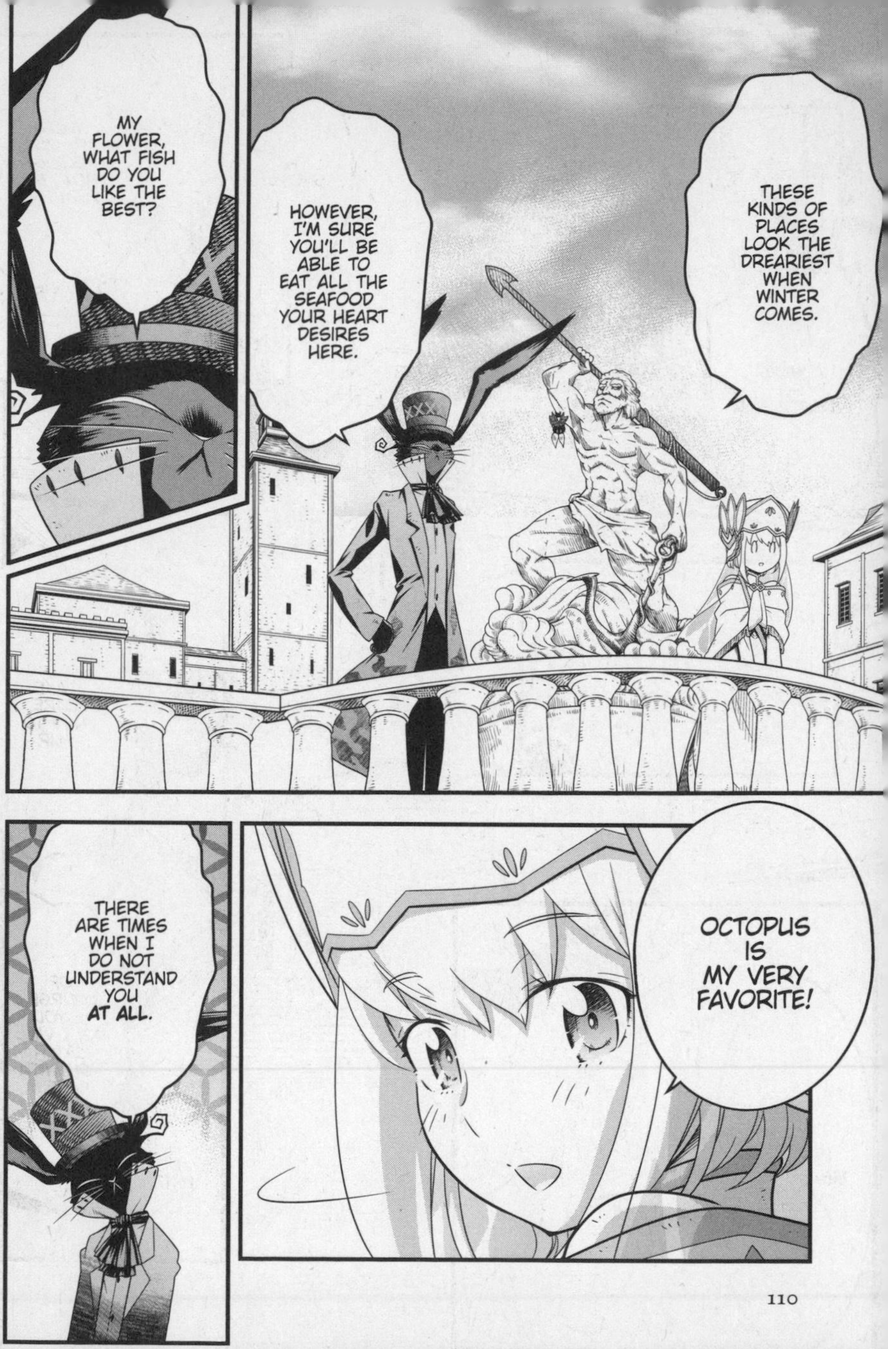
THESE KINDS OF PLACES LOOK THE DREARIEST WHEN WINTER COMES.
HOWEVER, I'M SURE YOU'LL BE ABLE TO EAT ALL THE SEAFOOD YOUR HEART DESIRES HERE.
MY FLOWER, WHAT FISH DO YOU LIKE THE BEST?
OCTOPUS IS MY VERY FAVORITE!
THERE ARE TIMES WHEN I DO NOT UNDERSTAND YOU AT ALL.

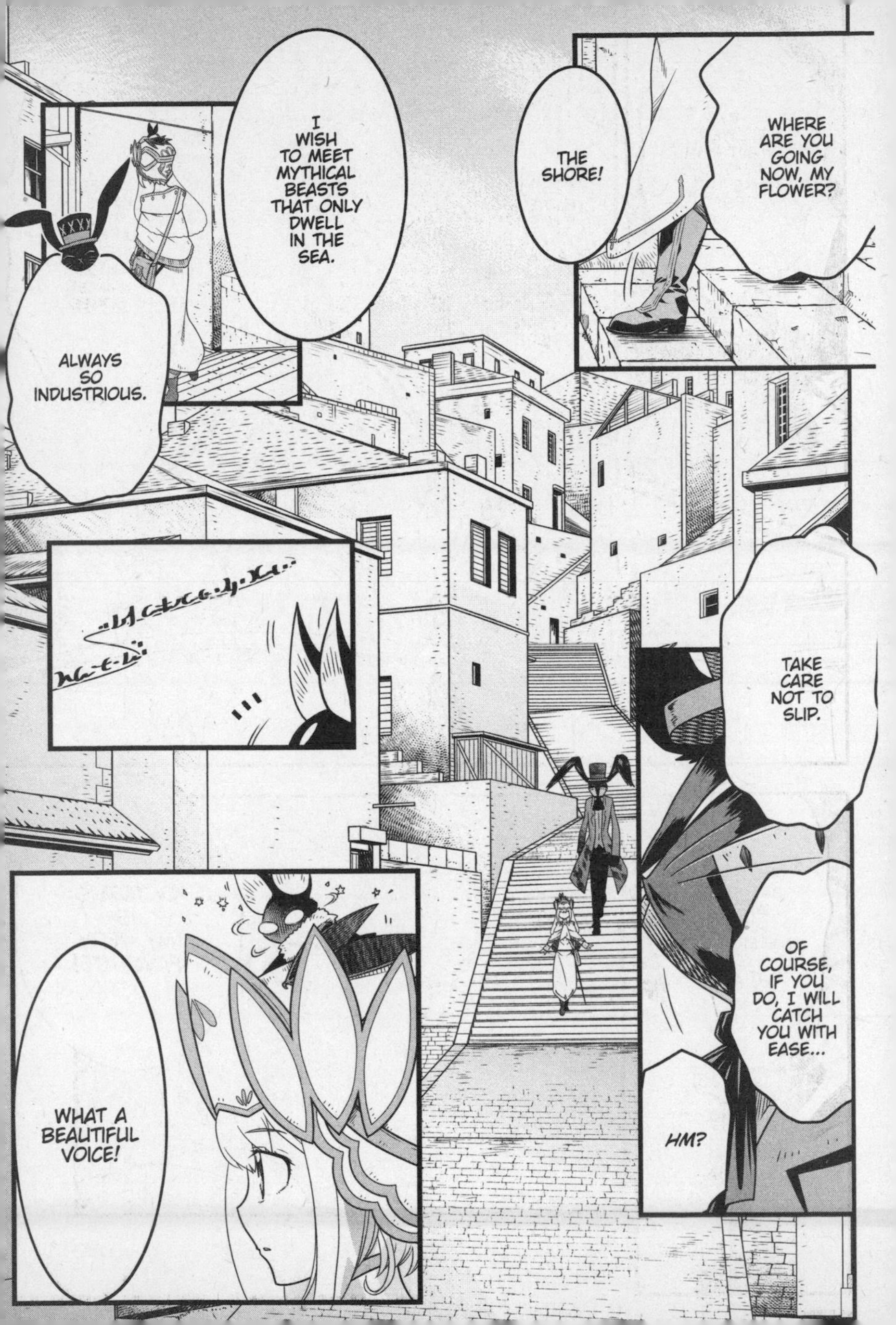
WHERE ARE YOU GOING NOW, MY FLOWER?
THE SHORE!
I WISH TO MEET MYTHICAL BEASTS THAT ONLY DWELL IN THE SEA.
ALWAYS SO INDUSTRIOUS.
TAKE CARE NOT TO SLIP.
OF COURSE, IF YOU DO, I WILL CATCH YOU WITH EASE...
HM?
...
WHAT A BEAUTIFUL VOICE!

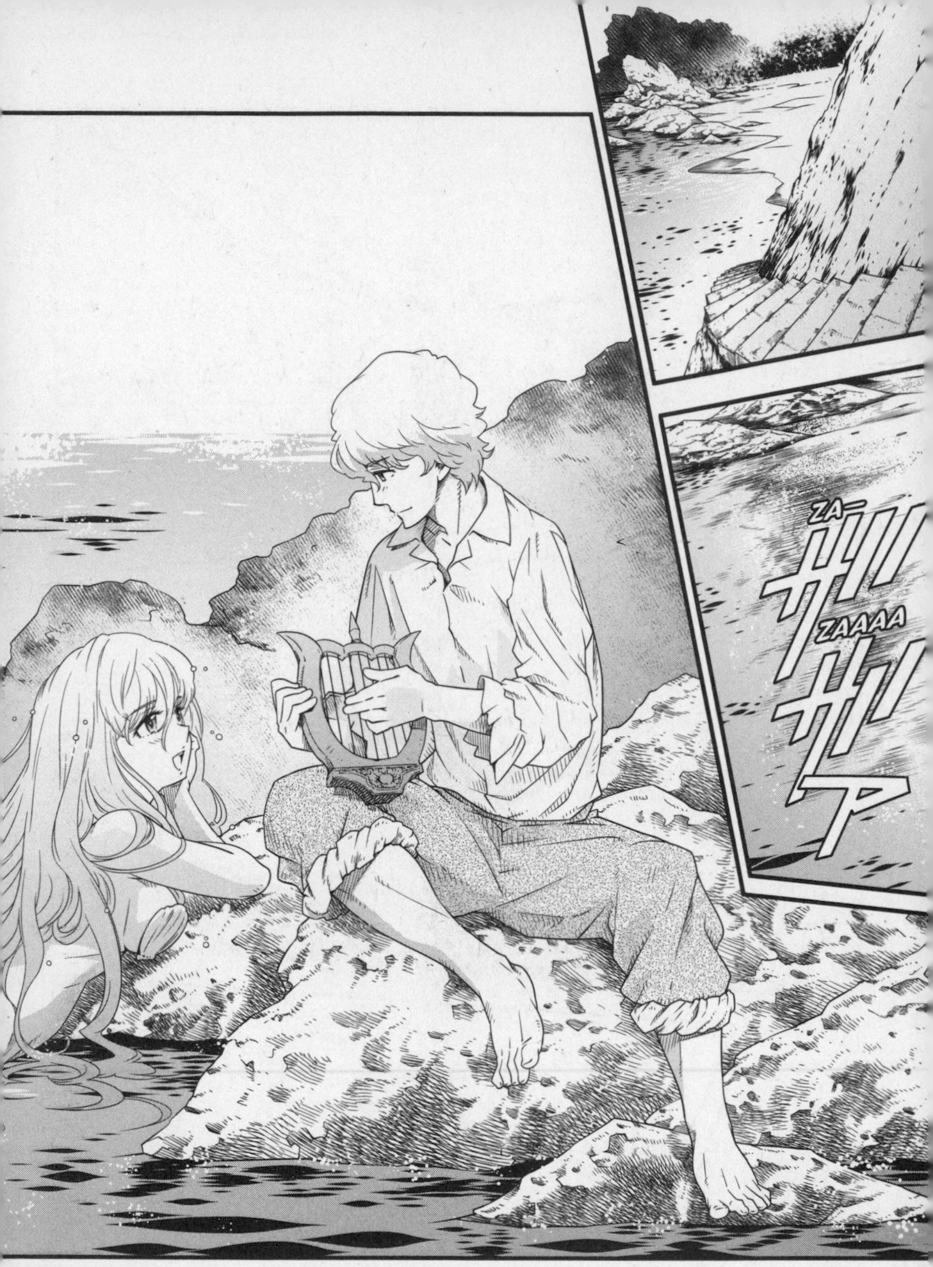
ZA—
ZAAAA

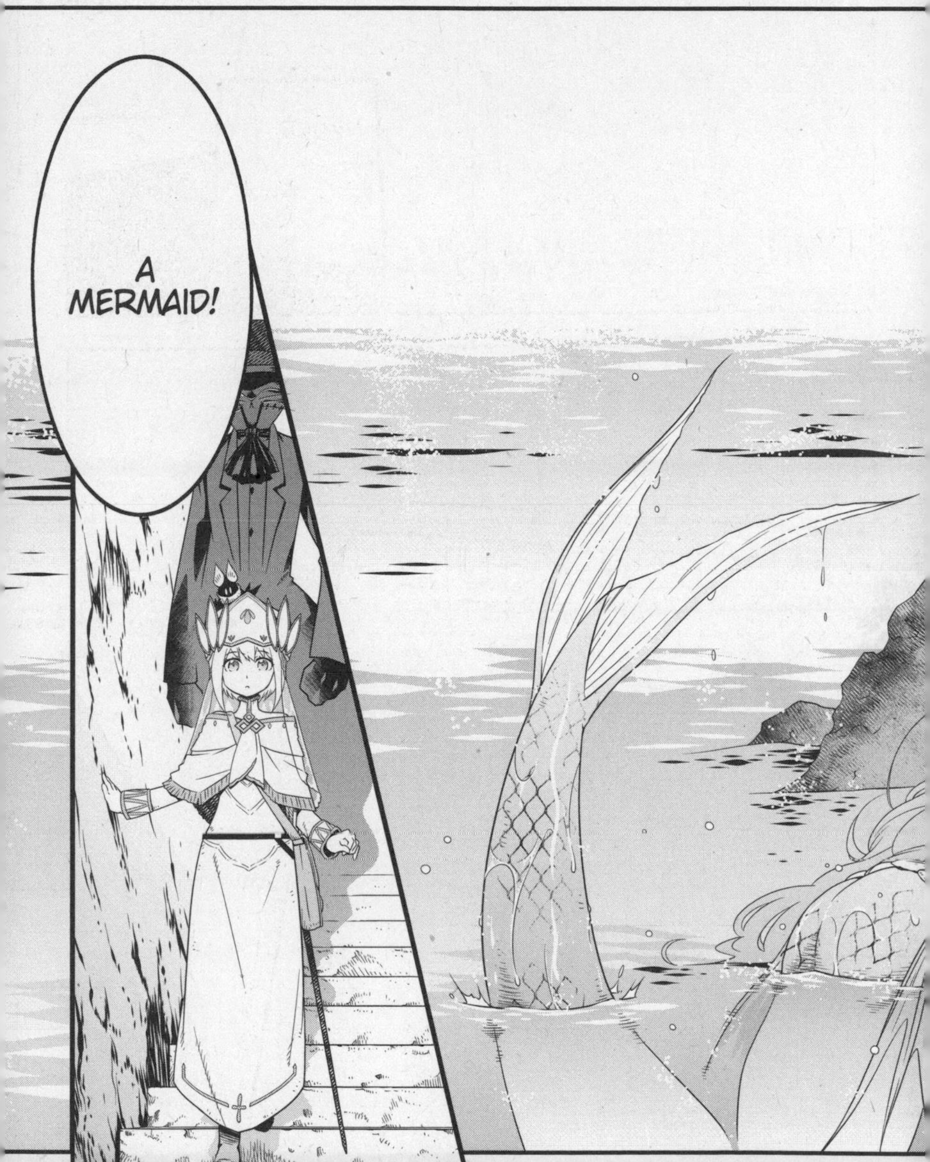
A MERMAID!

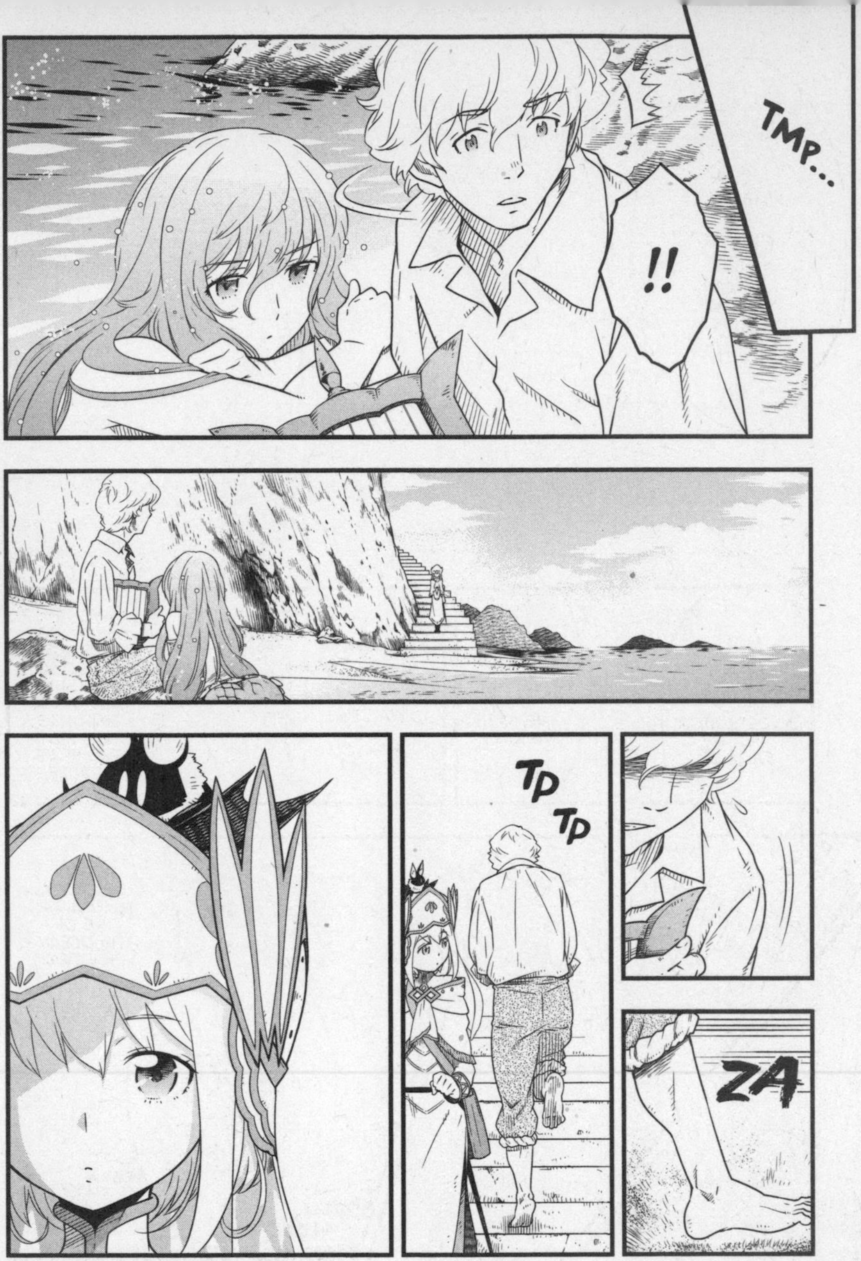
TMP...
!!
ZA
TP TP

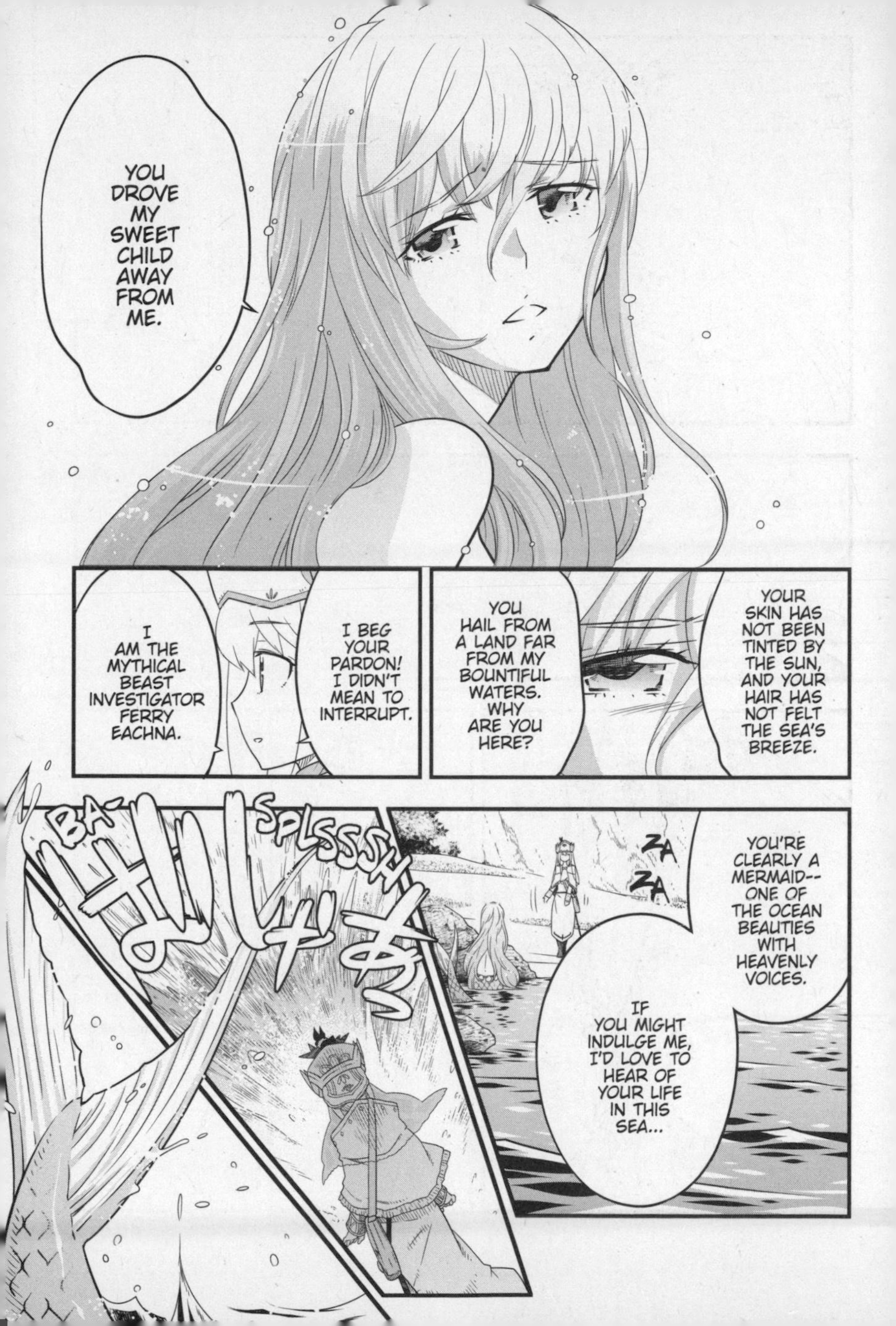
YOU DROVE MY SWEET CHILD AWAY FROM ME.
YOUR SKIN HAS NOT BEEN TINTED BY THE SUN, AND YOUR HAIR HAS NOT FELT THE SEA'S BREEZE.
YOU HAIL FROM A LAND FAR FROM MY BOUNTIFUL WATERS. WHY ARE YOU HERE?
I BEG YOUR PARDON! I DIDN'T MEAN TO INTERRUPT.
I AM THE MYTHICAL BEAST INVESTIGATOR FERRY EACHNA.
YOU'RE CLEARLY A MERMAID-- ONE OF THE OCEAN BEAUTIES WITH HEAVENLY VOICES.
ZA
ZA
IF YOU MIGHT INDULGE ME, I'D LOVE TO HEAR OF YOUR LIFE IN THIS SEA...
SPLSSSH
BA-

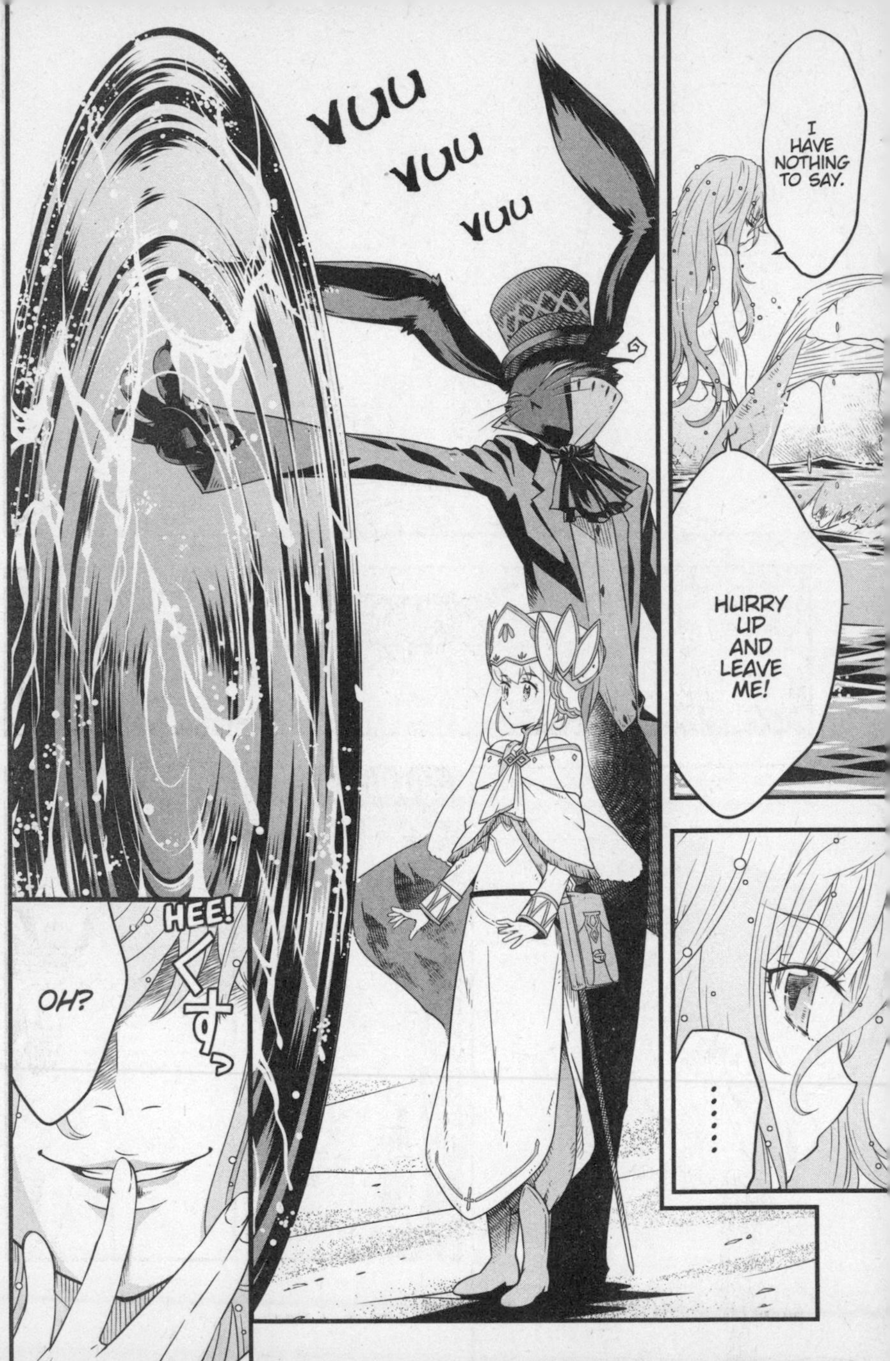
I HAVE NOTHING TO SAY.
HURRY UP AND LEAVE ME!
......
YUU
YUU
YUU
HEE!
くすっ
OH?

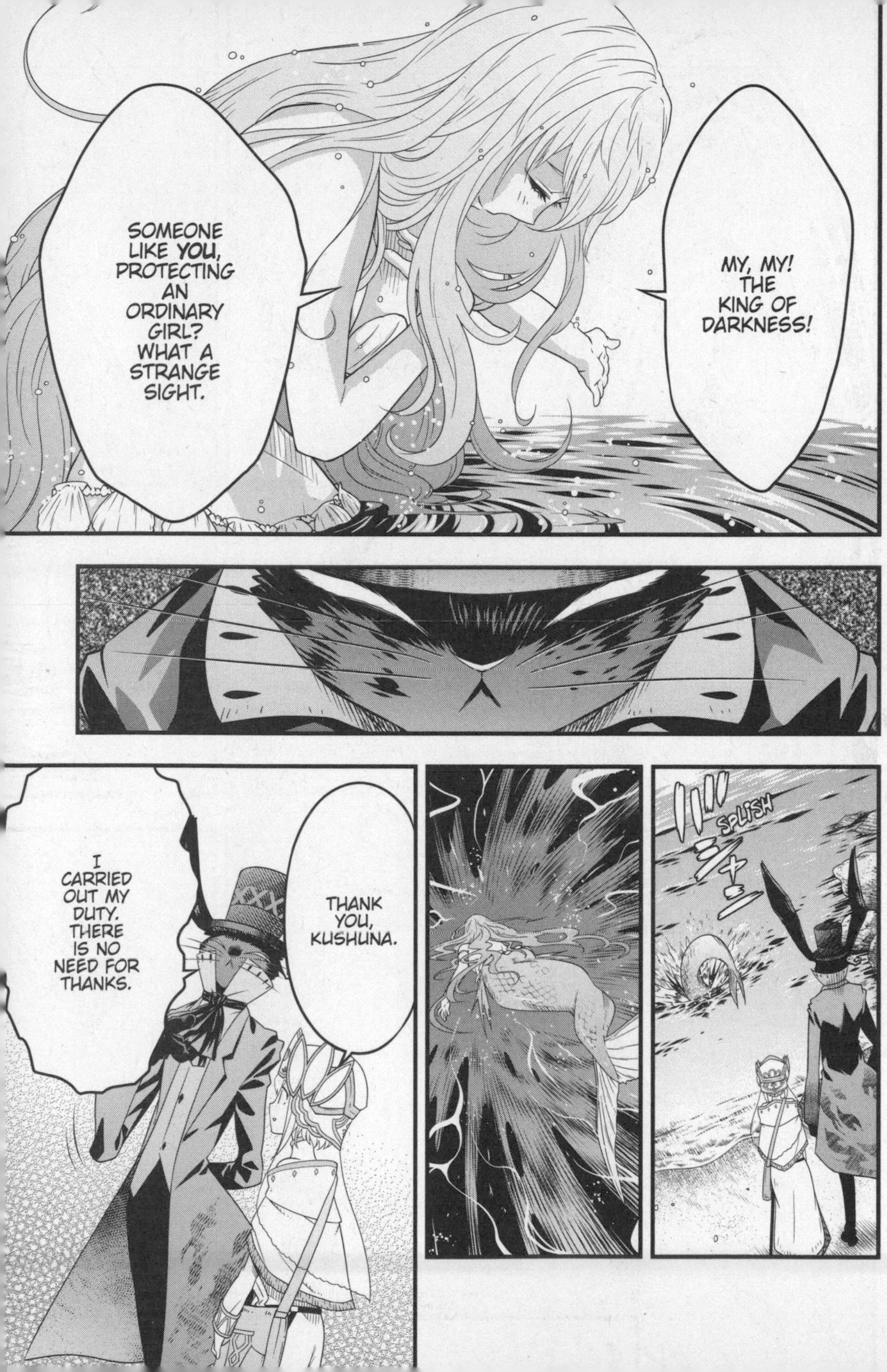
MY, MY! THE KING OF DARKNESS!
SOMEONE LIKE YOU, PROTECTING AN ORDINARY GIRL? WHAT A STRANGE SIGHT.
SPLISH
THANK YOU, KUSHUNA.
I CARRIED OUT MY DUTY. THERE IS NO NEED FOR THANKS.

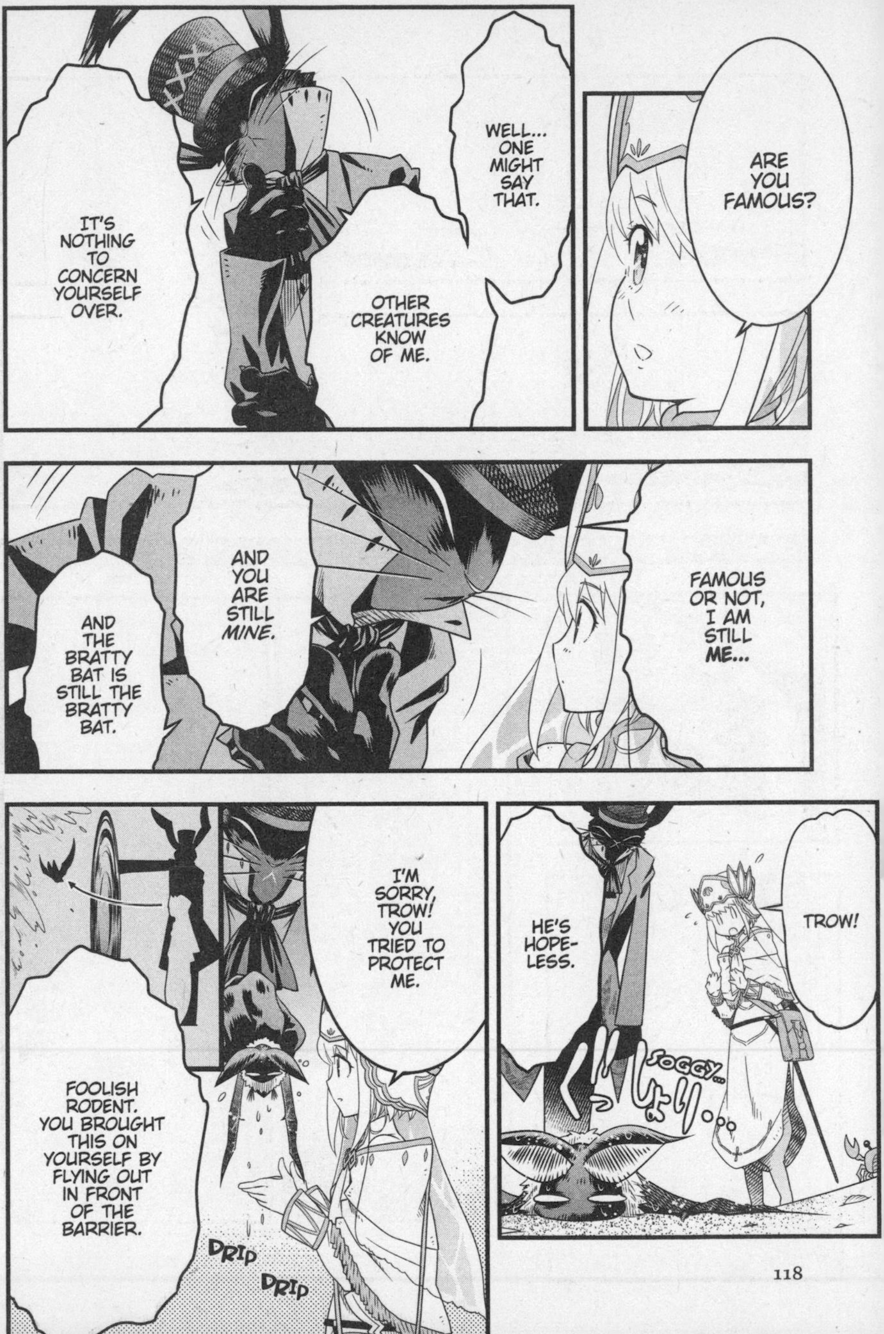
ARE YOU FAMOUS?
WELL... ONE MIGHT SAY THAT.
OTHER CREATURES KNOW OF ME.
IT'S NOTHING TO CONCERN YOURSELF OVER.
FAMOUS OR NOT, I AM STILL ME...
AND YOU ARE STILL *MINE.*
AND THE BRATTY BAT IS STILL THE BRATTY BAT.
TROW!
HE'S HOPE-LESS.
SOGGY...
I'M SORRY, TROW! YOU TRIED TO PROTECT ME.
FOOLISH RODENT. YOU BROUGHT THIS ON YOURSELF BY FLYING OUT IN FRONT OF THE BARRIER.
DRIP
DRIP

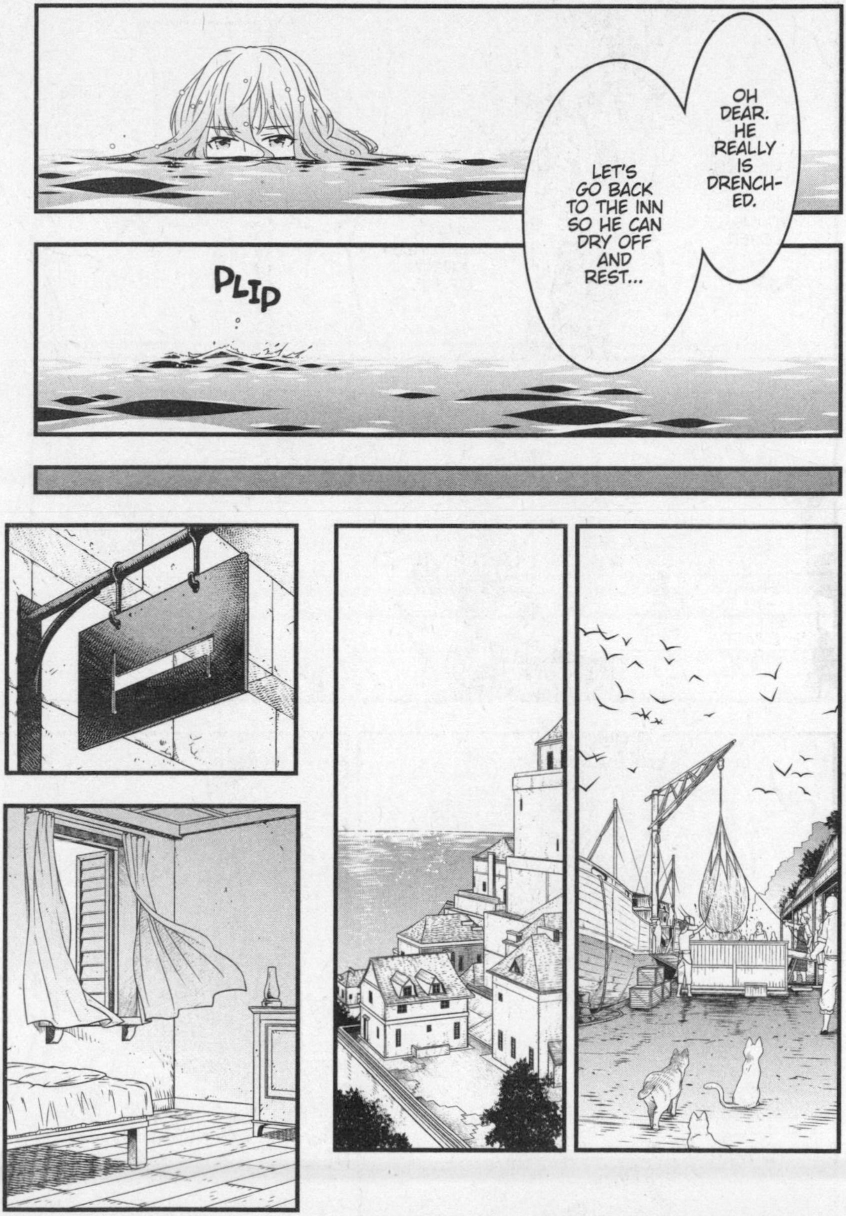
OH DEAR. HE REALLY IS DRENCH-ED.
LET'S GO BACK TO THE INN SO HE CAN DRY OFF AND REST...
PLIP

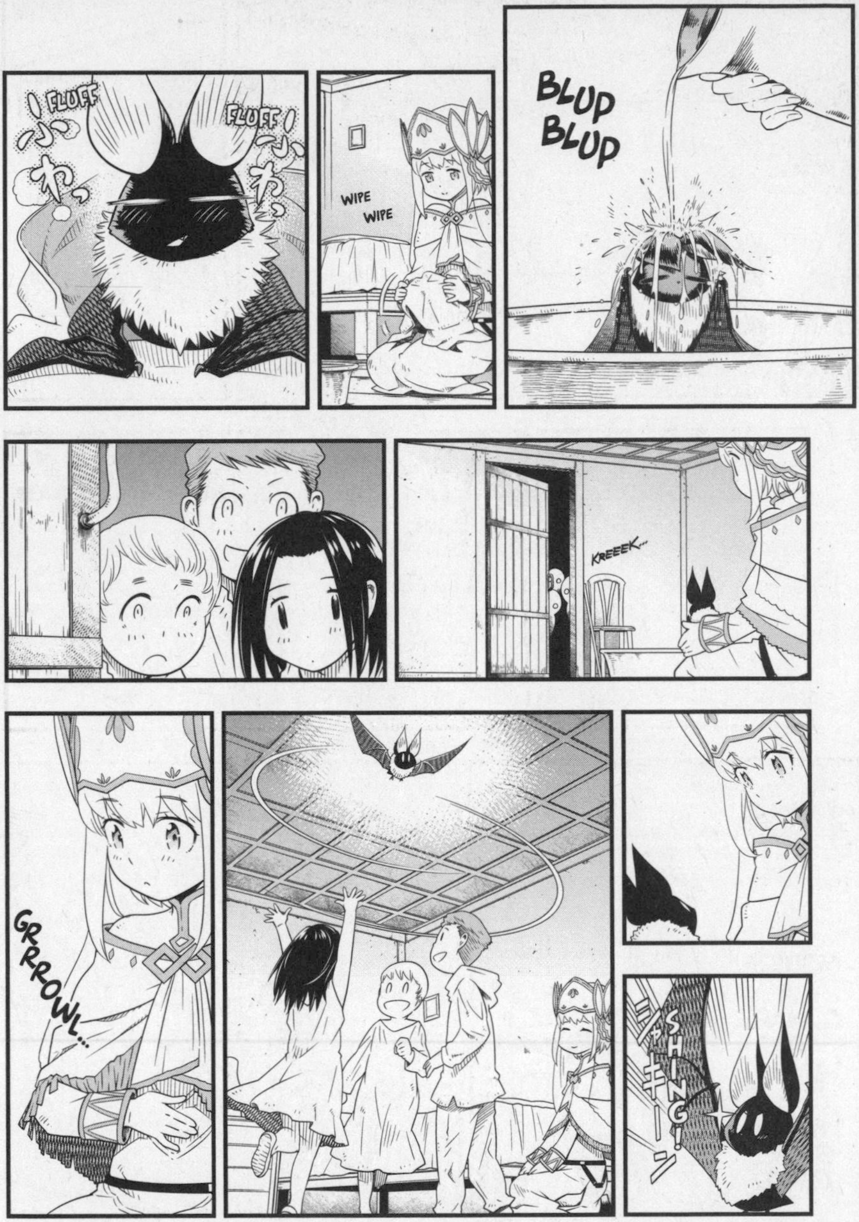
BLUP
BLUP
WIPE
WIPE
FLUFF
ふわっ
FLUFF
ふわっ
KREEEK...
シャキーン
SHING!
GRRROWL...

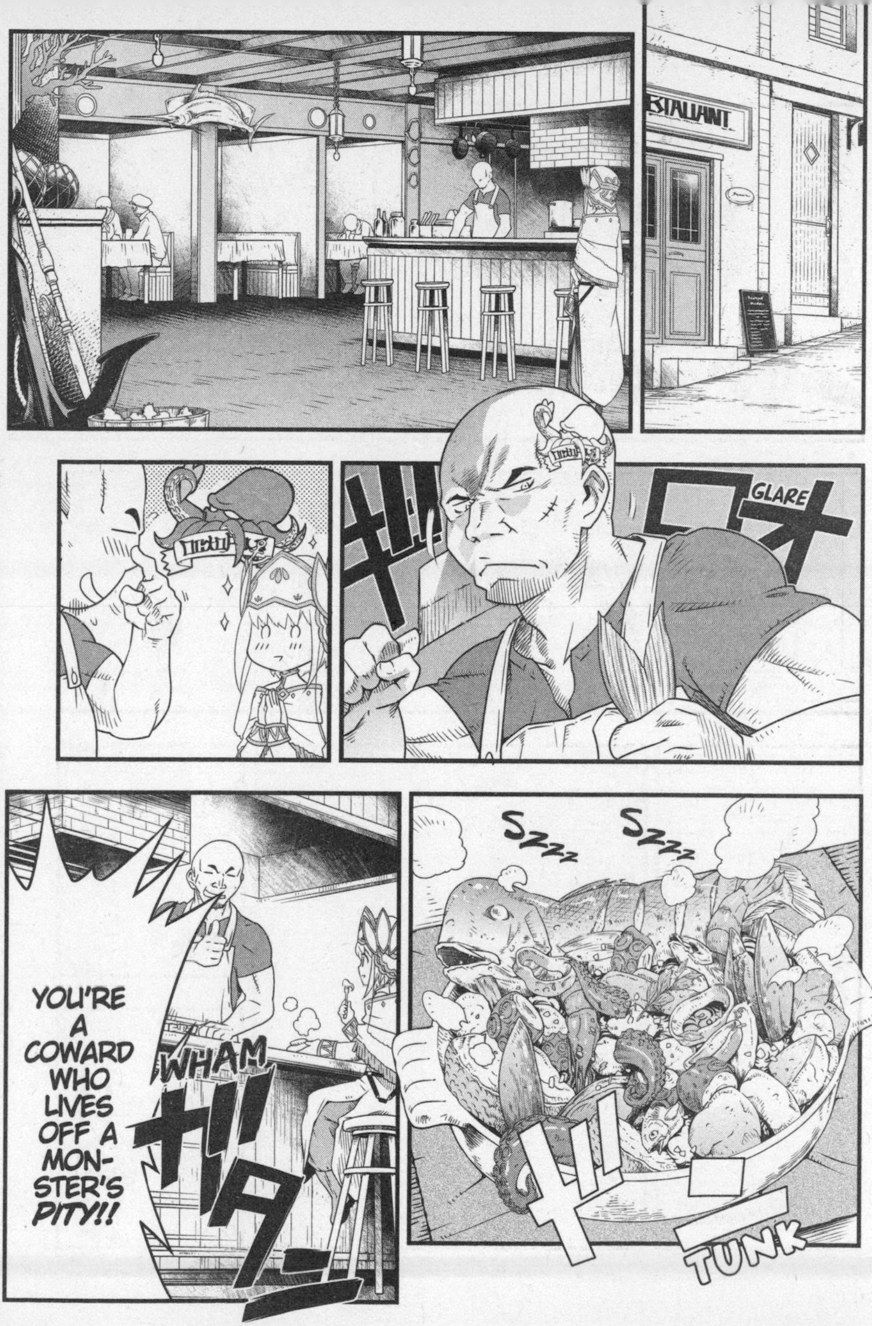
GLARE
SZZZZ
SZZZZ
TUNK
YOU'RE A COWARD WHO LIVES OFF A MON-STER'S PITY!!
WHAM

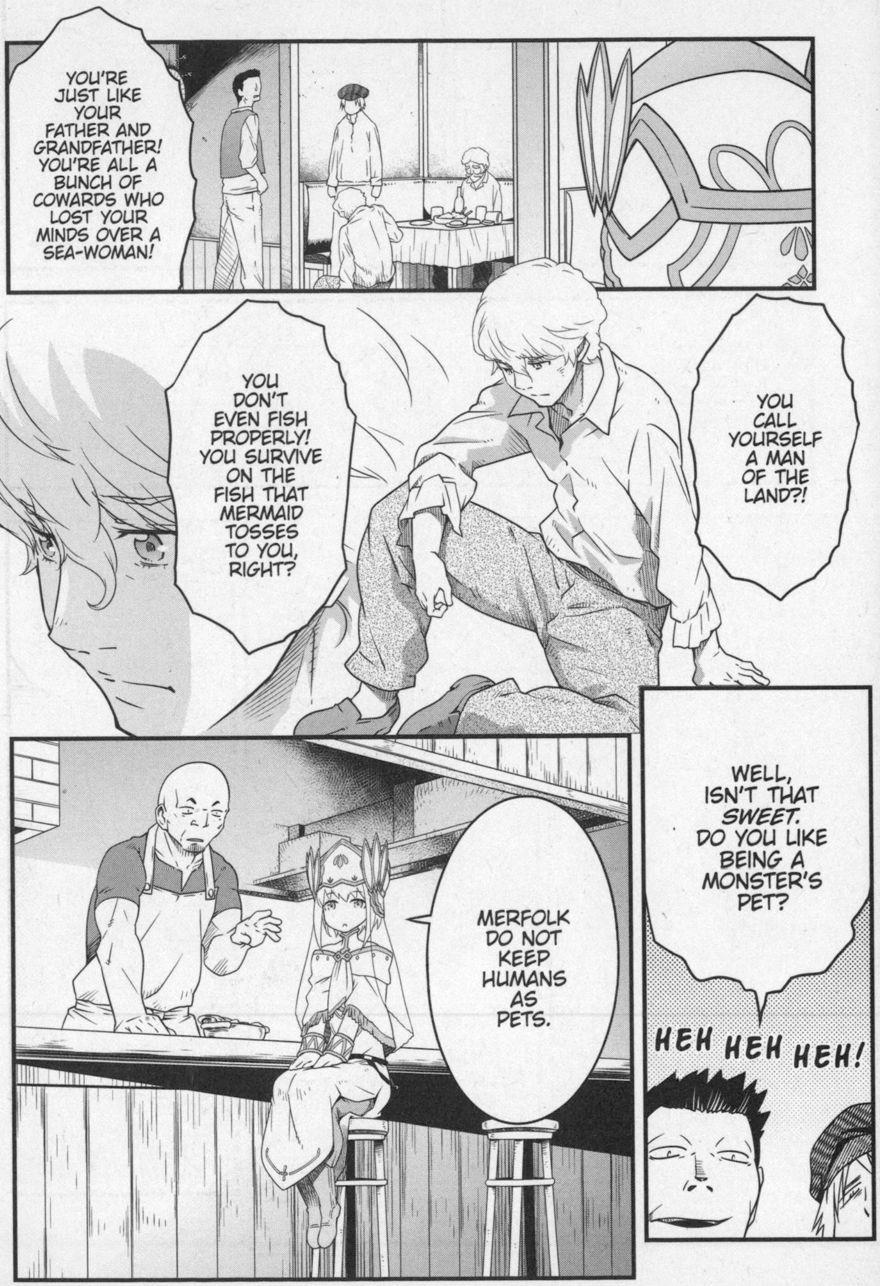
YOU'RE JUST LIKE YOUR FATHER AND GRANDFATHER! YOU'RE ALL A BUNCH OF COWARDS WHO LOST YOUR MINDS OVER A SEA-WOMAN!
YOU CALL YOURSELF A MAN OF THE LAND?!
YOU DON'T EVEN FISH PROPERLY! YOU SURVIVE ON THE FISH THAT MERMAID TOSSES TO YOU, RIGHT?
WELL, ISN'T THAT *SWEET.* DO YOU LIKE BEING A MONSTER'S PET?
HEH HEH HEH!
MERFOLK DO NOT KEEP HUMANS AS PETS.

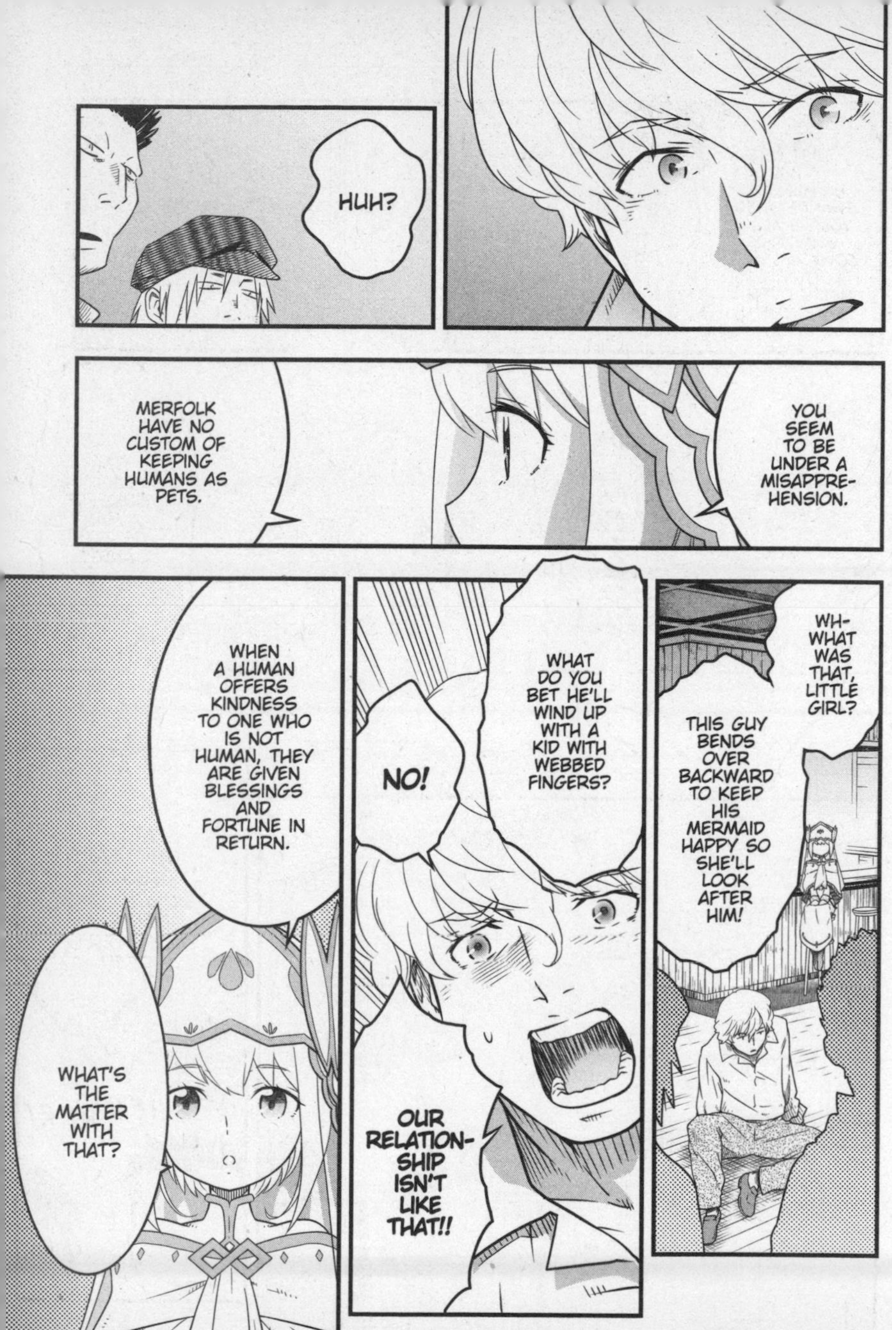
HUH?
YOU SEEM TO BE UNDER A MISAPPRE-HENSION.
MERFOLK HAVE NO CUSTOM OF KEEPING HUMANS AS PETS.
WH-WHAT WAS THAT, LITTLE GIRL?
THIS GUY BENDS OVER BACKWARD TO KEEP HIS MERMAID HAPPY SO SHE'LL LOOK AFTER HIM!
WHAT DO YOU BET HE'LL WIND UP WITH A KID WITH WEBBED FINGERS?
NO!
OUR RELATION-SHIP ISN'T LIKE THAT!!
WHEN A HUMAN OFFERS KINDNESS TO ONE WHO IS NOT HUMAN, THEY ARE GIVEN BLESSINGS AND FORTUNE IN RETURN.
WHAT'S THE MATTER WITH THAT?

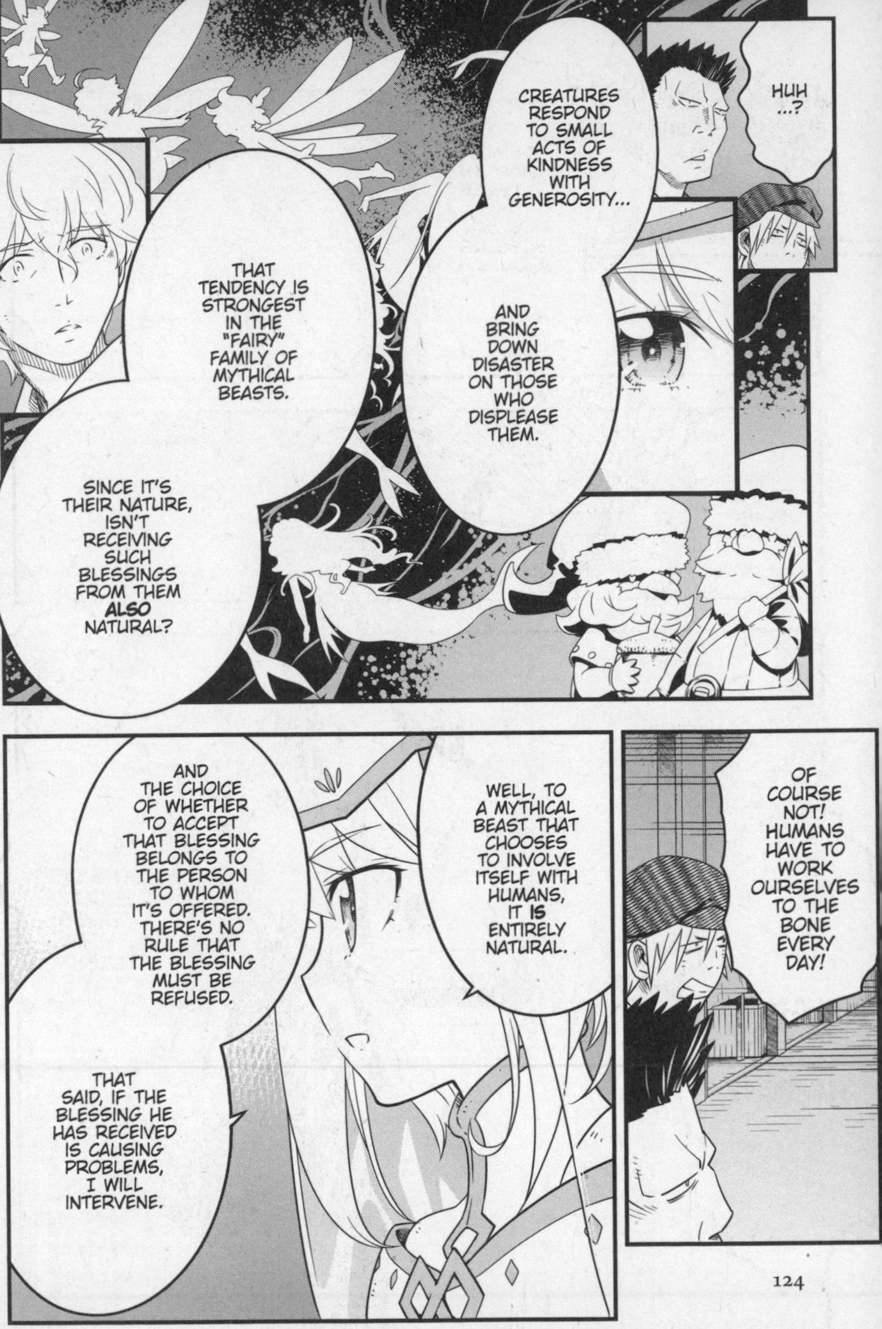
HUH ...?
CREATURES RESPOND TO SMALL ACTS OF KINDNESS WITH GENEROSITY...
AND BRING DOWN DISASTER ON THOSE WHO DISPLEASE THEM.
THAT TENDENCY IS STRONGEST IN THE "FAIRY" FAMILY OF MYTHICAL BEASTS.
SINCE IT'S THEIR NATURE, ISN'T RECEIVING SUCH BLESSINGS FROM THEM **ALSO** NATURAL?
OF COURSE NOT! HUMANS HAVE TO WORK OURSELVES TO THE BONE EVERY DAY!
WELL, TO A MYTHICAL BEAST THAT CHOOSES TO INVOLVE ITSELF WITH HUMANS, IT **IS** ENTIRELY NATURAL.
AND THE CHOICE OF WHETHER TO ACCEPT THAT BLESSING BELONGS TO THE PERSON TO WHOM IT'S OFFERED. THERE'S NO RULE THAT THE BLESSING MUST BE REFUSED.
THAT SAID, IF THE BLESSING HE HAS RECEIVED IS CAUSING PROBLEMS, I WILL INTERVENE.

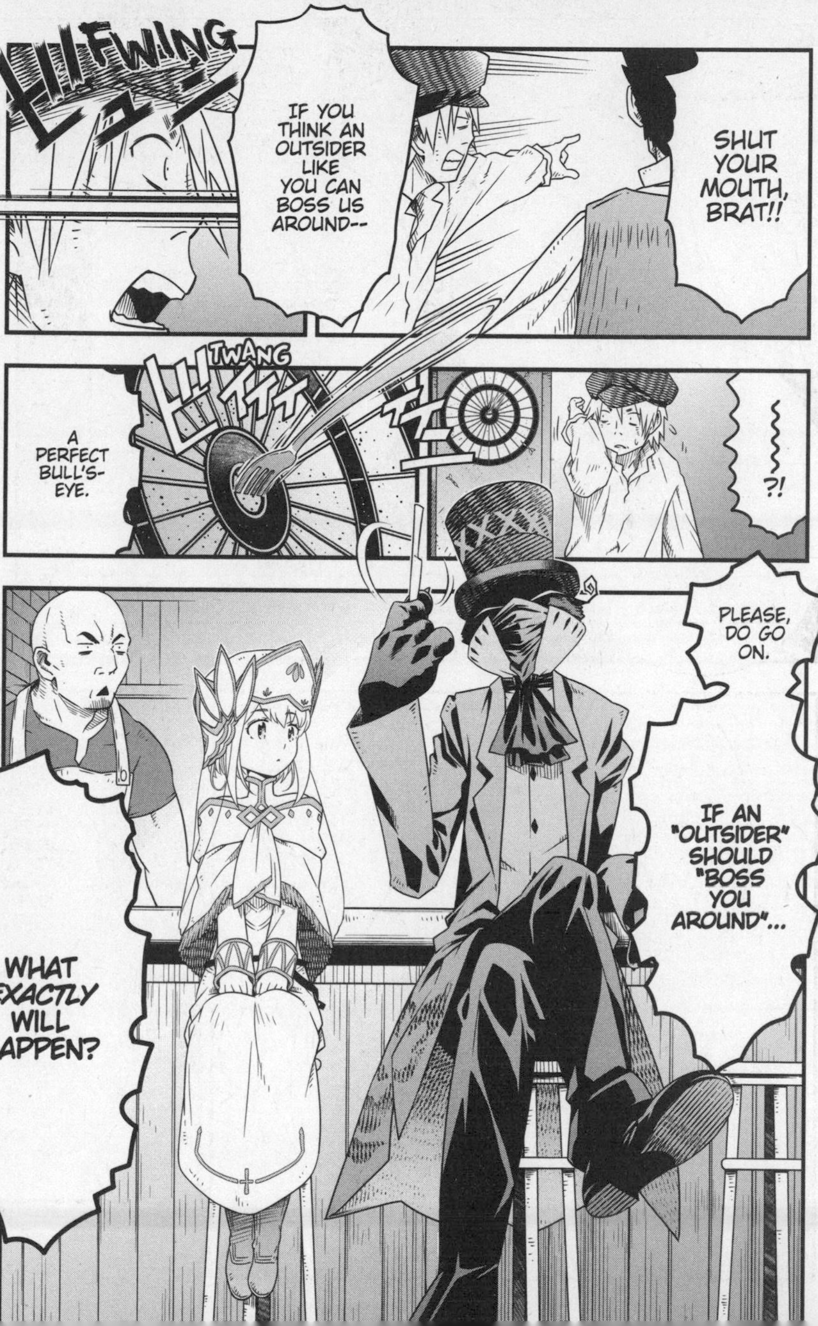
SHUT YOUR MOUTH, BRAT!!
IF YOU THINK AN OUTSIDER LIKE YOU CAN BOSS US AROUND--
FWING
......?!
TWANG
A PERFECT BULL'S-EYE.
PLEASE, DO GO ON.
IF AN "OUTSIDER" SHOULD "BOSS YOU AROUND"...
WHAT EXACTLY WILL HAPPEN?

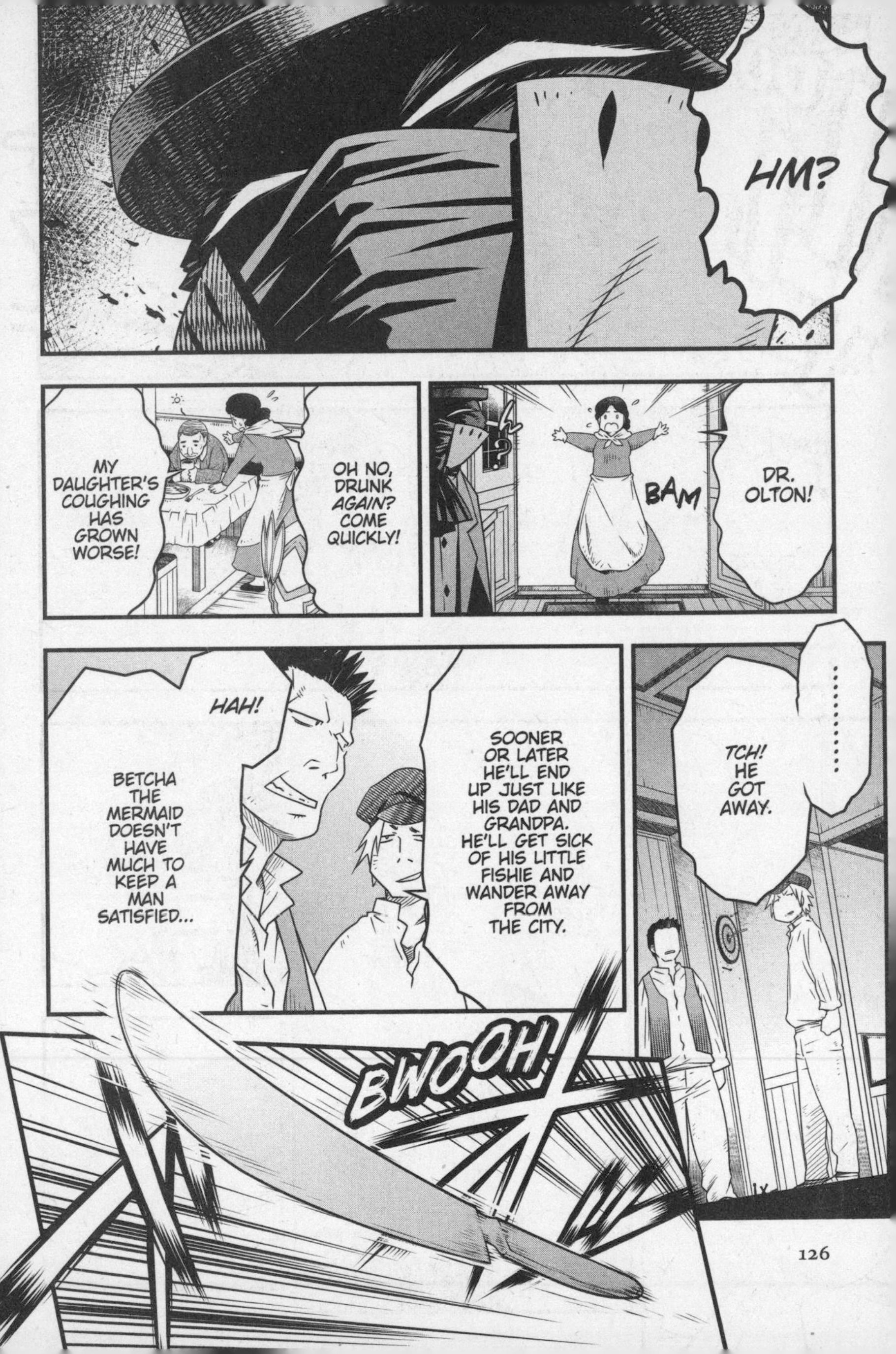
HM?
DR. OLTON!
BAM
OH NO, DRUNK AGAIN? COME QUICKLY!
MY DAUGHTER'S COUGHING HAS GROWN WORSE!
......
TCH! HE GOT AWAY.
SOONER OR LATER HE'LL END UP JUST LIKE HIS DAD AND GRANDPA. HE'LL GET SICK OF HIS LITTLE FISHIE AND WANDER AWAY FROM THE CITY.
HAH!
BETCHA THE MERMAID DOESN'T HAVE MUCH TO KEEP A MAN SATISFIED...
BWOOH

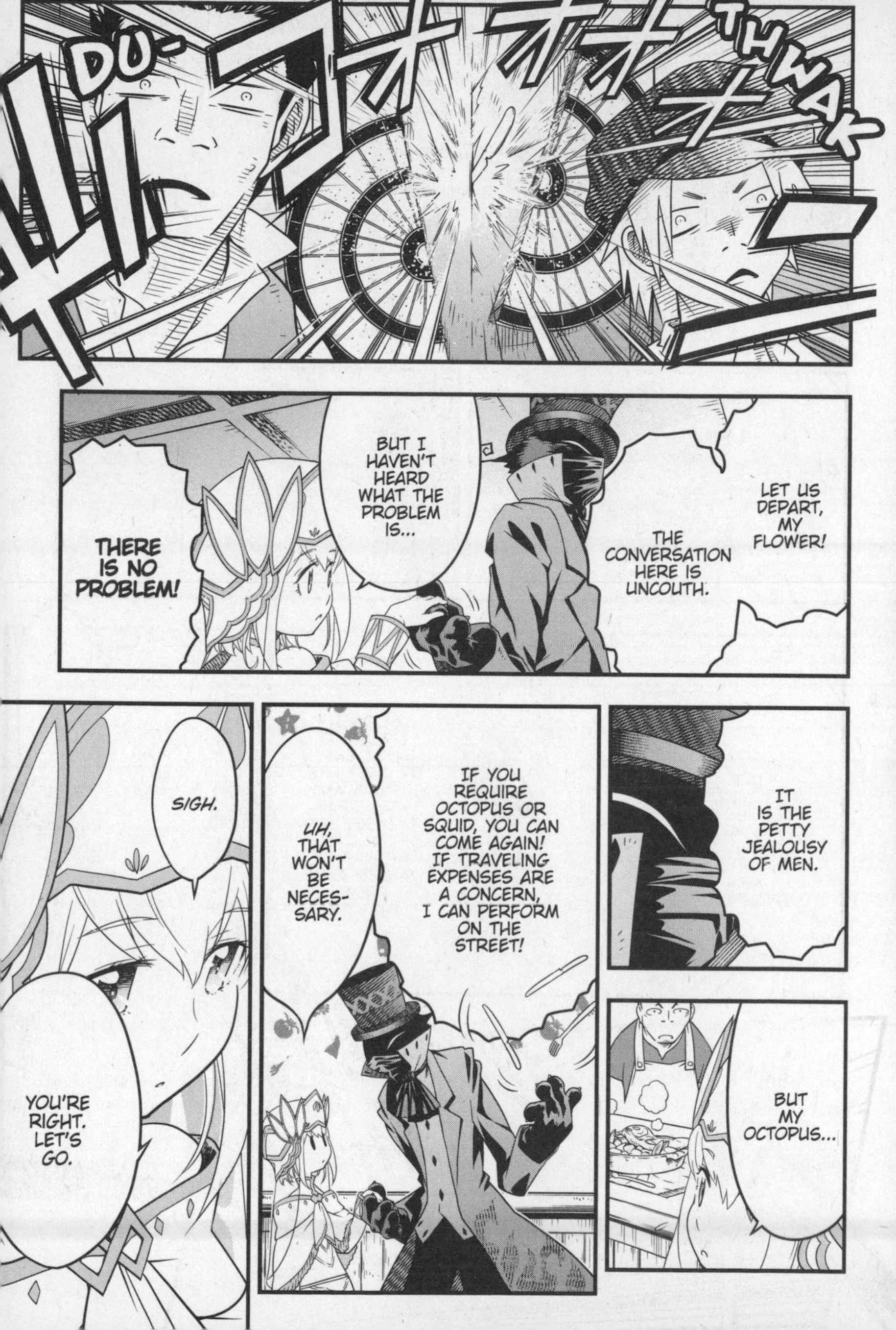
THWAK
DU-
LET US DEPART, MY FLOWER!
THE CONVERSATION HERE IS UNCOUTH.
BUT I HAVEN'T HEARD WHAT THE PROBLEM IS...
THERE IS NO PROBLEM!
IT IS THE PETTY JEALOUSY OF MEN.
BUT MY OCTOPUS...
IF YOU REQUIRE OCTOPUS OR SQUID, YOU CAN COME AGAIN! IF TRAVELING EXPENSES ARE A CONCERN, I CAN PERFORM ON THE STREET!
UH, THAT WON'T BE NECES-SARY.
SIGH.
YOU'RE RIGHT. LET'S GO.

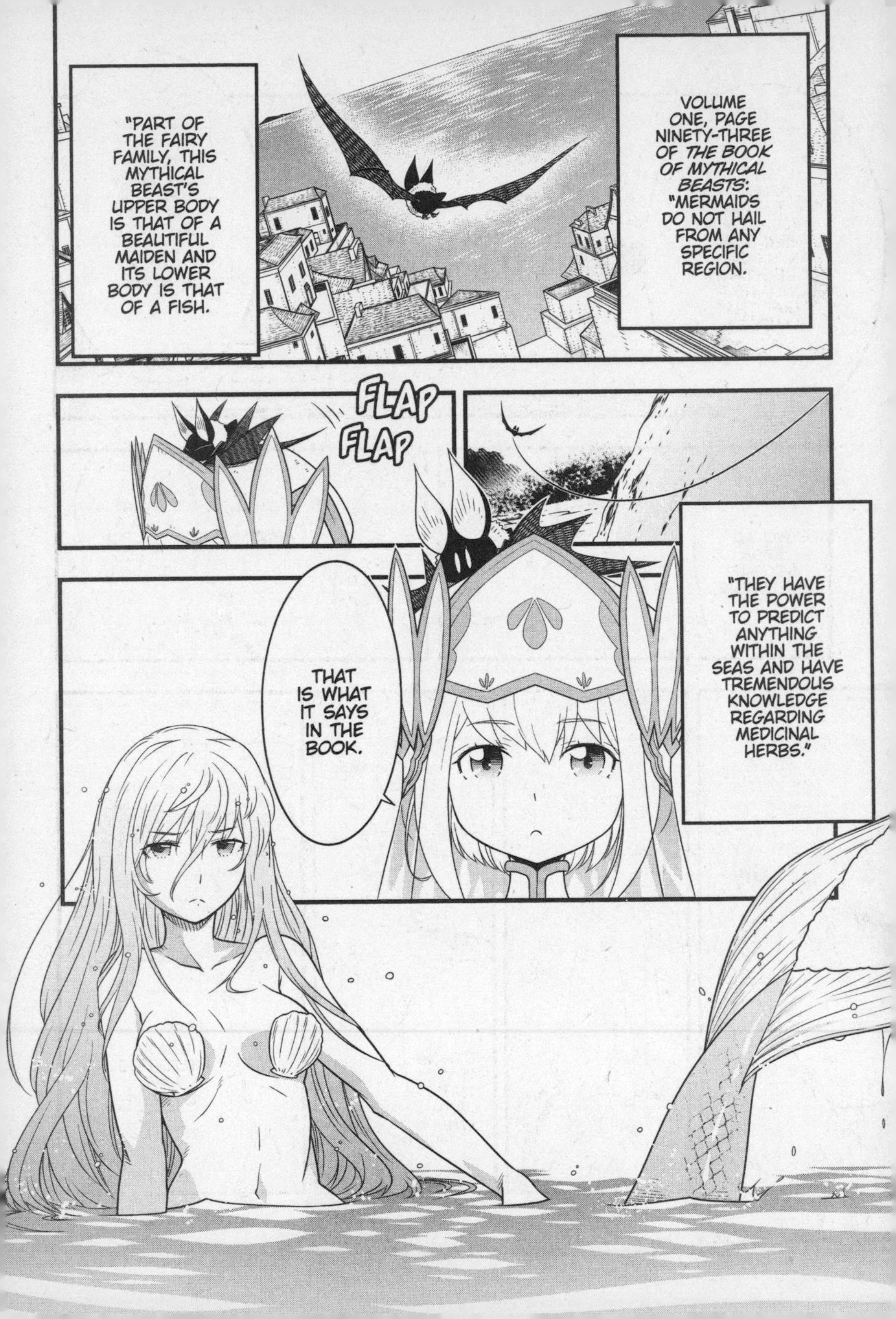
VOLUME ONE, PAGE NINETY-THREE OF *THE BOOK OF MYTHICAL BEASTS*: "MERMAIDS DO NOT HAIL FROM ANY SPECIFIC REGION.
"PART OF THE FAIRY FAMILY, THIS MYTHICAL BEAST'S UPPER BODY IS THAT OF A BEAUTIFUL MAIDEN AND ITS LOWER BODY IS THAT OF A FISH.
FLAP FLAP
"THEY HAVE THE POWER TO PREDICT ANYTHING WITHIN THE SEAS AND HAVE TREMENDOUS KNOWLEDGE REGARDING MEDICINAL HERBS."
THAT IS WHAT IT SAYS IN THE BOOK.

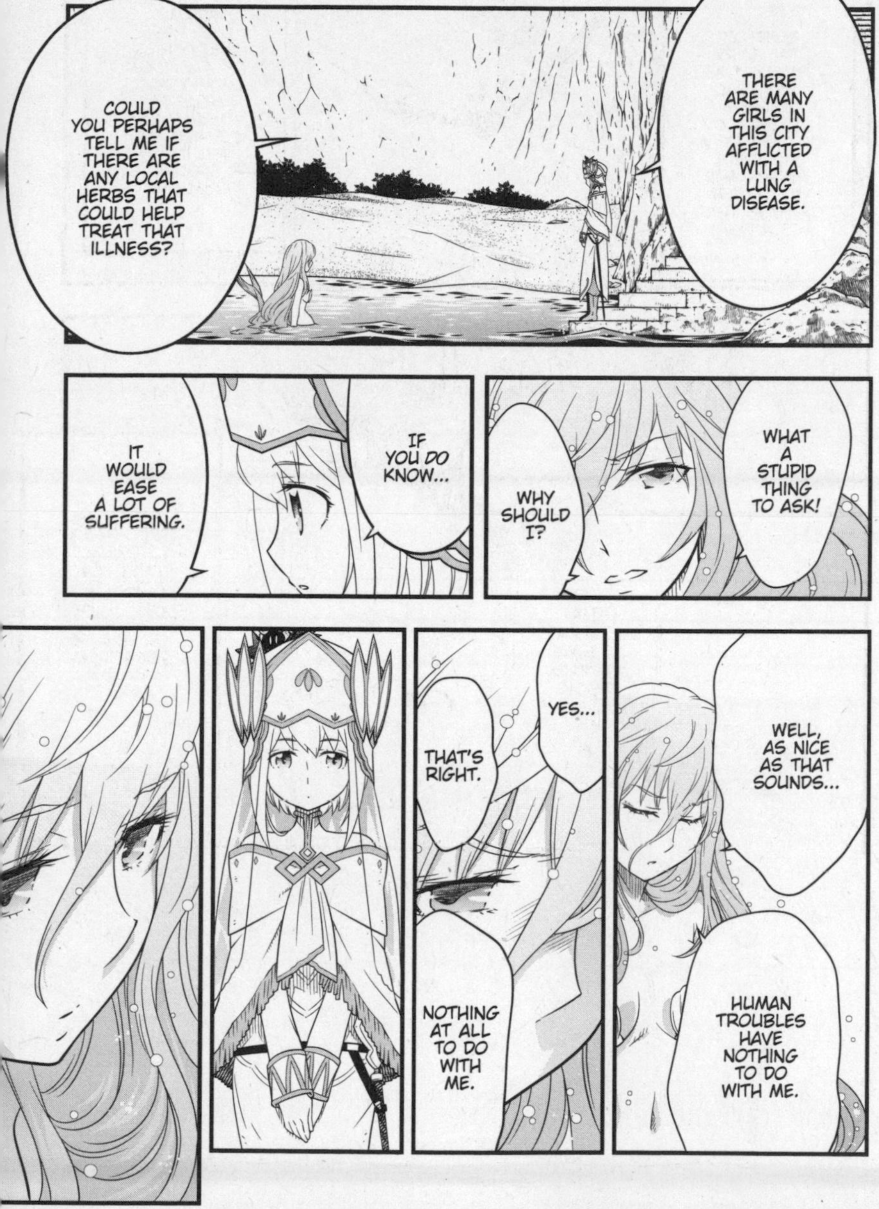
THERE ARE MANY GIRLS IN THIS CITY AFFLICTED WITH A LUNG DISEASE.
COULD YOU PERHAPS TELL ME IF THERE ARE ANY LOCAL HERBS THAT COULD HELP TREAT THAT ILLNESS?
WHAT A STUPID THING TO ASK!
WHY SHOULD I?
IF YOU DO KNOW...
IT WOULD EASE A LOT OF SUFFERING.
WELL, AS NICE AS THAT SOUNDS...
HUMAN TROUBLES HAVE NOTHING TO DO WITH ME.
YES...
THAT'S RIGHT.
NOTHING AT ALL TO DO WITH ME.

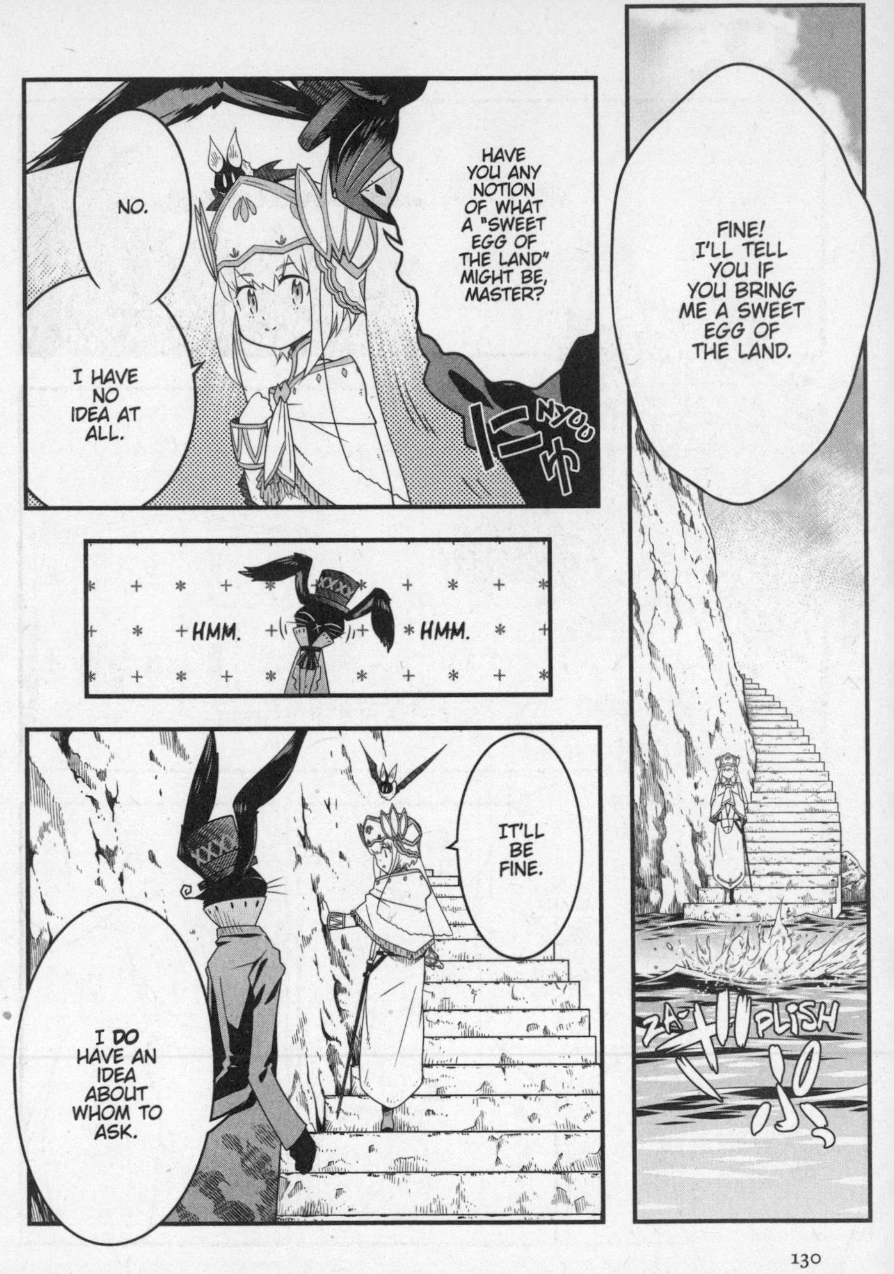
FINE! I'LL TELL YOU IF YOU BRING ME A SWEET EGG OF THE LAND.
ZA- PLISH
HAVE YOU ANY NOTION OF WHAT A "SWEET EGG OF THE LAND" MIGHT BE, MASTER?
NO.
I HAVE NO IDEA AT ALL.
NYUU
HMM.
HMM.
IT'LL BE FINE.
I DO HAVE AN IDEA ABOUT WHOM TO ASK.

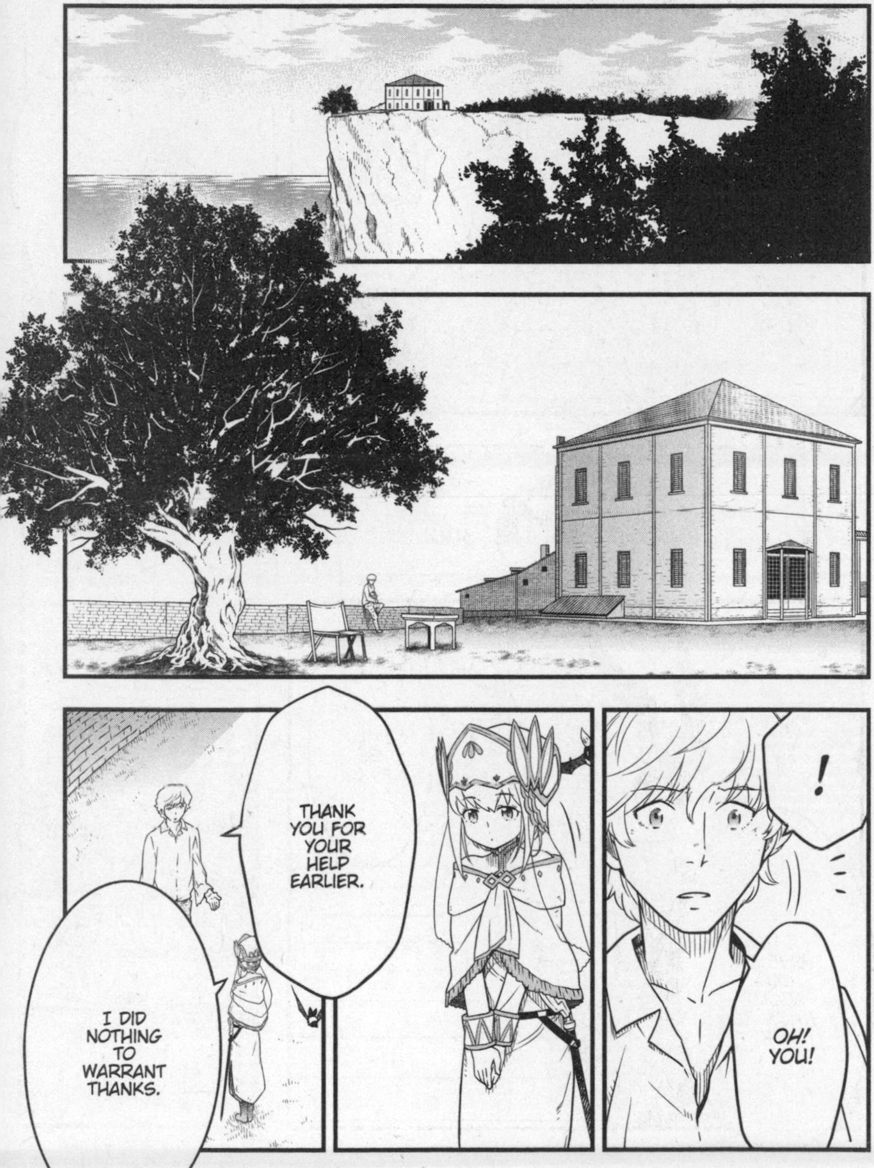
!
OH! YOU!
THANK YOU FOR YOUR HELP EARLIER.
I DID NOTHING TO WARRANT THANKS.

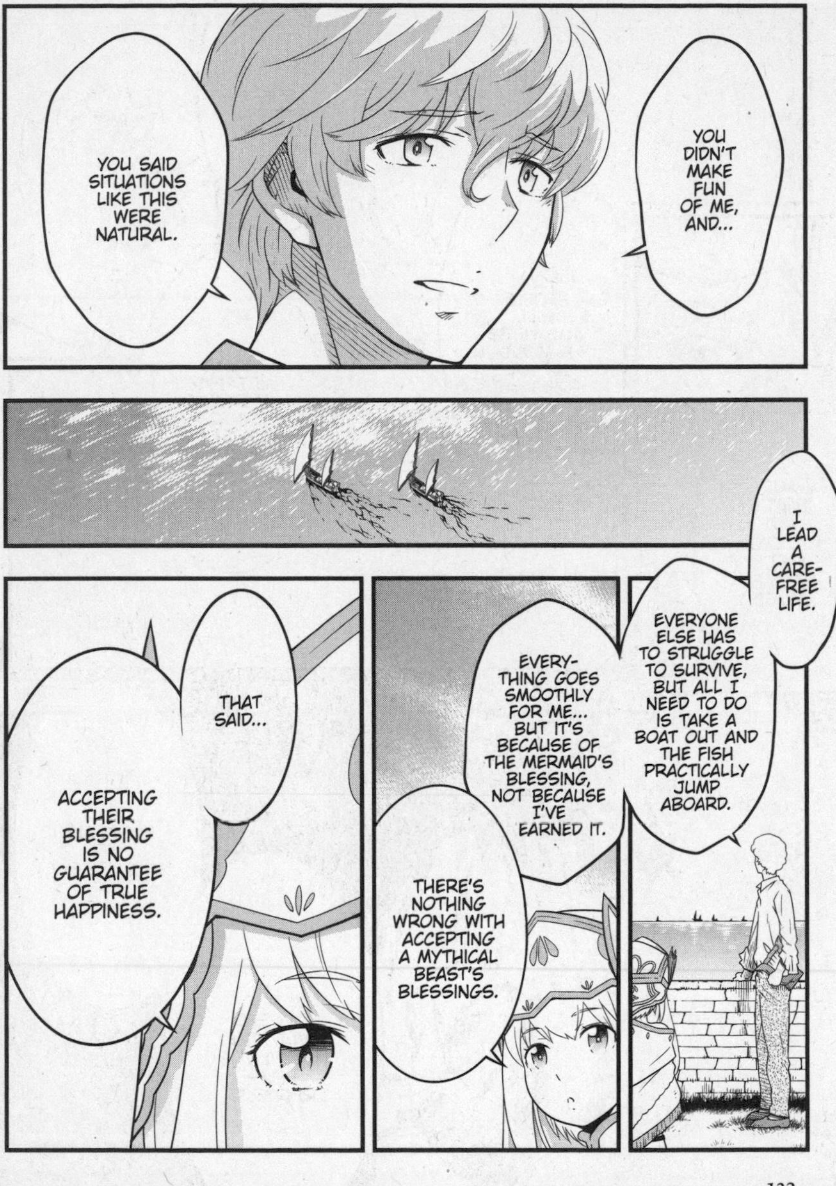
YOU DIDN'T MAKE FUN OF ME, AND...
YOU SAID SITUATIONS LIKE THIS WERE NATURAL.
I LEAD A CARE-FREE LIFE.
EVERYONE ELSE HAS TO STRUGGLE TO SURVIVE, BUT ALL I NEED TO DO IS TAKE A BOAT OUT AND THE FISH PRACTICALLY JUMP ABOARD.
EVERY-THING GOES SMOOTHLY FOR ME... BUT IT'S BECAUSE OF THE MERMAID'S BLESSING, NOT BECAUSE I'VE EARNED IT.
THERE'S NOTHING WRONG WITH ACCEPTING A MYTHICAL BEAST'S BLESSINGS.
THAT SAID...
ACCEPTING THEIR BLESSING IS NO GUARANTEE OF TRUE HAPPINESS.

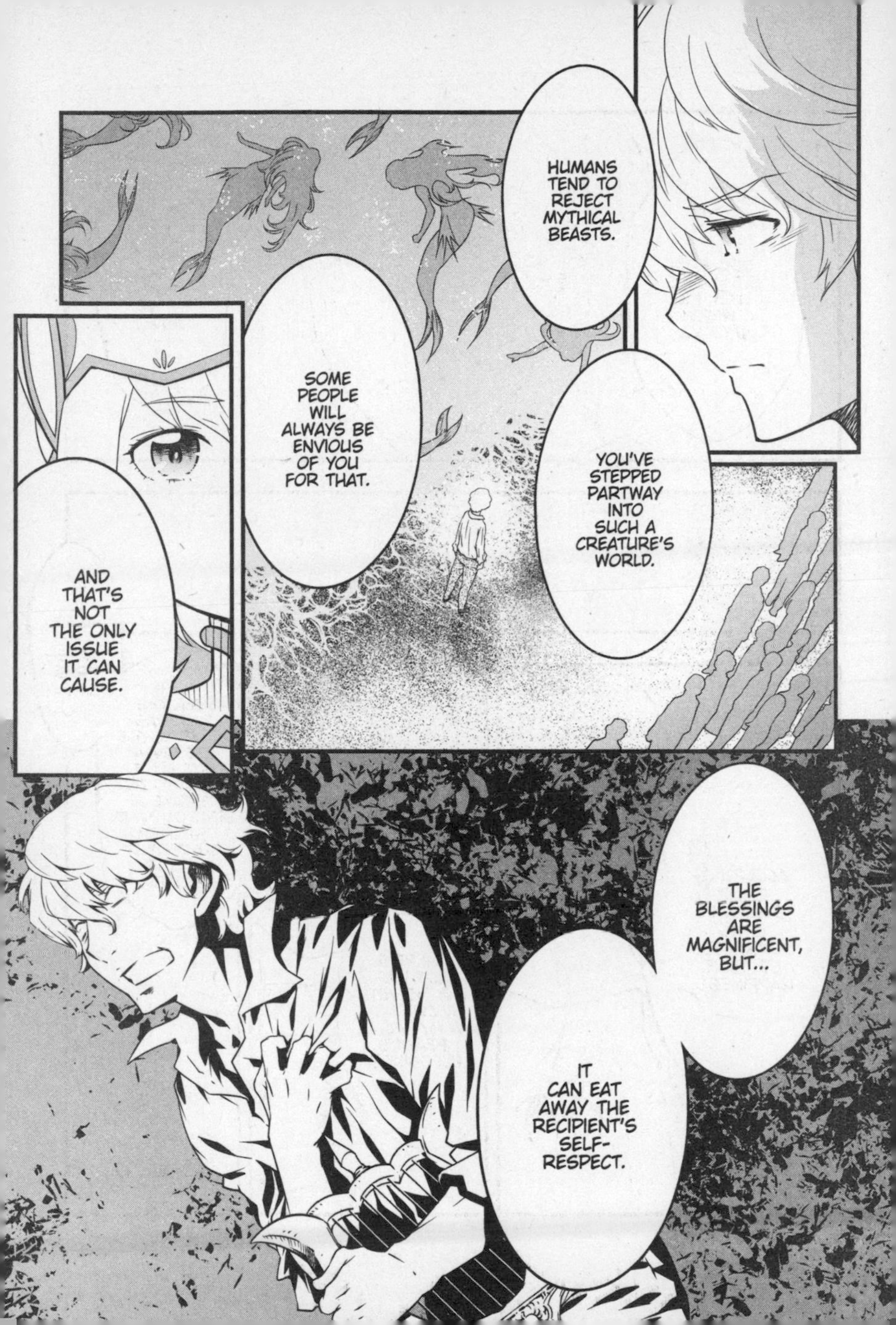
HUMANS TEND TO REJECT MYTHICAL BEASTS.
YOU'VE STEPPED PARTWAY INTO SUCH A CREATURE'S WORLD.
SOME PEOPLE WILL ALWAYS BE ENVIOUS OF YOU FOR THAT.
AND THAT'S NOT THE ONLY ISSUE IT CAN CAUSE.
THE BLESSINGS ARE MAGNIFICENT, BUT...
IT CAN EAT AWAY THE RECIPIENT'S SELF-RESPECT.

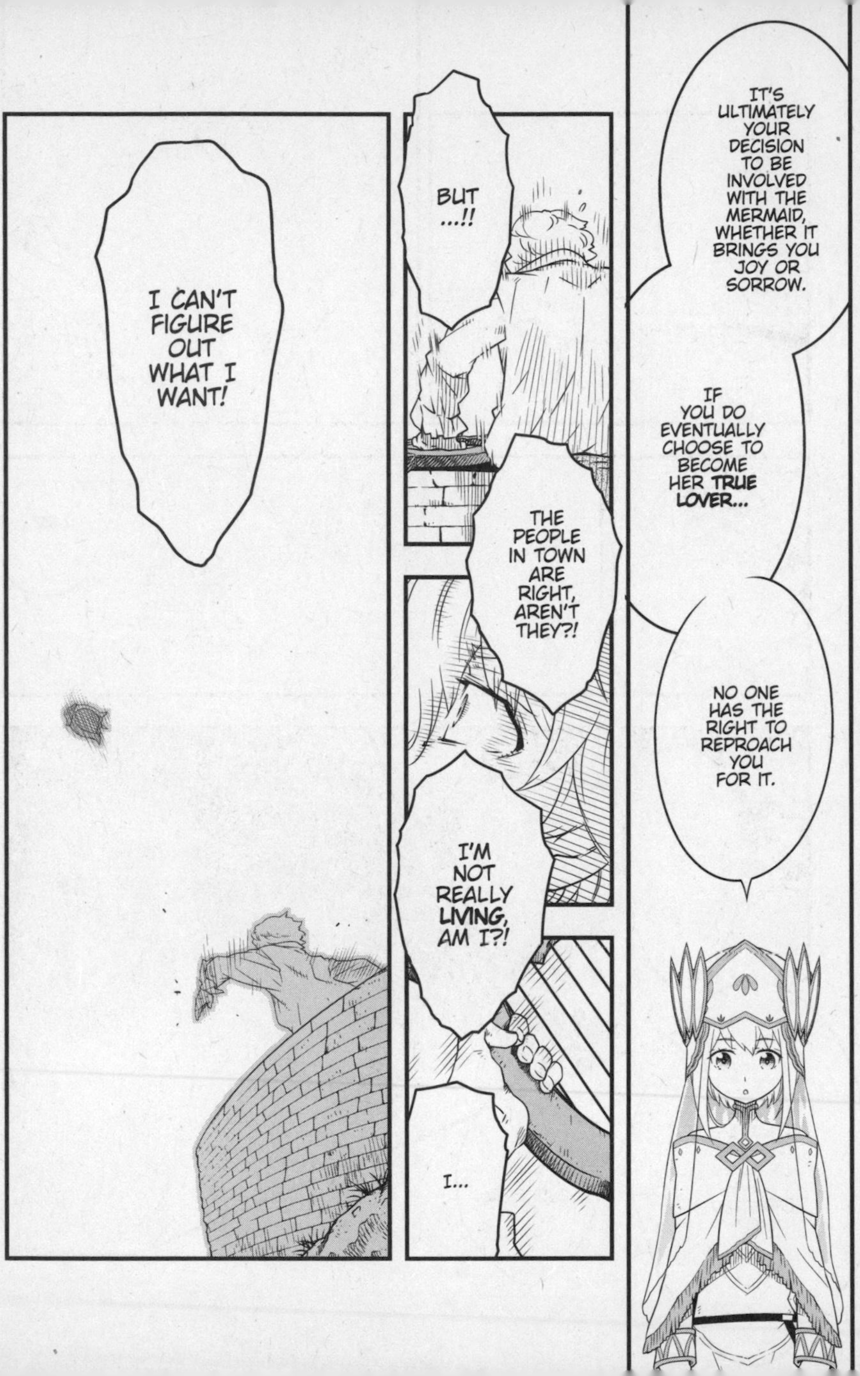
IT'S ULTIMATELY YOUR DECISION TO BE INVOLVED WITH THE MERMAID, WHETHER IT BRINGS YOU JOY OR SORROW.
IF YOU DO EVENTUALLY CHOOSE TO BECOME HER TRUE LOVER...
NO ONE HAS THE RIGHT TO REPROACH YOU FOR IT.
BUT ...!!
THE PEOPLE IN TOWN ARE RIGHT, AREN'T THEY?!
I'M NOT REALLY LIVING, AM I?!
I...
I CAN'T FIGURE OUT WHAT I WANT!

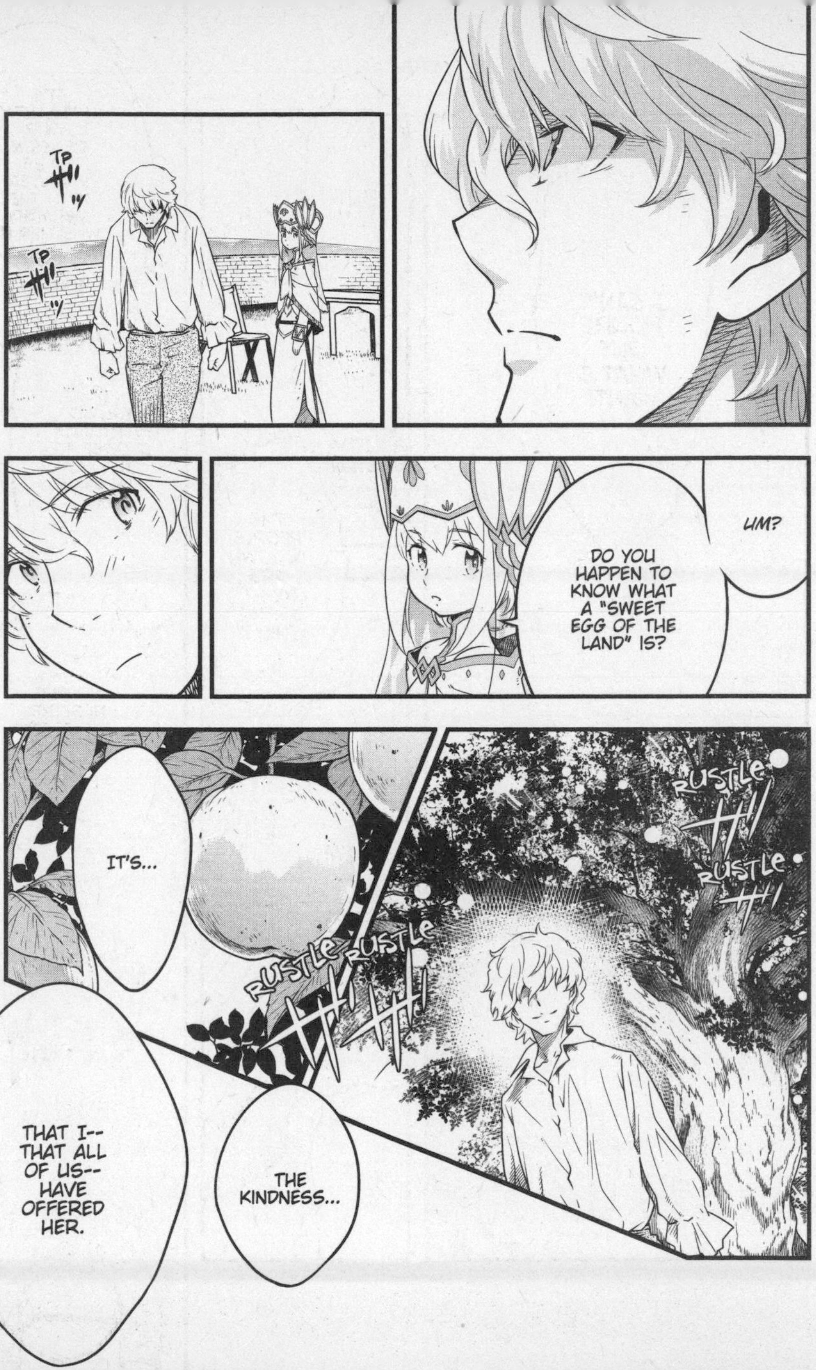
TP
TP
UM?
DO YOU HAPPEN TO KNOW WHAT A "SWEET EGG OF THE LAND" IS?
RUSTLE
RUSTLE
IT'S...
RUSTLE RUSTLE
THE KINDNESS...
THAT I-- THAT ALL OF US-- HAVE OFFERED HER.

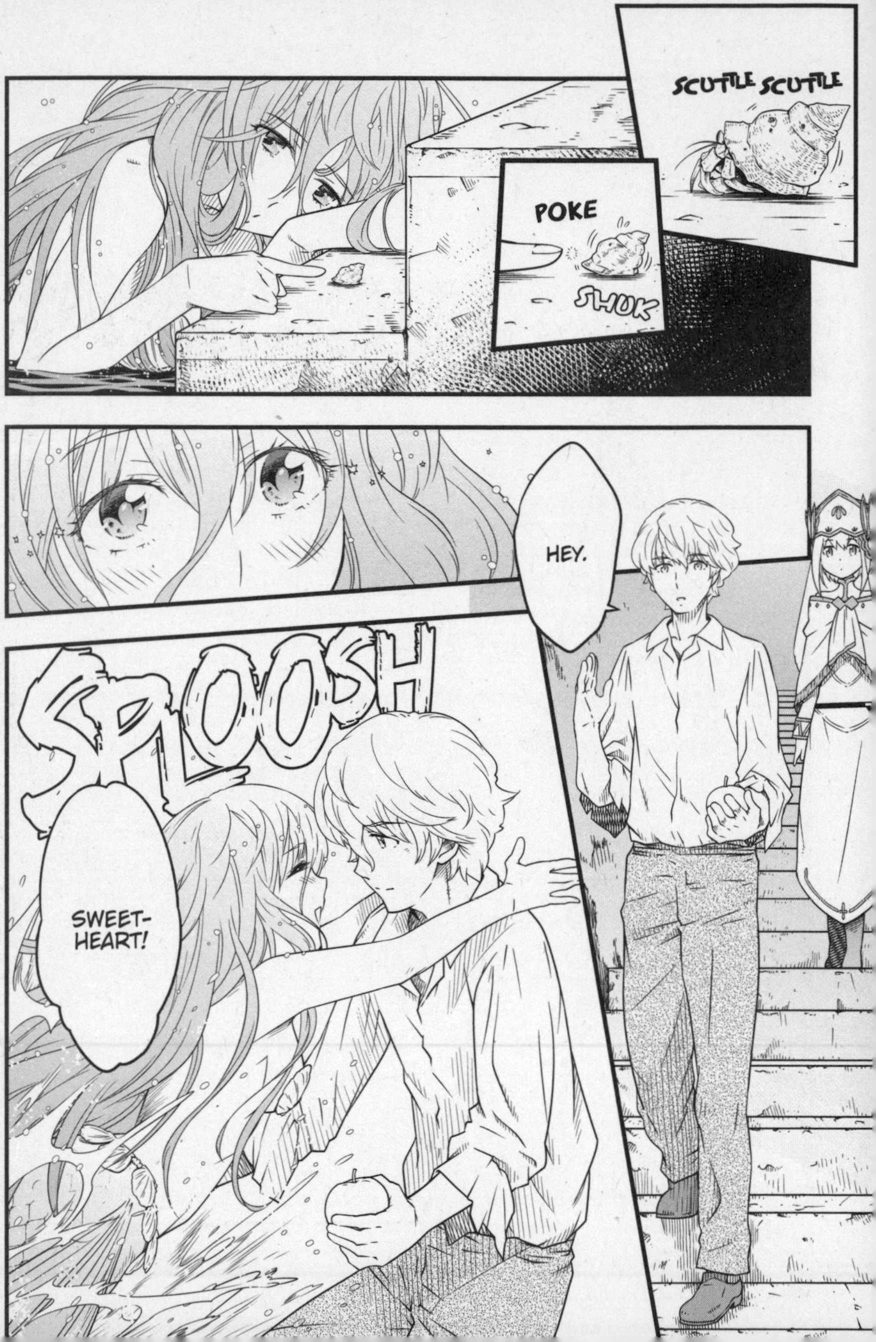
SCUTTLE SCUTTLE
POKE
SHUK
HEY.
SPLOOSH
SWEET-
HEART!

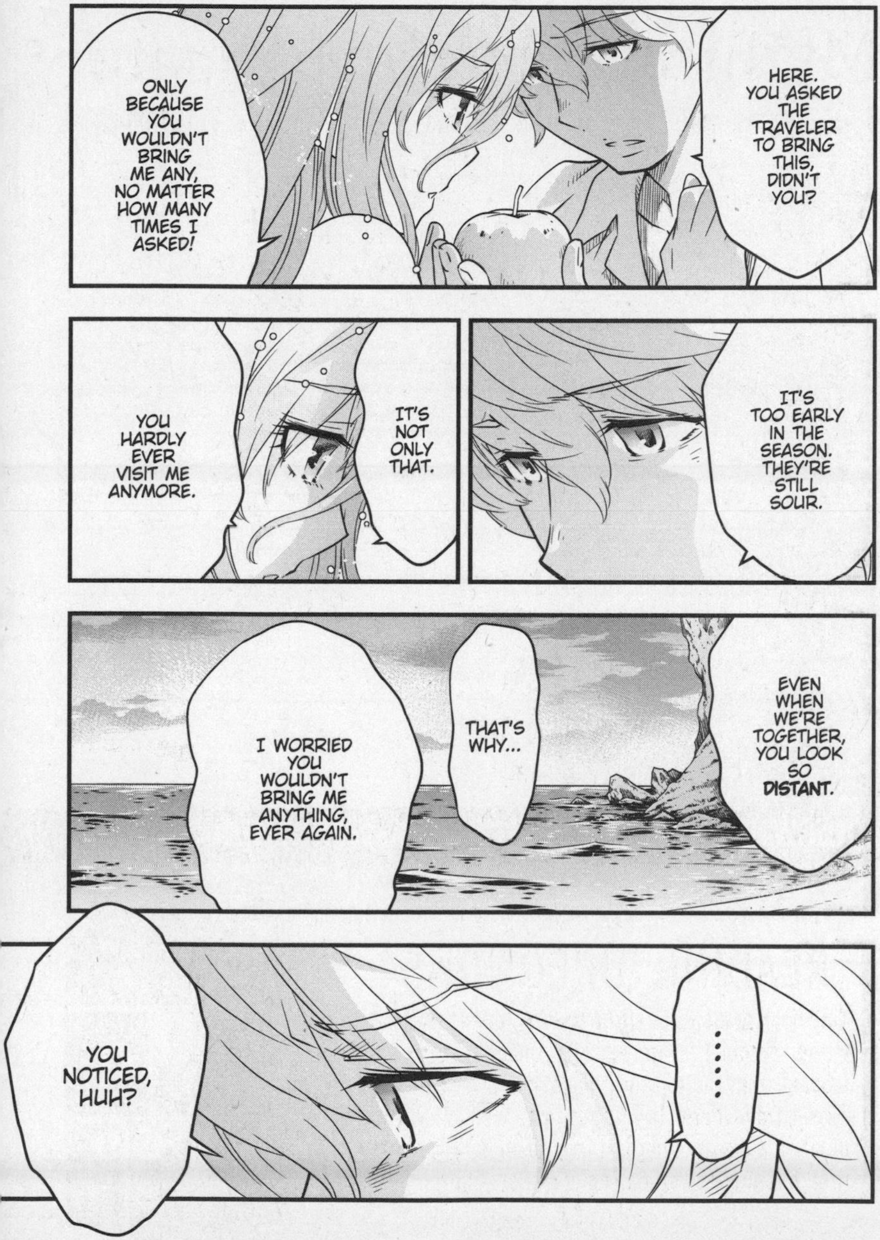
HERE. YOU ASKED THE TRAVELER TO BRING THIS, DIDN'T YOU?
ONLY BECAUSE YOU WOULDN'T BRING ME ANY, NO MATTER HOW MANY TIMES I ASKED!
IT'S TOO EARLY IN THE SEASON. THEY'RE STILL SOUR.
IT'S NOT ONLY THAT.
YOU HARDLY EVER VISIT ME ANYMORE.
EVEN WHEN WE'RE TOGETHER, YOU LOOK SO **DISTANT**.
THAT'S WHY...
I WORRIED YOU WOULDN'T BRING ME ANYTHING, EVER AGAIN.
......
YOU NOTICED, HUH?

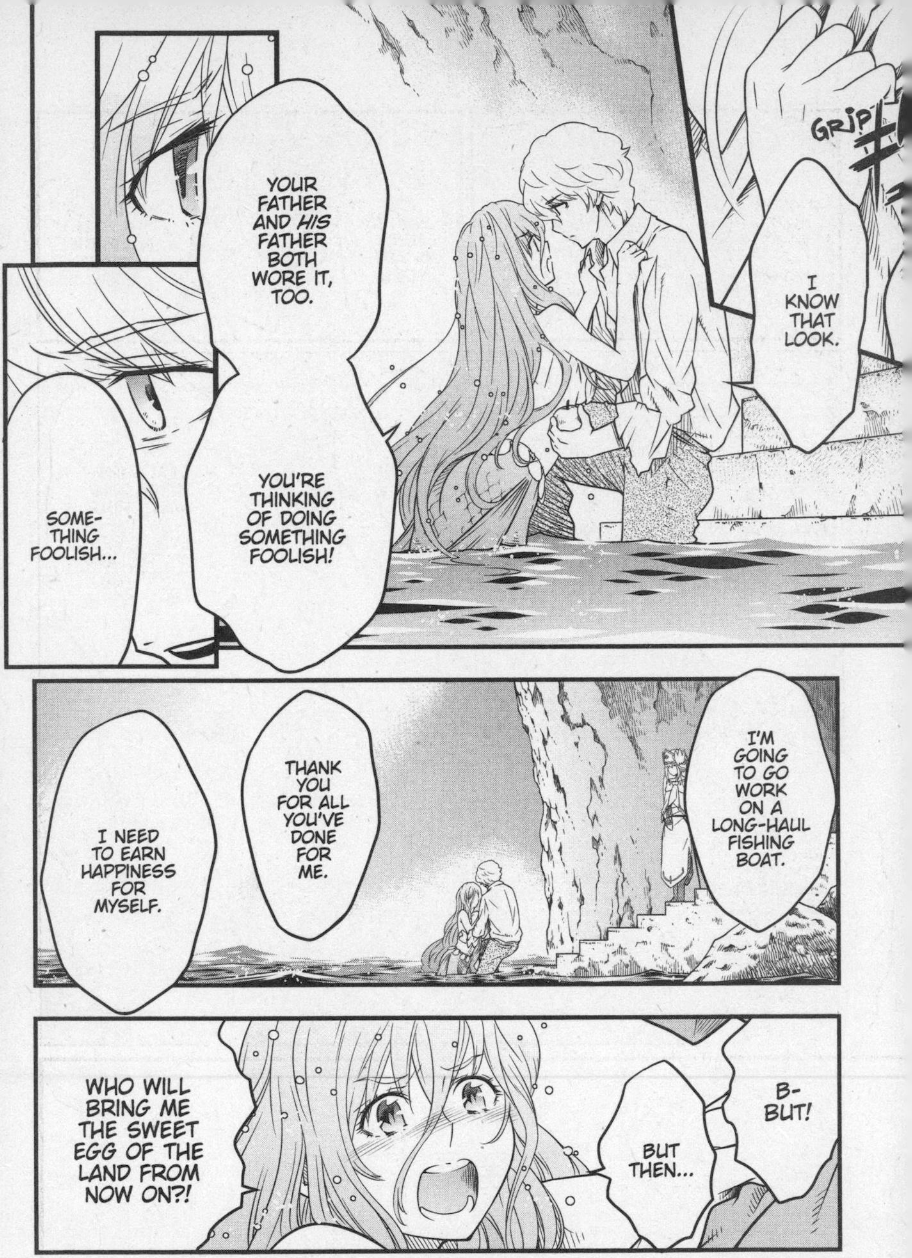
GRIP
I KNOW THAT LOOK.
YOUR FATHER AND HIS FATHER BOTH WORE IT, TOO.
YOU'RE THINKING OF DOING SOMETHING FOOLISH!
SOME-THING FOOLISH...
I'M GOING TO GO WORK ON A LONG-HAUL FISHING BOAT.
THANK YOU FOR ALL YOU'VE DONE FOR ME.
I NEED TO EARN HAPPINESS FOR MYSELF.
B-BUT!
BUT THEN...
WHO WILL BRING ME THE SWEET EGG OF THE LAND FROM NOW ON?!

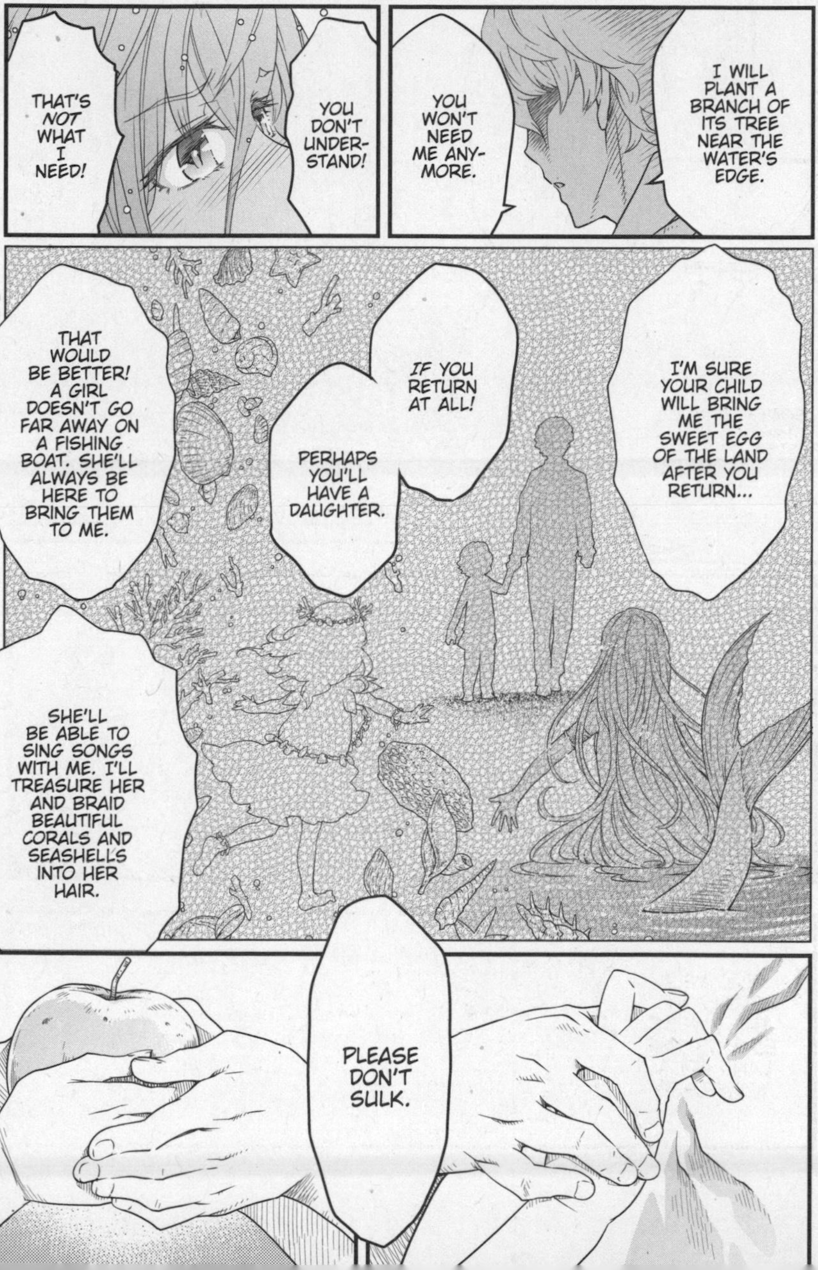
I WILL PLANT A BRANCH OF ITS TREE NEAR THE WATER'S EDGE.
YOU WON'T NEED ME ANY-MORE.
YOU DON'T UNDER-STAND!
THAT'S *NOT* WHAT I NEED!
I'M SURE YOUR CHILD WILL BRING ME THE SWEET EGG OF THE LAND AFTER YOU RETURN...
IF YOU RETURN AT ALL!
PERHAPS YOU'LL HAVE A DAUGHTER.
THAT WOULD BE BETTER! A GIRL DOESN'T GO FAR AWAY ON A FISHING BOAT. SHE'LL ALWAYS BE HERE TO BRING THEM TO ME.
SHE'LL BE ABLE TO SING SONGS WITH ME. I'LL TREASURE HER AND BRAID BEAUTIFUL CORALS AND SEASHELLS INTO HER HAIR.
PLEASE DON'T SULK.

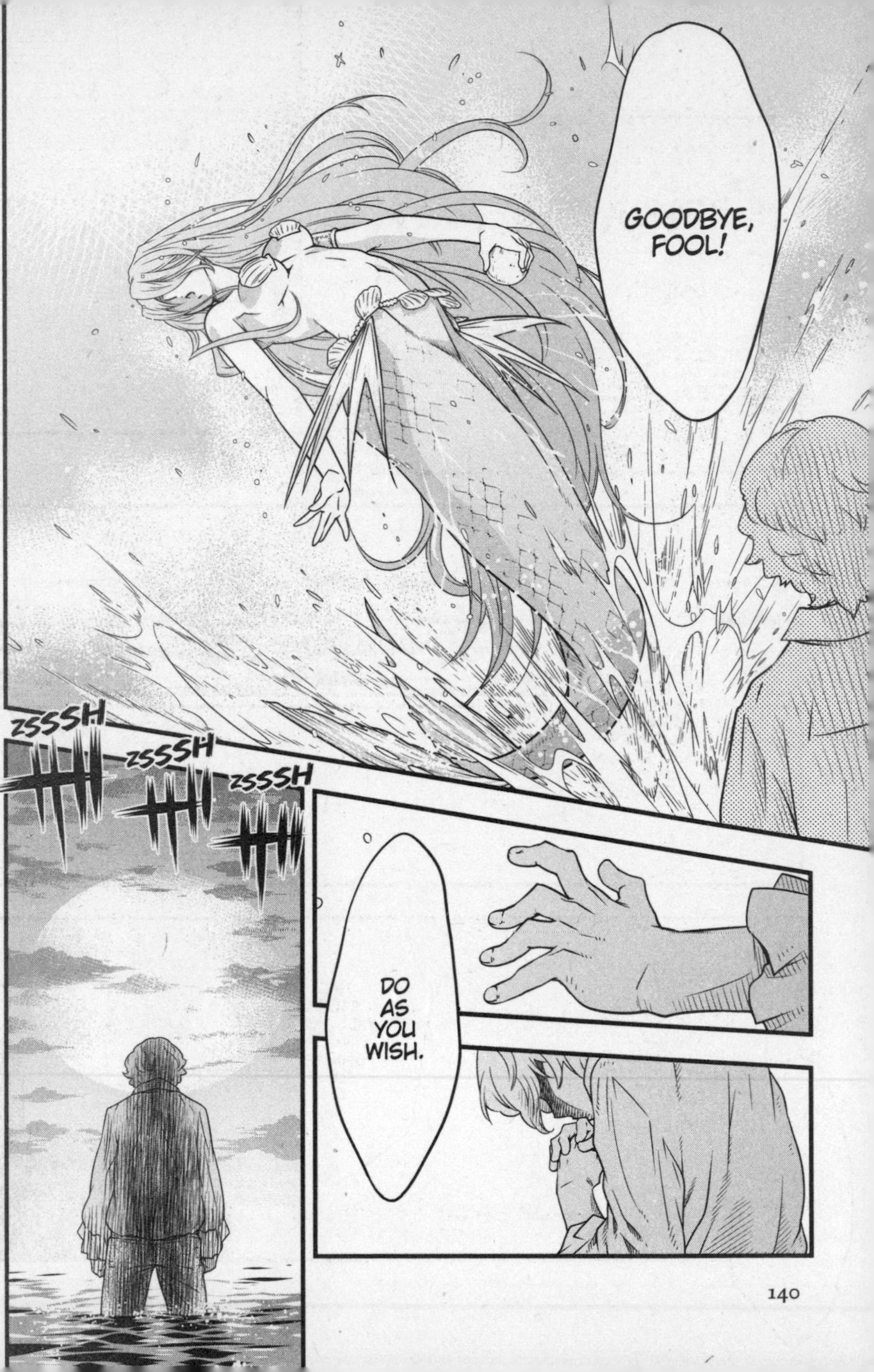
GOODBYE, FOOL!
DO AS YOU WISH.
ZSSSH
ZSSSH
ZSSSH

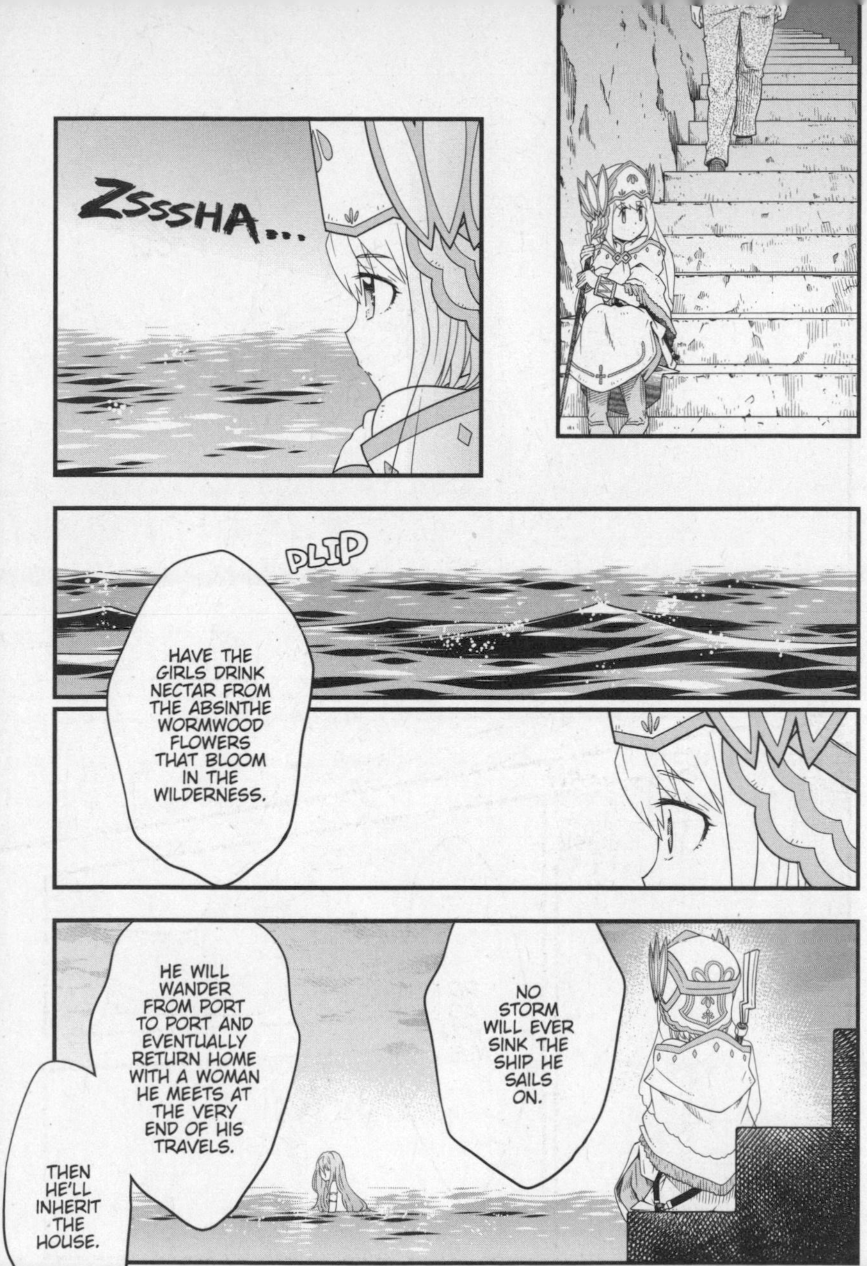
ZSSSHA...
PLIP
HAVE THE GIRLS DRINK NECTAR FROM THE ABSINTHE WORMWOOD FLOWERS THAT BLOOM IN THE WILDERNESS.
NO STORM WILL EVER SINK THE SHIP HE SAILS ON.
HE WILL WANDER FROM PORT TO PORT AND EVENTUALLY RETURN HOME WITH A WOMAN HE MEETS AT THE VERY END OF HIS TRAVELS.
THEN HE'LL INHERIT THE HOUSE.

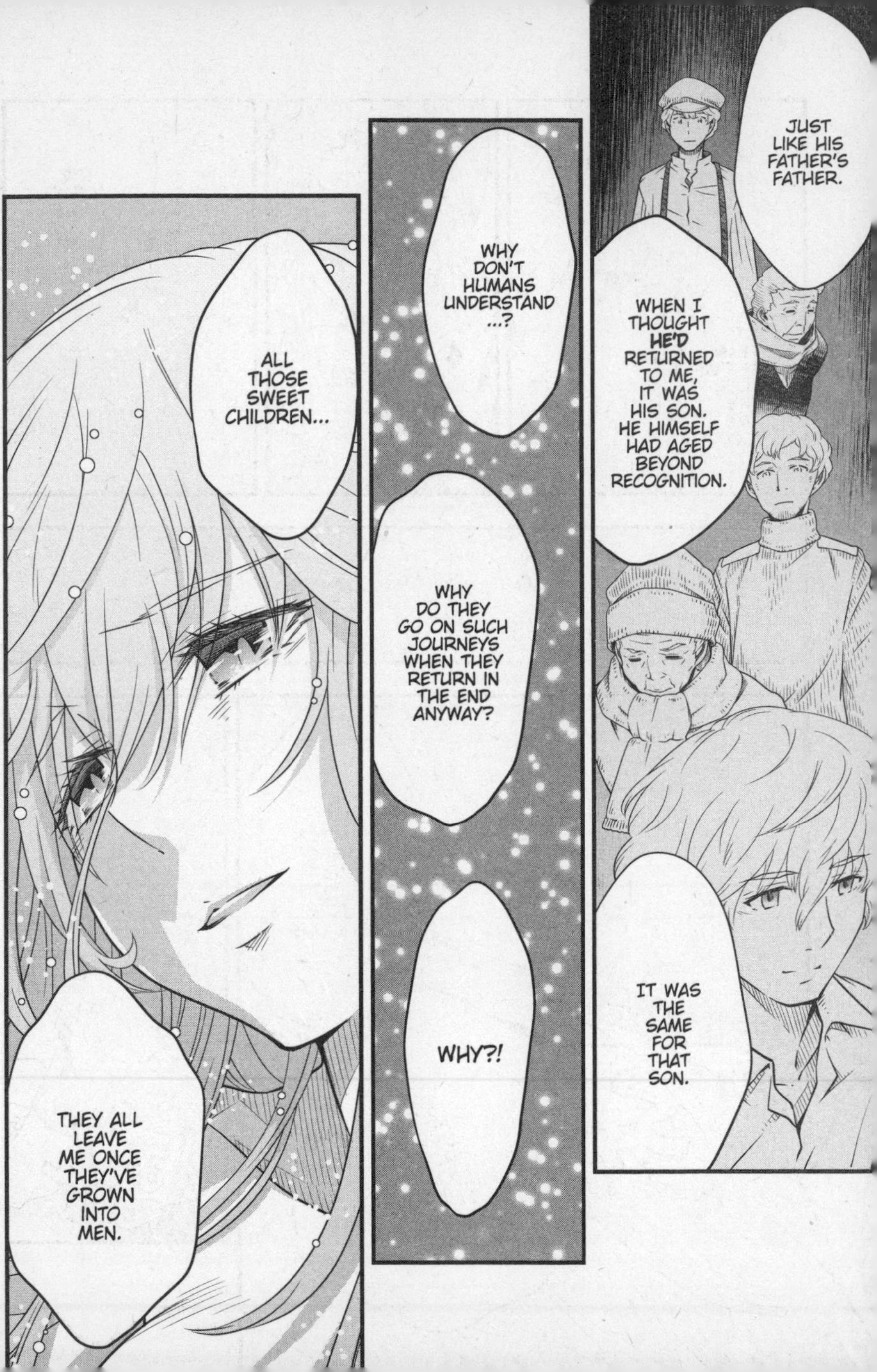
JUST LIKE HIS FATHER'S FATHER.
WHEN I THOUGHT HE'D RETURNED TO ME, IT WAS HIS SON. HE HIMSELF HAD AGED BEYOND RECOGNITION.
IT WAS THE SAME FOR THAT SON.
WHY DON'T HUMANS UNDERSTAND ...?
WHY DO THEY GO ON SUCH JOURNEYS WHEN THEY RETURN IN THE END ANYWAY?
WHY?!
ALL THOSE SWEET CHILDREN...
THEY ALL LEAVE ME ONCE THEY'VE GROWN INTO MEN.

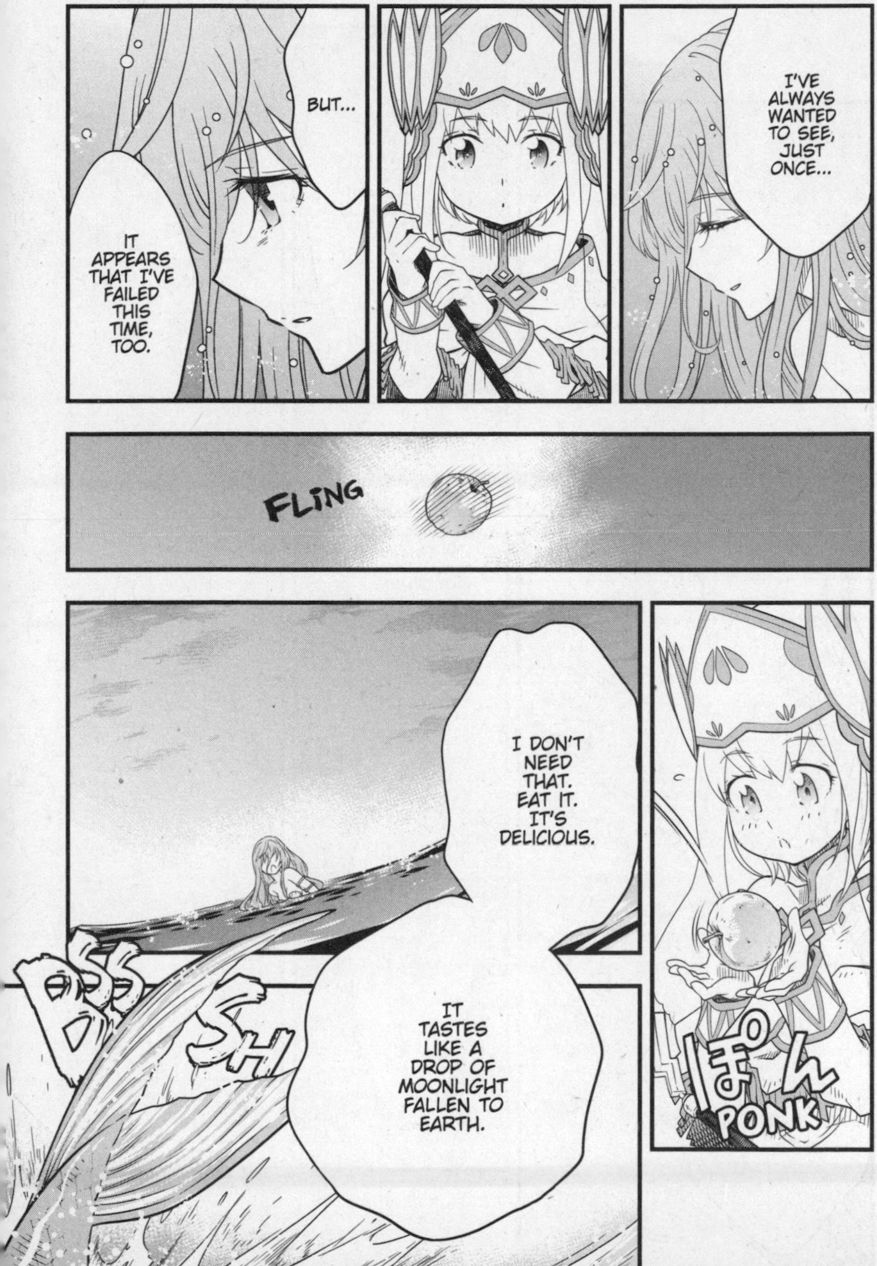
I'VE ALWAYS WANTED TO SEE, JUST ONCE...
BUT...
IT APPEARS THAT I'VE FAILED THIS TIME, TOO.
FLING
ぽん
PONK
I DON'T NEED THAT. EAT IT. IT'S DELICIOUS.
IT TASTES LIKE A DROP OF MOONLIGHT FALLEN TO EARTH.
BSSH

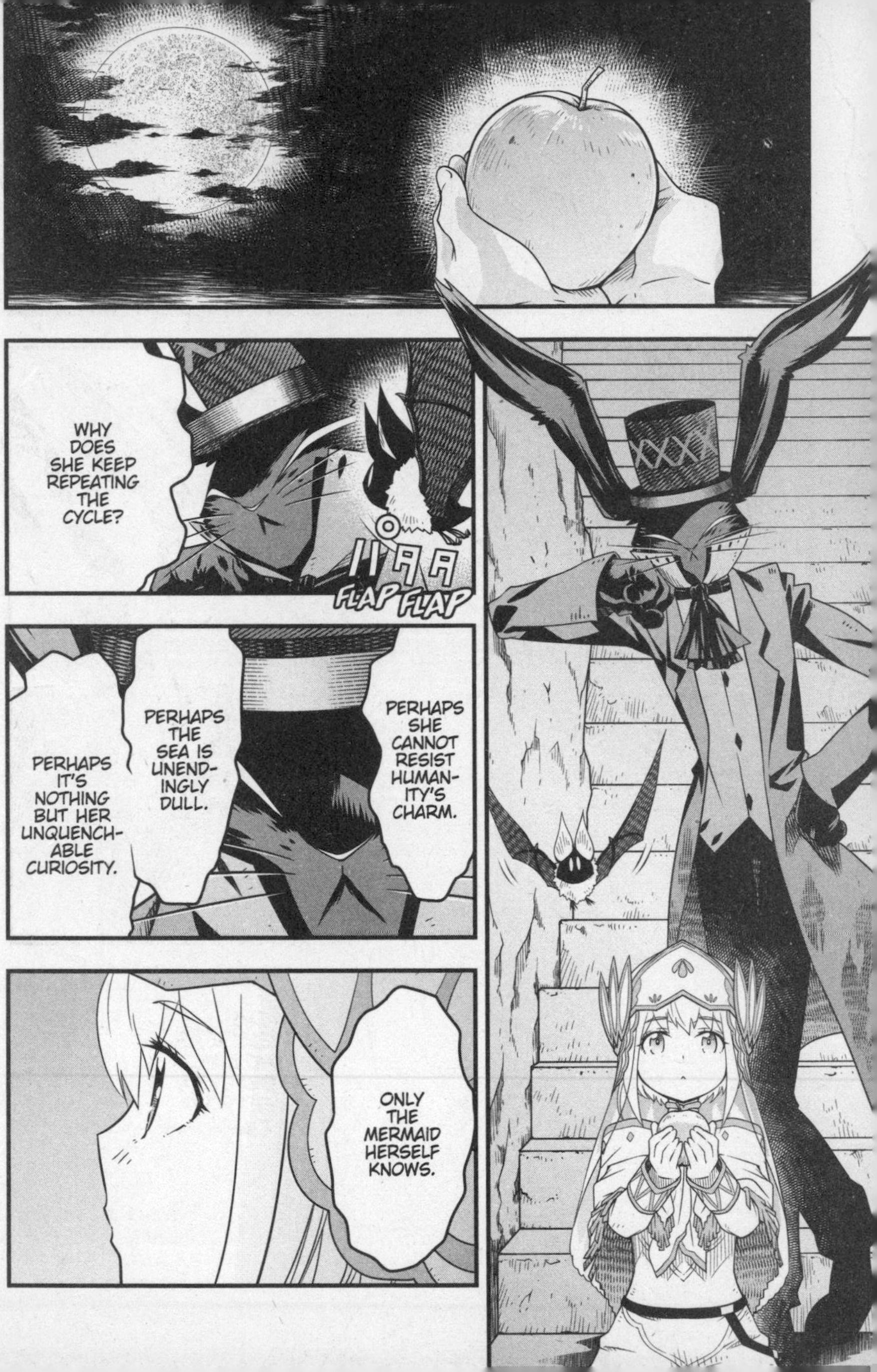
WHY DOES SHE KEEP REPEATING THE CYCLE?
FLAP FLAP
PERHAPS SHE CANNOT RESIST HUMAN-ITY'S CHARM.
PERHAPS THE SEA IS UNEND-INGLY DULL.
PERHAPS IT'S NOTHING BUT HER UNQUENCH-ABLE CURIOSITY.
ONLY THE MERMAID HERSELF KNOWS.

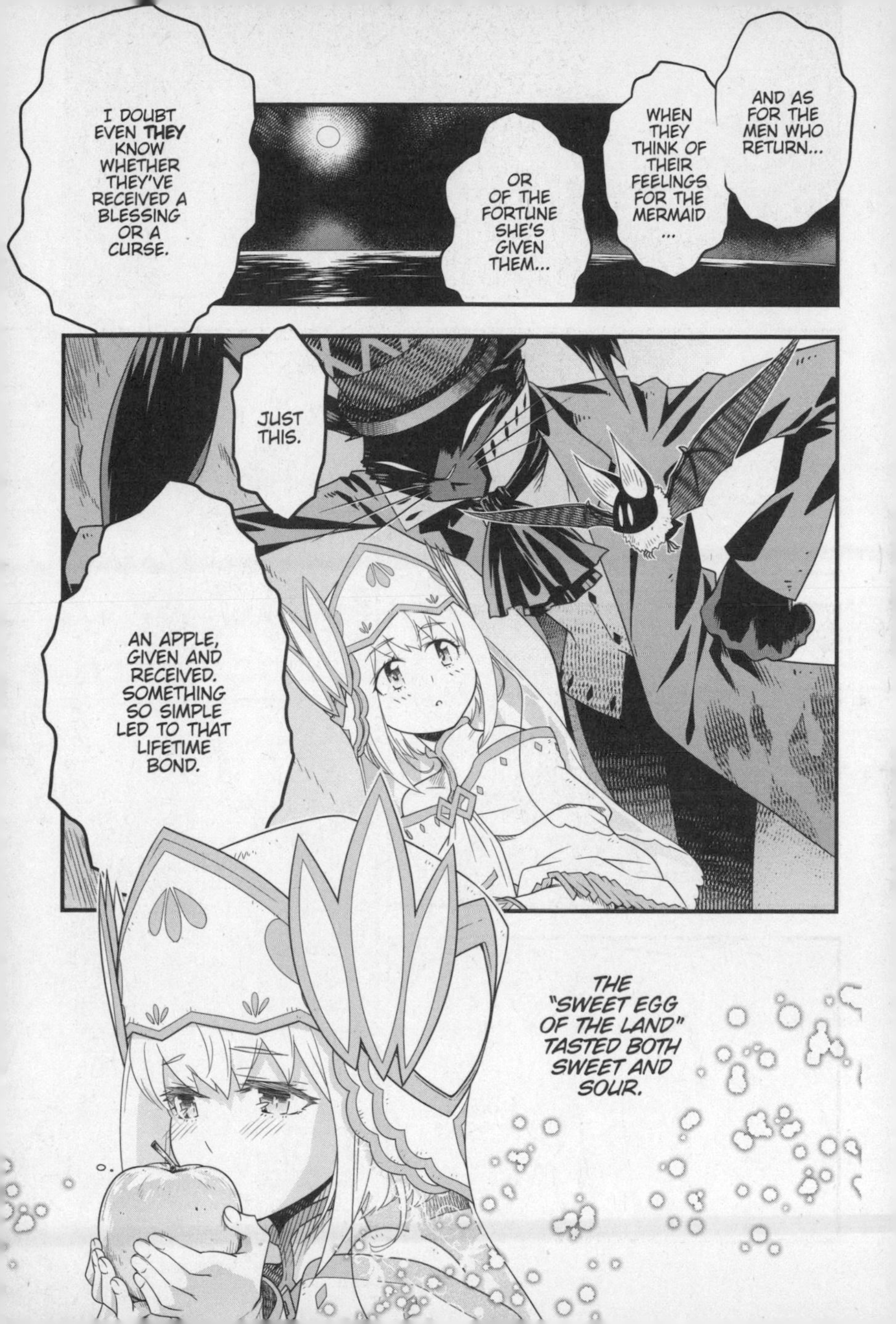
AND AS FOR THE MEN WHO RETURN...
WHEN THEY THINK OF THEIR FEELINGS FOR THE MERMAID ...
OR OF THE FORTUNE SHE'S GIVEN THEM...
I DOUBT EVEN THEY KNOW WHETHER THEY'VE RECEIVED A BLESSING OR A CURSE.
JUST THIS.
AN APPLE, GIVEN AND RECEIVED. SOMETHING SO SIMPLE LED TO THAT LIFETIME BOND.
THE "SWEET EGG OF THE LAND" TASTED BOTH SWEET AND SOUR.

Mythical Běast
≽Investigator≼

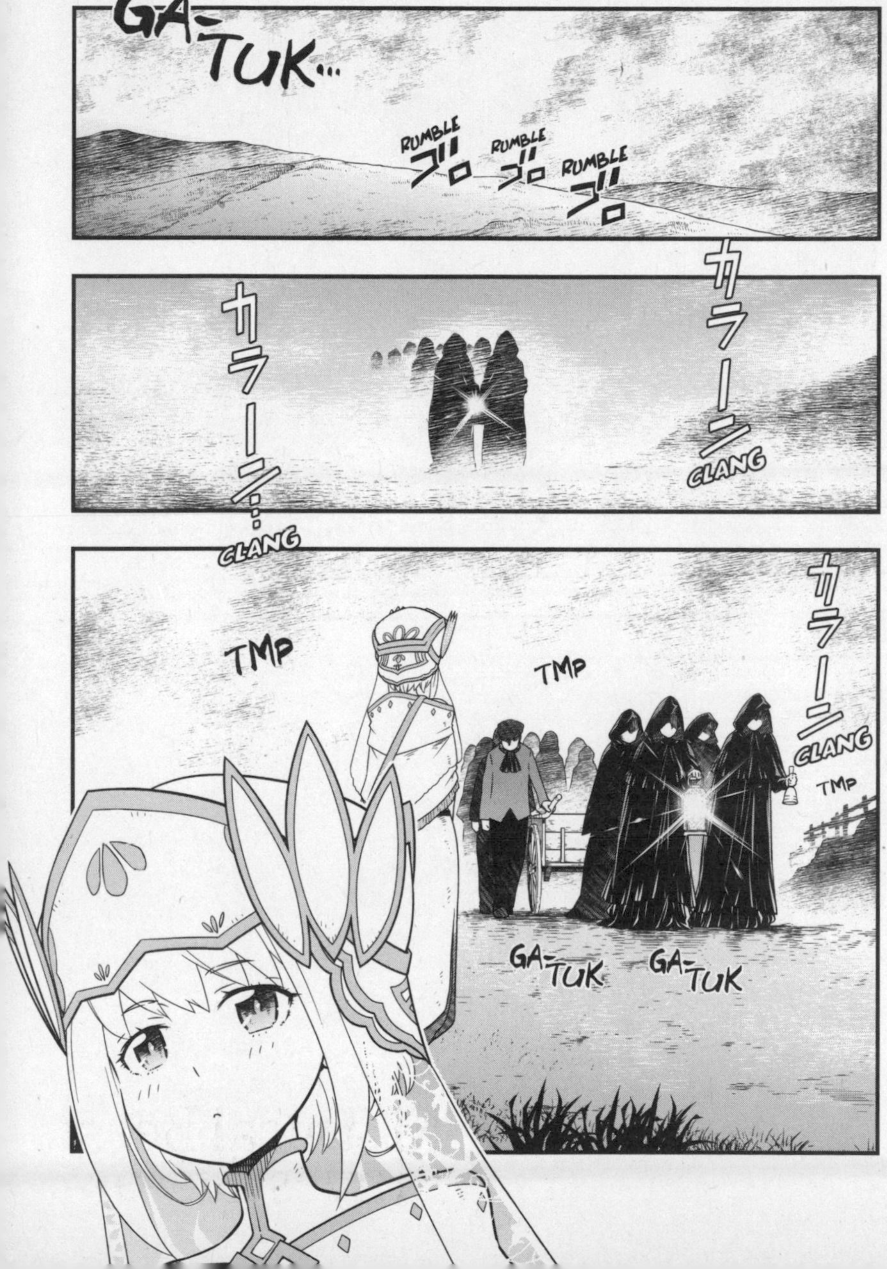
GA-TUK...
RUMBLE ゴロ
RUMBLE ゴロ
RUMBLE ゴロ
カラーン CLANG
カラーン… CLANG
カラーン CLANG
TMP
TMP
TMP
GA-TUK
GA-TUK

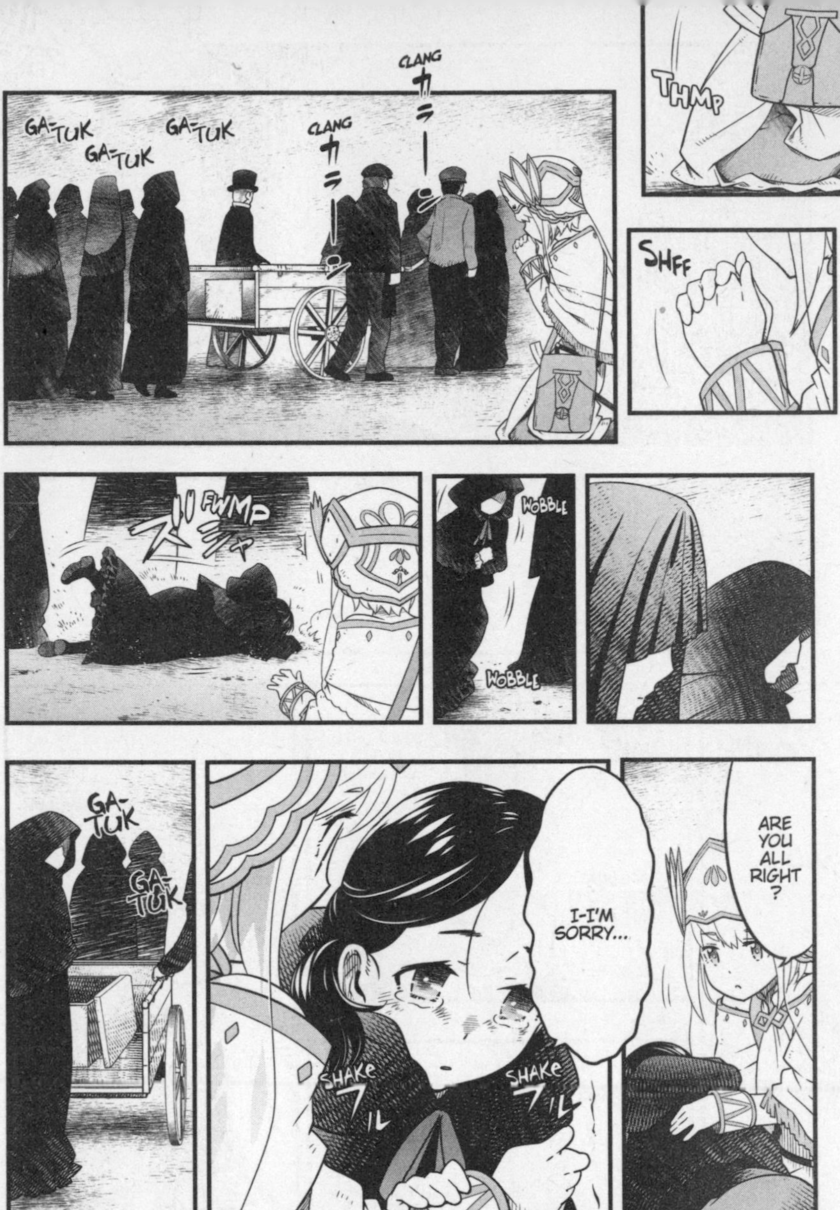
THMP
SHFF
CLANG
カラー
CLANG
カラー
GA-TUK
GA-TUK
GA-TUK
WOBBLE
WOBBLE
FWMP
ズシャ
ARE YOU ALL RIGHT?
I-I'M SORRY...
SHAKE
フル
SHAKE
フル
GA-TUK
GA-TUK

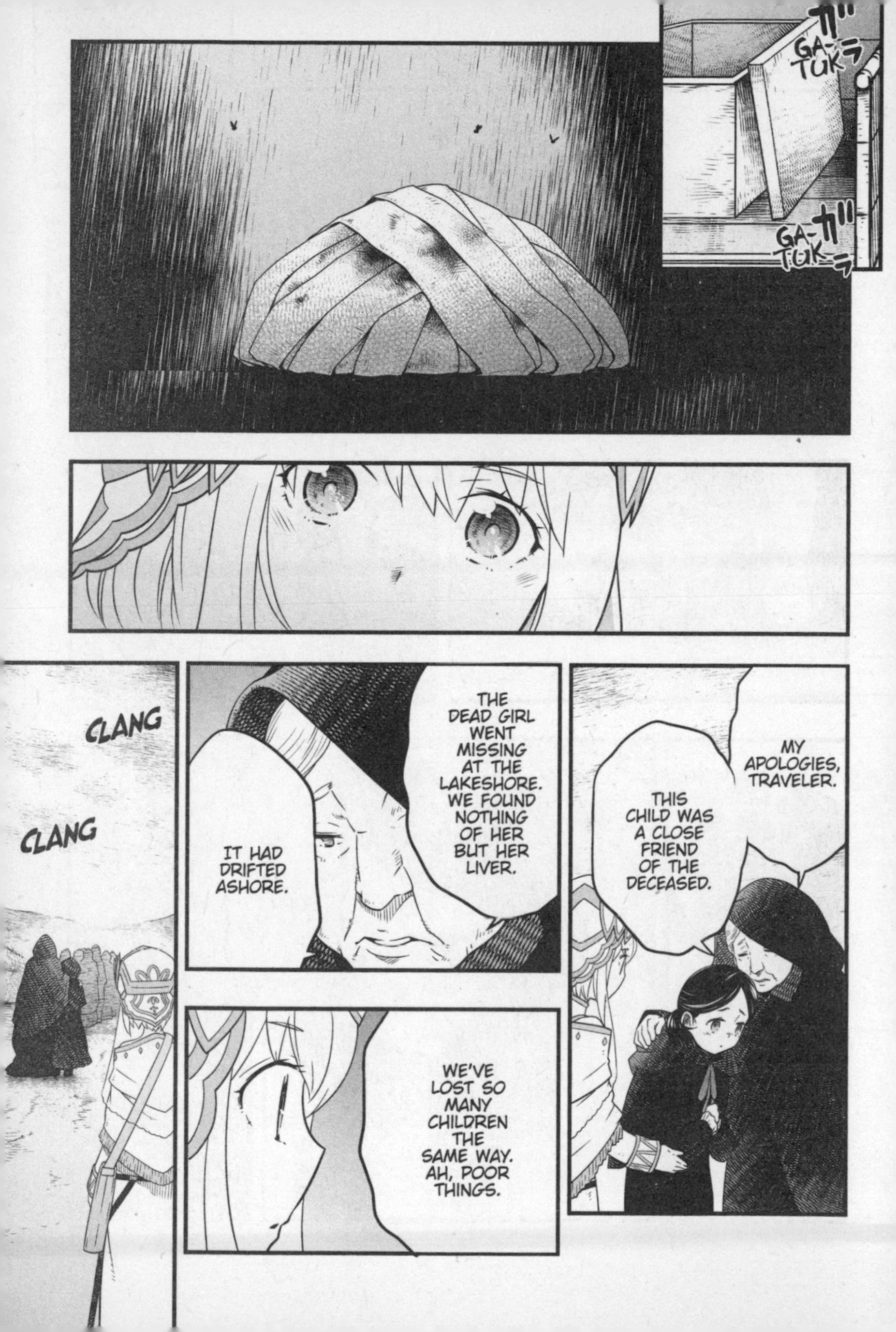
GA-TUK
GA-TUK
MY APOLOGIES, TRAVELER.
THIS CHILD WAS A CLOSE FRIEND OF THE DECEASED.
THE DEAD GIRL WENT MISSING AT THE LAKESHORE. WE FOUND NOTHING OF HER BUT HER LIVER.
IT HAD DRIFTED ASHORE.
WE'VE LOST SO MANY CHILDREN THE SAME WAY. AH, POOR THINGS.
CLANG
CLANG

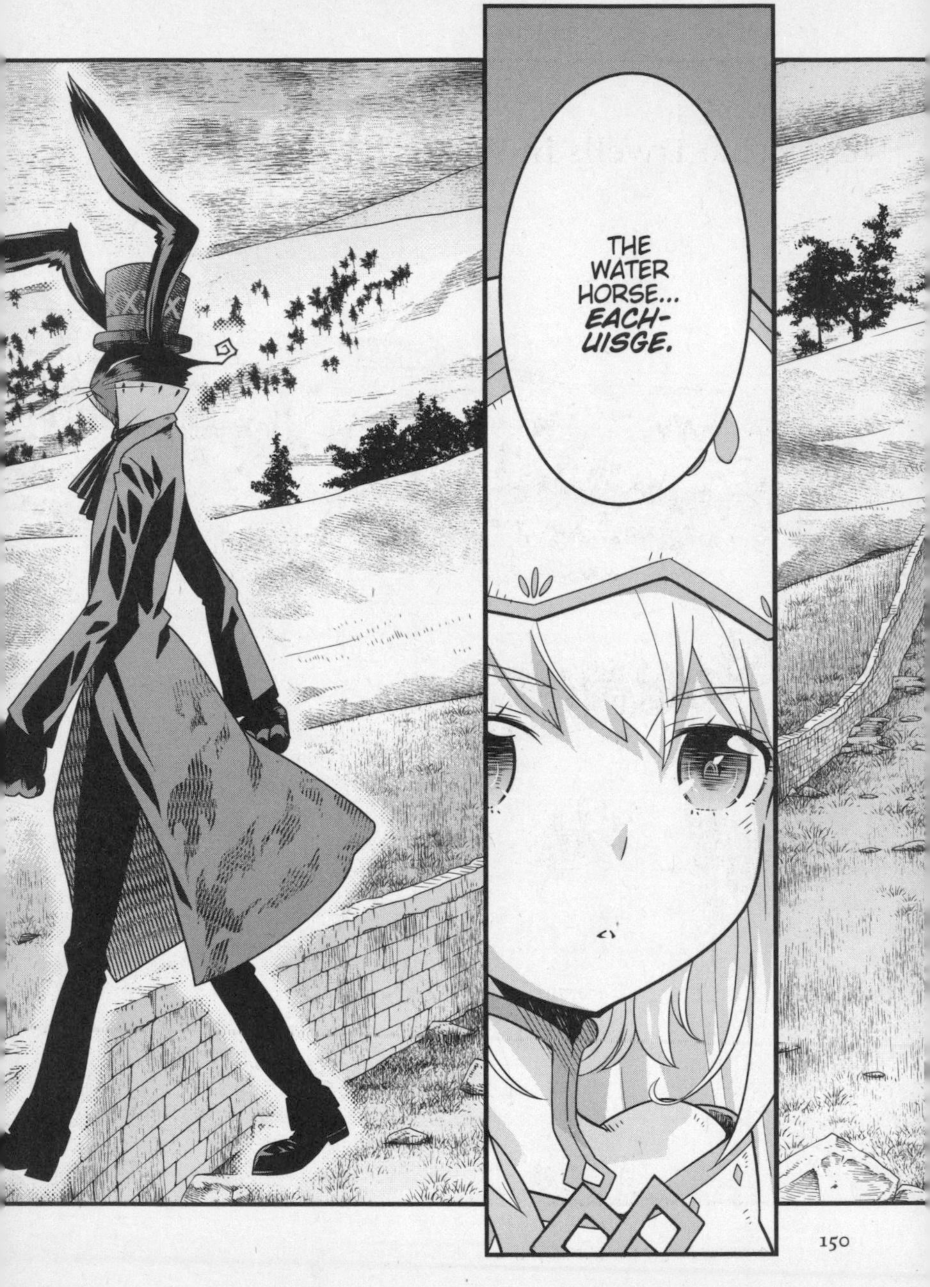
THE WATER HORSE... EACH-UISGE.

[Chapter 5]
Horse That Dwells in Water

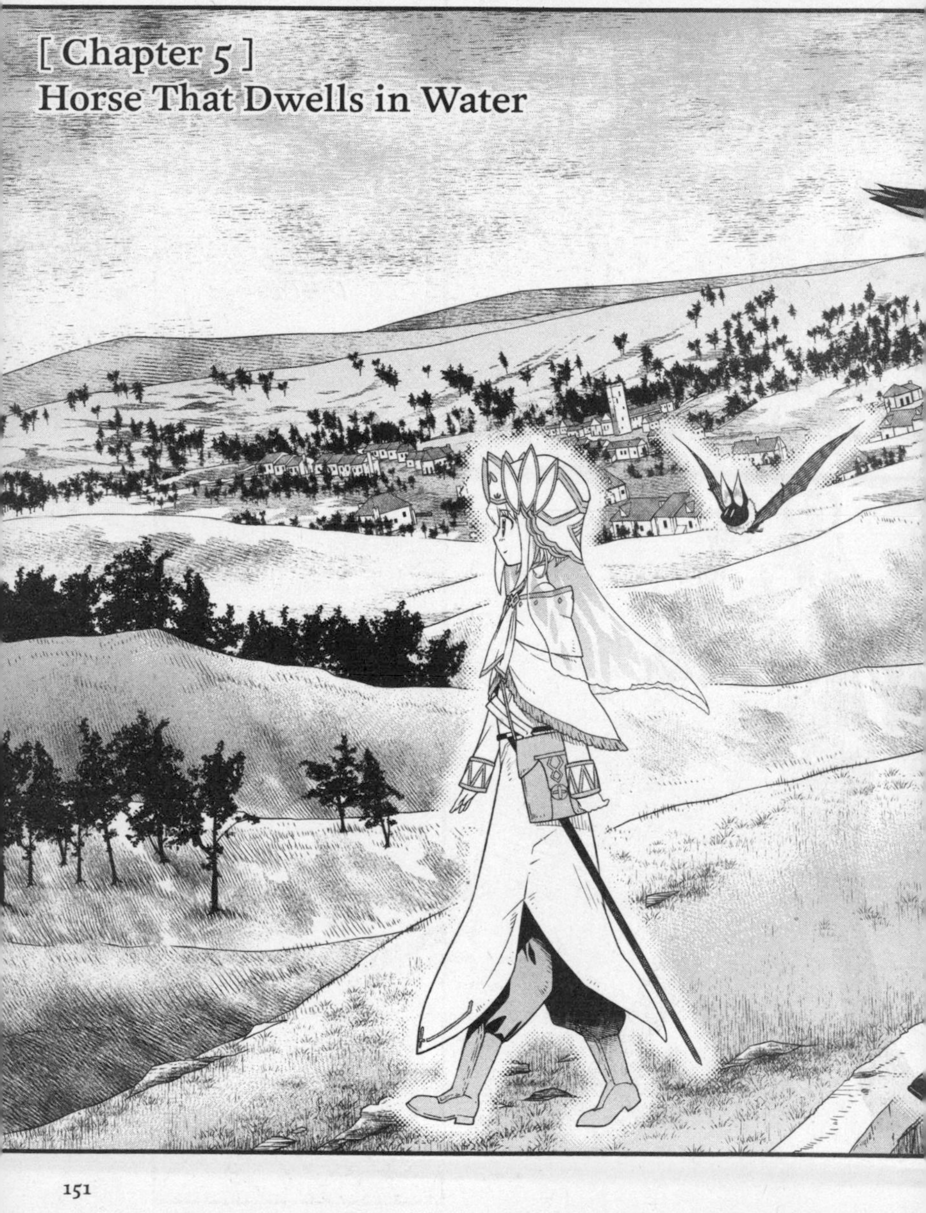

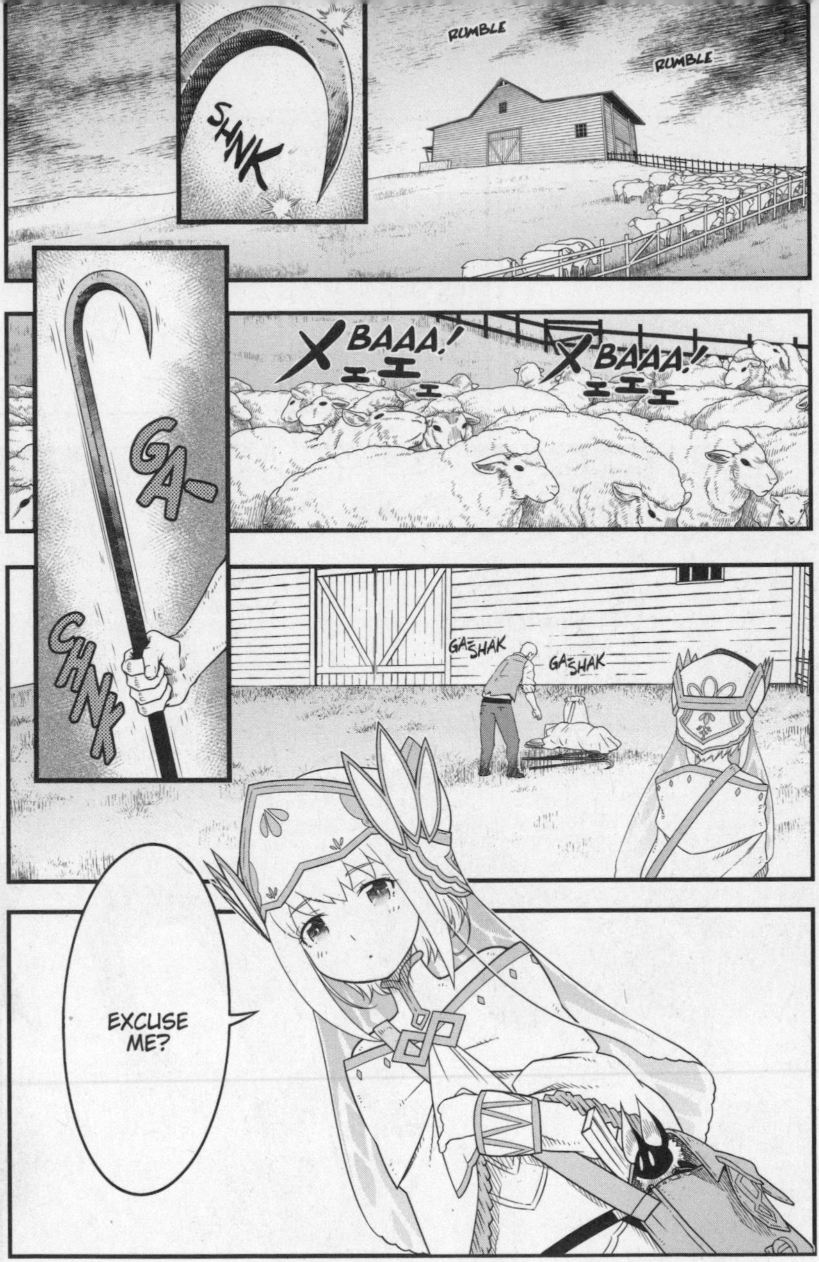
RUMBLE
RUMBLE
SHNK
BAAA!
BAAA!!
GA-SHAK
GA-SHAK
GA-CHNK
EXCUSE ME?

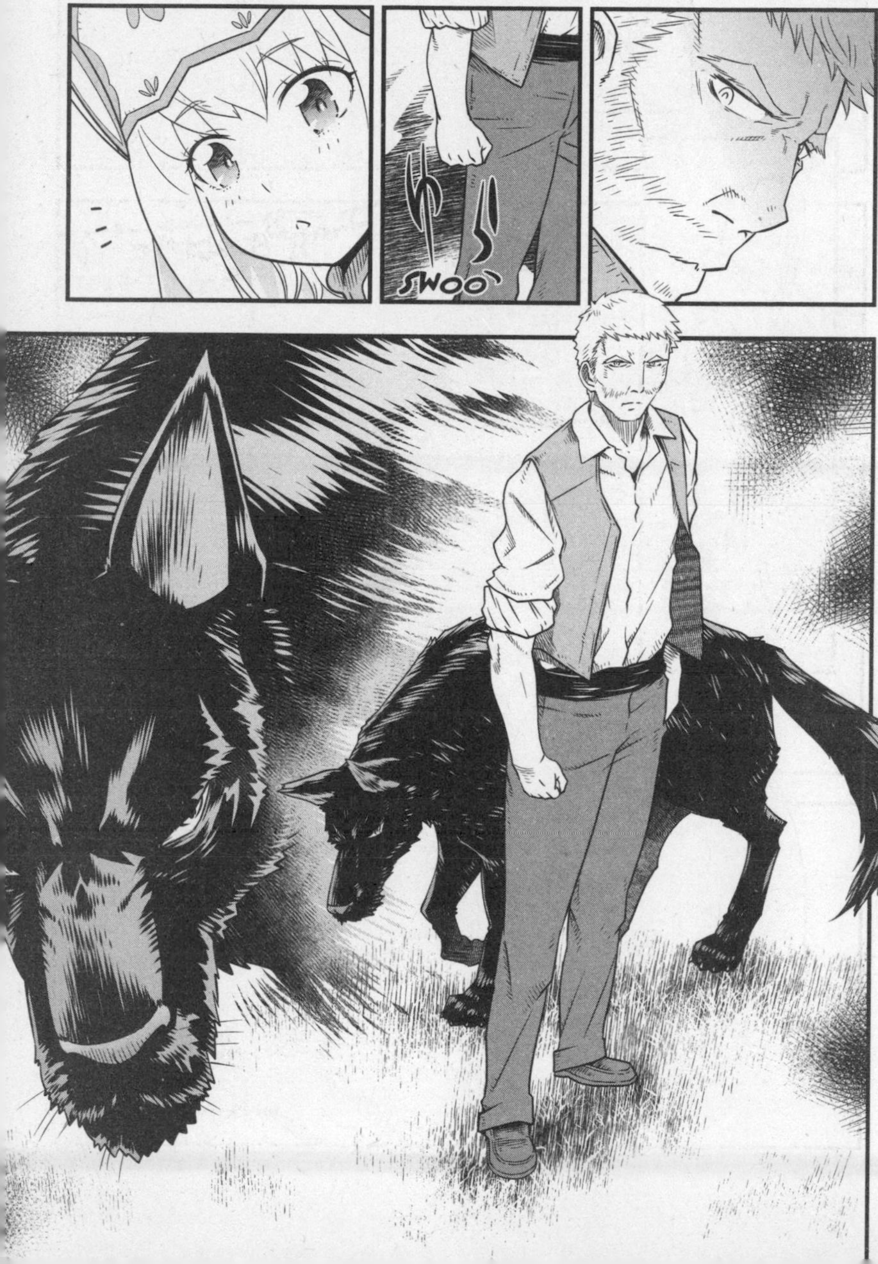
SWOO

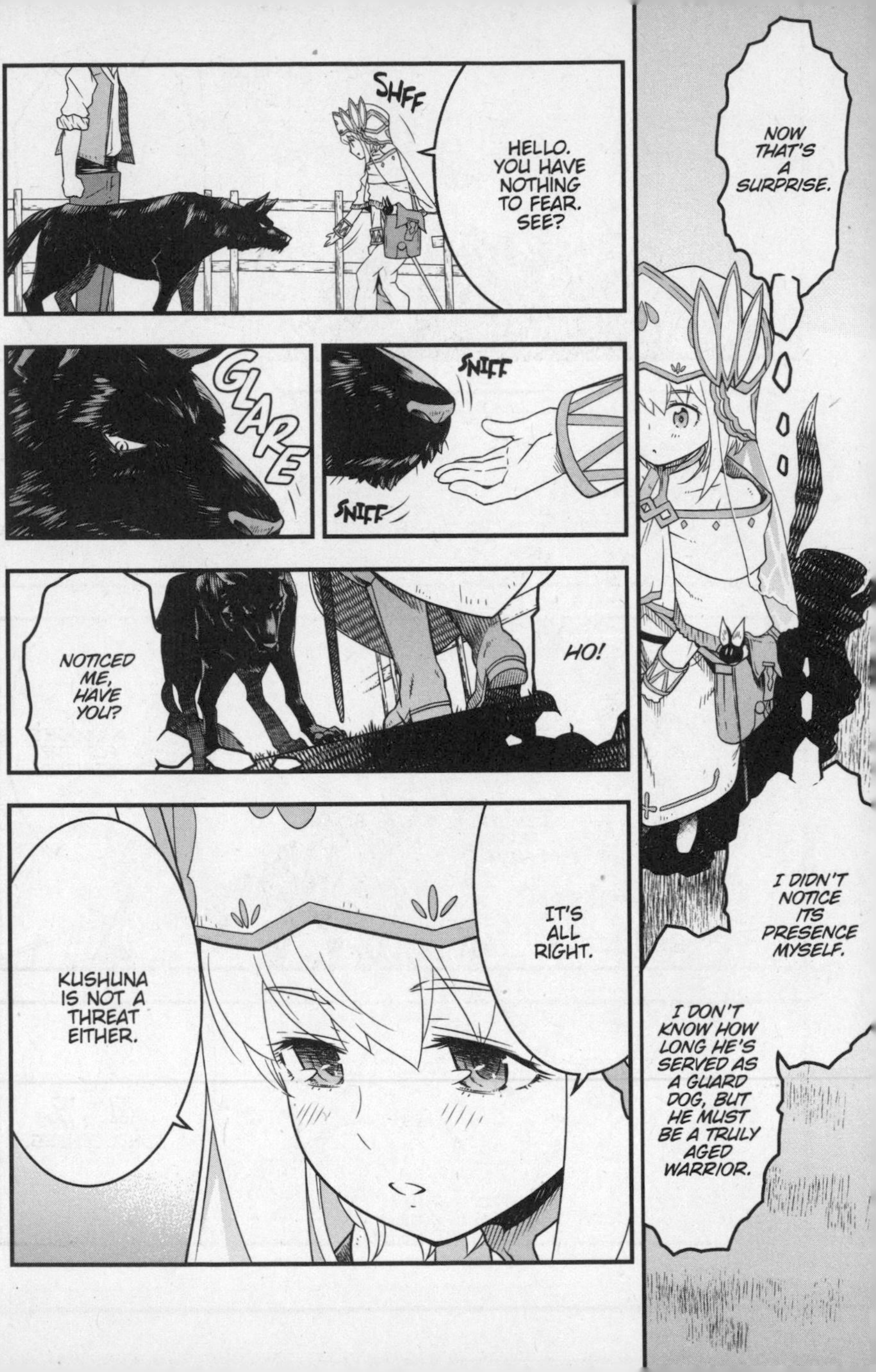
SHFF
HELLO. YOU HAVE NOTHING TO FEAR. SEE?
SNIFF
SNIFF
GLARE
HO!
NOTICED ME, HAVE YOU?
IT'S ALL RIGHT.
KUSHUNA IS NOT A THREAT EITHER.
NOW THAT'S A SURPRISE.
I DIDN'T NOTICE ITS PRESENCE MYSELF.
I DON'T KNOW HOW LONG HE'S SERVED AS A GUARD DOG, BUT HE MUST BE A TRULY AGED WARRIOR.

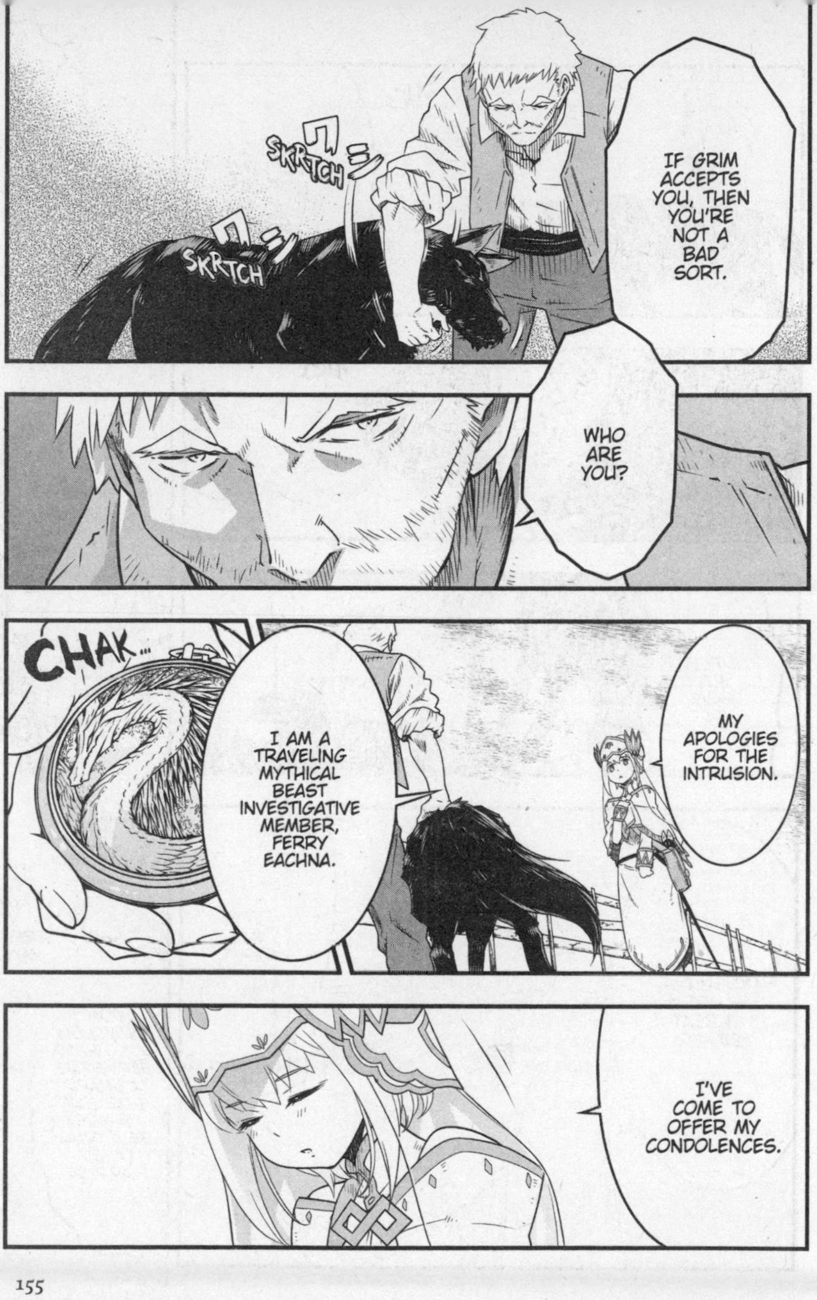
IF GRIM ACCEPTS YOU, THEN YOU'RE NOT A BAD SORT.
SKRTCH
SKRTCH
WHO ARE YOU?
MY APOLOGIES FOR THE INTRUSION.
I AM A TRAVELING MYTHICAL BEAST INVESTIGATIVE MEMBER, FERRY EACHNA.
CHAK...
I'VE COME TO OFFER MY CONDOLENCES.

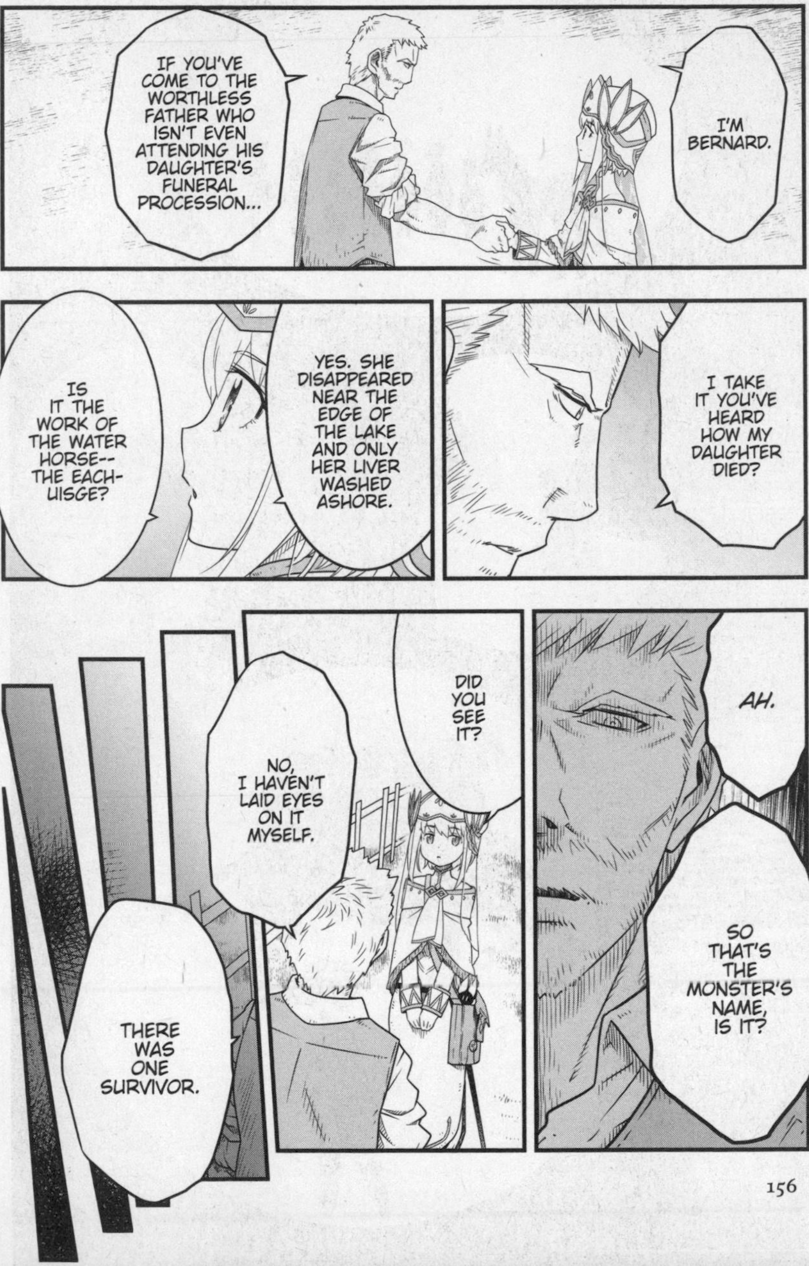
I'M BERNARD.
IF YOU'VE COME TO THE WORTHLESS FATHER WHO ISN'T EVEN ATTENDING HIS DAUGHTER'S FUNERAL PROCESSION...
I TAKE IT YOU'VE HEARD HOW MY DAUGHTER DIED?
YES. SHE DISAPPEARED NEAR THE EDGE OF THE LAKE AND ONLY HER LIVER WASHED ASHORE.
IS IT THE WORK OF THE WATER HORSE-- THE EACH-UISGE?
AH.
SO THAT'S THE MONSTER'S NAME, IS IT?
DID YOU SEE IT?
NO, I HAVEN'T LAID EYES ON IT MYSELF.
THERE WAS ONE SURVIVOR.

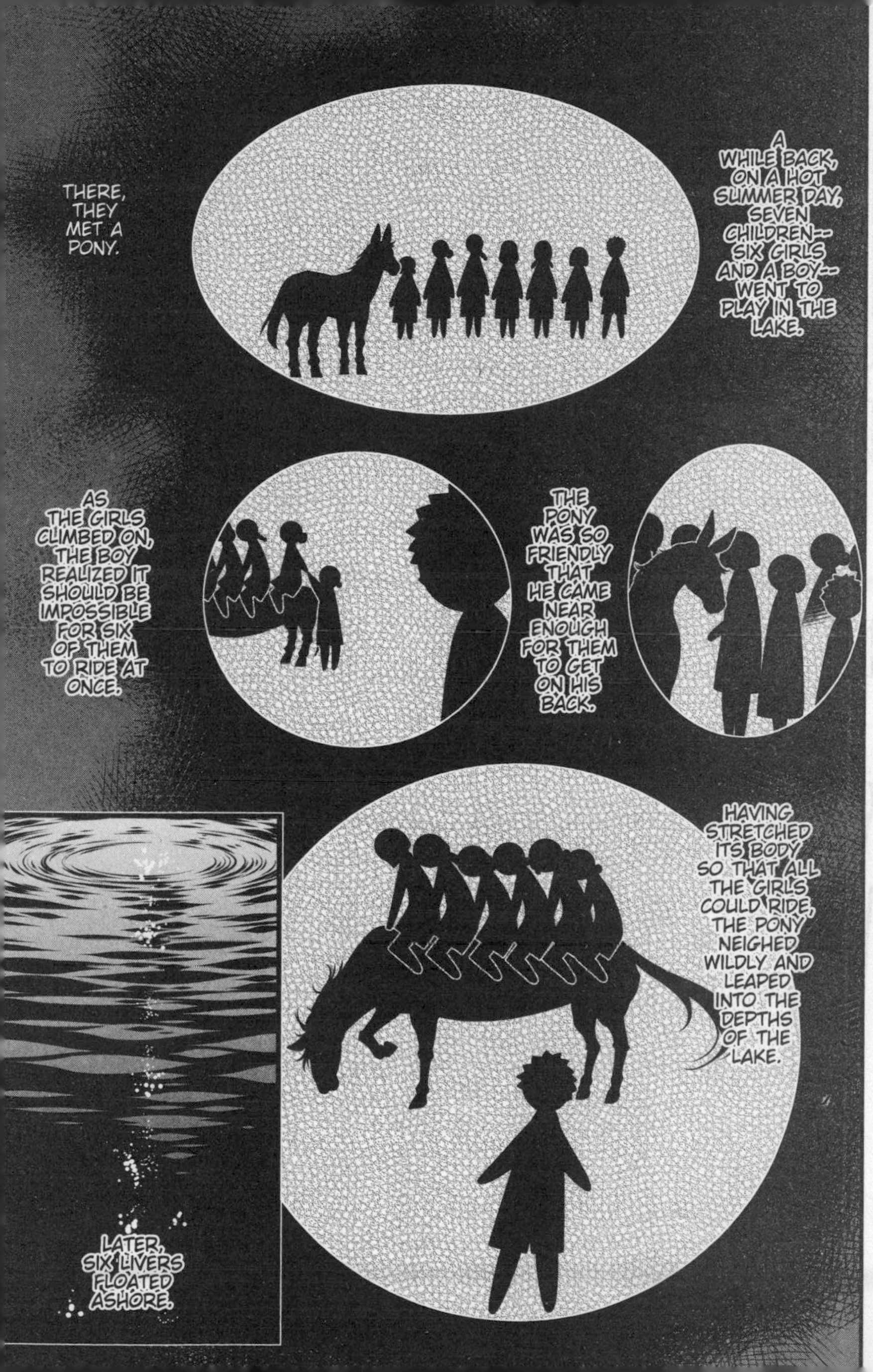
A WHILE BACK, ON A HOT SUMMER DAY, SEVEN CHILDREN-- SIX GIRLS AND A BOY-- WENT TO PLAY IN THE LAKE.
THERE, THEY MET A PONY.
THE PONY WAS SO FRIENDLY THAT HE CAME NEAR ENOUGH FOR THEM TO GET ON HIS BACK.
AS THE GIRLS CLIMBED ON, THE BOY REALIZED IT SHOULD BE IMPOSSIBLE FOR SIX OF THEM TO RIDE AT ONCE.
HAVING STRETCHED ITS BODY SO THAT ALL THE GIRLS COULD RIDE, THE PONY NEIGHED WILDLY AND LEAPED INTO THE DEPTHS OF THE LAKE.
LATER, SIX LIVERS FLOATED ASHORE.

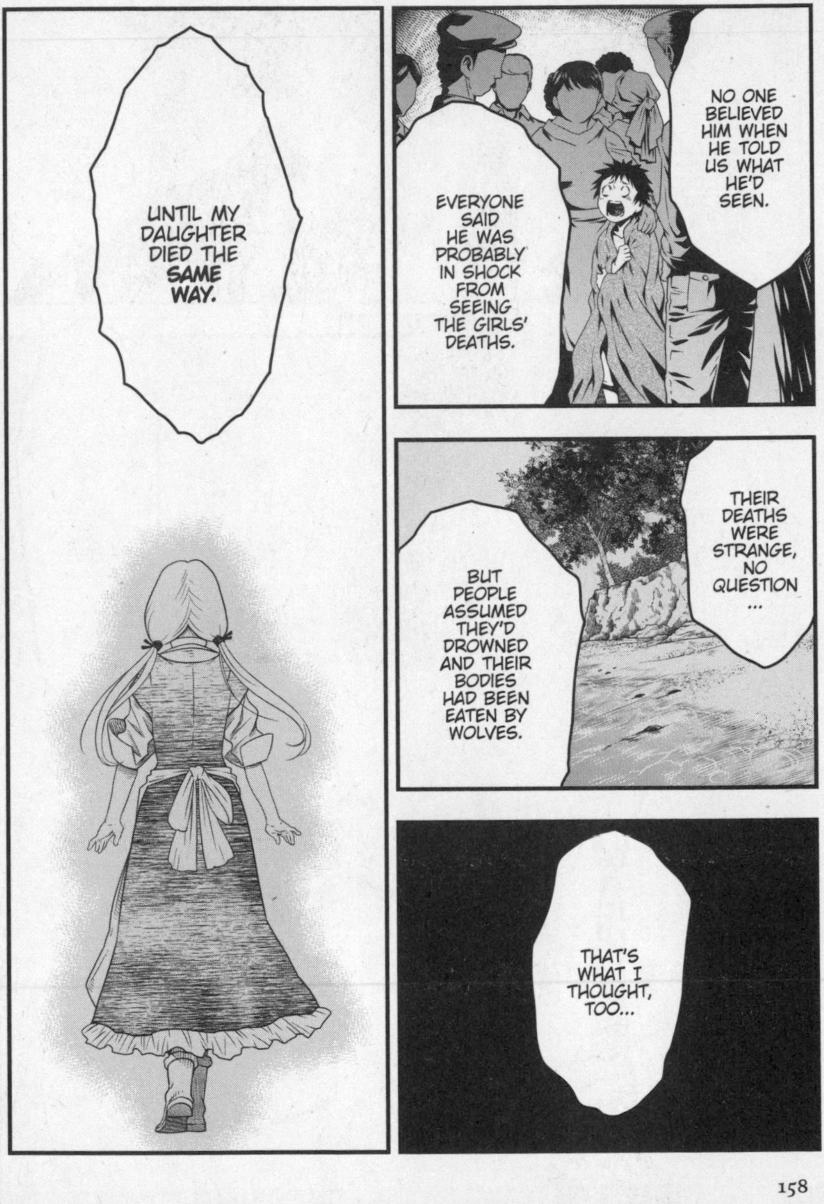
NO ONE BELIEVED HIM WHEN HE TOLD US WHAT HE'D SEEN.
EVERYONE SAID HE WAS PROBABLY IN SHOCK FROM SEEING THE GIRLS' DEATHS.
THEIR DEATHS WERE STRANGE, NO QUESTION...
BUT PEOPLE ASSUMED THEY'D DROWNED AND THEIR BODIES HAD BEEN EATEN BY WOLVES.
THAT'S WHAT I THOUGHT, TOO...
UNTIL MY DAUGHTER DIED THE **SAME WAY.**

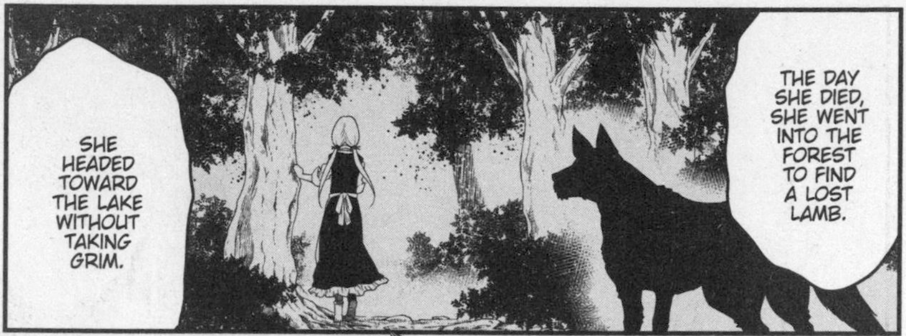
THE DAY SHE DIED, SHE WENT INTO THE FOREST TO FIND A LOST LAMB.
SHE HEADED TOWARD THE LAKE WITHOUT TAKING GRIM.
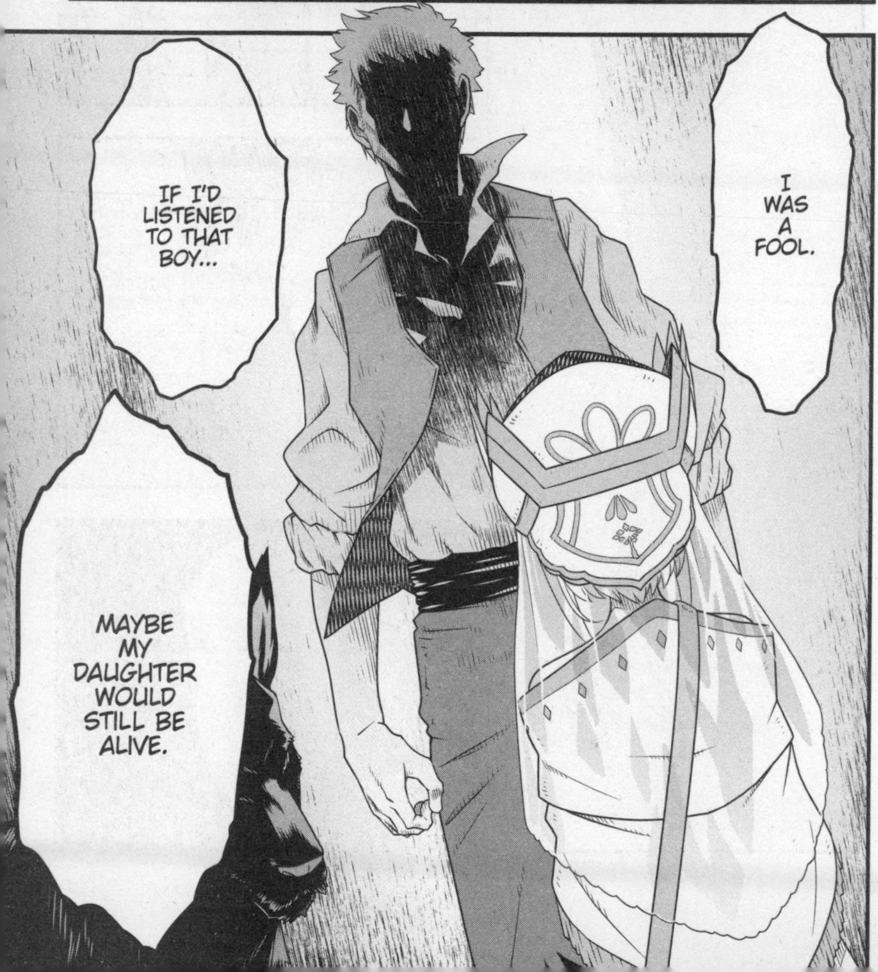
I WAS A FOOL.
IF I'D LISTENED TO THAT BOY...
MAYBE MY DAUGHTER WOULD STILL BE ALIVE.

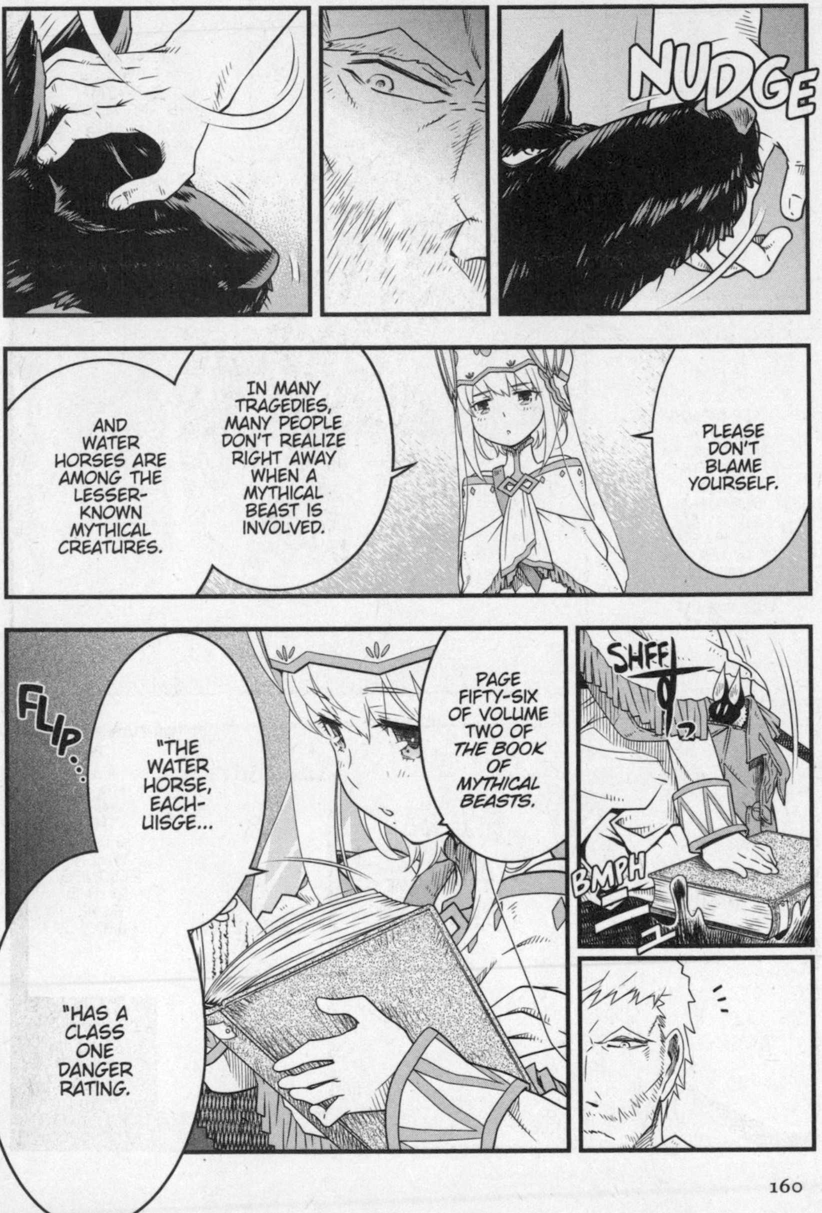
NUDGE
PLEASE DON'T BLAME YOURSELF.
IN MANY TRAGEDIES, MANY PEOPLE DON'T REALIZE RIGHT AWAY WHEN A MYTHICAL BEAST IS INVOLVED.
AND WATER HORSES ARE AMONG THE LESSER-KNOWN MYTHICAL CREATURES.
SHFF
BMPH
PAGE FIFTY-SIX OF VOLUME TWO OF *THE BOOK OF MYTHICAL BEASTS.*
FLIP...
"THE WATER HORSE, EACH-UISGE...
"HAS A CLASS ONE DANGER RATING.

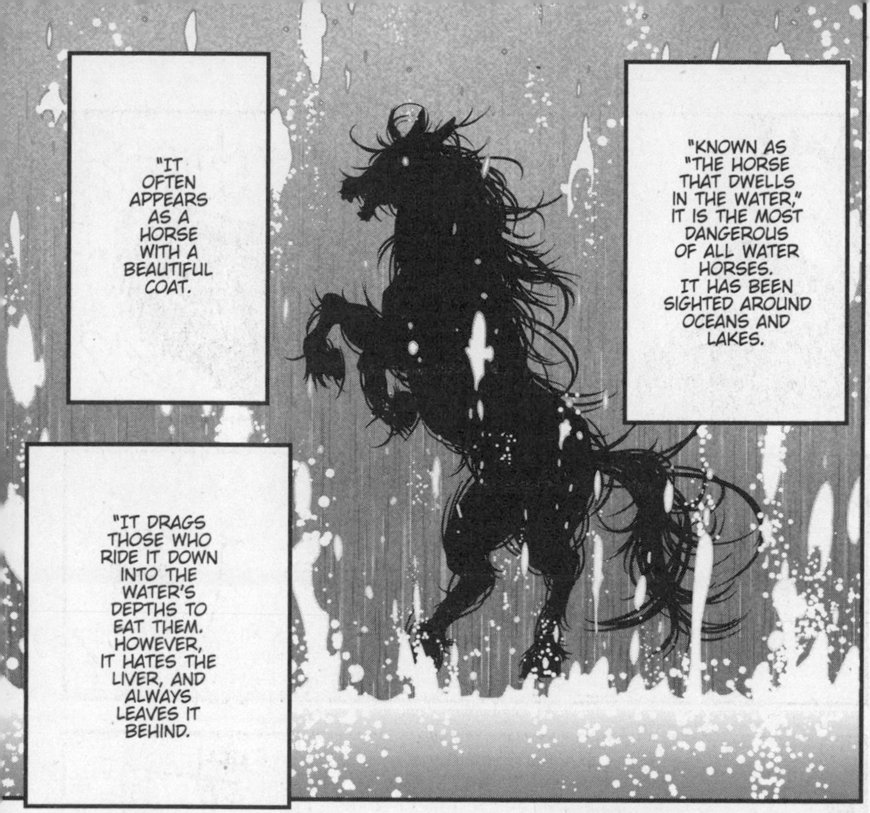
"KNOWN AS "THE HORSE THAT DWELLS IN THE WATER," IT IS THE MOST DANGEROUS OF ALL WATER HORSES. IT HAS BEEN SIGHTED AROUND OCEANS AND LAKES.
"IT OFTEN APPEARS AS A HORSE WITH A BEAUTIFUL COAT.
"IT DRAGS THOSE WHO RIDE IT DOWN INTO THE WATER'S DEPTHS TO EAT THEM. HOWEVER, IT HATES THE LIVER, AND ALWAYS LEAVES IT BEHIND.
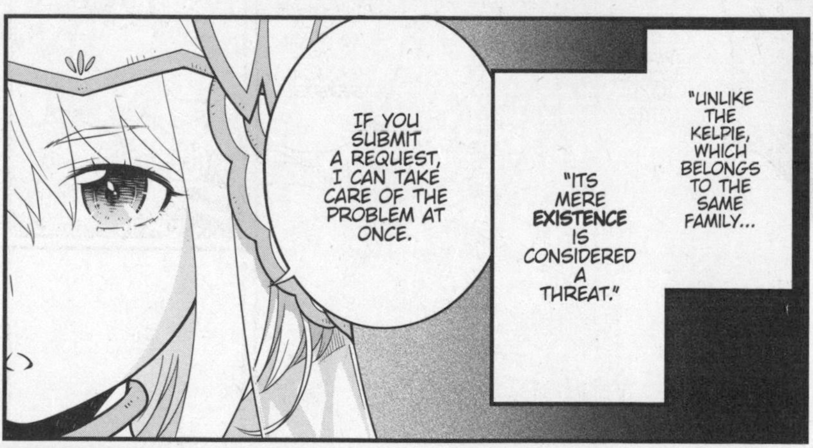
"UNLIKE THE KELPIE, WHICH BELONGS TO THE SAME FAMILY...
"ITS MERE **EXISTENCE** IS CONSIDERED A THREAT."
IF YOU SUBMIT A REQUEST, I CAN TAKE CARE OF THE PROBLEM AT ONCE.

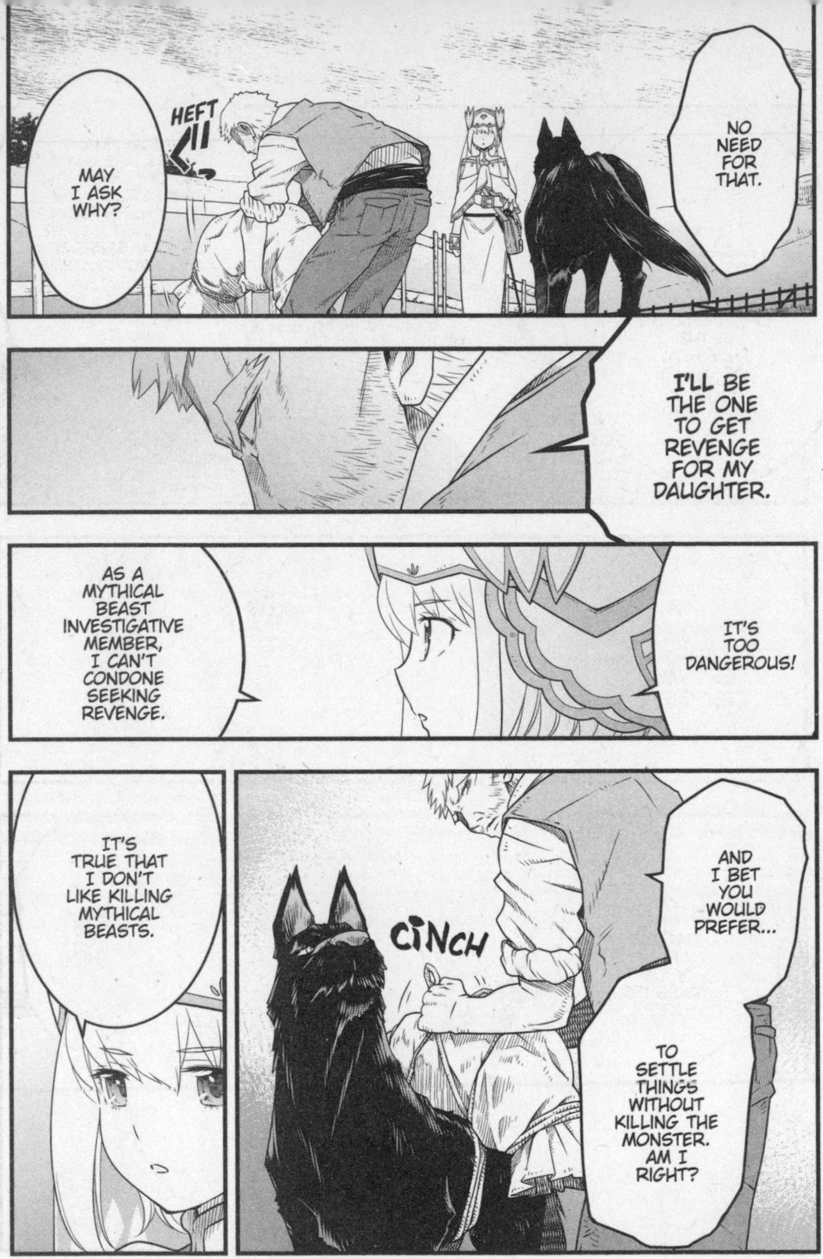
NO NEED FOR THAT.
HEFT
MAY I ASK WHY?
I'LL BE THE ONE TO GET REVENGE FOR MY DAUGHTER.
IT'S TOO DANGEROUS!
AS A MYTHICAL BEAST INVESTIGATIVE MEMBER, I CAN'T CONDONE SEEKING REVENGE.
AND I BET YOU WOULD PREFER...
CINCH
TO SETTLE THINGS WITHOUT KILLING THE MONSTER. AM I RIGHT?
IT'S TRUE THAT I DON'T LIKE KILLING MYTHICAL BEASTS.

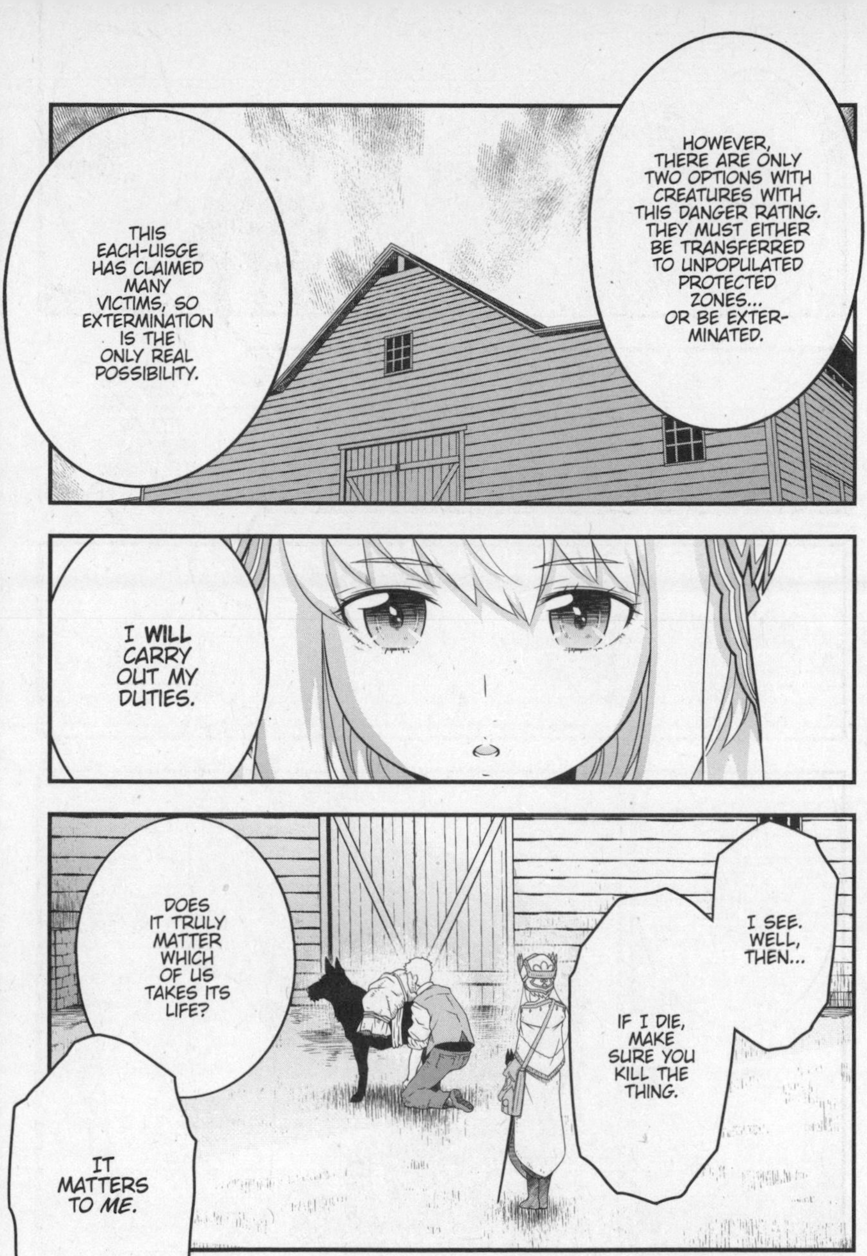
HOWEVER, THERE ARE ONLY TWO OPTIONS WITH CREATURES WITH THIS DANGER RATING. THEY MUST EITHER BE TRANSFERRED TO UNPOPULATED PROTECTED ZONES... OR BE EXTERMINATED.
THIS EACH-UISGE HAS CLAIMED MANY VICTIMS, SO EXTERMINATION IS THE ONLY REAL POSSIBILITY.
I **WILL** CARRY OUT MY DUTIES.
I SEE. WELL, THEN...
IF I DIE, MAKE SURE YOU KILL THE THING.
DOES IT TRULY MATTER WHICH OF US TAKES ITS LIFE?
IT MATTERS TO *ME*.

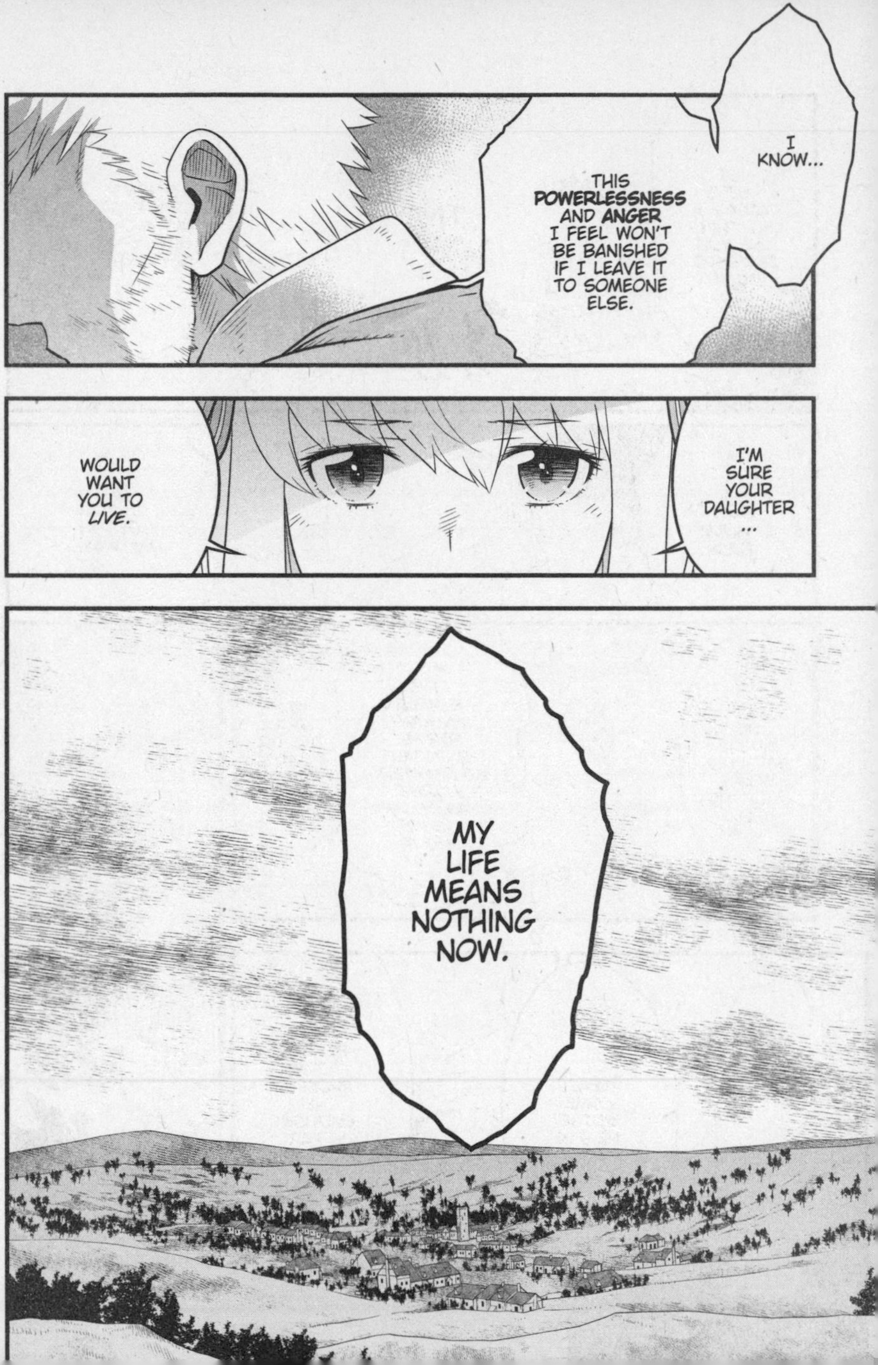
I KNOW...
THIS POWERLESSNESS AND ANGER I FEEL WON'T BE BANISHED IF I LEAVE IT TO SOMEONE ELSE.
I'M SURE YOUR DAUGHTER ...
WOULD WANT YOU TO LIVE.
MY LIFE MEANS NOTHING NOW.

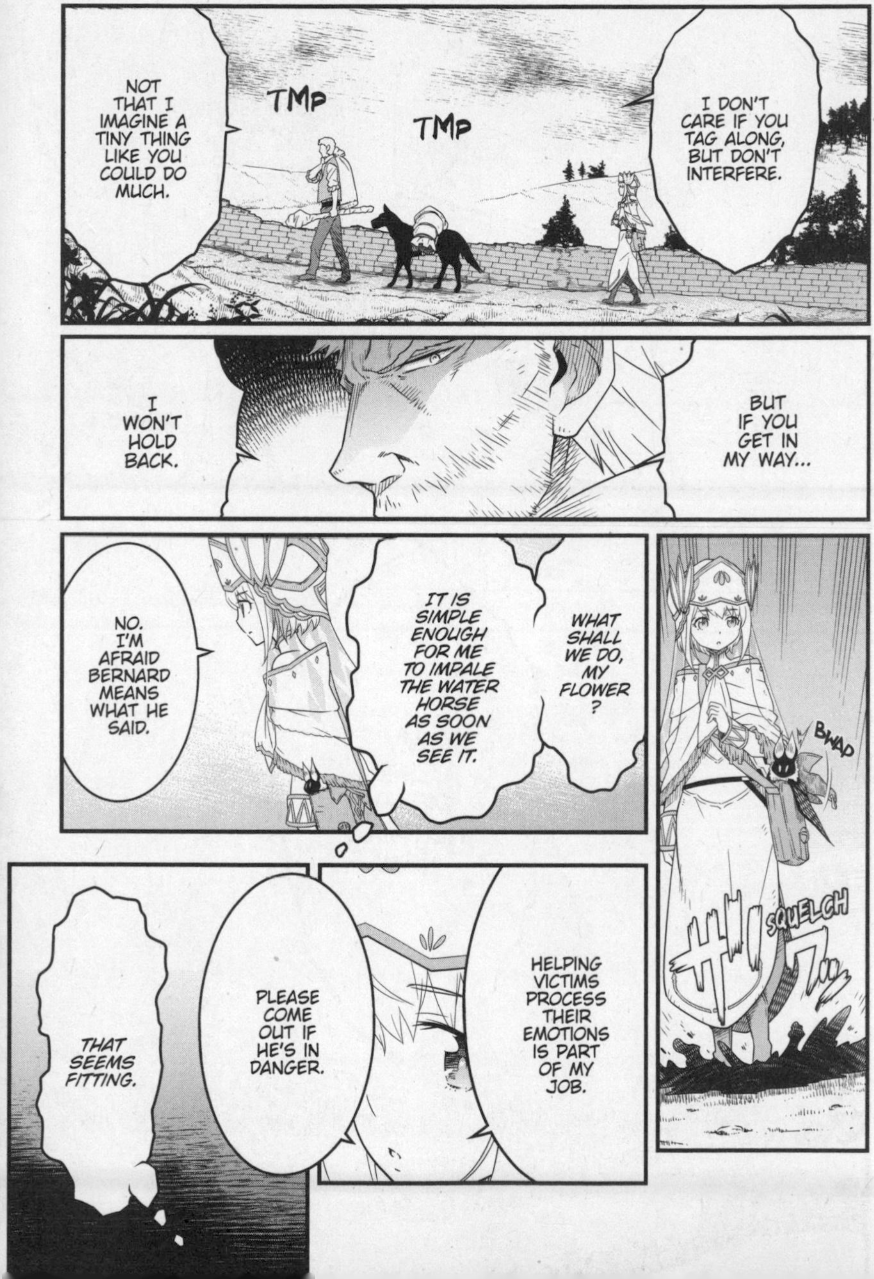
I DON'T CARE IF YOU TAG ALONG, BUT DON'T INTERFERE.
TMP
TMP
NOT THAT I IMAGINE A TINY THING LIKE YOU COULD DO MUCH.
BUT IF YOU GET IN MY WAY...
I WON'T HOLD BACK.
BWAP
SQUELCH
WHAT SHALL WE DO, MY FLOWER?
IT IS SIMPLE ENOUGH FOR ME TO IMPALE THE WATER HORSE AS SOON AS WE SEE IT.
NO. I'M AFRAID BERNARD MEANS WHAT HE SAID.
HELPING VICTIMS PROCESS THEIR EMOTIONS IS PART OF MY JOB.
PLEASE COME OUT IF HE'S IN DANGER.
THAT SEEMS FITTING.

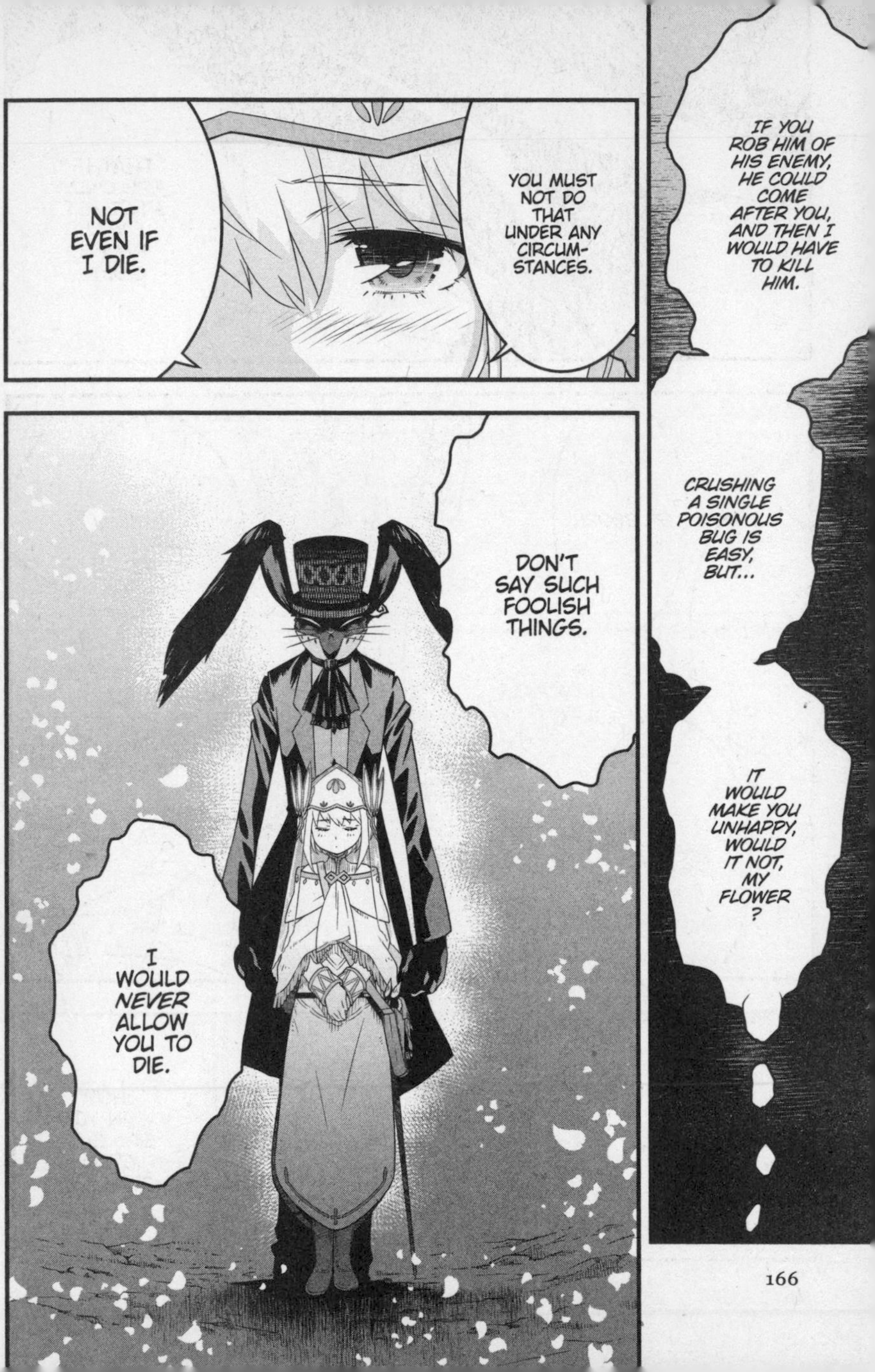
IF YOU ROB HIM OF HIS ENEMY, HE COULD COME AFTER YOU, AND THEN I WOULD HAVE TO KILL HIM.
CRUSHING A SINGLE POISONOUS BUG IS EASY, BUT...
IT WOULD MAKE YOU UNHAPPY, WOULD IT NOT, MY FLOWER?
YOU MUST NOT DO THAT UNDER ANY CIRCUM-STANCES.
NOT EVEN IF I DIE.
DON'T SAY SUCH FOOLISH THINGS.
I WOULD NEVER ALLOW YOU TO DIE.

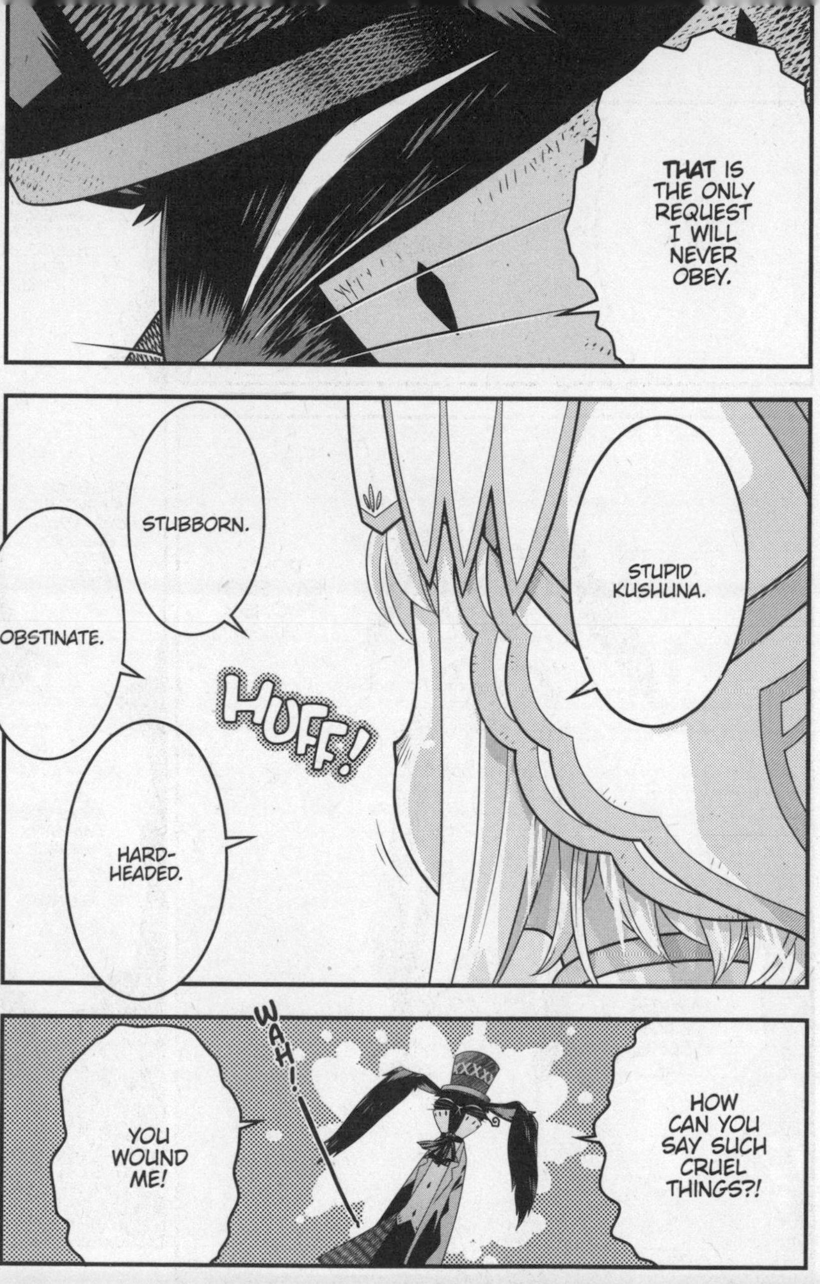
THAT IS THE ONLY REQUEST I WILL NEVER OBEY.
STUPID KUSHUNA.
HUFF!
STUBBORN.
OBSTINATE.
HARD-HEADED.
HOW CAN YOU SAY SUCH CRUEL THINGS?!
WAH!
YOU WOUND ME!

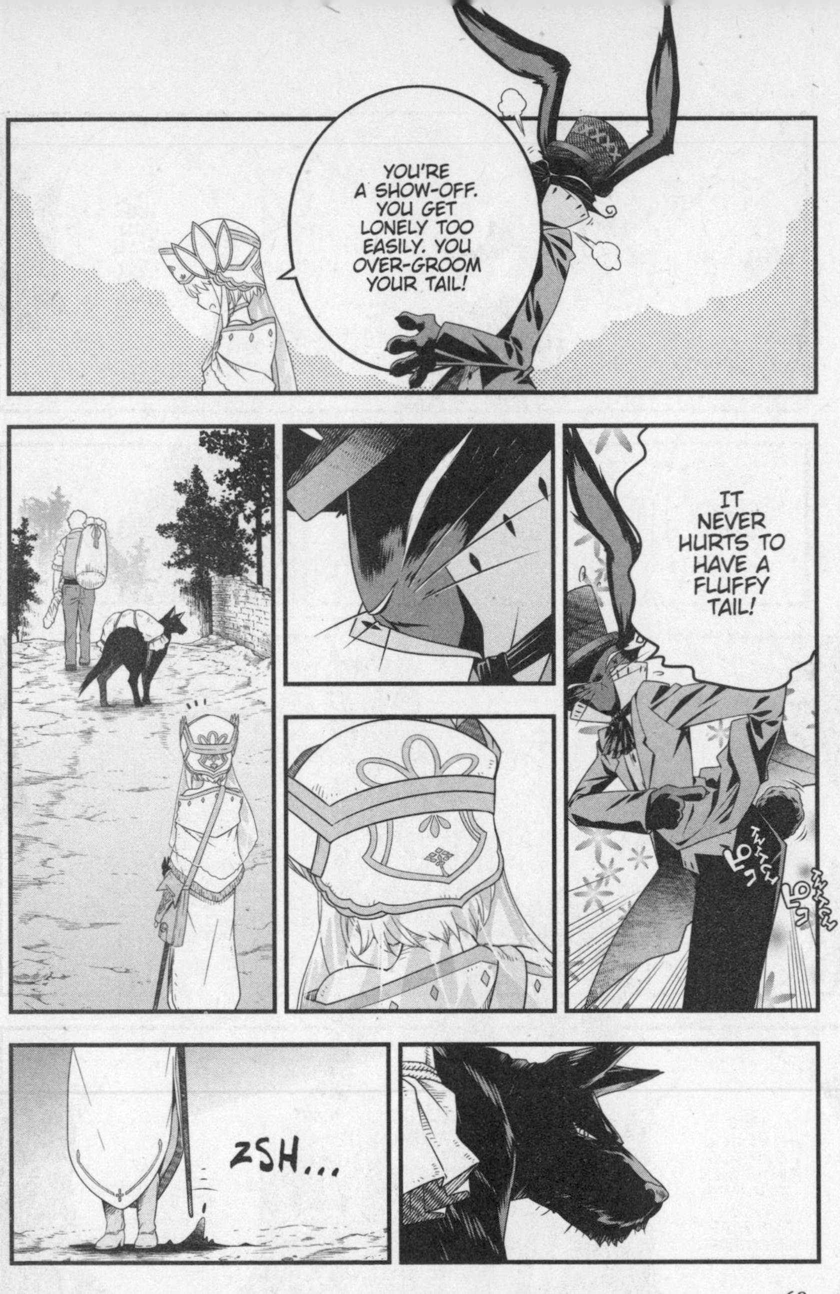
YOU'RE A SHOW-OFF. YOU GET LONELY TOO EASILY. YOU OVER-GROOM YOUR TAIL!
IT NEVER HURTS TO HAVE A FLUFFY TAIL!
TWITCH
TWITCH
ZSH...

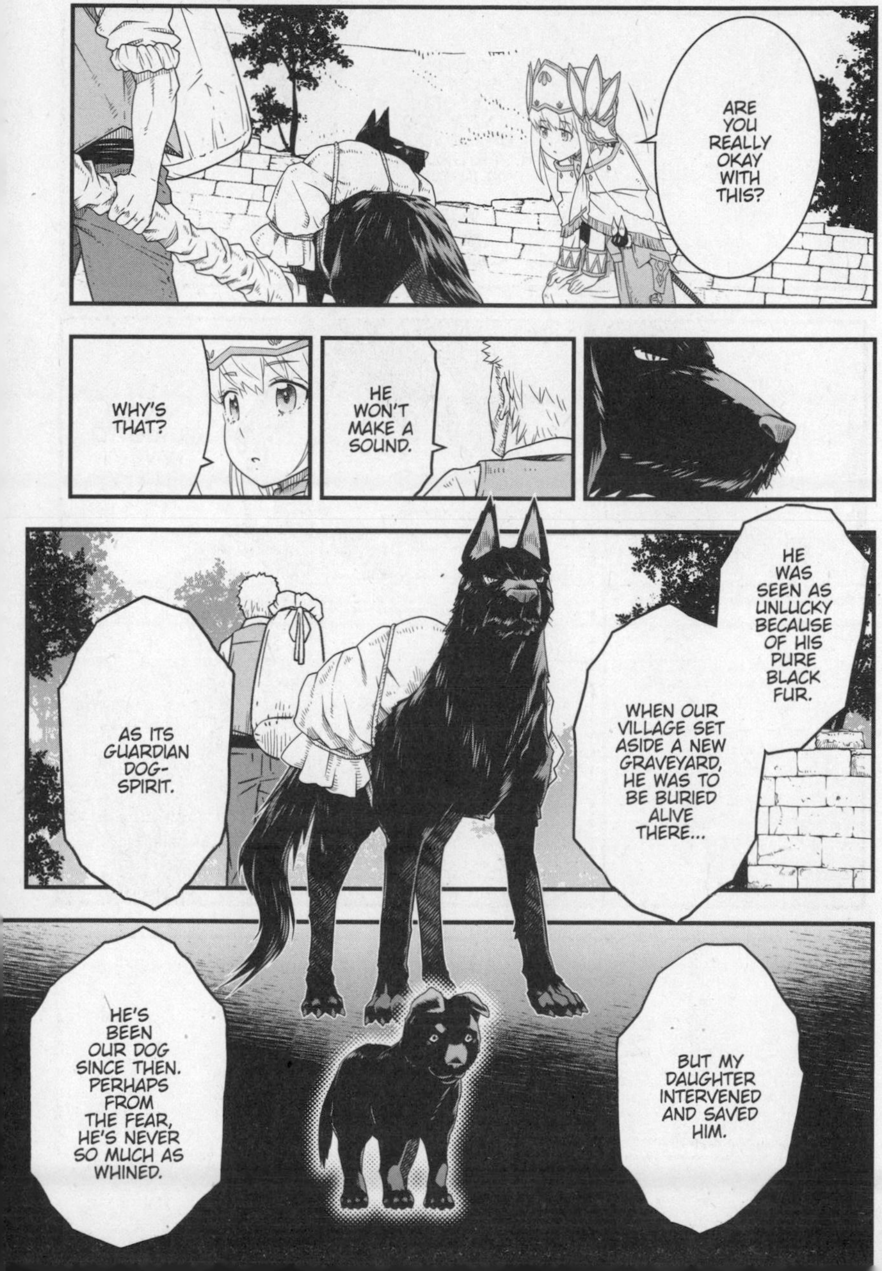
ARE YOU REALLY OKAY WITH THIS?
HE WON'T MAKE A SOUND.
WHY'S THAT?
HE WAS SEEN AS UNLUCKY BECAUSE OF HIS PURE BLACK FUR.
WHEN OUR VILLAGE SET ASIDE A NEW GRAVEYARD, HE WAS TO BE BURIED ALIVE THERE...
AS ITS GUARDIAN DOG-SPIRIT.
BUT MY DAUGHTER INTERVENED AND SAVED HIM.
HE'S BEEN OUR DOG SINCE THEN. PERHAPS FROM THE FEAR, HE'S NEVER SO MUCH AS WHINED.

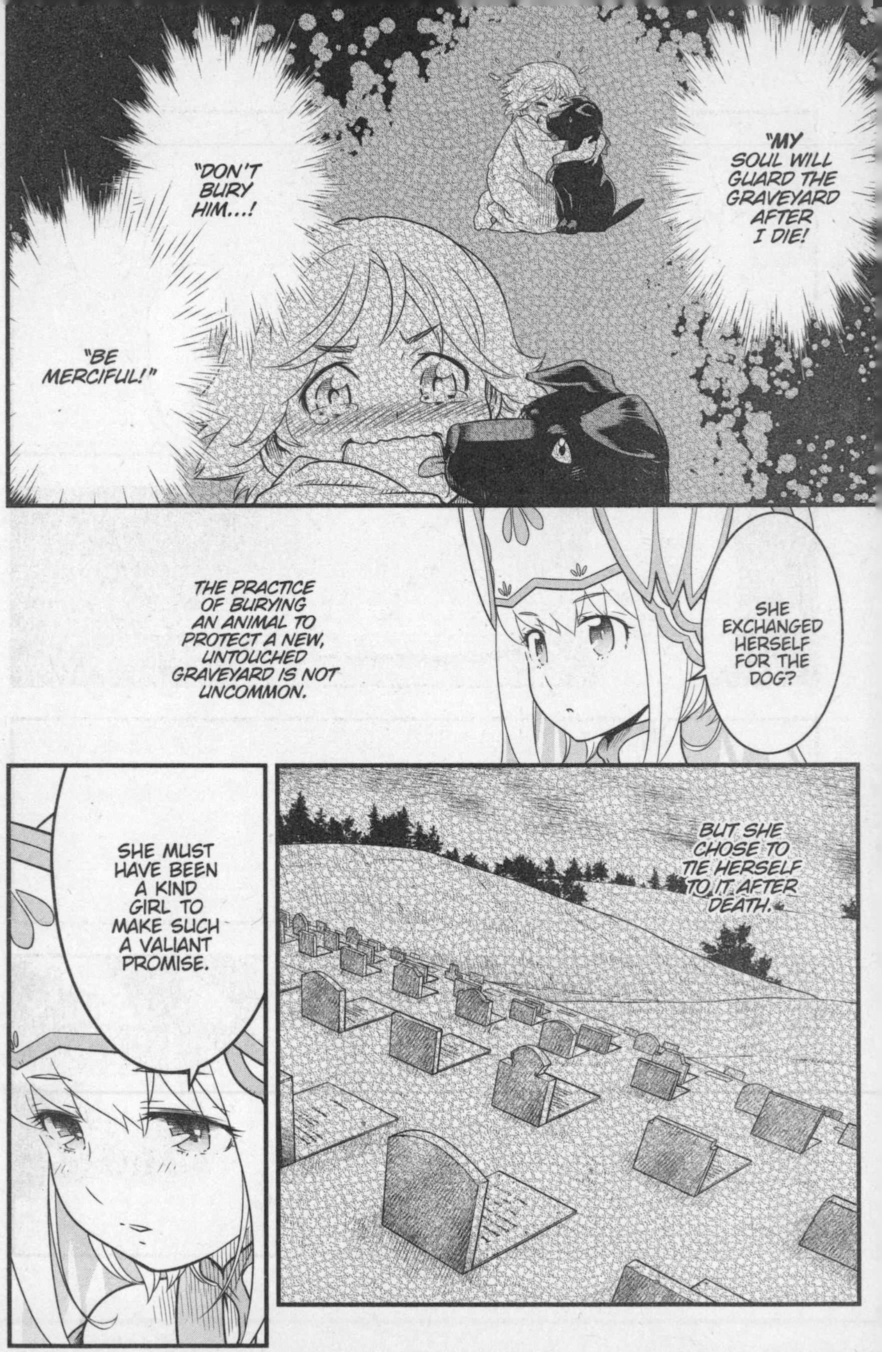
"MY SOUL WILL GUARD THE GRAVEYARD AFTER I DIE!
"DON'T BURY HIM...!
"BE MERCIFUL!"
SHE EXCHANGED HERSELF FOR THE DOG?
THE PRACTICE OF BURYING AN ANIMAL TO PROTECT A NEW, UNTOUCHED GRAVEYARD IS NOT UNCOMMON.
BUT SHE CHOSE TO TIE HERSELF TO IT AFTER DEATH.
SHE MUST HAVE BEEN A KIND GIRL TO MAKE SUCH A VALIANT PROMISE.

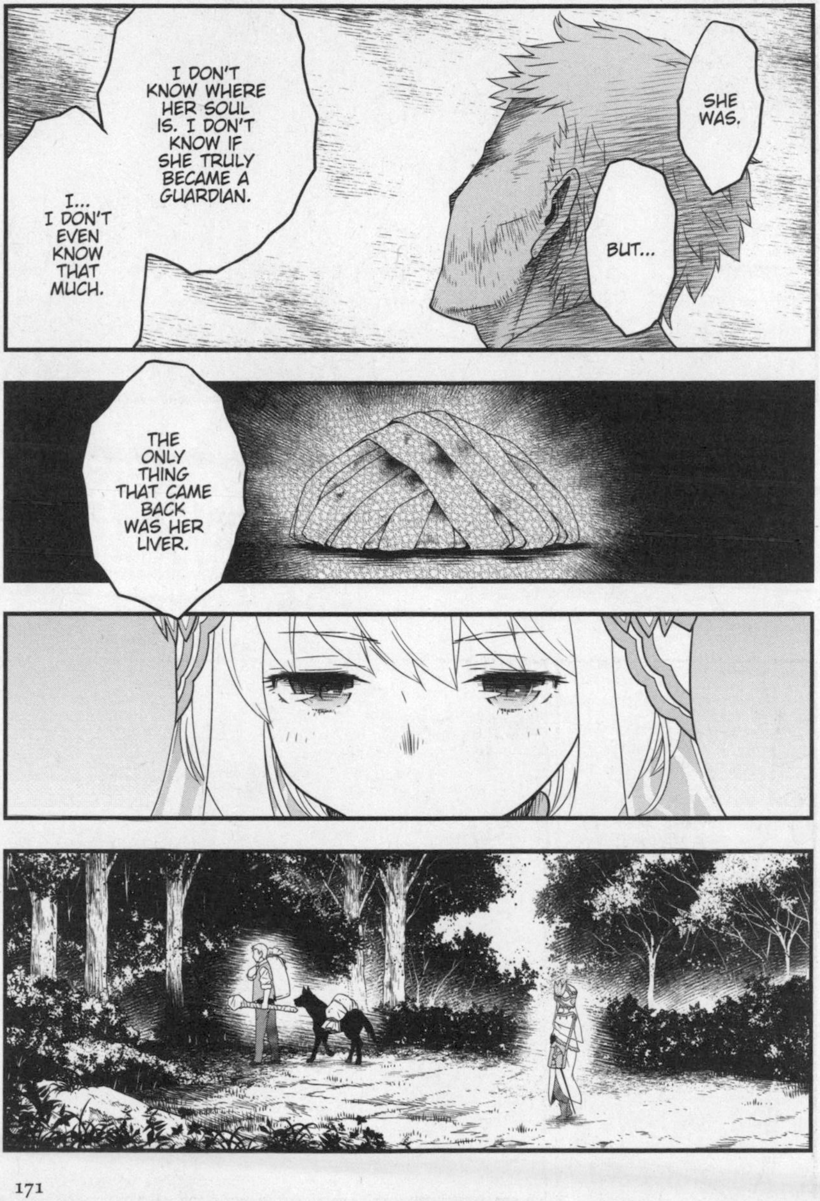
SHE WAS.
BUT...
I DON'T KNOW WHERE HER SOUL IS. I DON'T KNOW IF SHE TRULY BECAME A GUARDIAN.
I... I DON'T EVEN KNOW THAT MUCH.
THE ONLY THING THAT CAME BACK WAS HER LIVER.

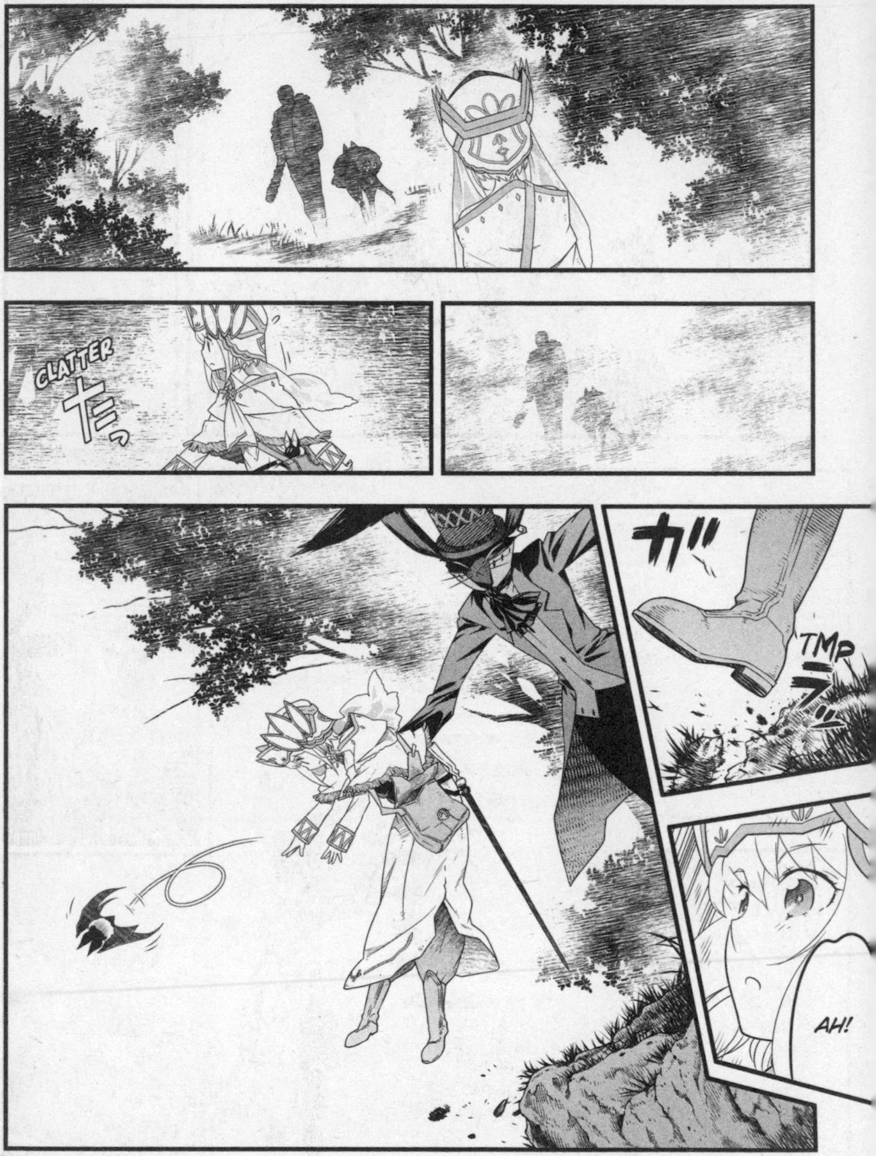
CLATTER
ガッ
TMP
AH!

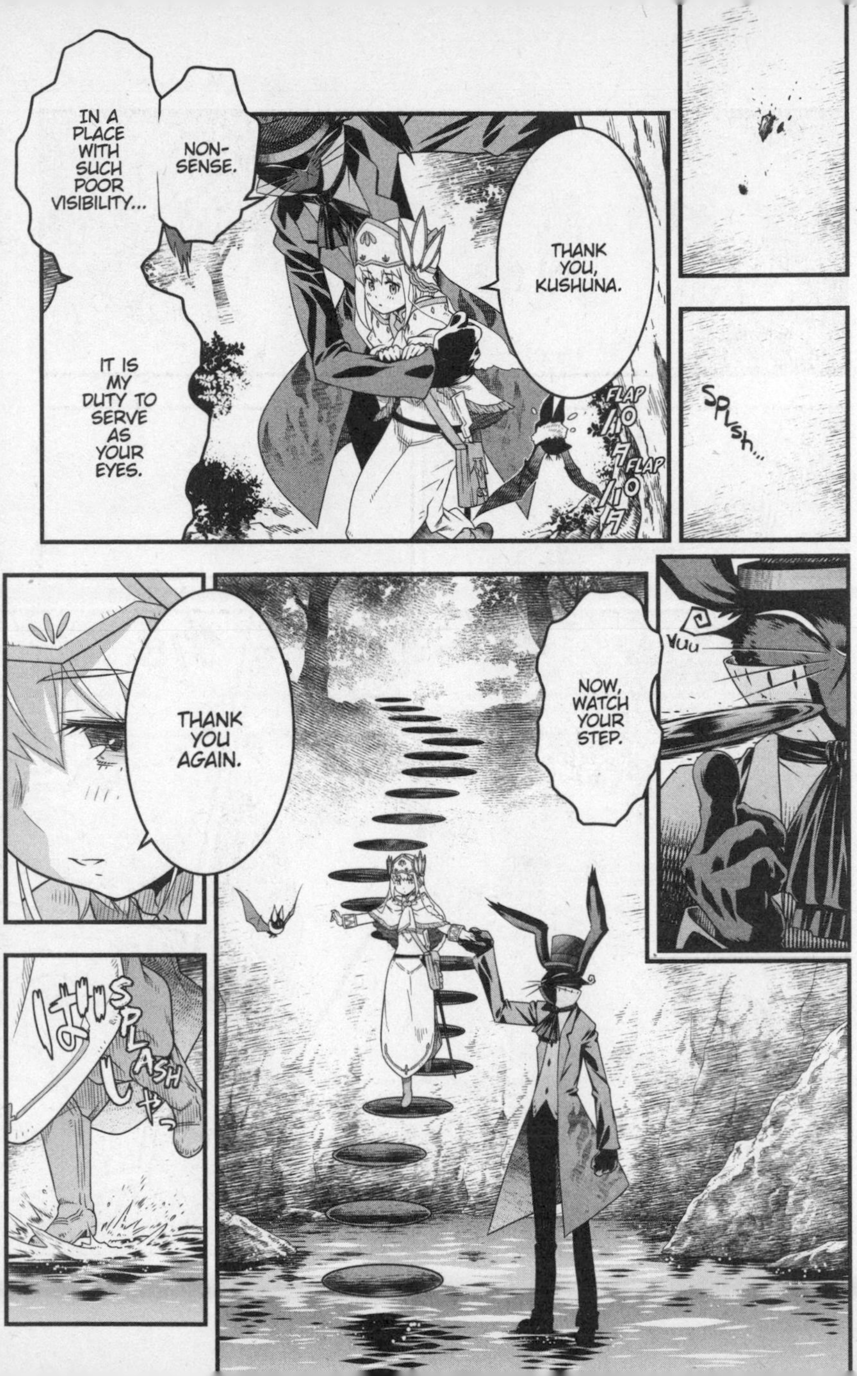
SPLVSH...
THANK YOU, KUSHUNA.
FLAP FLAP
NON-SENSE.
IN A PLACE WITH SUCH POOR VISIBILITY...
IT IS MY DUTY TO SERVE AS YOUR EYES.
VUU
NOW, WATCH YOUR STEP.
THANK YOU AGAIN.
SPLASH

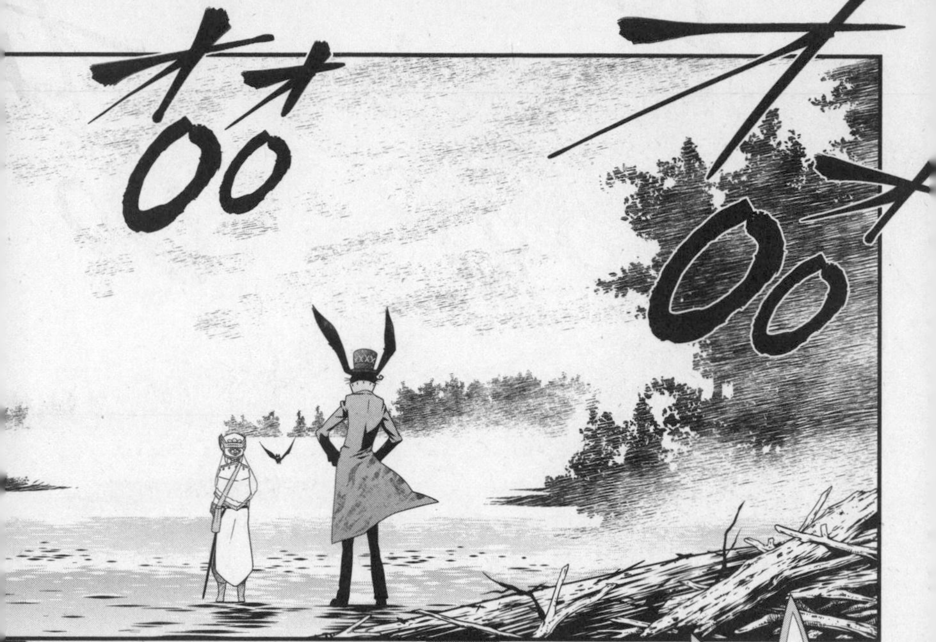
OO
OO
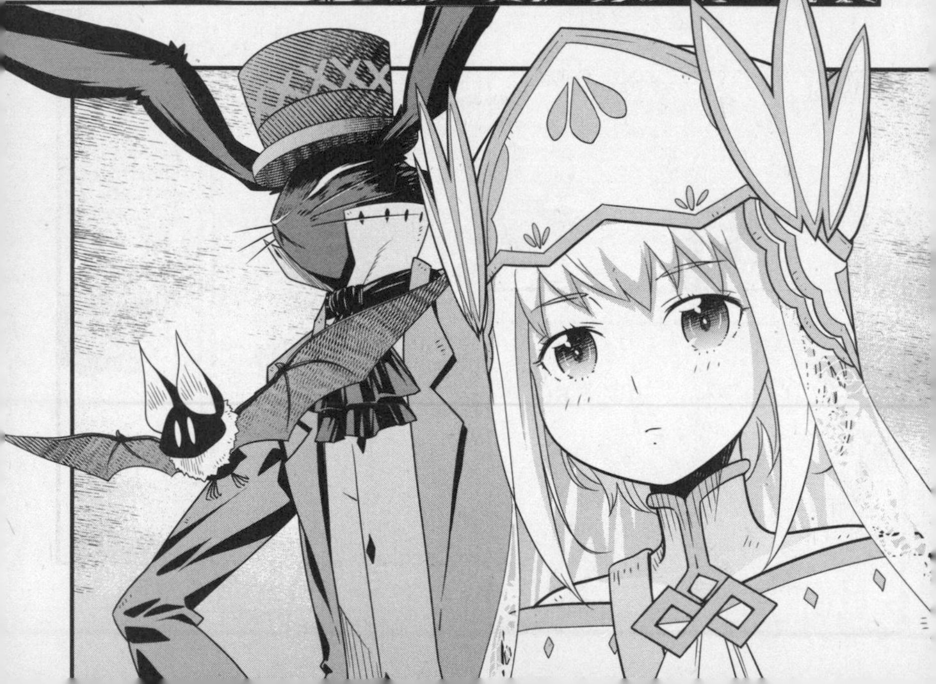

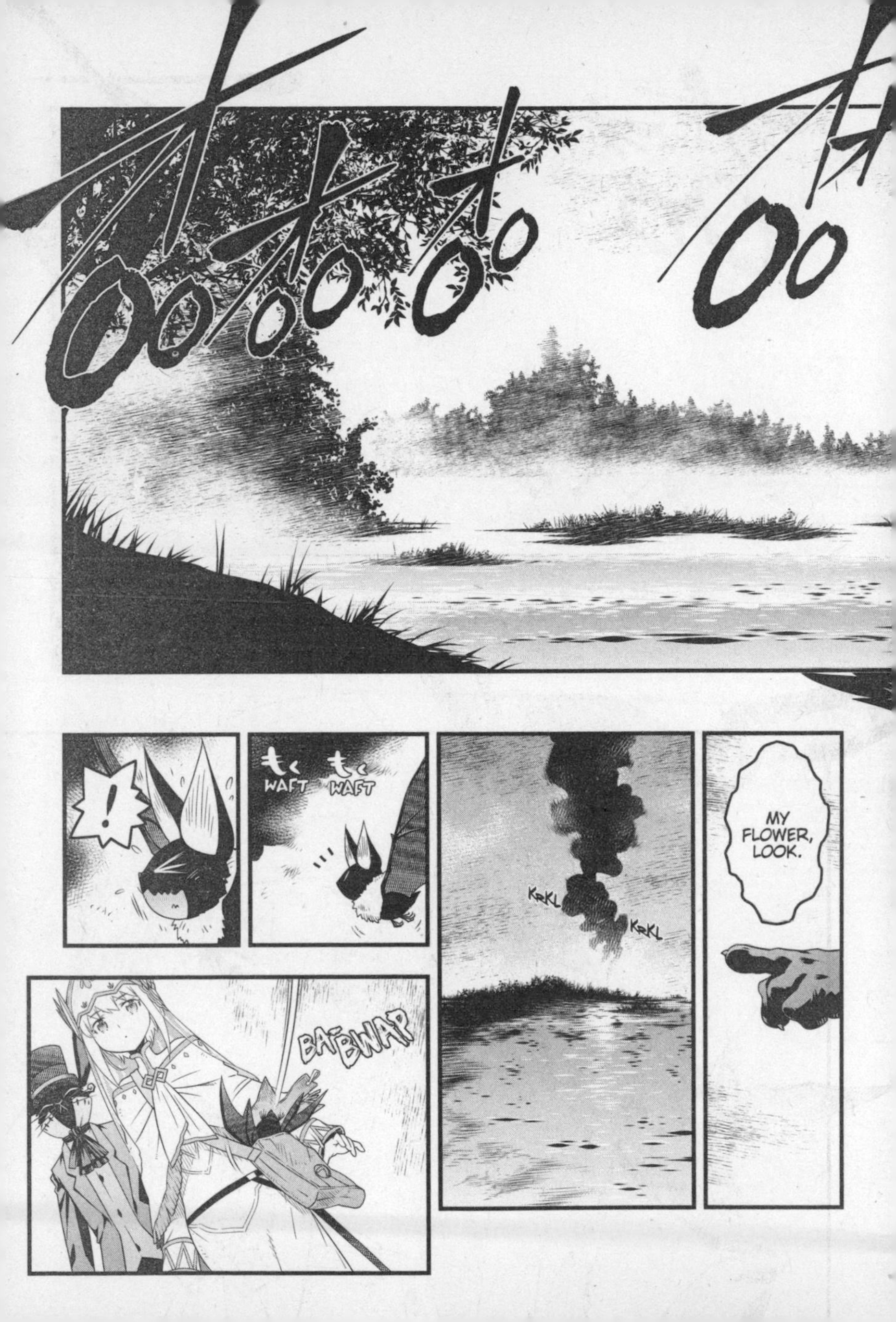
OOOOOOO
OO
MY FLOWER, LOOK.
KRKL
KRKL
もく WAFT
もく WAFT
!
BAFBWAP

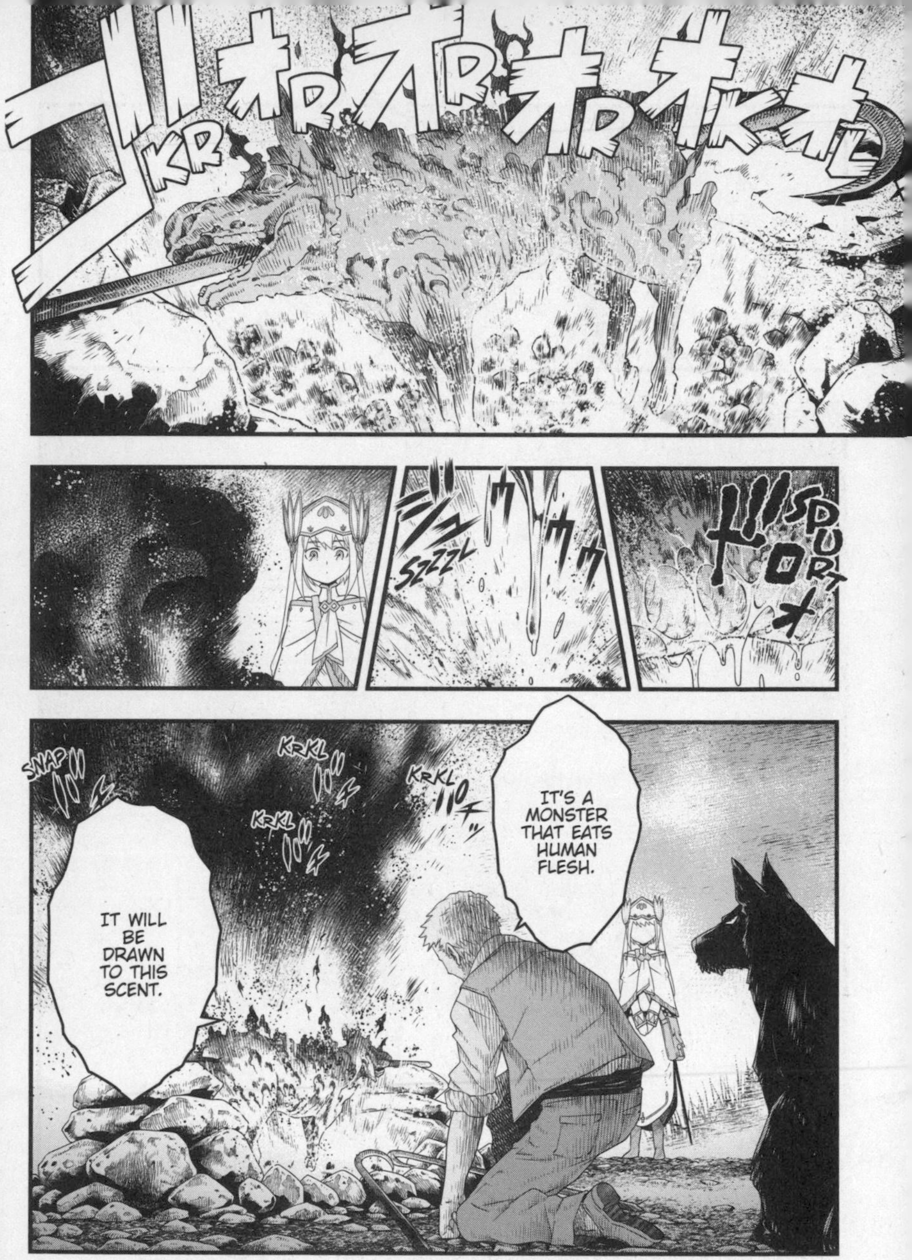
KR
KR
KR
K
L
SPURT
SZZZL
IT'S A MONSTER THAT EATS HUMAN FLESH.
KRKL
KRKL
KRKL
SNAP
IT WILL BE DRAWN TO THIS SCENT.

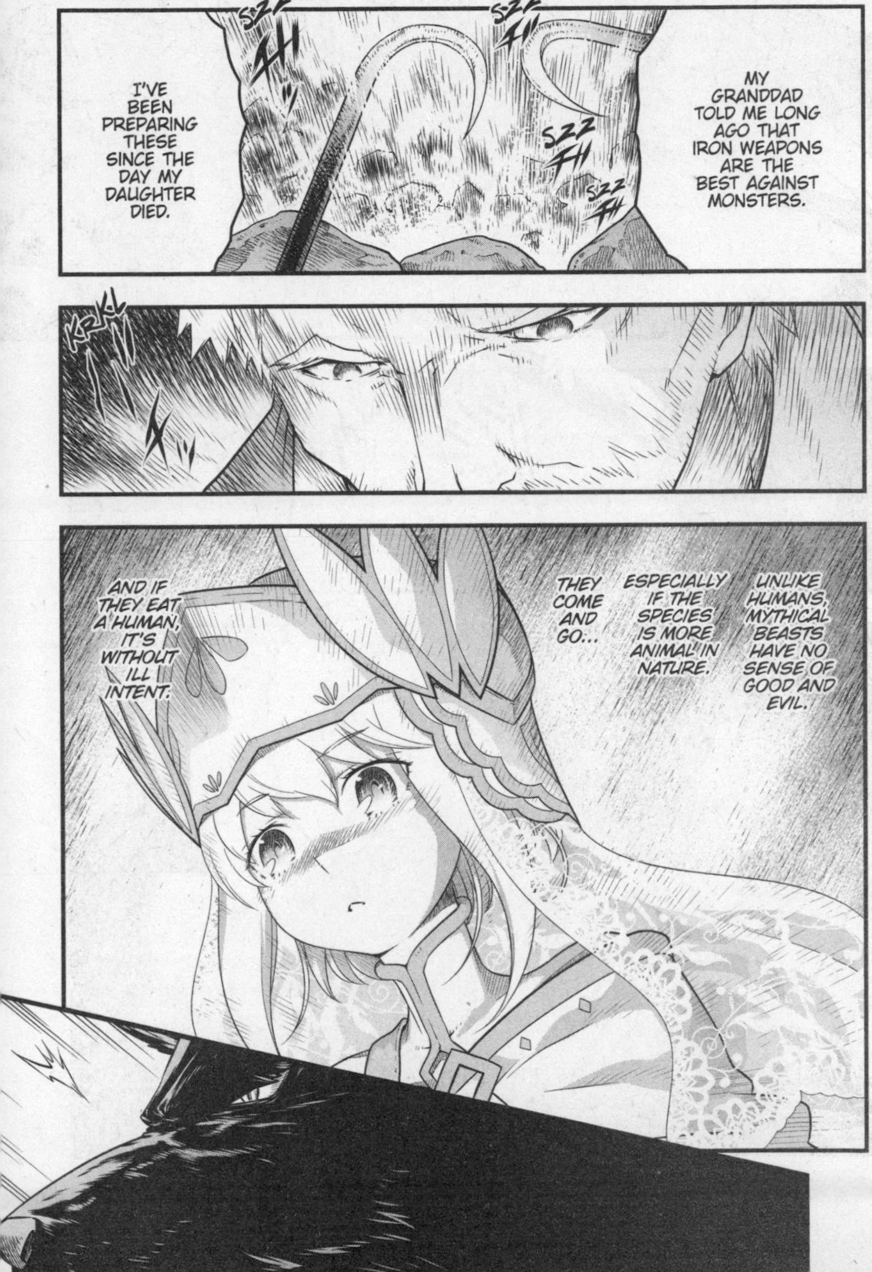
MY GRANDDAD TOLD ME LONG AGO THAT IRON WEAPONS ARE THE BEST AGAINST MONSTERS.
I'VE BEEN PREPARING THESE SINCE THE DAY MY DAUGHTER DIED.
UNLIKE HUMANS, MYTHICAL BEASTS HAVE NO SENSE OF GOOD AND EVIL.
ESPECIALLY IF THE SPECIES IS MORE ANIMAL IN NATURE.
THEY COME AND GO...
AND IF THEY EAT A HUMAN, IT'S WITHOUT ILL INTENT.

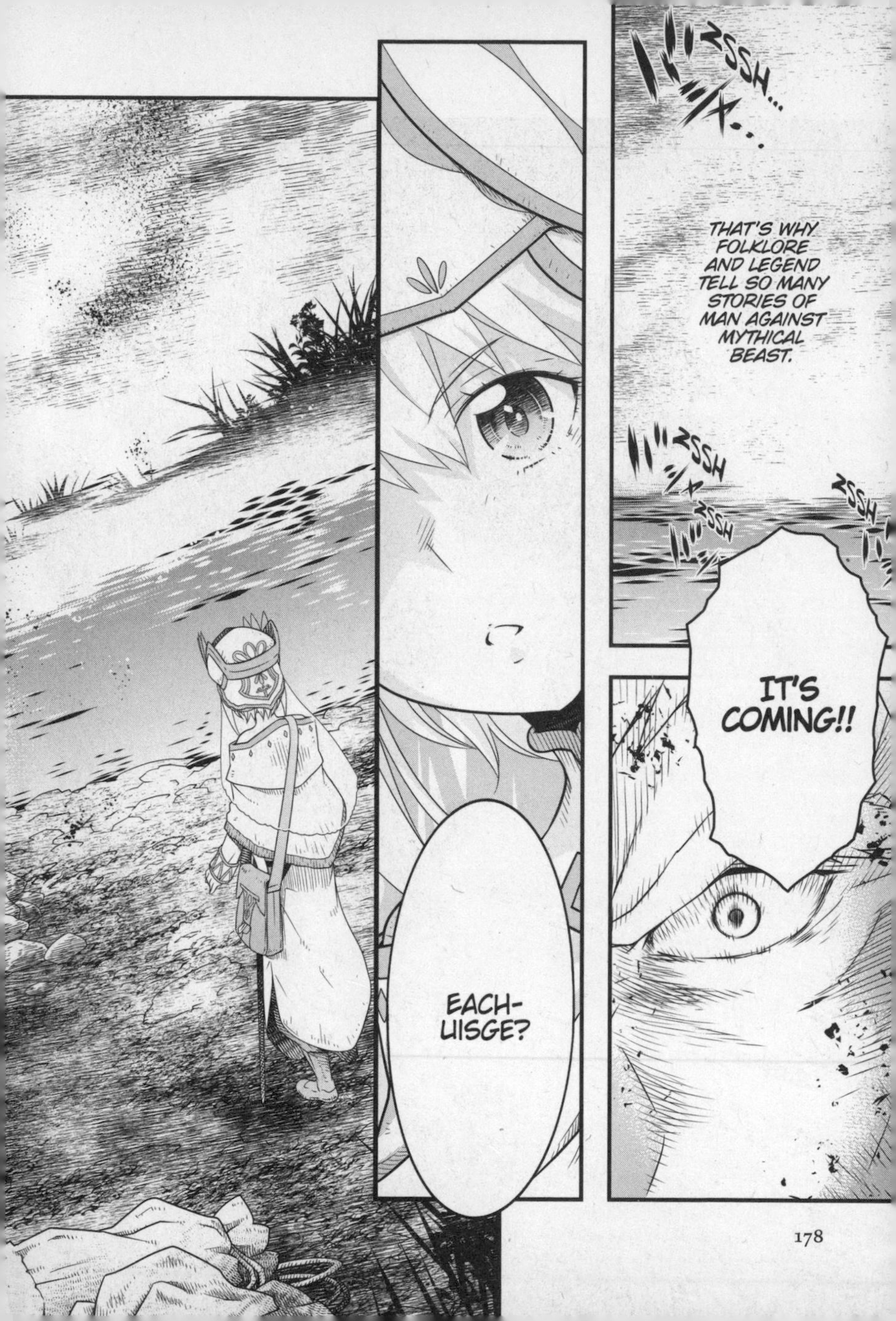
ZSSH...
THAT'S WHY FOLKLORE AND LEGEND TELL SO MANY STORIES OF MAN AGAINST MYTHICAL BEAST.
ZSSH
ZSSH
ZSSH
IT'S COMING!!
EACH-UISGE?

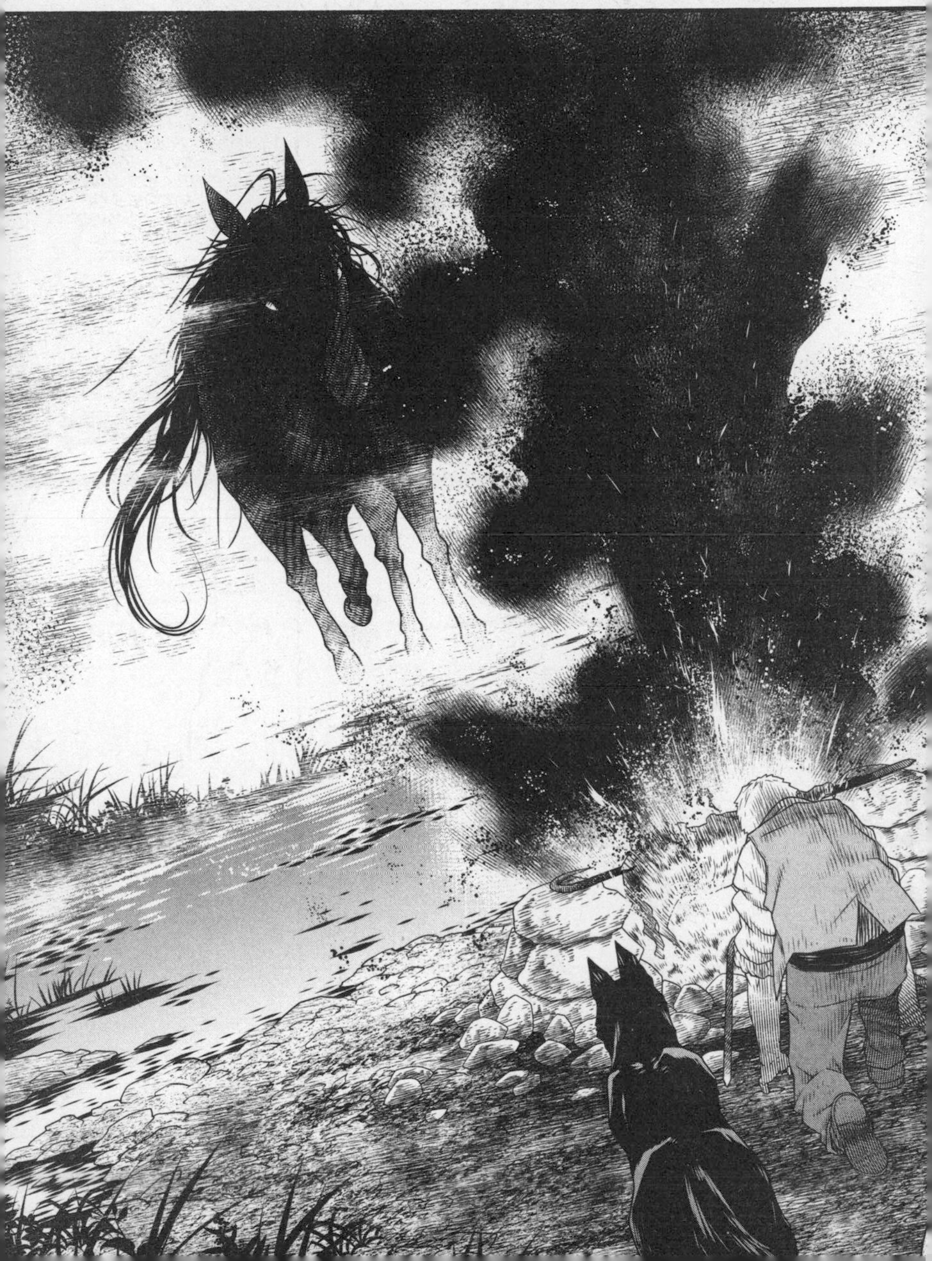

Mythical Beast Investigator

Afterword

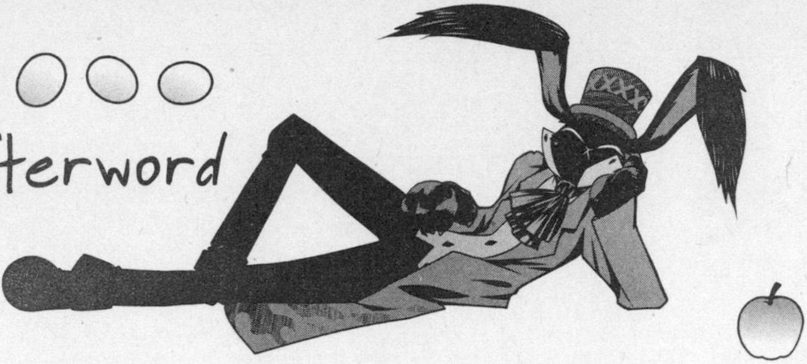

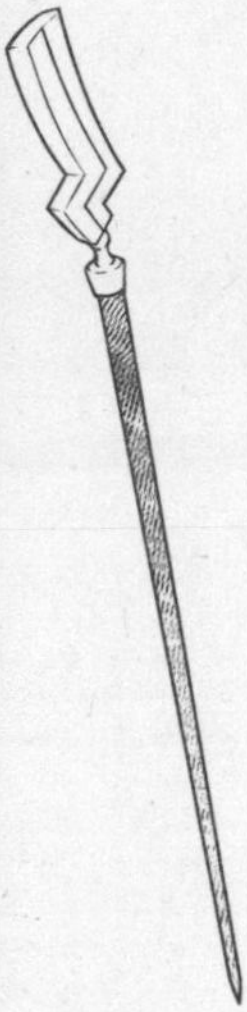

Hello, Hoshino here!
Thank you for picking up the first volume of the manga version of *Mythical Beast Investigator.*

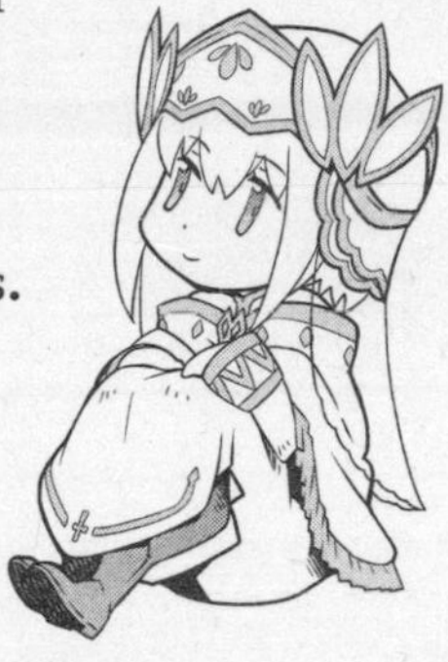

The world was created through Ayasato-sensei's words and lack-san's illustrations. I hope that this interpretation is a good gateway to help bring people to this marvelous world.

However...

As a reader, I want to talk to other people who've read *Mythical Beast Investigator!* I want to discuss chapters and scenes with other fans! *Ahh,* I'm going to pour all of these feelings into this manga! Please continue to take care of me!!

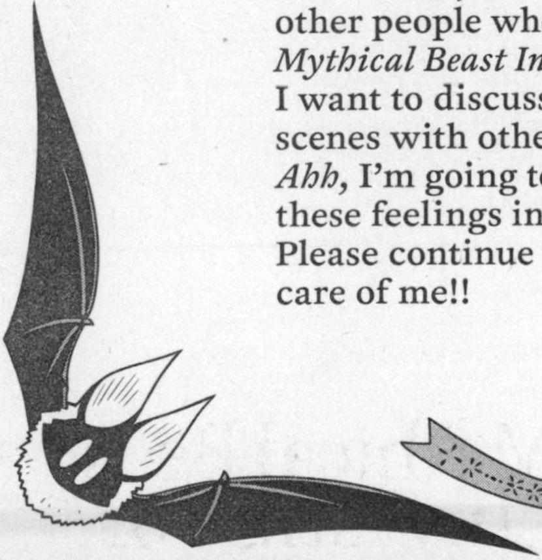

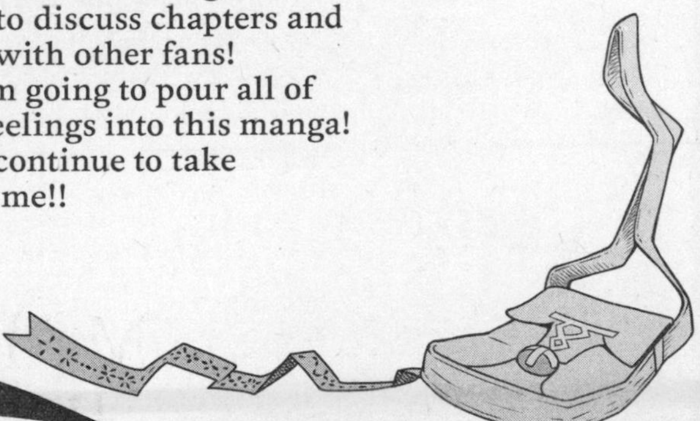

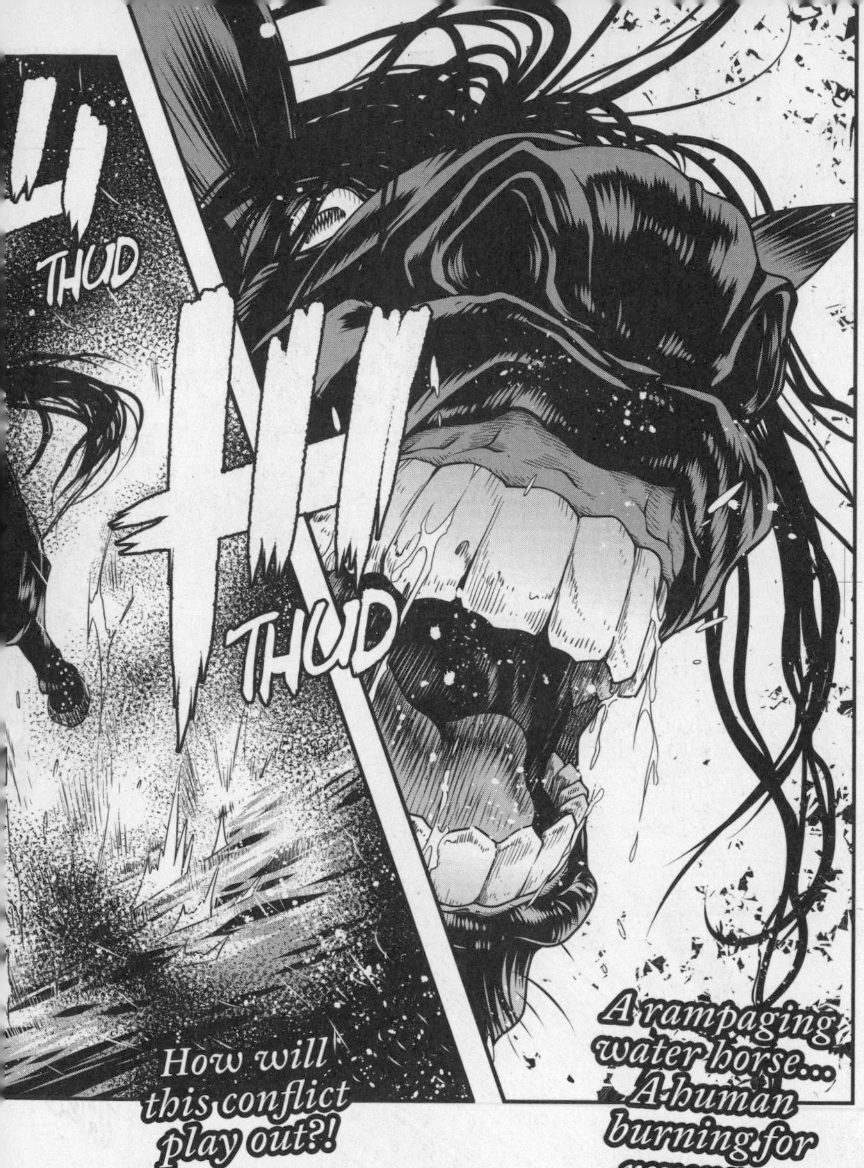
THUD
THUD
A rampaging water horse... A human burning for revenge...
How will this conflict play out?!

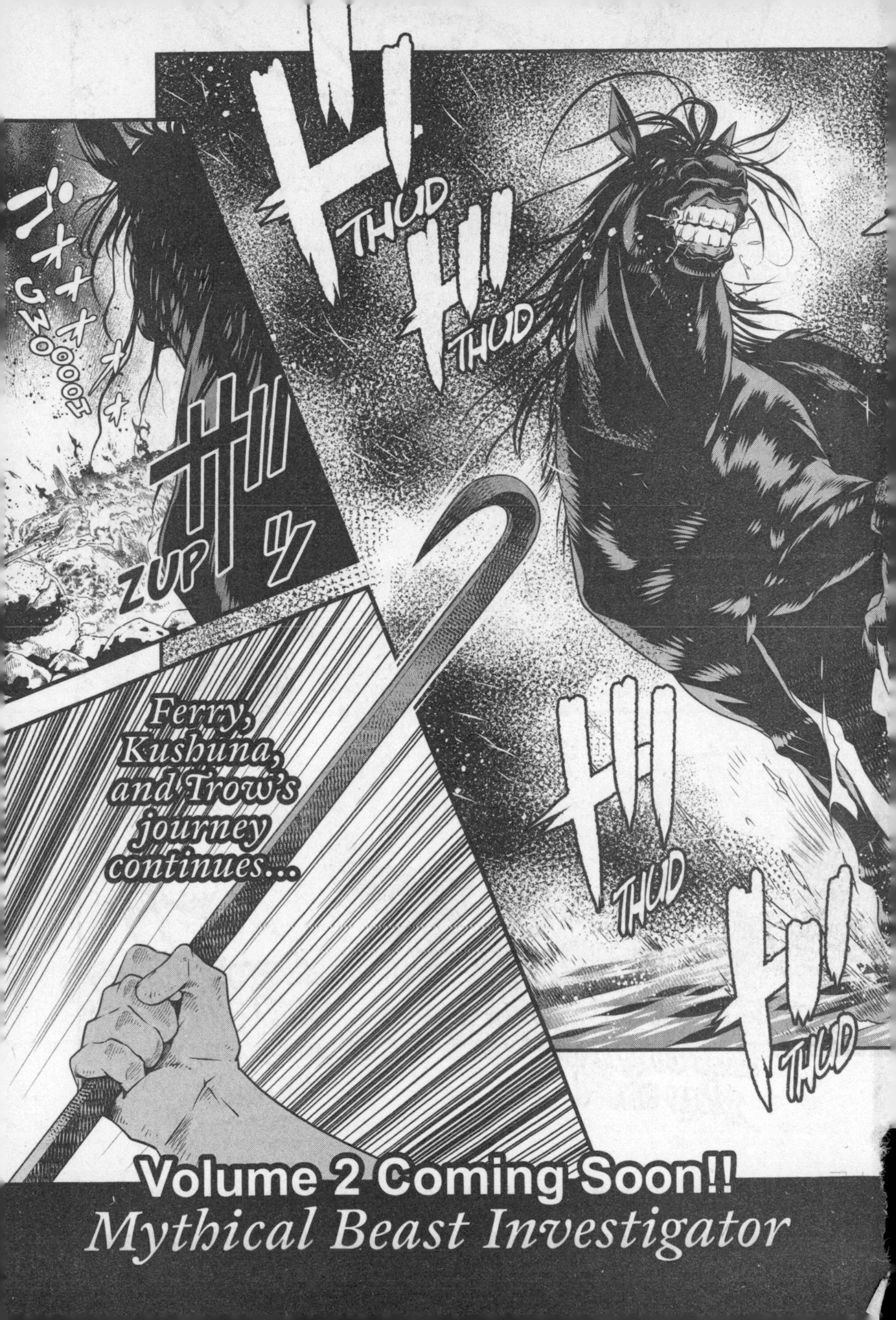
THUD
THUD
GWOOOOOH
ZUP
Ferry, Kushuna, and Trow's journey continues...
THUD
THUD
Volume 2 Coming Soon!!
Mythical Beast Investigator

SEVEN SEAS ENTERTAINMENT PRESENTS

⇝Mythical Bëast Investigator⇜

story: **KEISHI AYASATO** / art: **KOICHIRO HOSHINO** / character designs: **LACK**   VOLUME 1

TRANSLATION
Angela Liu

ADAPTATION
Ysabet MacFarlane

LETTERING AND RETOUCH
Simone Harrison

COVER DESIGN
KC Fabellon

PROOFREADER
Dawn Davis
Brett Hallahan

EDITOR
Shannon Fay

PRODUCTION MANAGER
Lissa Pattillo

MANAGING EDITOR
Julie Davis

EDITOR-IN-CHIEF
Adam Arnold

PUBLISHER
Jason DeAngelis

MYTHICAL BEAST INVESTIGATOR VOL. 1
© Keishi Ayasato 2018
© Koichiro Hoshino 2018
First published in 2018 by KADOKAWA CORPORATION, Tokyo.
English translation rights arranged with KADOKAWA CORPORATION, Tokyo.

Seven Seas press and purchase enquiries can be sent to Marketing Manager Lianne Sentar at press@gomanga.com. Information regarding the distribution and purchase of digital editions is available from Digital Manager CK Russell at digital@gomanga.com.

Seven Seas and the Seven Seas logo are trademarks of Seven Seas Entertainment. All rights reserved.

ISBN: 978-1-64275-053-9

Printed in Canada

First Printing: July 2019

10 9 8 7 6 5 4 3 2 1

FOLLOW US ONLINE: www.sevenseasentertainment.com

READING DIRECTIONS

This book reads from *right to left*, Japanese style. If this is your first time reading manga, you start reading from the top right panel on each page and take it from there. If you get lost, just follow the numbered diagram here. It may seem backwards at first, but you'll get the hang of it! Have fun!!

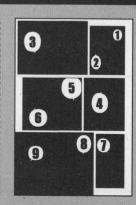